CONSUMER Superbrands

AN INSIGHT INTO BRITAIN'S STRONGEST BRANDS 2003

For Peter and Alice -
demonstrations of how precious life is.

FROM

The Independent Authority on Branding

Australia • Britain • Denmark • Egypt • France • Germany • Hong Kong • India • Ireland • Italy
Malaysia • The Netherlands • Philippines • Saudi Arabia • Singapore • Spain • UAE • United States

EDITOR-IN-CHIEF
Marcel Knobil

AUTHORS
James Curtis
Des King
Jane Simms
Delwyn Swingewood
Mark Tungate

MANAGING EDITOR
Angela Pumphrey

EDITORIAL ASSISTANT
Emma Selwyn

DESIGNER
Verity Belcher, Creative & Commercial Communications

ART DIRECTOR
Adam Selwyn, Creative & Commercial Communications

BRAND LIAISON DIRECTOR
Annie Richardson

Special Thanks to:
Bill Colegrave, Director; Richard Thomas, Director.
And **Mintel** for providing a considerable amount of market
research material.

For Superbrands publications dedicated to: Australia,
Britain, Denmark, Egypt, France, Germany, Hong Kong,
India, Ireland, Italy, Malaysia, The Netherlands, Philippines,
Saudi Arabia, Singapore, Spain, UAE and United States
email: brands@thebrandcouncil.org or
telephone: 0207 267 8899.

For Superbrands publications dedicated to Business-to-Business
brands, Cool BrandLeaders and to internet dedicated brands
email: brands@thebrandcouncil.org or telephone: 020 7267 8899.

Production by Pixel Colour Imaging Limited

Printed in Italy

ISBN 0-9541532-1-9

Contents

It is with great pleasure that the British Brands Group supports this collection of Superbrands. Each connects with the public to a remarkable extent, inspiring confidence, loyalty, and trust. It is a tribute to those who sought out consumer insights, applied their imagination and creativity, and made the investment necessary to build such sustaining and valued relationships.

In our world of choice, ever-rising expectations and intolerance of second best, the task of retaining the consumer's preference is increasingly challenging. Performance and value for money ceased to be sufficient years ago. Today, every encounter with the brand must be managed. How the company behaves – with all its stakeholders – is now important. And reading the future, which has perhaps never been so difficult, has never been so important.

The British Brands Group is committed to building an environment in the UK where brands such as these can continue to flourish, and new brands nurtured to bring delight and satisfaction to consumers.

JOHN NOBLE Director, The British Brands Group

Brands have become so central to our everyday lives that most of us cannot fail to be touched by them. The most powerful brands have become so well known that they not only occupy a special place in the hearts of millions, but have developed their own personality, and with it an entry in the lexicon of popular vocabulary.

The huge quantity of competing brands means that each one has to work even harder to capture the public's imagination and connect with customers. Many have succeeded, and a small number have done so spectacularly well.

CIM is delighted to endorse this publication, which has not only independently identified some of the UK's most popular brands, but has also dug down under the surface to uncover what truly makes them so powerful.

MIKE JOHNSTON International Chairman, The Chartered Institute of Marketing (CIM)

The fierce competition between brands, especially in consumer markets, means that the survivors have really served their customers well, otherwise they would have voted with their wallets and gone elsewhere. Great commercial communications are an essential part of the process whereby brands get 're-elected' by their customer 'electorate' on a daily basis. New product innovations are brought to market for trial, while existing ones are re-presented for affirmation or reappraisal. Price points are under constant attack and brands which behave badly in the 'social court' are increasingly brought to account. This new Superbrands book celebrates the winners: great brands whose total value proposition satisfies media savvy and discerning customers over and over again.

HAMISH PRINGLE, Director General of the Institute of Practitioners in Advertising (IPA) and author of two books on brands: Brand Spirit and Brand Manners.

Marcel Knobil

Chairperson, The Brand Council
Chairperson, Consumer Superbrands Judging Panel
Chairperson, Creative & Commercial Communications

70% of people think that their favourite brands would be better at running the country than the Government. And 66% of consumers feel that Britain's top brands are more trustworthy than the major political parties – with the majority in no doubt that brands are more likely to live up to their promises than political parties.

These results from an NFO WorldGroup survey commissioned by The Brand Council are illustrative of the immense respect that Superbrands command. The creation and stewardship of brands that have gained such admiration, fame and accomplishments is a tremendous achievement. The Brand Council is in the privileged position to pay tribute to, and provide case studies on them.

With the expert assistance of the Consumer Superbrands Judges we have been able to identify the most highly respected brands in the UK (listed on www.thebrandcouncil.org) and offer insight into the background, development and future of many of them. Each judge has a deep appreciation of what makes a great brand and keeps the following definition in mind: "A Superbrand offers consumers significant emotional and/or tangible advantages over its competitors which (consciously or sub-consciously) consumers recognise and want."

Judges do not score any brands that they are associated with or compete against.

I am extremely grateful to my colleagues on The Brand Council both in the UK and throughout the world as well as the judges who perform their roles voluntarily. It is through the hard work of individuals who truly appreciate the discipline of branding that we come to appreciate the role of branding and hence unanimously vote 'Yes Logo'.

The Superbrand Recipe

How to remain a Consumer Superbrand

John Ballington

Corporate & Consumer Affairs Director
Lever Fabergé

Throughout time the collision of people and technology has created seismic shifts re-drawing our social landscape. Brands are a relatively new invention but already one common thread unites the elite. It's their evolution. The ability to refresh their relevance to society without losing the clarity and consistency that made them great. Trust built painstakingly over decades on a shifting social topography is increasingly complex to maintain or extend. People are more empowered. Connectivity makes them more informed; more networked. Sceptics erase brand equity with the sweep of a mouse. That's why today's Superbrands only have a season ticket to greatness. Renewal comes from making sense of our society; weaving knowledge from the threads of data spun from our digital world. Tomorrow's elite will be those stepping back to see movements in the wider picture not those with atomised or narrow-cast views. We've already debunked the notion that the family is a broken institution, uncovered concepts like lifelong parenting and defined the new contract between parents and children.

It's time for brands to replace number crunching with curiosity and hunger for understanding modern life…ALL of it.

Quentin Bell

Founder
The Quentin Bell Organisation

To someone fortunate enough to have founded a successful business, I know: starting it is the easier bit. But to remain successful? It needs a tad more resolve.

And so it is with Superbrands. The trick is to remain one. Here are my five top tips:

(I discount, as read, having an initial ripping concept; adequate infrastructure; human resources, distribution etc):

1. INVEST and MONITOR your success, constantly and consistently, from the top: remember no profit, no Superbrand!
2. SURPRISE: customers and competitors must follow your lead!
3. DEMONSTRATE that (in an age where technology ensures PRODUCT parity) your unique BRAND values, vision and personality are UNASSAILABLE. It's the biggest test of how to remain a Superbrand: ensure these cannot be replicated by others!
4. CELEBRATE your successes, modestly, but for all to see!
5. REMEMBER: being 'serious' and having fun in business are compatible concepts!

Marcel Knobil

Chairperson, The Brand Council
Chairperson, Consumer Superbrands Judging Panel

When I asked the Marketing Manager of one of the world's most admired brands what his most significant contribution was during his tenure, he answered: "To do nothing to it". A tongue-in-cheek response, but with significant resonance.

It is critical that we recognise that the lives of Superbrands are invariably far more enduring then those of their guardians. A talented brand guardian will identify what is the heart and soul of a brand and ensure that all activities reflect it. Of course, the brand needs to be invigorated and refreshed on an enduring basis but the DNA of the brand must be recognised and respected.

Whilst it might be tempting for a new brand guardian to attempt to impose his/her personality onto a Superbrand and to make major changes, take heed. Superbrands have invariably earned immense popularity through offering consistency of communications and product delivery. A schizophrenic brand can rapidly lose its attraction.

David Mercer

Head of Design
BT

A successful brand is not a static thing – fixed in a moment in time. Brands must evolve, but never too fast or they will detach from their provenance, yet fast enough so they are always seen as being of the moment.

Brands must be relevant to the wider, interdependent world in which they exist, contributing to the pulse of society and its infinite onward movement. Brands must remain meaningful, demonstrating a point of view and command a clear difference in their respective markets.

Superbrands are brands, which consistently achieve all this and above all else, they continue to touch people and to involve the world they are irrevocably a part.

Drayton Bird

Chairman
The Drayton Bird Partnership

Many, if not most marketers, associate great brands with great advertising. And research shows that those firms that advertise more are more profitable – and those that rely on promotion are less so.

But this is only one element in lasting success. The Economist's advertising has been outstanding. But Proctor & Gamble or Wrigley advertising is generally pedestrian. They are just persistent, consistent and spend more.

Hoover managed to destroy its brand with one risibly unwise promotion, and the US car industry seems bent on destroying its famous brands by selling almost entirely on a cash-back basis.

I suspect brands are built more on word of mouth than advertising, but both call for a superior product or service. Once a brand becomes dominant finding new reasons for consumers to buy and keep buying is crucial – promoting Coke as a breakfast drink is a prime example.

Stephen Factor

Chief Executive
NFO WorldGroup UK

Brand management doesn't lend itself to clear and certain truth. If I spend X will I certainly gain Y? That's why maintaining a Superbrand year after year is such an epic task. Yet perhaps some truths about effective brand management are self-evident:

Never stop learning about your brand. Brands are organic and not static. They grow and evolve. Keep seeking knowledge.

Live the brand. Ensure every action is consistent with the brand's personality and culture. Brands are not infinitely elastic. A line-extension too far and the brand may snap.

Innovation isn't just the domain of new products. Longevity is the sum of many moments of creation. The true stars of brand management relaunch at the peak of success, before the brand starts sliding to oblivion.

In a world full of competition, in highly complex markets, the best advice is to put your money where your mouth is, maintain discipline and stay true to your brand.

Winston Fletcher

Chairman
Advertising Standards Board of Finance

The basic rules for remaining a consumer Superbrand are not dissimilar to those for becoming a Superbrand. A Superbrand must meet real consumer needs, both psychological and physical, and do so better than any other brand on the market. A Superbrand must offer great value. A Superbrand must successfully communicate its consumer benefits on pack, in advertising, and through every other means of marketing communication.

But having achieved Superbrand status these rules become increasingly difficult to apply. Superbrands get copied, so they must constantly ensure their formulation is superior to competitors'. Retailers may try to elbow them off their shelves, so Superbrands must constantly generate consumer demand through advertising and sales promotion. And then, of course, consumers are constantly in a state of flux, so Superbrands must adapt themselves to their ever changing demands. The two absolute constants are: Keep Close to the Customer, and The Customer is King. Superbrands that abide by those two principles stay Superbrands forever.

David Haigh

Chief Executive
Brand Finance

The core of every Superbrand is a package of trademarks and other legal rights which need to be actively managed and protected. A bundle of functional and emotional attributes are wrapped around this core to create psychological and emotional loyalty.

Superbrands display strong non-functional differentiation even in apparently commodity markets, leading to price premium, volume uplift and long term demand.

Superbrands are active and vigilant in defending and extending their Intellectual Property rights. They are equally robust in putting high quality brand management and marketing budgets behind the task of creating psychological and emotional power. They do not cut spend when the economy wobbles but invest continuously.

Superbrands need to have a strong and simple personality, remain focused in their positioning, simple in their promotional messages and above all maintain the trust and respect of their consumers. The future stream of revenues guaranteed by a Superbrand demands consistency combined with flexibility to meet changing circumstances. But like old friends what they stand for remains constant from one generation to the next.

Michael Peters OBE

Chairman and Executive Creative Director
Identica

At a time when the economy is suffering such a downturn, big ideas, communicated simply, are the way forward for consumer Superbrands. Many existing Superbrands are in danger of falling by the wayside unless they are more innovative.

The IBMs of tomorrow will be born because they are fresh and energetic, and unless Superbrands that dominated the twentieth century adopt similar strategies, I believe that many of them are in danger of becoming extinct and will not be able to compete in the marketplace.

The real test will occur during the next five years. If the Superbrands of today rest on their laurels, they may be bitten by the aggressive newcomers to the market whose approach to brands will determine the course of global business in the twenty first century.

Chris Powell

Chairman
BMP DDB

Don't get carried away with thoughts of the power of branding:
- keep your product or service better than the competition
- freshen the brand's presentation
- don't get too greedy with line extensions, forgetting the need to nurture the core brand.

But, remember that if you do muck up, the trust you've built up will sustain an inferior brand for a few years.

If you get lost, go back to the beginning. Understand what has made the brand successful in the past and re-interpret it to suit the future.

Tim Sutton

Chairman
Orpheus Group

"And we are here as on a darkling plain swept with confused alarms of struggle and flight where ignorant armies clash by night." Matthew Arnold was referring to the decline of religious faith, rather than having prescience of today's confusing and bewildering world of consumer choice with all its competing claims and counter claims. But in a world of overload information and personal insecurity, the words still have resonance.

Not for nothing do out of town supermarkets simulate the appearance of modern cathedrals. They are a modern faith and Superbrands are the high priests – the guiding lamps through the darkness and the guardians of the sacred flame. We trust Superbrands because they maintain authenticity and integrity. Like all symbols, they ascribe meaning to aspects of our life. But of course we have to be careful because the very act of trying to analyse and deconstruct symbols can lead to their impotence.

Will Whitehorn

Brand Development & Corporate
Affairs Director Virgin Management Ltd

These are challenging times for Superbrands. Scandals such as Enron, Pyco and Worldcom have made consumers all over the world more cynical than they were at the start of the decade. It is at times like these when brand management and the management of the business need to work hand in hand. The aim of every Superbrand must be to put both their people and the customer ahead of short-term considerations. The relationship with the general public is the most important asset that a Superbrand possesses. The difficulties of the last eighteen months have made it clearer than ever to me that that relationship in all its manifestations from customer service to product quality needs direct board level representation. Most of all, Superbrands need to remember that they have to think as carefully about the next five years, as the next six months.

Abbey National®
because life's complicated enough.

Market

The retail financial services market has changed rapidly over recent years. The UK financial services sector was at one time characterised by a combination of regulatory restrictions and functional demarcation.

In the past two decades successive governments have continued to deregulate the industry, largely in response to past recessions and to support structural change by improving the efficiency and competitiveness in both the public and private sectors.

In addition to this, technological advances have fuelled competition in almost every sector of the financial services market. Furthermore, banks and building societies have been joined in the UK retail banking and financial services marketplace by a diverse range of new entrants such as internet banks, supermarkets, insurance companies, credit card providers and consumer finance groups.

Abbey National and its subsidiaries constitute a major financial services group in the UK. With total assets of £215 billion and income before taxes of £1,938 million as at December 31st 2001, the Abbey National Group is ranked as the 6th largest banking group in the UK in terms of total assets. It is the UK's second largest residential mortgage lender and retail deposit taker. Furthermore, Abbey National has a relationship with one in three UK households.

Achievements

In 1989 Abbey National became the first building society to convert to banking status with the intention of becoming 'the' outstanding financial services provider in the UK.

Since it was founded in 1944, Abbey National has enabled thousands of people in the UK to own their own homes and save for the future. One of Abbey National's chief achievements has been to combine the best of its building society heritage with its banking status.

Terry Burns, Chairman of Abbey National plc, says: "Abbey National is focused on providing its customers with a quality range of retail financial services, from traditional mortgage and savings businesses to personal and small business banking, and consumer credit, investment, protection and insurance."

Since conversion in 1989, the Abbey National Group has acquired major operations in life assurance, personal finance and point of sale finance businesses – among others.

The Abbey National Group also has an overseas presence predominantly serving the offshore market.

Abbey National has been at the forefront of introducing new technology to enhance its customer propositions. For example, Abbey National's retail customers were the first in the world to be able to access their accounts via the internet and through digital television. Abbey National's e-banking service is at the heart of the Groups' 'bricks & clicks' strategy, designed to give customers choice about how they deal with the bank, whether over the

"Mortgage expert-ease"

Peter. Abbey National Customer

Our **Mortgage Specialists** can make moving home easier and could **save you money**

YOUR HOME IS AT RISK IF YOU DO NOT KEEP UP REPAYMENTS ON A MORTGAGE OR OTHER LOAN SECURED ON IT.

telephone, at a cash machine, in a branch, through digital TV or over the internet.

The Abbey National Group's separately branded internet bank, cahoot, went live in 2000, offering a competitively priced credit card and current account. cahoot has since successfully launched flexible loan, travel insurance and savings and investments accounts.

Abbey National was awarded Best Overall Lender 2001-2002 by 'Your Mortgage' magazine and Best Bank in 1999-2000 and 2000-2001.

History

Abbey National was formed in 1944 following a merger between the London-based Abbey Road Building Society, founded in 1874, and the National Building Society, established in 1849. There was large-scale public demand for housing in post-war Britain, which Abbey National helped to meet with the provision of mortgages.

At first, Abbey National focused on savings accounts and mortgages, but during the 1960s and 1970s a wider range of financial services was gradually introduced. By 1989, Abbey National was officially recognised as a bank by the Bank of England and had 681 branches nationwide – a huge leap from 1960 when the building society had just 60 branches. Unlike other banks that were actively cutting the number of branches at the time, Abbey National continued to increase its number of outlets and in 2002 the bank had over 750 branches.

Abbey National's transition to plc status in 1989 was strongly supported by its members. Up to five million voted their approval in a secret ballot. Almost overnight, the total number of private shareholders in the UK rose from six million to nine and a half million. Today, the Abbey National Group has just over two million shareholders, of whom a large number have held shares since 1989. Abbey National's change to bank status also resulted in the formation of its wholesale banking arm, Abbey National Treasury Services plc.

Product

Abbey National's retail bank offers a whole range of financial services, such as banking services, market leading in-credit and overdraft rates, a variety of loans to reflect varying needs, mortgages, insurance and financial planning. Indeed, Abbey National now has a level of service in place to act as a 'one-stop-shop', for all its customers'. Their financial needs are met through its network of branches, telephone services, cash machines and e-banking facilities.

Mortgages have always been the backbone of Abbey National's business. It is the second largest mortgage lender in the UK, assisting more than two million people to buy their homes. It offers an extensive range of different mortgages including fixed, capped and now Flexible Mortgages, which enable customers to stop, start and vary their payments. Advice on mortgages is available face to face in the branch or over the phone from Abbey National's financial planning advisors – on hand to guide customers through a lifetime of financial needs.

Abbey National acquired Scottish Mutual in

1992. As well as selling pensions and investment products through intermediaries, Scottish Mutual also provides protection products under the Scottish Provident brand name.

Abbey National also offers a full range of banking services, including a bank account, credit card, savings accounts and a variety of loans to reflect different needs. Abbey National's user friendly bank account offers market leading in-credit and overdraft rates.

Other features include a 24-hour telephone banking service. AbbeyLink automated teller machines (ATMs) linked to over 28,000 cash machines and account access via the internet and digital TV.

Abbey National continues to add to its range of saving and investment accounts for people with anything from £1 to £2 million to invest. These accounts range from instant access through to a range of fixed rate bonds to ISAs and other Stockmarket-linked products.

Recent Developments

Abbey National has developed its convenience retailing strategy introducing innovative partnerships with third parties such as Costa Coffee and Homebase. It is offering customers a choice of convenient time saving 'touchpoints' at alternative venues other than the 'traditional' bank environment to satisfy their financial needs. It is also the first UK bank to implement franchising, with over half the branch network now operating in this way. This allows the local market to be more responsive to their individual market conditions. Credit card provision has been outsourced to MBNA and has accelerated the introduction of highly competitive cards.

In addition, the bank's e-commerce offering has been overhauled and now provides e-mortgage and e-credit card management facilities.

In 2002, Abbey National became the first UK high street bank to offer a fund supermarket with the launch of FundsCentre, offering a choice of 280 funds from 24 leading fund managers.

FundsCentre is a gateway to the UK's leading fund providers, offering easy access, choice and convenience. It is available to investors online, by telephone and by post.

In September 2002 'Abbey National for Intermediaries' was created to bring the intermediary brands of Scottish Mutual, Scottish Provident, James Hay and Cater Allen Private Bank under one umbrella. By January 2003, intermediaries were able to access all of Abbey National's UK intermediary products, services and brands through a single point of contact.

Promotion

Abbey National Retail Bank repositioned its brand in December 1997 following extensive consumer and staff research. The vision statement was 'to make its customers lives easier by delivering products and services in a straightforward, unstuffy, astute, friendly and 'can-do' manner that suits individual needs.' These sentiments are reflected in the strapline 'because life's complicated enough.'

A campaign featuring Alan Davies was used to communicate this positioning until 2001. The work used Davies to personify customers, showing the potential confusion money matters could cause and illustrated how Abbey National could make managing one's finances more straightforward.

In 2002, the communications strategy was refreshed – while keeping the idea of making customers' lives easier at its core, the new work reinvigorates the creative look and feel of the brand.

The Abbey National Group supports charitable organisations and equal opportunities for disabled members of the community. Abbey National also supports education, training and employment for disadvantaged groups in society. Furthermore, the Abbey National Group made a community contribution of £3.9 million in 2001.

Brand Values

Abbey National retail bank's positioning in the financial services market is typified by its mission statement which reflects the company's desire to blend the old with the new. Its intention is to 'achieve above average growth in shareholder value over the long term, which can be achieved only if it meets the needs of its customers, its staff, and all the other stakeholders in the business'.

This approach, combined with listening to and understanding its customers and staff is what 'because life's complicated enough' is all about.

www.abbeynational.co.uk

Things you didn't know about
Abbey National

About one in seven mortgages in Britain is provided by Abbey National, making it the second largest mortgage lender in the UK.

Branch staff carry out around 98 million transactions for customers every year.

In November 1984, Abbey National became the first building society to offer a £100 cheque guarantee card.

In 1989, Abbey National became the first UK company to sell mortgages over the telephone.

During the 1989 ballot to decide Abbey National's conversion to plc status, there were three flights a day to Germany to pick up ballot boxes billeted at the British army bases.

Market

The sports clothing and footwear market has grown significantly over recent decades, with a marked increase in products being worn beyond the traditional sporting environments. An effect of this increased popularity is that sports companies have become much more aware of the image and perception of their brand and products, as well as their on-field performance.

As one of the biggest sporting occasions in the world, the 2002 World Cup attracted the attention of each of the major global sports brands. However, only adidas can lay claim to a heritage in the tournament stretching back more than 40 years. In 2002, the event generated such interest that it pushed the growth of the sports industry to new levels.

For adidas, 2002 also witnessed a fundamental shift from the traditional footwear and apparel structure used by most sporting goods companies to a new, three-way approach which enables adidas to address the needs of its consumers in a very focused way. The adidas brand is segmented into three divisions: adidas Sport Performance (products developed for the sports performance market), adidas Sport Heritage (adidas Originals products) and adidas Sport Style. Both the Sport Performance and the Sport Heritage business already show strong results, and adidas is hoping for the same success from adidas Sport Style since its introduction in 2003. Medium to long term, the adidas Sport Style division should account for as much as 5% of total adidas brand sales. Sales in the Sport Performance division should represent at least 65-70% of adidas brand sales while the Sport Heritage division will have a share of 25-30%.

Achievements

Despite continued competition across all categories, ongoing success in football is down to the company's passion for frequently making and marketing technically superior products. adidas believes that its leadership in football, combined with its new structure, will result in significant advances in market share across all categories.

adidas continues to focus on, and believe in, a 'performance' philosophy. In practice, this means supporting the best athletes, teams and competitions across the globe. With this in mind adidas has cultivated and extended partnerships with the likes of David Beckham (football), Zinedine Zidane (football), Sergio Garcia (golf), Maurice Green (athletics), The New Zealand All Blacks (rugby), Real Madrid (football) and the former World and reigning European football champions – France. The brand also has a long and rich association with the Olympic movement. It is extremely proud of the fact that it supports 26 of the 28 Olympic disciplines, something no other brand has achieved. Indeed, 2002 has seen the continued development of new technologies that will be used in Athens in 2004.

In the marketing of its products, adidas has once again led the industry with award winning advertising and public relations campaigns in support of its FIFA World Cup sponsorship and its technology launches for a3 and ClimaCool.

As well as earning Superbrand status again in 2002, adidas was voted as being a Cool BrandLeader in 2001 by the Superbrands Cool Council – the 'cool' factor now being key to brands, particularly those operating in the youth market.

History

Adi Dassler, a shoemaker from the village of Herzogenaurach, Bavaria, created the very first

adidas sports shoe in 1920. From humble beginnings the adidas corporation has expanded into a global company synonymous with world sport. Many of the fundamental principles upon which the first shoes were built, remain firmly rooted in the company philosophy of today.

Dassler was an athlete as well as a shoemaker and applied his knowledge and skills to producing products for athletes that helped improve performance at the highest level.

Dassler's efforts in the service of sport earned him more than 700 patents and other industrial property rights, many of them for revolutionary new products.

The company was, and remains today, committed to reacting to athletes' requirements and using their experiences to develop ever better performance footwear and clothing.

The phrase 'listen, test, modify' which was first used by Dassler himself, remains the key to the company's research and development operation.

Technical innovations over the years include the world's first football boot with screw-in studs, spiked track and field shoes and the present day development of ClimaCool, a shoe that allows ventilation of the feet. Since adidas equipped the first athletes at the Olympic Games in Amsterdam in 1928, over 800 world records and medals have been won by athletes using adidas footwear and apparel at Olympic Games and World Championships.

Product

Since the introduction of Dassler's first sports shoe in the 1920s, the adidas brand has expanded to such an extent that products are now available for almost every sport.

adidas designs both its apparel and footwear ranges with athletes' needs today in mind. Design concepts begin with the athlete and as a result, top competitors past and present, confirm that adidas equipment always takes into account the latest developments in modern technology. For example, in preparation for the 2002 FIFA World Cup, adidas put its apparel and footwear through eighteen months of athlete and laboratory testing to ensure the best possible performance under extremes of heat and humidity.

Looking forward to the Olympic Games in 2004, adidas is again involved in a lengthy development process. With Olympic records broken by hundredths of a second, adidas is determined to develop a new range of clothing and footwear that will give their athletes the necessary edge to challenge the boundaries of sporting achievement.

Recent Developments

2002 was a hugely significant year for adidas. Firstly, the World Cup in Japan and Korea was the stage for adidas to launch revolutionary clothing, ball and boot technologies that would help their teams and players perform to the very best of their ability. The Predator Mania is a re-engineered football boot that provides more swerve, increased accuracy, greater ball control and improved power transfer that results in greater comfort. It proved to be a big success with consumers and players alike. In the France '98 tournament, 55 players chose to wear the latest Predator football boot. In Japan and

Korea that number almost tripled, with 155 players wearing Predator Mania as their boot of choice.

In addition, adidas revealed the adidas Fevernova as the official Matchball of the FIFA World Cup. Launched as the most accurate and fastest ball adidas has ever produced, the Fevernova also proved a big hit with consumers as record global sales made it adidas' most successful ball ever. Using a revolutionary syntactic foam layering system, the ball returns energy in equal measures in all parts of the ball, making its flight more accurate and predictable than ever.

adidas also launched its team clothing range, Dynamic Layering Concept (DLC). It has been developed to provide physiological support to football players from head to toe, with each individual garment scientifically designed to provide the best possible support. DLC is ultra-lightweight and provides 'moisture management' and features 'graduated muscle compression'. Scientific evidence shows that DLC can improve a footballer's physiological performance. In the World Cup, nine teams wore DLC clothing including Argentina, France, Germany and Japan.

Sports Performance is the heart of the brand. Formally known as Forever Sport, this division features products developed for the performance sports market but has design appeal, encouraging consumers to wear the products both on and off the court or playing field. 2002 saw the launch of ClimaCool and a3 running shoes. Both were developed within the adidas innovation team. The aim for ClimaCool was to develop a functional shoe that featured a ventilation system. Tests proved that ClimaCool kept feet 20% cooler and drier than conventional footwear. a3 (pronounced a-cubed) is the culmination of five years development and is the most advanced training shoe technology that adidas has ever produced. The a3 concept is simple. Whereas most trainers offer just one heel technology, a3 combines three which

cushion, guide and drive the foot forward giving runners, as adidas' scientists would say, the 'perfect footstrike'. Both trainers have enjoyed very successful debut years in the marketplace.

The Sports Heritage division contains products that were once functional, now fashionable. In the 1970s and 1980s they were chosen by top athletes around the world as the performance product of choice. The range remains the same but through adidas Sports Heritage will be re-invented for the fashion arena using the authentic heritage of the adidas brand in sport performance.

Design and functionality are already strong aspects in the two existing adidas divisions and will be continued with an even stronger focus in the newly introduced Sport Style division designed by Yohji Yamamoto.

Promotion

adidas continues to acknowledge communication's pivotal role in the ongoing success of the brand. The brand now has a wholly integrated approach to all its marketing activity. The most significant of adidas' publicity activities is the high profile brand advertising. Recently, a number of key symbols and teams have featured in media campaigns targeted at both the sports and wider 'youth' audiences.

performance products for athletes.

The brand mission is quite simply to become the 'leading sports brand in the world'. It aims to do this by becoming the best performing brand in all sporting goods categories. To achieve this, the brand continues to produce the highest quality performance products possible at marketplace prices. Furthermore, products will continue to be designed and developed to enhance the performance of all who participate in sport, irrespective of their age, gender or ability.

www.adidas.com

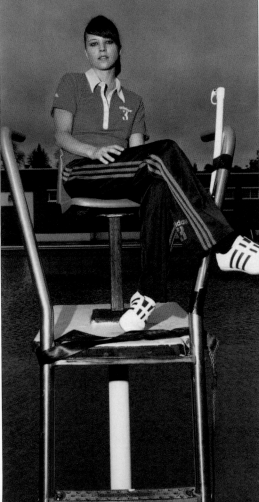

adidas is committed to incorporating new and developing media into the mix, a strategy that has seen everything from utilising the world's biggest advertising hoarding in Birmingham during the World Cup, to communicating the brand's target audience via the internet and email.

Continuing sponsorship and support of some of the world's top athletes and teams has also helped adidas successfully position itself as the brand of choice in sport.

Underpinning all of this high level activity, are extensive 'grassroots' sports programmes where adidas, along with some of the nations best coaches, help athletes of all ages get the most they can from their sport. Recently adidas took this one stage further with the launch of adidas Team Football — a schools initiative designed by teachers to help make learning more fun for children. It does this by encouraging and measuring their teamwork and fair play in a new and exciting way through science, literacy, numeracy and citizenship. The scheme is linked to the National Curriculum at Key Stages one and two. With David Beckham as the ambassador and support from the English Schools Football Association, The Schools Consortium and Sportsmatch, the scheme is being taken up by thousands of school children aged eight to ten.

Brand Values

adidas' brand positioning is clear and distinct. adidas has a genuine and far-reaching respect for sport and this is manifested in the company's devotion to making the best possible

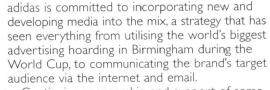

Market

Today's busy lifestyles, coupled with an explosion in consumer information about health, are driving factors behind the rise in self-medication and the consequent growth of over the counter (OTC) medicines. In the UK alone, the OTC sector is worth £1.75 billion (Source: Mintel). A breakdown of the figures indicates that pain relief ranks highly in the nation's health care priorities. The total analgesics market was worth an estimated £377 million in 2002 (Source: Mintel 2002), representing a 19% increase in real terms on sales in 1997.

Next to the cold, the headache is today's most frequent ailment. They may be minor ailments but they have one thing in common – Pain. Analgesics remain the most effective remedy for pain relief. A range of analgesics is available OTC, differentiated not only by their active ingredients but by their formats.

Anadin is at the forefront in providing effective pain relief. Over the years the brand has taken advantage of industry innovation and incorporated other ingredients such as paracetamol and ibuprofen into its portfolio, enabling it to offer a range of targeted and effective solutions to combat pain.

Achievements

Anadin is the most famous OTC brand in the UK with over 90% consumer awareness (Source: RSGB). It has mass market appeal with users of all ages from sixteen upwards. Changes in legislation in the 1990s enabled the brand to extend its product range while maintaining its position as a leading pain killer brand which delivered a range of long standing values to the consumer. Today Anadin is the second biggest selling branded analgesic in the UK and its product range is worth £45 million.

History

Originally launched in the US as Anacin, the brand appeared in the UK in 1932 under the Anadin name. It is owned by Wyeth and has always communicated that its key task is to defeat pain quickly. Widely respected by health care professionals and consumers alike, Anadin has used several different slogans to press home its message over the years.

These range from the famous 'Nothing Acts Faster than Anadin' slogan, which was introduced in 1955, to the recent 'Headache! What Headache?' and 'When only fast will do'.

Anadin has successfully steered its way through the growth of Own Label products during the 1990s – which resulted in many consumers switching from branded goods to retailers own lines, including health care products – by innovating and providing solutions relevant to its target market.

Product

Anadin is one of the UK's oldest and best known oral analgesics and a firm family favourite. The original aspirin-based formula provides fast, effective relief for a wide range of everyday aches and pains including headaches, period and dental pains, as well as the symptoms of colds and flu. The range has evolved into a portfolio of six UK variants delivering pain relievers in a variety of formats comprising caplets, tablets, liquid capsules and soluble tablets. Anadin Extra, containing aspirin, paracetamol and caffeine was launched in 1983. Its counterpart, Anadin Extra Soluble, which was unveiled in 1992, is ideal for those finding tablets difficult to swallow. The formula is more readily absorbed into the bloodstream enabling it to act faster. In 1988, Wyeth launched Anadin Paracetamol, a formulation suitable for children from the age of six, which is designed to reduce temperature and is therefore especially beneficial in the treatment of feverish colds and flu. In 1997, Anadin Ibuprofen was introduced. Coated for easy swallowing, it is formulated to relieve rheumatic or muscular pain, backache and period pain whilst actively reducing inflammation.

Recent Developments

The last three years have witnessed continuing innovation. As a result of the launch of Anadin Ultra in September 1999, sales grew at a double-digit rate. Anadin Ultra contains an ibuprofen solution in an easy to swallow, soft gelatine capsule allowing it to be rapidly absorbed into the bloodstream, combating pain more than twice as fast as tablets. In a move to benefit consumers and trade, the entire range received a new look in July 2002. Key features included a new embossed Anadin logo which reflects a more modern and dynamic image. In addition, Anadin Ultra and Extra packs were foiled to differentiate these variants as the most premium within the range. The effect of these changes has added branding consistency across the entire product range, ensuring stronger impact when the variants are grouped together. This improved on-shelf stand-out conveys to consumers that in an increasingly competitive

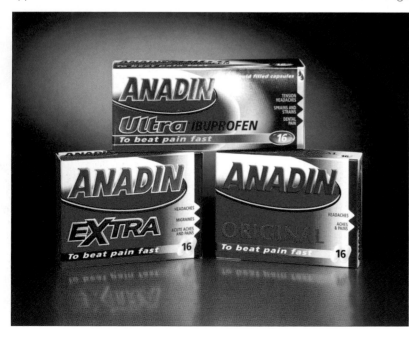

market, Anadin offers a range of premium quality products.

For consumers, the new design aims to 'take the pain out of choosing a painkiller' while communicating the modernity of the brand. Key indicators on the front of packs encourage analgesic users to identify the best product for their specific type of pain. Additionally, the use of consumer friendly language on the back of packs and on information leaflets further simplifies product selection and usage. Careline details are also included on packs, allowing consumers to receive further advice and guidance about the range.

Promotion

Anadin's familiar logo is synonymous with its brief to tackle everyday aches and pains swiftly and effectively since its launch more than 70 years ago. It is important for the brand to be at the forefront of product development and to inform the public about the benefits these products can bring. Therefore, advertising is key to Anadin's promotional strategy. In September 2002 it launched a terrestrial and satellite television campaign for Anadin Ultra. The campaign avoided the scientific angle taken by some other brands and opted for a humorous, slice-of-life approach featuring the 'Twice as Fast' strapline with the consumer message that Anadin Ultra's liquid ibuprofen capsules could hit pain more than twice as fast as their tablet equivalent. The 'Bus Stop' creative focuses on a typical British scene – a bus queue. The woman at the front of the queue announces, "It's gone!" leaving everyone to assume she means the bus. Confused they leave. She is in fact showing her surprise at how rapidly her headache has cleared. 'Submarine' features a crew of submariners tracking an enemy vessel. Suddenly the radar technician again says the line "It's

When only fast will do.

gone!" leaving a bewildered captain. He is also referring to the swift departure of his headache.

The commercials formed part of a £6 million television push which launched in December 2001 with 'Locker Room' and 'Detective'. Both were shot in black and white to reinforce Anadin Extra's position as a strong, efficacious painkiller. The creative executions clearly struck a chord with consumers, achieving 17th place in the Marketing NOP adwatch survey for best advertising recall and pole position for best OTC advertisement in the TNS Omnimas Survey in July 2002. Following the burst of advertising in June/July, RSGB studies revealed a 40% growth in consumers considering Anadin as 'a brand I might buy'.

In addition to television, Anadin deploys a variety of promotional activities to maintain brand awareness. To underline Anadin Ultra's speed of delivery, it sponsored a car in the prestigious 2002 British Touring Car Championship. The event attracts 200,000 visitors during the season and receives extensive television coverage with average viewing figures of one million per programme. As a result, Anadin's prominently branded car benefited considerably and the driver of the Anadin Ultra Honda Accord secured third place overall in the product category. Further consumer support for the sponsorship included Anadin branded give-aways at each event and a series of competitions in consumer and retailer magazines offering the chance to win a VIP trip to the championships.

Public Relations is another effective part of the brand's communications mix. To coincide with the 2002 pack relaunch, Anadin ran a consumer PR campaign that highlighted how the affects of modern life are causing stress related pain and affecting daily life. Research commissioned by Anadin revealed that the strain of modern living is increasingly detrimental to the sex life of UK males. Three quarters of men in the UK felt life was more stressful than five years ago and 63% said that they were suffering from frequent headaches at bedtime as

a direct result. Press coverage was considerable. The story ran with the brand mentioned in five national and 25 regional newspapers. The campaign was supported with nationwide radio interviews and an Anadin leaflet drop in five major cities which gave consumers the opportunity to win a Spa weekend break.

As well as offering consumers in-store leaflets about pain relief, Anadin has a website www.anadin.co.uk which offers product information and other details about combating pain.

Brand Values

Anadin has a brand heritage which delivers substantial consumer confidence. The Anadin range is regarded as a trustworthy, reliable, safe, no-nonsense method of delivering pain-relief. Its ability to offer effective treatment for all types of pain is reinforced by its status as a big brand because it is one of the most famous OTC brands with over 90% consumer awareness (Source: RSGB). Each sub-brand has its own positioning. Anadin Original is a tried and trusted traditional family product, used to combat milder forms of pain. Anadin Extra, designed for people who haven't the time or inclination to let minor discomfort trouble them, has a dynamic profile delivering a speedy strong remedy for really severe pain such as migraine. Anadin Ultra offers a modern, premium fast acting form of relief and appeals to the consumer who is abreast of the latest developments and trends.

www.anadin.co.uk

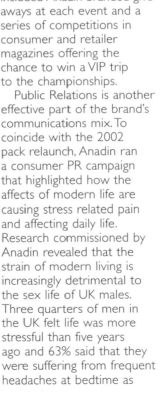

Anadin* Ultra's* liquid filled Ibuprofen capsules could hit pain more than

twice as fast

as normal Ibuprofen tablets.

Ultra

FAST

ANADIN
Ultra IBUPROFEN
To beat pain fast

Wyeth

Always read the label
Contains Ibuprofen

Soft Strong and Long
TOILET TISSUE

Market

Glamorous it may not be but, as an essential household purchase, toilet tissue is one of the UK's largest grocery product categories – and it is a sector that is increasingly diverse and competitive. Consumers spend some £815 million on toilet tissue annually (Source: Kimberly-Clark). UK toilet tissue is generally recognised as the softest in Europe and, as such, it is often used for 'secondary' functions such as make-up removal and nose blowing. All products in the category have improved, becoming softer, more absorbent and offering better wet strength. Due to such improvements, toilet tissue has become less restricted to the main purpose for which it is bought. The result has been heightened competition in both the toilet tissue and facial tissue markets, in addition to an increased number of players in these sectors.

Some 99% of the UK market favours soft toilet tissue, with 46% of the market preferring coloured toilet tissue, as consumers still find it important to match their toilet tissue with the décor of their bathroom. This use of coloured toilet tissue shows a huge increase from 1957 when it accounted for just 25% of the total market. In the 1950s the product was sold mainly through chemists, today however it achieves nearly 90% of its sales through major grocery multiples (Source: ACNielsen 2000).

When consumers were asked by Andrex® what they would be most likely to look for in a toilet tissue, softness emerged as the most important factor.

Achievements

Andrex® has been the leader in the toilet tissue market for over 40 years and has consequently become a household name – driven by high profile advertising.

2002 marked 30 years of the Andrex® puppy winning the hearts of the nation. Famous as the star of the UK's longest running consistent television advertising campaign, the puppy has now stolen the show in well over 100 commercials.

Despite its longevity, Andrex® is still recording significant growth. Between 2001 and 2002 independent sources attributed a 16.6% increase

in value to Andrex®, ranking it the UK's fifteenth fastest growing brand (Source: ACNielsen 2002).

Andrex® achieved the number six position in Marketing magazine's 'Biggest Brands' listing in August 2002 – based on ACNielsen's annual Top 50 ranking of UK brands. Andrex® was placed ahead of such brands as Ariel, Pampers and Robinsons with sales in excess of £240 million, a figure that was beaten only by Coca-Cola, Walkers Snack Foods, Müller, Nescafé and Stella Artois. Having been listed behind Persil in 2001, Andrex® emerged from the latest ranking as the UK's biggest non-food brand (Source: ACNielsen 2002).

Product development and innovation is a consistent focus for the brand. In 1992, Andrex® successfully launched a moist toilet tissue variant which contributed to a 45% growth in the moist category during its launch year. Andrex® Moist toilet tissue has been brand leader since 1993 and enjoys a 61% value share within the moist category (Source: ACNielsen August 2002).

Most recently, in 2001, Andrex® launched an Aloe Vera variant of the brand invigorating a totally new category in the paper products market. The same year, through relaunching the core brand with product improvements, fewer sheets per roll and a lower pack price, Andrex® achieved significant increases in sales and overall volume share – which was up to 25.8% in June 2002 from 21.8% the previous year (Source: ACNielsen August 2002).

History

Andrex® was developed from a design for gentlemen's disposable handkerchiefs that were sold exclusively in Harrods, London's famous department store. The tissue took its name however from St Andrew's Mill in Walthamstow, where it was first produced in 1942. Before soft toilet tissue such as Andrex® was introduced, the market consisted of much harsher products often known as 'shinies', which were sold mainly through chemists – famous brands included Bronco and Izal.

Andrex® was endorsed by Hollywood film stars of the day who demanded that studios stock softer toilet tissue rather than the ubiquitous 'shinies'. By 1961 the brand achieved market

leadership; a position it has retained ever since.

The Andrex® toilet tissue range has been greatly extended in recent years. It can be purchased in a range of colours and pack sizes which have been continuously developed since 1957 when Andrex® launched its first colour variant; Magnolia. In 1966 a full range of coloured variants were introduced.

The famous Andrex® puppy commercials were first screened in 1972. The original concept included a little girl running through her house trailing a roll of Andrex®. However, this was blocked by television regulators who believed it would encourage children to be wasteful. So the little girl was replaced by a playful Labrador puppy and the campaign went on to become one of the best-known commercials throughout the country.

In 1978 the manufacturer of Andrex® was awarded Royal Warrants of Appointment.

By 1991 over 81% of Andrex® sales were generated through multiple grocery outlets. A growing concern at this point was the increase in 'green' products made from recycled paper, which then accounted for 20% of the market. Andrex® responded by informing consumers through its advertising that it was an environmentally aware brand and took part in a programme of planting new trees. In addition Andrex® mass production facilities converted to non-chlorine gas bleached pulps.

Product

Kimberly-Clark Ltd, the manufacturer of Andrex® toilet tissue, is committed to maintaining its number one position in the marketplace.

Goes a long long way

Andrex
Luxury Toilet Tissue

Development is continuously underway to improve product quality – a priority due to the rising competition from retailers' own brand and other named brands. A number of relaunches have strengthened Andrex® considerably. The 1996 'New Feel' relaunch reintroduced 1.5 million consumers to the product, resulting in a 7% rise in value (Source: ACNielsen 1996). The 'Softest Ever' relaunch in January 1999 achieved a further 7% growth within the year (Source: ACNielsen 1999). In addition, the 2001 product enhancements and simultaneous change in price drove a 4% increase of the brand's volume share (Source: ACNielsen 2002).

Andrex® has maintained its reputation as one of the highest quality products on the market. There are six colours in the range and three standard pack sizes – two roll, four roll and nine roll.

The newest extensions to the Andrex® brand share the key attributes of softness and strength that have made the parent brand so successful. Andrex® Moist toilet tissues, with natural aloe, are lightly moistened to cleanse and refresh, and are available in both tub and refill formats. Andrex® Aloe Vera, available in four and nine-roll packs, has soft ripples that are enriched with both aloe and vitamin E for an extra level of care.

Recent Developments

In 1999, after over 25 years of successful puppy advertising, it was felt that a new approach was needed in order to re-establish the well-known brand icon. That year, Andrex® offered consumers the chance to apply for an exclusive Andrex® Bean Puppy. More than one million buyers responded to the offer, helping to raise over £110,000 for the National Canine Defence League. It also reaffirmed the popularity of the puppy amongst customers. The promotion was awarded the Institute of Sales Promotion (ISP) Grand Prix Award for the most successful promotion of 1999 and helped reassert

the position of Andrex® as the UK's favourite toilet tissue brand. When, in 2001, the promotion was offered to customers again, Andrex® still received over half a million applications for Bean Puppies.

The Andrex® puppy has also now found a kennel on the internet. Consumers can meet the puppy and play online games and collect tokens for merchandise at the award winning www.andrexpuppy.co.uk. The site has the younger visitor in mind and in addition to the other activities available, gives visitors the opportunity to email comments about their puppies in the 'bark back' section of the site.

In 2001 Andrex® was relaunched with new look packaging which replaced the Andrex® logo with one of three phrases, inviting customers to 'Hold me', 'Feel Me' and 'Touch Me' in order to experience product improvements first hand.

Promotion

The Andrex® puppy has become inextricably linked with the brand itself, symbolising the qualities of softness and strength that are at the core of the Andrex® brand.

The puppy has featured in nearly 120 commercials to date, generally appearing in the family home but also with various other animals including an elephant and a giraffe.

It was not until 1991 that the product was actually shown in the bathroom. The 'Little Boy' execution was one of the most successful in the history of Andrex® advertising and was voted the favourite commercial of 1991 by the public. It is still recalled by consumers, despite the fact it has not been televised for over ten years.

As a brand icon, the puppy is also used in a variety of other marketing and promotional devices. This has included calendars as well as a joint activity with Disney's 101 Dalmatians, and several soft toy promotions. In 1999 the Andrex® Puppy Appeal raised £110,000 for the National Canine Defence League which helped them care for over 11,000 dogs.

To celebrate the 25th year of puppy advertising, Andrex® sponsored an appeal for the Guide Dogs for the Blind Association, raising £270,000 for

the charity. Andrex® continues to work with the National Canine Defence League and a new fundraising partnership with the Irish Guide Dogs for the Blind was announced in 2002.

Significant investment was made in sales promotion activity focusing on the puppy to support the 30th Anniversary celebrations in 2002. A national, on-pack 'Finders Keepers' promotion rewarded customers with the opportunity to win one of 30,000 special prizes 'buried' by the puppy.

Brand Values

Despite an unglamorous product category, Andrex® has achieved a remarkable position as the UK's number one non-food brand, its sixth largest grocery brand and the market leader for over 40 years. Moreover, the brand is still growing. Andrex® has always developed high quality products that aim to provide the best value for families due to its key attributes: softness, strength and length. The renowned puppy advertising has been running successfully for over 30 years and ensures the brand is instantly recognisable.

www.andrexpuppy.co.uk

Things you didn't know about Andrex®

2002 marked 60 years of the brand and 30 years of the Andrex® puppy, which first made its debut on our TV screens in 1972, in an advertisement entitled 'Puppy'.

The name Andrex® comes from the St Andrew's Mill in Walthamstow, London where it was first produced in 1942 (rolled toilet tissue was invented in 1879).

In an NFO WorldGroup survey commissioned by Superbrands, the Andrex® puppy was found to be the most preferred guest to attend a wedding.

The first press advertising for Andrex® appeared in the early 1960s and featured the James Bond star George Lazenby holding a baby.

Around 1.5 million rolls of Andrex® toilet tissue are sold in the UK each day – enough tissue to encircle the world one and a half times.

The Andrex® commercial 'Little Boy' was the first of its kind to show the product in situ. It has also been the most successful puppy commercial in the history of Andrex® advertising.

One third of Andrex® purchasers never buy any other toilet tissue.

Feel different about new Andrex®

Feel Me New ANDREX® Toilet tissue is now even thicker and it's more absorbent too.

Touch Me New ANDREX® Toilet Tissue is so soft and gentle against your skin.

Hold Me and see for yourself how much ANDREX® Toilet Tissue has improved.

Andrex® with Aloe Vera Toilet Tissue is enriched with extracts of Aloe Vera and has Soft RIPPLES™ to give you an extra level of care for all the family.

ASDA Price

Always LOW PRICES

Market

It is 40 years since a couple of Yorkshire brothers opened a small supermarket in the town of Castleford when such stores were in their infancy. Today supermarkets have come of age and grown out of all recognition from their early days in terms of size and range of products. The Big Five alone, which includes ASDA, account for combined sales of £62 billion (Source: Mintel 2002).

The twenty first century shopper is more affluent, sophisticated and food conscious with higher expectations and needs than his/her predecessor and willing to experiment with a range of foods and lines which, 40 years ago, were considered not only 'exotic' but also prohibitively expensive, except to the fortunate few.

Food accounts for 16% of the average household's weekly outgoings (which is £385) with the majority of the population (50.3%) doing their shopping once a week. A smaller group (14.6%) shop two or three times weekly (Source: Mintel 2002). The rise in the number of homes with fridges, freezers and microwaves, coupled with the growth of car ownership has revolutionised how, when and where we shop. Additionally, in this time conscious age the supermarket's one-stop shop ethos is lost on few consumers. Out-of-town developments have helped remove the headache of congested city-centre shopping for those favouring a more leisurely, family oriented approach to buying everything from their weekly groceries to clothes for the children.

Interestingly, ASDA has found that even in a climate of greater economic prosperity, consumers now perceived getting good value for money as a sensible and acceptable thing to do. A cultural shift towards rising aspirations and higher expectations of material well-being is also taking place. This has led to the majority of people aiming towards making their disposable income go further. British shoppers value supermarkets. It is hardly surprising that ASDA and the Every Day Low Pricing (EDLP) policy is a firm favourite with shoppers making it the UK's third largest supermarket group.

Achievements

ASDA is the UK's best value food and clothing superstore. Average prices at ASDA, which carries out more than eleven million transactions a week offering an unmatchable mix of fresh food, grocery, clothing, home, leisure and entertainment goods, are over 10% lower than competitors. ASDA has received countless accolades. For the fifth consecutive year in 2002, it was voted 'Britain's best value supermarket' by The Grocer magazine and the UK's favourite store for range, price, service and reliability in a survey by ACNielsen. Over the years ASDA has raised millions for charities as well as being involved with local communities. In 2001 staff raised £3.5 million for local good causes and spent over 67,000

hours undertaking voluntary work. A crowning achievement for such efforts has been the Nestlé Social Commitment Award.

As well as looking after its customers and the local community, ASDA cares equally for its staff who are known as 'colleagues' and suppliers. In 2002 it topped a Sunday Times employee survey – Britain's Top 100 Companies to Work For. Such prizes have been underlined by The Castle Award recognising ASDA's commitment to providing equal pay and opportunities for women through innovative working practices ranging from introducing the first supermarket store manager job share scheme at Barnsley in

1999 to the 'School Starter' programme which allows parents to take a half day holiday on their child's first day at school. ASDA has also been named top employer by Personnel Today magazine and won awards for its innovative share schemes, 11,000 employees pocketed £14.5 million worth of shares in 2002. ASDA places great importance on using local suppliers, working with more than 2,600 and buying £1.1 billion in produce from them annually. Its own Code of Trade Practice, goes farther than the industry standard with special provisions for small and developing suppliers.

History

ASDA came into being in 1965 although its roots are firmly embedded in the Yorkshire dairy business of the 1920s when the Stockdale family operated its own milk wholesaling business.

The Stockdale's joined forces with other local farmers and through a process of acquisition and diversification became a public company. Associated Dairies & Farm Stores Ltd was formed in 1949. Enterprising brothers Peter and Fred Asquith joined the company in the 1950s and began developing a supermarket concept. Their first supermarket, aptly named 'Queen's' opened at the former Queen's Theatre in Castleford, Yorkshire, offering 'permanent reductions'. Two years later the Asquiths opened the third store under the ASDA name. The 1970s and 1980s witnessed a period of further growth with the purchase of furniture retailer MFI, Allied Carpets and the Gateway stores chain.

Amid much attention from the press, the US food retailing giant, Wal-Mart, bought ASDA for £7 billion in 1999. As part of the Wal-Mart family ASDA has retained its identity and remained true to its principles of better value and always backing British farmers and growers. The union has been very successful and ASDA has since gained one million new customers. Six thousand price cuts were made in 2000 and the following spring ASDA cut shoppers combined grocery bills by a further £52 million.

Product

ASDA today has more than 250 stores throughout the UK. It has a flexible approach to store sizes which vary from between 10,000 and 100,000 square feet, aiming to place the right development in the right catchment. The largest units or Supercentres, offer food, general merchandise, clothing and white/brown goods. The superstore is a mini-equivalent of its big brother. Small stores do not come any smaller than Billingham's 8,000 square foot, but are designed to suit the urban commuter who might need a sandwich for lunch or last minute ingredients for that evening's meal.

Its own label brands – Smart Price, ASDA Brand, Good For You! Organic and Extra Special, are best selling brands in their own right and have been developed to meet specific customer needs. In response to consumer demand ASDA implemented a three year pledge to ensure its own label products were healthier reducing fat, sugar and salt levels by 10% and in the process taking out 900 tonnes of salt without compromising on price, quality or shelf-life. The initiative includes removing allergenic ingredients like gluten and milk and lowering levels of additives linked to hypersensitivity in children. ASDA has been at the forefront of developing in-store 'food-to-go' counters introducing Curry Pot in 1996. This success prompted the superstore to launch Tex-Mex, Chinese, fish and chips and rotisserie chicken ranges.

In striving to serve all customers ASDA has been truly innovative. Schemes for the using disabled range from using Braille guns to label tinned goods, electric shopping scooters and 'trolley-vators' which lift shoppers to the higher shelves. The UK's first multi-lingual superstore in Bradford featured customer signage in Urdu, Punjabi and English. The brand's online home shopping service, asda.com, launched in 1998 and is operational in more than 30 stores throughout the UK with coverage constantly growing. The service offers a range of more than 11,000 products delivered to customers in temperature-controlled vans. ASDA offers competitively priced online travel and pet insurance, whilst its 'Calltime' programme offers an alternative service to BT with reduced-rate phone calls.

character pyjamas from £6

Recent Developments

ASDA works constantly to improve product and services while delivering its promise of Every Day Low Prices (EDLP). It has embarked on a multi-million pound review of its own label business which accounts for just over half of total sales. In true ASDA style the review has resulted in reducing prices while increasing volume. In 2002 alone the meat, fish and poultry section alone witnessed a £750,000 investment in rolling back prices.

ASDA also continues to drive down non-food prices. In May 2001 the superstore was victorious in its six-year campaign to abolish retail

price maintenance (RPM) for over the counter (OTC) medicines. The campaign ended a practice which meant consumers were paying in excess of £300 million on OTC branded products annually. ASDA celebrated by cutting prices by 50% on 36 healthcare items. In endeavouring to maintain lower prices whilst retaining quality, ASDA broke the Net Book agreement and bought better value books and reduced the price of comics.

ASDA has relaunched its general merchandise departments with 5,000 new lines delivering previously unheard of prices in the UK with toasters, kettles and irons under £8 and microwaves for less than £40. In parallel it expanded into new speciality areas like opticians, pharmacies, jewellery and photo departments, the latter offering prices 30% less than the high street. By the end of 2002 ASDA was the UK's sixth largest chain of opticians and ready to accelerate its pharmacy development, should it win its battle to relax the UK pharmacy opening controls.

The George clothing range which now encompasses everything from babyware to beachware launched in only five stores in 1990 has grown to a £600 million business and is the UK's second biggest fashion retailer. George Essentials launched in 2001 with prices averaging 30% lower than standard ranges with no compromise on quality. George Fast Fashion appeared the following April. It captures the latest styles and trends as they come off the catwalk with a brief to produce clothes from design to store in only seven weeks. The ranges are refreshed every four weeks reflecting the growing desire of shoppers to be inspired by new and fresh fashion items every time they shop.

Promotion

ASDA has invested heavily in promotional and advertising activity spending £18 million annually on television alone. Commercials which underscore ASDA's great value use the 'pocket the difference' tagline while featuring ordinary shoppers and staff in every day situations.

A variety of in-store publications – ASDA Price News, George Magalogues and ASDA Magazine – keep customers informed of new products while broadening their understanding of the non-food range. ASDA Magazine, with a readership of five million is the UK's most popular women's monthly. ASDA has also made clever use of below the line advertising using rickshaws to publicise the launch of its Dewsbury store.

As part of its promotional strategy the superstore has run a variety of entertainments or 'retailments' for customers. These included drive-in movies, fireworks parties and skating nights. ASDA was a key sponsor of the 2001 Commonwealth Games and part of its commitment to the regeneration of Manchester was the opening of a superstore.

Brand Values

ASDA is a people focused company with a caring nature. Central to the brand's personality is its aim to maintain a genuine interest in what customers think and feel so it can be prepared to do the best for them. ASDA hopes to be perceived as consistent and trustworthy and present customers with an offer where they can expect low prices whenever they shop and whatever they shop for whilst ensuring quality is not sacrificed.

www.asda.com

Market

Rarely have we witnessed a market grow at such a pace and on such a scale as that of the internet. By the second half of 2002 over twenty million adults in Britain were regular online users, compared to just four million five years before. More and more people are making purchases on the web, using it for online banking, booking holidays, looking for jobs, staying in touch with friends, family, business contacts and countless other uses.

But what is growing at an even faster rate is the number of website pages and amount of information available. In the days when people invariably went to a library, used a phone directory or their office filing system to look up information, everything they wanted was filed and indexed by subject and in alphabetical order. This is not so with the internet. Literally billions of pages are freely available but with no formal index system to tell people what information there is, or where it can be found. It is little surprise, therefore, that after email the second most popular use of the internet is to search. Various studies show that over 75% of web users in the UK visit a search engine at least once a month, and millions are searching online every day.

Achievements

The search market has changed dramatically over the past five years and the landscape has become dominated by a small handful of players. In terms of pure search, the online brand with the highest awareness among UK adults is Ask Jeeves, www.ask.co.uk (Source: RSL Capibus April 2002).

The origins of web search were fairly rudimentary and results returned were often wildly inaccurate. A system using 'Boolean Logic' symbols was introduced to narrow down the search as the number of web pages grew. But for most users, going online for the first time and getting the right combination of text, punctuation and mathematical symbols was too complicated. It was Ask Jeeves that broke the mould by making the search experience more user-friendly. The brand set out to provide a more efficient and 'guided' search, pioneering the notion of letting people ask questions in plain English to help them find the right answers. In recent years web users in general have become more skilled and rely on a simple phrase or keyword to make a search – even with Ask Jeeves. Ask Jeeves remains in the enviable position of being one of the first places surfers go for help finding what they are looking for on the net.

Ask Jeeves UK was launched at the beginning of 2000, and by the end of 2002 over six and a half million people were visiting every month.

The brand has very quickly become established and has built a reputation for ease of use, helpfulness and friendliness – attributes that many people look for as they try to navigate their way around the web. With its distinctive style and use of a 'virtual butler', Ask Jeeves owns the 'guided search' space. It addresses the mass market, from the experienced web user to the novice and attracts all age groups. Women in particular show an affinity to the 'avuncular' Jeeves, and the site reaches more of the general female market than any of the leading magazine titles.

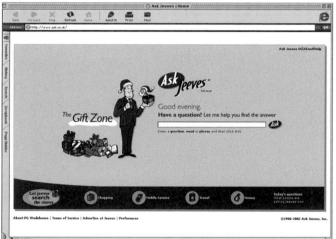

History

In 1996, David Warthen, creator of a natural language technology, joined forces with Garrett Gruener, a venture capitalist and together they created Ask Jeeves. In April 1997, www.askjeeves.com was launched to provide web users with a more user-friendly, natural way to find answers. In 1998, the company launched Ask Jeeves for Kids (www.ajkids.com) – a fun and child-friendly version of the original that allows kids to use the same natural-language approach but with added safety features.

Ask Jeeves grew quickly from a small enterprise to an international organisation. In February 2000, Ask Jeeves UK was launched (www.ask.co.uk) – initially as a joint venture between Ask Jeeves International, Carlton Communications plc and Granada Media Group, but later becoming wholly owned by Ask Jeeves, Inc in February 2002.

The site is regularly audited by ABC Electronic. In October 2001 Ask Jeeves, Inc acquired Teoma, a powerful new index search technology. Teoma searches and categorises sites on the web in a different way to other engines, enabling it to find the most relevant results amongst the billions of pages on the web. Not only does it find sites that are more relevant, but it also identifies which of these sites are an authority on the subject in question and is therefore more likely to provide the best answer or help with a query.

This next generation technology has been integrated into Ask Jeeves which has improved search results provided by the site.

Product

Ask Jeeves is a search engine that helps web users find what they are looking for on the internet. For many people it is their first port of call for when they need to find information, compare prices, book tickets, search for goods and services before making a purchase, and so on. Through a combination of leading edge technology and human editorial selection, users are presented with a set of the most relevant results in response to their request for information or help. Whether they ask a whole question or simply use a phrase or keyword, users always receive a selection of sites that will help them find what they are looking for, delivered in a friendly, helpful way.

Over six and a half million people in the UK use Ask Jeeves every month and the site receives more than a million queries or requests for help every day. Popular topics include shopping, travel, education, health, automotive, entertainment, finance and leisure. Included on the site at www.ask.co.uk are a number of channels that make it easier for people to browse and search for ideas, inspiration and information on specific products and services. The Shopping Channel for instance offers over one hundred different product categories to help users find what they are looking for – from electronic games, CDs and garden equipment, to food, groceries and fashions.

For added reassurance, all sites selected in any section of the channel will have undergone a strict selection process to make sure that they offer the best possible shopping experience. For instance, Ask Jeeves editors check each site against criteria such as ease of use, security, choice and customer care before allowing that site to be

A comparison tool helps surfers choose for instance, which of the 4,000 plus mortgages available is right for them or who is offering the most competitively priced travel insurance. If the user knows the company that they want to check out, a category by category suppliers list is available to help find the right website addresses.

The Ask Jeeves Mobile Service was launched to provide quick access to a wide range of services for mobile phones. Catering for the rapidly increasing trend in mobile downloads, the Mobile Service has a wide range of popular ringtones, logos or icons and picture messages that people can download to their own phone or send to a friend. With literally thousands of these being sent or exchanged every week, the Mobile channel has proved to be an extremely popular addition to the site.

a pre-determined question. 'The Magic Word' promotion in which four winners successfully guessed the right keyword in response to a set of clues won between them a trip to a diamond mine in South Africa, a trip to Florida, a VIP visit to Le Mans and a luxury shopping trip in Paris.

Brand Values

One of the reasons Ask Jeeves has established itself so quickly as a successful brand lies in the fact that the company and the site itself was given a character and a personality that befitted the service. The phrase 'Ask Jeeves' has begun to enter the vernacular as a common response to questions posed between family members, friends or business colleagues. And in becoming a celebrity figure in his own right, Jeeves the butler has helped bring the brand to life. As the 'world's first internet butler' and instantly recognisable, Jeeves embodies service delivered in an efficient, helpful, easy to use, reliable and friendly way.

www.ask.co.uk

Recent Developments

Since the launch of www.ask.co.uk in February 2000 a number of major enhancements have been made to the site. These include added functionality – such as the Channels – and more recently, some major design improvements to enhance the user experience and make it easier to find what one is looking for online. The results reply page has been simplified to present a cleaner, easier to use interface, that visitors to the site have responded to well. Emphasis has also been put on providing users with a 'guided' search experience – helping them when they are not quite sure what they are looking for or where to find it.

Relevancy of answers is the key requirement web users have when it comes to search. Thanks to the integration of 'Teoma' on the site, Ask Jeeves has the cutting edge technology to provide the most relevant results more of the time.

Promotion

Ask Jeeves continues to maintain its high profile presence across a range of media including TV, radio and press as well as online with integrated campaigns of brand advertising, tactical promotions and awareness campaigns. Major promotions of note designed to drive traffic and build awareness and frequency of use have included the '£1 Million Question' where entrants stand a chance of winning £1 million in cash or a number of exclusive prizes by guessing

part of the Ask Jeeves Shopping channel. For those users who are more concerned about security on the web, the channel also has a step-by-step guide with hints and tips to buying safely over the internet.

As an ever-increasing number of people take better control over their personal finances, the Jeeves Money Channel has been designed to help users compare terms and shop around for the best rates of interest. Armed with this resource, users are able to more competently review their investments or find the best deal on their home utilities, for example.

AVIS

Market

Avis is synonymous with vehicle rental. Alongside other major players such as Hertz, Budget, Europcar and new entrant, easyCar it dominates the sector. Indeed, Avis is the car hire market leader in the European, African and Middle Eastern markets, with around eight million customers annually (Source: Mintel).

In addition, Avis has the largest fleet and widest choice of vehicles with 34% of its total income derived from leisure use of its vehicles. This accounts for the biggest segment of its yearly revenue, ahead of corporate operations and prestige vehicle hire.

As a whole, the UK car hire industry has had to battle with a series of problems in recent years, including the fuel crisis of autumn 2000 and car-pricing realignment affecting supply chains. However, over a five year time frame, growth has still been seen in this market.

Achievements

From humble beginnings at Detroit Airport, Avis has built itself into a world-leading brand and is an instantly recognisable name to consumers and business users all over the world.

Avis has successfully pioneered car rental in several international markets, including Central and Eastern Europe, where it subsequently expanded its operations. It was the first car rental company to open an office in East Germany after the fall of the Berlin Wall – a move that helped it springboard into neighbouring former eastern bloc territories, like the Czech Republic and Romania. It has achieved a similar goal in the former Soviet Union and, when it opened an office in the Ukraine in 1997, became the first and only car rental company to have an office in every European country. This gives it an unrivalled European network – including a presence at 75 major European airports.

The brand has been similarly pioneering in Africa, where it now has representation in over 85% of the region. Again, this has given it greater coverage than any of its competitors. In the Middle East, it is represented in 90% of the region and in Asia, is licensed to operate in 27 territories.

Avis has been similarly pioneering in its commitment to high customer service levels since the mid 1960s including the introduction of the first computerised reservation system Wizard, in 1972. It has also built one of the best partnership structures in the business, with almost 50 airline partners.

History

Warren Avis opened the first Avis office at Willow Run airport, Detroit, in 1946. At that time, he had a grand total of three cars, but it was the world's first ever car rental operation at an airport.

By 1953, Avis was the second largest car rental company in the US and already expanding overseas, opening franchised operations in Mexico, Canada and Europe. By 1963 it was struggling with a 10% US market share, compared to 75% for Hertz. It launched an advertising campaign that proved crucial in turning its fortunes around. The slogan, 'We're only No.2. We try harder' emphasised its commitment to customer service and remains at the core of its brand today. The slogan has subsequently

been recognised as one of the ten best of all time.

In 1965, Avis officially launched Avis Europe to look after its growing operations in Europe, Africa and the Middle East. By 1973, it was market leader in these areas – a position it still holds today.

Avis entered a worldwide advertising and marketing agreement with General Motors in 1979 and began featuring GM cars in its fleet worldwide. In 1986, Avis Europe legally separated from its owner, Avis Inc, and became the first ever car company to float in the London Stock Exchange. In three years, it tripled its market value, before reverting to private ownership again in 1989.

In 1987, Avis Inc became employee-owned, with a £1.2 billion Employee Stock Ownership Plan – this made it the largest employee owned company in the US and a role model for other companies to follow.

The brand's impressive technological track record continued and in 1996 it became the first car rental company to launch a website – www.avis.com, allowing customers to make or modify a booking online. The following year, Avis Europe re-floated on the London Stock Exchange to fund expansion of the business.

In March 2000, an all-new central reservations centre, based at Salford Quays in Manchester, went live. Staffed by 250 agents, the centre takes over two and a half million calls and makes over 150,000 outbound calls every year. Agents can speak English, French, German, and also handle fax, post and email reservations.

Product

Worldwide, Avis has 5,100 rental locations and a fleet of 370,000 vehicles in over 170 countries. Annually, it completes around sixteen million rental transactions, generating annual gross revenue of approximately £1.7 billion.

The company maintains relationships with more than 50 of the world's airlines. Its network of outlets is split between those wholly owned by the company and licensees.

Avis was an early leader in technical support systems, with the introduction of its Wizard computerised reservation system in 1972. This is still in operation today and is the most extensive online, real time reservation, rental and management information system in the industry. Wizard controls the fleet, knowing where every car can be found, who they are rented to and when they will be returned. Wizard is also invaluable when it comes to managing company fleet costs and travel policy. Reports can be customised for corporate customers so they can optimise the management of their rental costs.

Thanks to partnerships with major airlines, Avis offers streamlined services at airports. For instance, with British Airways at Heathrow, customers can return their car and check-in for an onward BA flight at the same desk. With services like Avis Preferred, customers can enjoy some of the quickest service in the industry. Having completed a personal profile just once, customers can call ahead and then arrive at a Preferred desk to find a car pre-assigned with all the paperwork completed. Returning a car is just as quick – the Rapid Return Service allows the vehicle details to be entered into a hand held terminal, which automatically calculates the bill and issues a receipt before the customer even reaches the desk. Prestige Cars offers customers top of the range vehicles from a Jaguar X type to a Porsche Boxster and its Chauffeur Drive service offers limousines with uniformed drivers.

Avis also provides services tailored for business users, like Avis Advance, and Maxi-Rent – a flexible programme for long term rentals designed to facilitate fleet management.

Recent Developments

Avis is continuing to promote responsible car usage. A core element of this is its partnership with Future Forests, an environmental task force planting trees to offset carbon emissions. Avis is the only car rental company working with Future Forests. Since 1999 Avis UK has been 'carbon neutral' planting sufficient trees to offset the carbon emissions of the head office operations.

In 2002, the brand announced two major initiatives furthering its relationship with Future Forests. Firstly that all European operations are also to become carbon neutral and secondly car rentals booked online during the second quarter of 2002 had the carbon emissions offset automatically. Following the initial three-month promotion, online customers can offset their carbon emissions on their rentals for £1.

Avis has also introduced a car-sharing scheme, called Urbigo. This allows members, who pay an annual membership fee, to pick up cars from specially allocated points as and when they need them. It is designed to be a cost-effective alternative to car ownership or long-term rental. The scheme started in Oxford, but has now been developed in several locations in the London area.

Promotion

Avis is one of the most promotionally active of the major car rental brands, making extensive use of media including press, outdoor, radio and the internet. Campaigns are run on a national, regional or local level, with additional promotional activity with key partners and on the web.

Recent national campaigns included a Jubilee promotion in the summer of 2002, to coincide with the Golden Jubilee celebrations. On a more localised level, to celebrate the Commonwealth Games in Manchester in August 2002, customers who booked a car at Avis in Manchester Airport during the Games received an Avis cool bag.

Joint campaigns with partners such as bmi british midland include direct mail, joint advertising, or most recently, email activity. In July 2002, bmi and Avis used a customer relationship management (CRM) campaign via email to inform all bmi passengers and loyalty club members of their services.

Avis also uses product placement as a branding tool, with inclusion in films such as James Bond's Tomorrow Never Dies.

Brand Values

The company is driven by a singular vision which was established in 1965 – 'to be the best and fastest growing company with the highest profit margins in the car rental business'. These values are encapsulated in the 'We Try Harder' slogan. From the 1960s, when Avis made a virtue of being second biggest but the best in terms of service, it has put the customer at the centre of the business. Empathy (understanding customer needs), Honesty (value for money and integrity) and Humanity (putting the customer first) underpin the 'We Try Harder' philosophy. These values have contributed to Avis having one of the strongest and most consistent corporate cultures in the world.

www.avis.co.uk

The Brand Council

BBC

Market

The twenty first century technological revolution is dramatically changing the broadcasting and media environments, as telecommunications, IT and broadcast media converge.

Digital broadcasting has led to the launch of hundreds of new niche and broad-based entertainment and educational channels. Established broadcasters now face unprecedented competition, with over 40% of homes in the UK now receiving digital channels.

The internet has been another catalyst for radical change and has lead to the creation of global giants, for example, the merger between AOL and Time Warner. 40% of homes have access to the web and broadband services, which offer a much quicker connection speed, now reach 8% of homes.

Interactive and digital television, EPGs (electronic programme guides), WAP phone technology and digitally enhanced video recorders are further providing audiences with more choice than ever before.

The challenge for established and new broadcasters and service providers alike is to ensure brand presence and standout across a broad range of multi-media. The need for relevant, focused and clearly positioned brands and marketing strategies has never been greater.

Achievements

The BBC has been the most significant British broadcaster for over 78 years and continues to

In 2001 BBC One overtook ITV as the most-watched terrestrial network. In addition, during 2001/02, BBC television and radio programmes and web content won a string of major national and international awards. These include; 22 Gold Awards at the Sony Radio Academy Awards, ten BAFTA Television Programme Awards; seven BAFTA Television Craft Awards, six BAFTA Children's Film and Television Awards, four British Comedy Awards, four Golden Rose of Montreux Awards and three Emmy Awards.

The BBC is the broadcaster that audiences turn to at times of national significance. During the 2002 World Cup, audiences overwhelmingly turned to BBC One for all of the crucial England matches. For news of the Queen Mother's death and coverage of her funeral, again the BBC was the broadcaster of choice for three-quarters of the audience. And almost half the population watched some of the Queen's Jubilee coverage from the BBC. When whole communities came under the unprecedented threat as the blight of foot-and-mouth disease destroyed thousands of livelihoods in 2001, BBC local radio stations became the focal point around the clock for news.

The BBC World Service is stronger than ever, reaching over 150 million homes. Its global presence enhanced by BBC America and BBC World channels, ensuring there is a major British voice in an increasingly global media market.

During World War II the BBC established itself as the voice of the nation in the UK and of resistance in Europe, marking key historical moments, including the declaration of war by Prime Minister Neville Chamberlain, as well as King George VI's and Winston Churchill's speeches to the nation.

BBC television began broadcasting with the launch of its first channel in 1939. Transmissions were closed down during the War, but resumed in 1946 and continued to capture moments of national and historical significance with the transmission of live pictures of Queen Elizabeth II's coronation from Westminster in 1953 and man's first steps on the moon in 1969.

The BBC's second television channel, BBC Two, was launched in 1964. Full colour television transmissions, again pioneered by the BBC, began in 1967, together with the launch of BBC Radio 1 and local radio. Other major developments included Ceefax (1974), breakfast television (1983), Nicam Stereo (1980s) and the introduction of BBC World Service television in 1991.

In September 1955, the launch of ITV, a national advertiser-supported channel made up of regional franchises, provided the BBC's first commercial broadcasting rival. This duopoly lasted until the launch of Channel 4 in 1982 and domestic competition increased further in 1997 with the launch of Channel 5, the latest terrestrial player.

The most significant development in the industry, however, has been the explosion of

deliver the corporate challenge laid down by its first Director General, John Reith, 'to educate, entertain and inform'.

The BBC has become a national institution, universally recognised for the depth, breadth and quality of its award-winning news, sport, drama, comedy, natural history, music, online and factual programming.

Today's BBC has a tri-media offering, including TV, Radio and Interactive services; with an emphasis on connecting with its audiences.

The BBC caters for audiences of all ages and ethnic backgrounds in every part of the country. Its response to devolution and regional diversity has moved beyond news and political reporting to entertainment and factual programming. For example, increased investment in local television output and 37 'Where I Live' community websites across England form a major expansion of the BBC's local internet presence.

History

Formed in October 1922, the British Broadcasting Corporation was originally launched as a commercial radio broadcaster. Five years later it received its Royal Charter, establishing it as the UK's public service broadcaster.

The BBC now offers a range of multi-media broadcast services providing not only groundbreaking programming but pioneering technological and broadcasting innovation to all its licence fee payers.

From its early years the BBC began creating enduring institutions, such as the time 'pips' which have been used on the hour, every hour since 1924. 'The Week in Westminster', launched in 1930, is still broadcast weekly on BBC Radio 4.

1932 saw the launch of the Empire Service (a forerunner to today's BBC World Service) and the BBC's first major live outside broadcast was of George VI's coronation in 1937.

cable and satellite channels, dominated in the UK by BSkyB, launched in 1989.

Product

The BBC's public services are funded by an annual licence fee and carry no advertising or sponsorship. The BBC is committed to providing an innovative and dynamic mix of national and regional programming, some of which would be commercially unattractive to independent channels, in order to meet the requirements of its audiences.

The BBC makes use of its archive and brand portfolio on a commercial basis to supplement the licence fee. This is achieved though programme and publishing sales and commercial joint ventures from which the profit is reinvested into the core licence fee service.

Despite increasing demands on leisure time, the BBC reached 93% of the UK population in

2001/02 in some form. Indeed, its services include two national television channels, BBC One and BBC Two; five national radio stations, BBC Radio 1, BBC Radio 2, BBC Radio 3, BBC Radio 4, BBC Radio Five Live; 39 local radio stations, and dedicated services for listeners in Scotland, Wales and Northern Ireland.

Since 1997 it has also launched, six digital television channels; BBC News 24, BBC Choice (relaunched as BBC Three in October 2002), BBC Knowledge (relaunched as BBC

A new digital TV channel
www.bbc.co.uk/bbcfour

BBC FOUR
EVERYBODY NEEDS A PLACE TO THINK.
SAM TAYLOR-WOOD, ARTIST. REGENT'S PARK, LONDON.

Four in March 2002), BBC Parliament, CBBC and CBeebies, as well as three digital radio networks BBC 6 Music, BBC Five Live Sports Extra and BBC 1Xtra. The BBC Asian Network also went digital nationally in October 2002.

BBC World Service radio broadcasts in 43 languages and has a global audience of 150 million people, listening at least once a week. The World Service won the top Sony 2001 award for its coverage of September 11th and Afghanistan.

The BBC's educational role now sits at the heart of its public service remit. The primary challenge is to develop the learning dimension across all BBC output, harnessing new technologies as well as traditional ones, and creating popular and effective forms of learning for twenty first century Britain. Indeed, 10,000 people have gained an NVQ accreditation in internet literacy after completing the BBC's 'Becoming Webwise' online course, developed in partnership with Further Education colleges. 'Skillswise', launched during 2002, allowed people to improve their literacy and numeracy skills online, supporting the national drive to raise standards.

As both a broadcaster and a responsible and

ethical employer, the BBC engages directly in the life of the communities in which it operates. This involvement takes many different forms, some based on partnerships with other organisations, and all reflecting the social and environmental responsibility which the BBC, sees as an essential part of its public service role.

BBC Open Centres aim to expand the scope of the BBC's relationship with local communities. The concept was launched in Blackburn in 2001; each Open Centre offers opportunities for local people, on a drop-in basis or through more formal courses, to learn about the media, acquire IT skills and become involved in community broadcasting.

Recent Developments
Original and inspiring content and programming are key to the delivery of the BBC's public service remit and it continues to provide a rich variety of exceptional factual, drama and comedy content.

All internet and interactive services across the BBC were rebranded as BBCi in November 2001 to critical and popular success, with more than eight million viewers accessing one of its new services. During 2001/02 BBCi won nine major awards, including two BAFTAs, a Promax, an EMMA, a Sports Industry Award and the Prix Europa (for the BBC Radio 1 website). BBCi is also the most visited content site in Europe, achieving up to 700 million page impressions a month.

CBeebies (already the number one channel for younger children) and CBBC launched in February 2002, both carry much higher levels of original British-made programming than any of the commercial channels.

Recent landmark specialist factual programmes have included 'The Blue Planet', 'Walking with Beasts' (which attracted thirteen million viewers) and 'Your NHS', a major collaboration between BBC One, News, Regional networks, Radio and New Media.

One programme which defined BBC Two in 2001 was the innovative workplace comedy series 'The Office', starring Ricky Gervais. It won a total of seven major awards, including two BAFTAs and was voted best new comedy of 2001 at the British Comedy Awards in December 2001.

The BBC is also actively involved in charity activities. 'Sport Relief' raised more than £10 million in 2002 and the annual 'Children in Need' appeal raised a record £25 million.

Promotion
The letters B, B, C have become instantly recognisable to audiences worldwide as a trademark of quality broadcast services. In 1997 the BBC relaunched its corporate identity to take it into the digital age of broadcasting. A simpler logo was devised and implemented across all BBC sub-brands, services and channels, to ensure consistency of communication and to strengthen and protect the core BBC brand – one of the corporation's most valuable assets.

The BBC's logo is one of its most effective promotional devices and is used extensively and creatively across television and radio channels, online services, microphones, merchandising, cameras, books, CDs and videos around the world.

Both of the BBC's terrestrial analogue channels, BBC One and BBC Two, have their own individual identities, which enable them to communicate their own specific personalities and style under the core BBC brand. New logos for BBC One and BBC Two were implemented at the end of 2001; the former was also refreshed with new idents.

The BBC uses a variety of on and off air media to support its channels, services and programmes. Television trails are commonly used to provide details of forthcoming programmes and features.

January 2002 saw the BBC embark on a new Marketing and Communications strategy that

focuses support behind key priorities from across the whole of the BBC. As part of this strategy, each month a single priority receives unprecedented levels of support, including on air trails across television and radio, posters, pro-active publicity, online banners, a launch event and much more, via a totally integrated marketing and communications campaign. The campaigns are all informed by genuine consumer insights and are evaluated through extensive quantitative and qualitative research.

The World Cup campaign during May/June 2002 was an example of this strategy in action and promoted the BBC's tri-media coverage. The Manga animation that was the core idea behind 'The Winning Team from the BBC' campaign was used throughout all the activity on and off air, online, and in press coverage. As a result the campaign reached 99% of the UK's adult population and was recognised by Caitlin Moran in The Times as including) "the coolest adverts ever made, anywhere on earth without exception".

Brand Values
Since it received the Royal Charter in 1927, the BBC has remained true to its core purpose of informing; educating; entertaining and, more recently, connecting. Through the explosion of new technology, the BBC has ensured it has delivered its public service remit and communications have exploded in recent years, as generations of audiences have grown up to be replaced by new audiences with their own specific needs. The BBC has consistently delivered original, inspiring programme content and production values and achieved an unrivalled reputation for quality, impartiality and integrity all of which have helped make it one of the world's leading media brands.

www.bbc.co.uk

BLACK & DECKER

Market

There are many factors that affect the health of the DIY market; from the state of the housing market, the performance of the economy, to weather conditions and the media. The increasingly competitive DIY industry is fairing well compared to other sectors after suffering badly in the uncertain economic climate of the late 1980s. Throughout the early 1990s the industry struggled to find its feet due to the scarcity of new homeowners and a subsequent slump in the home improvement market.

This situation was further exacerbated by an influx of brands from the Far East. However, the mid 1990s saw early signs of recovery in the market place and since then, the industry has gone from strength to strength.

The buying and selling of houses has not only helped sustain the DIY and decorating market, but has helped encourage more activity within the sector. People generally view DIY and decorating as an investment when selling their home. Alternatively, homebuyers want to redecorate their new home in a style akin to their tastes.

Other factors aiding the growth of the market include the change in the traditional make-up of

the family which has taken place in recent years. A rise in the number of people separated or divorced has meant that more people are living on their own. In addition to this, people are having children later in life, which means that they are staying in the pre-family lifestage for a longer period.

Gardening and DIY are now amongst the nation's favourite pastimes. This upsurge in fortunes has been aided by media programmes and lifestyle magazine coverage of DIY such as the BBC programme Changing Rooms. This has helped to introduce new users to the market with a 'Do it now' attitude to style and decoration. DIY is now being perceived as being more of a leisure activity than a chore.

In the power tools market in which Black & Decker operates, 5.3 million items were sold in the UK in 2001, with the greatest growth area being in drills and circular saws. First time buyers accounted for 48% of these purchases (Source: ConsumerSCOPE).

Women now represent 15% of main users compared with 9% in 1996 (Source: ConsumerSCOPE Quarterly) with 48% considering themselves active or very active in DIY activities (Source: ConsumerSCOPE Monthly). In addition, 35% of power tools are purchased by women (Source: ConsumerSCOPE Quarterly).

Achievements

Black & Decker is the UK's most popular power tool brand with a 36% market share (Source: ConsumerSCOPE). Furthermore, it is the biggest manufacturer of power tools in the world with an unsurpassed global distribution network. It is one of the leading manufacturers of lawn and garden power tools, power tool accessories and handheld vacuum cleaners. This is reflected in the fact that eight out of ten households in the UK own a minimum of one Black & Decker product.

The brand continues to place emphasis on the importance of design, research and development. This has led to Black & Decker receiving numerous awards with special recognition for the Quattro® Multi-tool as one of its best selling tools. In 1999 the product was awarded Millennium Product status by the Design Council.

As well as introducing new tools to the market place, old favourites from its range are updated to meet ever-increasing consumer demands. Black & Decker was the first company to develop cordless tools and the classic Workmate® Workbench.

History

Black & Decker began life in 1910, when two young Americans, Duncan Black and Alonzo Decker formed their own manufacturing company. To raise the initial capital needed for their fledgling enterprise, Duncan Black sold his treasured Maxewell-Briscoe car, whilst Alonzo Decker borrowed an equal sum.

With their US$1200 investment they leased premises in Baltimore, and began contract machine work.

The early Black & Decker products ranged from equipment for the US mint, to bottle capping machinery. In 1914 the first hand-held power drill was patented with its pistol grip,

trigger switch and universal motor. Black & Decker had now begun to produce the goods for which it would subsequently become world-renowned. Early successes such as this, and the Lectroflator – an electric air compressor used to inflate tyres – pushed sales to above US$1million, which enabled the company to expand. Service centres were opened in Boston and New York and a new factory was built in Towson, Maryland, to cope with the phenomenal growth. In 1922 another milestone was reached when the first subsidiary outside the US was formed in Canada. And in 1928 the first factory was built in the UK, in Slough. This factory produced a range of heavy-duty tools including tappers, screwdrivers and grinders. The outbreak of World War II proved a testing time for the new UK business, though it aided the general war effort by manufacturing armaments from its factories. The scarcity of metals at the time forced a rethink in the design of its tools. Products were soon being manufactured with plastic housings.

In 1946, it came to Black & Decker's attention that industrial tools were going missing – often ending up in workers' homes. This alerted Black & Decker to the possibility of creating a home tools market. The company decided to make tools specifically aimed at this market – a major decision that was to change the face of the company and created what we now know as the DIY market. This move was to form its core

business for the next 50 years.

The extraordinary growth in sales that this decision prompted, ensured continuous expansion. By 1957, sales had exceeded £25 million.

The 1960s saw further expansion, with the opening of new branches in Scandinavia as well as in the UK, and the opening of new headquarters in Maidenhead.

At the end of the 1960s, Black & Decker turned its hand to 'space development' in association with the National Aeronautical and Space Agency (NASA). Black & Decker devised a cordless zero-torque space tool, used on the Gemini project, and in the early 1970s, a Black & Decker moon drill was used to remove core samples from the lunar surface.

Black & Decker has launched a variety of innovative new products over recent years. This includes the award winning Mouse®. This is a compact decorating and sanding tool which sands down a variety of surfaces including paint and varnish. It also cleans and polishes metal and plastic surfaces, as well as being used for rust removal.

In summer 2000 the Scorpion® powered hand saw was added to the Black & Decker sawing range. Its launch made a traditionally hard working tool, into a safe and efficient one with three blades for different sawing needs.

In Spring 2003, the popular Quattro® Multi-tool was relaunched. The 14.4V Quattro® Multi-tool is an all-in-one answer to the four key DIY tasks – drilling, sanding, screwdriving and jigsawing – achieved with its interchangeable heads. With its soft grip handle and powerful battery pack, the Quattro® Multi-tool is one of the most successful and easy to use power tools on the DIY market.

Product

Black & Decker produces a wide range of tools and products for the home and garden. Black & Decker's power tools range includes cordless drills, jigsaws and sanders. This range is broken down to target three groups of consumers. The Jade range is the entry price point range – affordable but well specified. The Silver & Black range is

the user with flexibility when cleaning.

In 2002 Black & Decker relaunched the brand with a new branding statement, 'make it your own home™' with new packaging and a new advertising strategy. The move was instigated following a research and development programme.

Since its conception Black & Decker has continued to introduce stylish, effective, and easy-to-use equipment to the marketplace with constant design and product development playing a key role.

Recent Developments

Product innovation and development is at the heart of the Black & Decker brand. New products include the Sandstorm®, a multi-purpose sanding and decorating tool. Features include a range of separate bases to cope with a variety of tasks, as well as a 'finger sanding' attachment which enables the user to sand difficult to reach places. It also has a built in dust extractor.

Another significant development to the brand's range is the Esprit® Cordless Drill-Screwdriver. Part of the easiDIY™ range, it is suitable for tackling many tasks. Features include its 180° rotating head (giving five different drilling positions from 0°-180°) a pull down button to allow the quick release of the drill head, as well as an integrated battery which makes the tool more compact and balanced.

in-store demonstrations, videos and direct email marketing campaigns. This is backed up with give-aways and 'tried and tested' features in consumer and national media.

Brand Values

Black & Decker prides itself on being able to offer innovative products and value for money, whilst maintaining high quality.

With the improvement in imported products, Black & Decker has increased its strong hold over the rest of the market by developing its multi-functional tools range. As well as offering

known as the easiDIY™ range; aimed at first time DIYers, products are lightweight and have features which aim to make tasks as easy as possible. The Intense Orange range is the premium range of tools, designed with the more confident user in mind. Products are highly specified with many features.

The Workmate® Workbench, is a classic piece of equipment that needs no introduction. It is still the ultimate accessory for all serious DIYers.

In its garden range Black & Decker supplies a range of equipment including mowers, trimmers, shredders, chainsaws and the multi purpose 'Mastervac'® Garden Vac. 2003 saw the development of a new innovative Hedge trimmer that has a rotating handle for greater reach.

For the home, Black & Decker produces a range of 'Dustbuster'®, hand held vacuum cleaners. 50 million Dustbuster® are sold wordwide each year, and the range continues to find new audiences due to consistent improvements in power, attachments and colour.

Dustbuster® Plus 3 in 1 Cordless Vac is the latest innovation which combines a handheld cordless cleaner and a upright vacuum cleaner to provide

Promotion

One of Black & Decker's earliest examples of television advertising was in 1928. A specially fitted out six-person monoplane was used as a flying showroom to demonstrate how Black & Decker power tools could be used in the reconditioning of aircraft engines.

The company's first network television advert came in 1955 with a series of ads for its power tool range. Since then, Black & Decker has used a combination of television advertising, in-store promotions and publicity campaigns to keep in touch and lead the way with consumer requirements.

A key time in Black & Decker's promotional strategy is the run up to Christmas. It is important to maximise sales around this time, with an estimated 11% of all Christmas presents in the UK being power tools. For Christmas 2002, Black & Decker's TV advertising showed DIY tasks being successful undertaken using Black & Decker tools. And the ads were spiced up with humorous touches.

To assist first time buyers, Black & Decker launched a number of in-store promotional catalogues which explain the benefits of the tools in layman's terms, using easy-to-understand dialogue that avoids clumsy and confusing technical dialogue. This userfriendly approach is reinforced by a series of detailed illustrations and graphics.

In the UK, the promotion of Black & Decker products also relies on

quality and innovative tools, Black & Decker guarantees to give reassurance to the most nervous customers.

Being a visionary, customer focused brand, Black & Decker aims to ensure that its products are both exciting and challenging, but remain the best tools for the job.

www.blackanddecker.co.uk

Things you didn't know about
Black & Decker

Power tools account for 11% of all Christmas presents, with household 'powered tools' accounting for 9%.

The Black & Decker Workmate® – the multi-purpose workbench – was invented by Ron Hickman, designer of the Lotus Elan sports car, in 1961.

Black & Decker research has found that a large percentage of the younger generation solve their DIY problems by getting their dads to do the work for them – rather than tackling jobs themselves.

Despite overall growth in the market, male and female roles have remained largely unchanged. At no point in the last five years has the percentage of women to men using tools exceeded 15%.

BRITISH AIRWAYS

Market

Air travel generates over £200 billion in revenues and provides at least 28 million jobs around the world. It is an extremely competitive market, with over 260 airlines fighting to win a slice of 1.6 billion passenger journeys per year.

Historically, airline passenger numbers have grown rapidly, with traffic on scheduled airlines rising at an average annual rate of just under 5%, while cargo volumes have increased even faster.

British Airways is the largest international airline in the world, carrying more international passengers than any of its competitors. Last year over 44 million passengers flew on 499,000 British Airways' international scheduled services. That is the equivalent of 80 passengers checking in every minute, 24 hours a day, and a British Airways flight taking off and landing every 60 seconds.

One of the main stimuli to air travel has been the privatisation and deregulation of the industry. One feature of this changed landscape has been the emergence of the 'no-frills' airlines, which have achieved rapid growth in market share in the US domestic and short haul European markets.

A second feature of this has been the formation of global alliances between carriers – allowing them to co-operate on such activities as marketing, ticket booking and frequent-flyer programmes.

The airline industry suffered a major shock in 2001, with the combined forces of a global slowdown and the use of commercial aircraft in the September 11th terrorist attacks. The effect on the industry was a sharp drop in passenger demand, and 2001/02 was forecast to see airlines sustaining large losses as the industry dealt with the biggest challenge it has faced for a decade. A year on from September 11th, the airline market was still a long way from making a full recovery, although the current opinion is that these events will not dent the industry's longer-term growth trend or its economic importance.

Achievements

One of British Airways' key achievements of 2002 is a new short haul pricing structure for the UK and European markets. The airline's new commercial proposition promotes competitive low cost fares with a full service offering.

Introducing lower starting fares and the removal of restrictions such as the Saturday night stay rule; provides the customer with a choice of greater flexibility and value for money, enabling British Airways to offer more competitive options for both its business and leisure customers. This heralds a fundamental shift in British Airways price advertising strategy. British Airways now offers fares starting from £59 return on domestic flights and £69 return to Europe.

British Airways received numerous awards in 2002, including Best Airline in Western Europe,

Best Transatlantic Airline and Best International First Class by the OAG. Also Best Airline, Best First Class, Best Business Class, Best Shorthaul Flights, Best Frequent Flyer Programme, Best Cabin Staff and Most Innovative Airline by the Business Traveller Magazine. Also in 2002, British Airways received the NOP World Business Superbrands Award for being 'Best Community Member'.

History

British Airways origins date back to the pioneering days of civil aviation, following the end of World War I. Its forerunner, Aircraft Transportation and Travel Limited (AT&T), launched the world's first daily international scheduled air service between London and Paris in 1919. The single-engined de Havilland biplane carried just one passenger and took two and a half hours to reach Le Bourget. In 1924, AT&T merged with three other fledgling British airlines to form Imperial Airways Limited. During the 1920s and 1930s services were offered to Egypt, India, South Africa, Singapore and West Africa. Meanwhile, a number of other UK air transport companies merged to form the original privately owned British Airways Ltd in 1935.

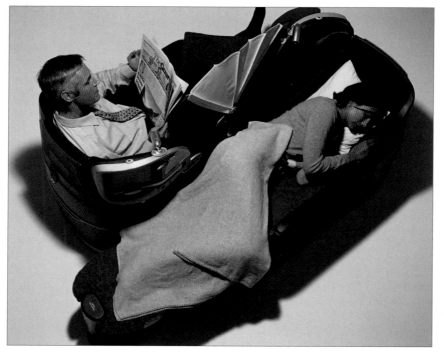

Imperial Airways and British Airways were nationalised in 1939 to form British Overseas Airways Corporation (BOAC).

The 1950s saw the dawn of the passenger jet age and BOAC led the way flying a Comet to Johannesburg in 1952, halving the previous journey time. BOAC also operated the first transatlantic jet services in 1958, with two Comets flying simultaneously between New York and London.

In the 1960s, other British airlines began to offer competing services. In 1967, the government unified these independents into a third carrier, British Caledonian. In 1972, the boards of BOAC and BEA were combined and, in 1974, the two formally merged to become British Airways. Continuing its pioneering spirit, British Airways launched the world's first supersonic passenger service, simultaneously with Air France in January 1976.

In February 1987, British Airways was privatised. Over one million applications were received for shares, making the floatation eleven times over subscribed. The oneworld™ alliance came into operation in February 1999 and combines the services of British Airways, Aer Lingus, American Airlines, Cathay Pacific, Finnair, Iberia, and Lan Chile, serving more countries than any other airline alliance.

British Airways has developed a strong relationship with Qantas, operating a joint service agreement, which allows sharing of revenues on Europe - Australia services. It also has simple code-sharing arrangements with several other airlines outside the oneworld alliance. Taken together with its extensive network, these partnerships increase the scale of British Airways' presence in the major world airline markets.

Product

British Airways has a fleet of over 220 aircraft including 56 Boeing 747s, 45 Boeing 777s, seven Concordes and 38 Airbus A319/320s.

The airline's offering is organised around a portfolio of products and services developed in order to meet customer's needs.

Concorde is the flagship of British Airways fleet and its passengers receive priority treatment wherever possible, with exclusive lounges at London Heathrow and JFK, and specially trained crew to ensure the premium level of service is delivered superbly.

FIRST, described as the 'ultimate in privacy and control' has been refreshed and enhanced since its original launch. The tailored service and personal space offered by FIRST allows travellers to work, rest and dine at any time during their journey. The cabin layout provides a private environment and seats which converts to a six foot six inch flat bed.

New Club World provides the first fully flat bed in business class. Each seat benefits from in-seat phone and laptop power, a movable privacy screen, improved in-flight entertainment and flexible dining options – including pre-flight dining on selected routes. Club World also gives travellers access to over 200 airport lounges worldwide. 75% of the British Airways long haul fleet is now fitted with FIRST, New Club World and World Traveller Plus cabins. British Airways intends to fit all 747 aircraft from London Heathrow with these cabins and also to introduce them to the Gatwick fleet.

World Traveller Plus is a premier economy cabin with a maximum of five rows of seats and increased legroom. It offers more space and a quieter, separate cabin, ergonomically designed seats and redesigned cabin interiors.

World Traveller has a comprehensive range of services and benefits for customers flying long haul in economy. It has a family focus (including 'Feed

If you won't fly to your client, who will?

It's better to be there **BRITISH AIRWAYS**

kids first' and children's activity packs) aiming to make long haul travelling easy.

Club Europe services are available on European flights and enables travellers to choose from a variety of check-in options and ground services. British Airways offers the best network, schedule, and frequency available.

Euro Traveller has the same choice of check-in options, network, schedule and frequency as Club Europe, but offers a premium yet value-for-money service.

Within the UK, the brand offers more flights to more destinations with the best punctuality.

The British Airways Executive Club is an established loyalty programme with over three million members worldwide. Benefits include dedicated phone and web facilities, priority boarding and the ability to earn BA Miles when using British Airways or any airline, hotel or car hire partner.

On Business is a loyalty programme for small to medium sized companies. Companies can earn points for flying with British Airways which they can then exchange for free British Airways flights and other cost saving rewards.

A range of check-in options are available when flying with British Airways, including telephone, online, self-service and London Paddington and airport departure gate check-ins. Online check-in gives travellers the opportunity to save time at the airport by checking in via the internet before they leave the office or home.

British Airways e-ticket can be amended up to 30 minutes before check-in and gives passengers the opportunity to avoid airport queues by using a British Airways Self-Service Check-In machine.

As well as a full range of customer services, British Airways supports a dedicated extranet site for the travel trade that provides information on all British Airways products and services, including any promotional offers. The extranet site also supports the highly successful functionality 'Ask BA', which allows users to ask a question that is answered instantly online.

Recent Developments

British Airways recently re-designed its website home page to make www.ba.com easier to use and more appealing in the very competitive online selling arena. The new look home page is aimed at helping new and existing customers have a better 'online' experience. Links to British Airways' special offers and the Executive Club, plus advice on how to access British Airways new cheaper fares are in place.

The website is now the most popular way for passengers in the UK to book their tickets directly with over one million visitors a week and a weekly average of £6.4 million revenue generated.

Promotion

British Airways' marketing campaigns have won numerous awards including, in 2002, CIMTIG Gold awards for Best Creative Media Plan, Best Television

Brussels return from £69

Have you seen how small our prices are?

For this and many more destinations book at ba.com   **BRITISH AIRWAYS**

Advertisement – Business, Best Outdoor Advertisement, Best Business Press Campaign.

Recent promotions include the highly successful 'Be There' campaign (January 2002), which concentrated on the fact that it is better to do business face to face. This promotion won the Best Television Advertisement – Business in the CIMTIG 2002 awards.

British Airways has a dedicated B2B sales force and marketing team, building stronger links between the airline and its corporate customers. The marketing team have recently developed newly designed corporate communications to ensure consistency of the brand is delivered.

From September 2002, British Airways mounted its largest and most sustained advertising and marketing campaigns, in which price was made the hero of all communications. The campaign line 'Have you seen how small our prices are?' launched on September 16th 2002. It also represented one of the broadest campaigns ever, designed to reach consumers across a wide mix of media and channels with TV, press, radio, outdoor, online and innovative ambient advertising such as laser projections across

London and advertising on cash point machines. The adoption of TV for this campaign marked the first return to price led advertising on TV for over four years. The campaign aimed to force a reappraisal of British Airways; to get British Airways back on the consideration list of customers who had been attracted to the 'no-frills carriers'. The second advertisement with the strapline – 'There's other ways and there's British Airways' – was the second phase of the short haul brand re-assertion. The advertisement demonstrates that British Airways offers value added services that some 'no-frills' airlines fail to provide.

British Airways also launched its first ever broadcast sponsorship – 'The British Airways Destinations Report' on Sky News – airing five times a day, 365 days a year.

Brand Values

Customers look for airlines that inspire confidence and that they can trust. British Airways responds to this with the twofold promise of reliability and reassurance.

Its reliability is reflected in the scale of operations and presence in the market place that the British Airways infrastructure allows. The choice of destinations and size of the fleet mean customers value British Airways' schedules as well as trusting the airline to have enough planes to keep a service running.

Reassurance is underpinned by safety and security – from baggage handling to punctuality, cleanliness and schedules, through to products and services. The airline's heritage, quality standards and attention to detail also supports this.

These traditionally British values are a fundamental part of the British Airways brand identity. As national flag carrier, British Airways' UK customers voice the statement "travel the world and feel at home". International customers, who place similar emphasis on such values, echo this sentiment just as strongly. What they are looking for essentially is a British experience in the air.

www.ba.com

Market

The UK's telecommunications market is one of the most competitive in the world, with over 200 different operators vying for a slice of the residential and business sectors. In 2000, telecoms watchdog Oftel estimated the market to be worth around £28 billion.

BT has been providing the UK with telecommunications services since the mid twentieth century and today provides over 28 million lines to customers' homes and businesses throughout the country.

BT is synonymous with phones and phone lines, and we all recognise BT Payphones in streets, stations and shopping centres. But people are less aware that BT is involved in such diverse activities as handling calls for the Nectar loyalty rewards scheme, providing transmission services for the broadcast of the US Open Tennis Championships, and distributing Reuters data to the African continent.

BT has a 73% share of the residential, fixed voice call market in the UK, and a 48% share of the business market. Despite stiff competition, the number of residential BT lines actually increased slightly over the 2001/02 period, as customers installed second lines and returned to BT from other operators.

In such a competitive market, BT has had to develop some innovative pricing packages to keep ahead of the pack. The company has developed its pioneering BT Together package which offers reduced call rates and other benefits for a fixed monthly fee. By the end of March 2002, more than ten million customers had signed up for the package, and 71% of residential customer call minutes were made by BT Together subscribers.

Looking forward, BT predicts that broadband will be the future for the communications market. Broadband provides customers with always on, high-speed direct access to the internet over a single phone line. By November 2002, BT had connected over 400,000 people to ADSL, the technology behind broadband, and hopes to secure one million customers by summer 2003 and five million by 2006.

Achievements

BT is one of the best known and most powerful brands in the UK. In research, the BT brand scores highly in terms of awareness, and has been one of the most consistently strong performers in Marketing magazine's Adwatch survey.

But it isn't just BT's advertising which forms public perceptions of the company — everything it does touches peoples' lives. Each year, MORI conducts a public survey on corporate social responsibility. 2001 results showed that the importance of social responsibility continues to grow, and that BT is among the handful of 'responsible companies' mentioned. BT was ranked ninth out of over 40 companies and was associated with helplines and prominent TV events – Children in Need and Comic Relief, for example.

In September 2002, for the second year running, BT topped the Dow Jones Sustainability index for the telecoms sector worldwide. Earlier in the year, BT was rated number one in the private sector in Race for Opportunity's Benchmark Report on race and diversity in the UK. Race for Opportunity surveyed 99 private and public sector organisations covering 2.75 million workers in the UK, and BT was shown as the overall top performing company.

BT's innovative approach to flexible working won it the accolade of UK Employer of the Year 2001 in the Parents at Work/Lloyds TSB Employer of the Year Awards, supported by the DTI. The company was specifically rated for its policies and practices in helping employees achieve a work/life balance.

BT operates one of the most sophisticated and well-maintained networks anywhere in the globe. The company's UK network is the country's largest, with the greatest geographical reach and customer coverage. With 120 million copper pair kilometres and six million optical fibre kilometres, it has the ability to touch virtually every home and business in the country. Its 900 local and trunk exchanges handle an average of 300 million calls daily.

History

For many years, the UK's telephone service was provided by the General Post Office. In 1969, the Post Office became a state public corporation and was split into two separate entities. The corporation responsible for telecommunications took on the trading name British Telecommunications and, in 1984, British Telecom, as it was then popularly known, was privatised. British Telecommunications plc was the first privatised company of its kind in Europe.

In 1991, the company was restructured and relaunched as BT with new branding and a new logo. A clear mission of putting customers first was demonstrated by the introduction of the Customer's Charter, and such advertising favourites as Busby and Beattie were introduced to the public.

Over the next ten years, BT established a number of joint ventures and alliances worldwide. With the liberalisation of the European telecoms market in 1998, BT was poised to take advantage of all the opportunities this market presented.

A radical restructuring in 2000 saw BT split into lines of business which are successfully in place today: BT Retail, BT Wholesale, BT Openworld and BT Ignite. Yell, the directories business, was sold in 2001 and BT Wireless, which incorporated mobile network BT Cellnet, was demerged in November 2001, and now trades wholly separately from BT under the name mmO2 plc. BT also exited a number of its worldwide ventures in order to focus on the UK market, and now trades under the name of BT Group plc.

Today, BT is a multi-billion pound company, with 104,000 staff generating an annual turnover in 2001/02 of £18.4 billion.

Product

BT's principal activities include local, national and international telecommunications services, higher-value broadband and internet products and services, and IT solutions. The company also provides network services to other licensed operators.

Some of BT's customers' communications needs are simple, and some complex. BT's job is to find the most effective way to meet those needs, no matter how diverse.

BT's Select Services have been around since the late 1990s, and originated with the eponymous 1471 service. They now include, for example:

Call Diversion – calls that can't get through to your home phone will still reach you on another fixed line or mobile of your choice; Call Minder – a messaging service that takes your calls when you are surfing the net, on the phone, or unable to get to the phone; Ring Back – which redials an engaged number; and BT Answer 1571, a free messaging service.

BT Openworld, the company's mass market internet division, is one of the UK's leading internet service providers (ISPs) and the UK's number one in unmetered access. It delivers broadband and narrowband services to more than 1.7 million business and residential customers in the UK. BT Openworld offers a wide range of internet access packages. Broadband packages include BT Openworld Home 500 Plug & Go and Business 500 Plug & Go, which are popular self-install broadband products. BT Openworld also provides broadband over satellite for business users.

Narrowband products include BT Openworld Anytime which provides unmetered access to the internet 24/7, and Pay-As-You-Go services.

BT also provides broadband services via its BT Broadband offering, launched in September 2002. BT Broadband is a revolutionary, 'no frills' product, leaving the user to decide on added services such as email or web space, and providing high speed access at low cost.

BT Ignite is BT's business services and solutions division, serving customers worldwide. As an information and communications technology service provider, BT Ignite provides integrated data and value-added services to meet the European needs of global multi-site corporates and the global needs of European corporates.

The BT Ignite portfolio ranges from desktop and network equipment and software, transport and connectivity, IP-based e-business solutions, managed network services and systems integration to consultancy for complex global requirements.

BT Wholesale manages BT's networks and has a turnover of around £12 billion a year. The division provides network services and solutions in the UK to communications companies, network operators and service providers.

Recent Developments

Recently, both BT and its marketplace have transformed dramatically.

In the 2002 financial year, BT undertook the UK's largest ever Rights Issue, raising £5.9 billion from shareholders. In 2001, BT sought its shareholders' approval to demerge its mobile operations, known as BT Wireless at the time. Shareholders unanimously agreed that BT's fixed and mobile operations would be better managed, and offer increased value, separately and, in November 2001, the business was demerged. This created two new companies – BT Group plc and mmO2 plc. Trading as O2, mmO2 plc now operates completely separately from BT, although the two companies do work together on certain mobile offerings for customers.

Having purchased the assets of Scoot, BT announced plans to re-enter the directories market in 2002. Using the new number 118 500 or the web, customers can get directory enquiries, classified listings and information ranging from weather forecasts to share prices.

In summer 2001, BT made public wireless LAN broadband a reality with the launch of BT Openzone. Hilton Hotels, Bluewater and Earl's Court Olympia became the first site partners for the BT Openzone 'hotspots'. BT aims to run more than 4,000 in the future to give business travellers the chance to experience the flexibility of mobile working combined with the power and speed of BT's broadband network.

For the first time ever, BT changed the colour of thousands of its high street phone boxes from red to bright blue in autumn 2002. All 1,000 of BT's modern phone boxes fitted with

BT Broadband. Leaves normal internet standing.

0800 800 060 BT.com/btbroadband BT

new public internet terminals were given the blue makeover, and this will increase to 8,000 blue boxes by the time the programme is completed in 2007. A further 20,000 'e-payphones' are planned in locations such as shopping centres, airports, rail, tube and bus stations, creating the world's largest network of public internet kiosks.

Promotion

Since privatisation, BT has maintained a high profile in marketing communications and, in recent years, has regularly been one of the highest spending advertisers in the UK. Its two lead agencies in 2002 were Abbott Mead Vickers and St Luke's.

In 1999, Abbott Mead Vickers developed a campaign for BT introducing the theme 'Stay in touch', using ET as the central character. Unlike the previous 'It's good to talk' campaign, it featured email and internet call stimulations.

The strapline 'Bringing people together' was introduced in 2001. Advertising focused on using

ordinary people and BT's ability to 'bring them together' – achieving 'connectedness'. A brand campaign, 'More connections. More possibilities' launched in September 2001 with the 'Stadium' execution, which was hugely popular, projecting BT's stature and forward thinking at the same time.

Using the same strapline, BT launched the UK's most intensive television campaign to help double broadband connections in September 2002. The company spent £10 million over ten days between September 22nd and October 2nd to advertise the potential of broadband. The campaign, called 'Broadband has landed', featured singer Jarvis Cocker, cartoon pigs on motor bikes and a giant rhino.

Brand Values

The beginnings of the now familiar BT identity and the first steps towards establishing a BT brand were taken in 1988. Since then, the

brand has been carefully developed and, in 1997, was valued for the first time. A value of £5.7 billion was ascribed to the BT brand and, when undertaken again in 2000, the brand was valued at a staggering £9.4 billion. BT runs a brand web site at www.btbrand.bt.com, as well as a freefone Brand Helpdesk, to help ensure that the value of its brand is maintained.

A second brand valuation followed a major project to redefine BT's core brand proposition in the UK. The brand proposition developed was 'BT is your guide to the potential of communications, today and for the future, wherever you are, whatever you need'.

The fundamental human need that the new brand proposition sought to address was 'connectedness' meaning both the functional connectedness which BT's network offers, and emotional connectedness which enables people to enrich their lives and achieve their goals.

By autumn 2002, the brand proposition had evolved to 'BT's purpose is to co-create and host the new communicating society, stimulating participation at every level.'

www.bt.com

CLASSIC *f*M

Market

Today Classic FM is the largest commercial radio station in the UK broadcasting to 6.8 million adults every week and over a quarter of a million children.

Alongside Classic FM there are now 261 independent radio licences in addition to the BBC's 49 stations.

New technology is revolutionising the radio broadcast market. The advent of digital radio is already delivering its promise of up to 200 new services broadcasting via digital audio broadcasting (DAB), cable and satellite, whilst the internet has fuelled a global explosion of some 9,000 online radio services.

Digital is the future for radio in the twenty first century. Classic FM was the first commercial station to go digital in 1999 and the brand has since expanded into new platforms and technologies to reach younger audiences.

More than half a million people now log on to classicfm.com every month to listen and interact with the station. A further 300,000 people tune into Classic FM radio via their digital televisions.

Achievements

Classic FM's pioneering approach to its programming, advertising and marketing has won the station many accolades, including more than ten Sony Awards. Classic FM has been voted UK Station of the Year three times, and has been nominated for the award on four occasions. It has won two Gold Awards for On Air Station Sound and has also been voted Campaign Medium of the Year.

The Classic FM brand has also won much praise across the world of marketing. In 2002, Classic FM was highly commended by Marketing Week as Media Brand of the Year and awarded UK's Brand Development of the Year by the Marketing Society. Classic FM is also the current holder of Arts and Business Champion of the Year Award, in recognition for its projects encouraging children to make music.

History

Something strange was afoot one summer's day in 1992. As listeners across the UK tuned in between 100 and 102 MHz, they found themselves listening to birdsong. Nothing else – just birdsong. Then, just before 6am on the morning of September 7th, instead of starlings and sparrows, the sound of classical music poured out of radios across the country. Classic FM was born.

From day one, media pundits and classical music buffs alike were ready to laugh off air the idea of

Take a load off your mind this Christmas.

CLASSIC *f*M
smooth classics
for rough days
3CDs

out

The perfect Christmas present.
Out now from all good record stores.
Suggested retail price £14.99

a commercial station playing classical music. However within months of launch, Classic FM had achieved double BBC Radio 3's audience figures, with many listeners coming to classical music for the first time in their lives. Eleven years on, Classic FM has now more than three times as many listeners as BBC Radio 3.

From the beginning the vision was to treat Classic FM not simply as a radio station but as a brand in its own right. This philosophy has driven forward a number of new and successful ventures over the years.

Classic FM's main record label, launched in 1994, has to date sold over a million CDs. The biggest seller being the latest release, Smooth Classics for Rough Days, which has already 'gone gold' twice over.

The first issue of Classic FM Magazine rolled off the presses in 1995. It is now the biggest-selling classical music magazine on the news-stand, with more than a quarter of a million readers a month.

Add to this, live concerts and events across the UK, the Classic FM Credit Card, and Classic FM People – the brand's personal introduction service, and Classic FM has transformed itself into one of the UK's premier lifestyle brands.

Product

Classical music is at the heart of everything Classic FM stands for. With a CD library of more than 150,000 tracks of the world's finest classical recordings, the station has a passion to make classical music an accessible part of everyone's lives.

Listeners also play an active part in choosing the music that is played on the station. Daily shows like Lunchtime Requests and the internet driven chart, Classic FM Most Wanted, let the audience vote or request their favourite tracks to be played on air.

Since 1996, more than a million votes have also been cast through the annual Classic FM Hall of Fame poll, making the chart the biggest regular survey of classical music tastes anywhere in the world. This chart is featured every morning on Henry Kelly's Hall of Fame Hour.

Classic FM music is programmed with the broadest audience in mind, and the station is continually attracting new younger listeners.

For this reason music education in schools is an important part of the station's work.

The Classic FM Music Teacher of the Year Awards, now in their fourth year, actively support the inspirational work of teachers who keep music-making alive in schools.

Classic FM has also joined forces with Yamaha, the Purcell School and players from top London orchestras, the London Symphony and Royal Philharmonic, to give youngsters from across the UK the chance to come together for an unforgettable weekend of music-making at the Yamaha-Classic FM School of Music.

Classic FM's National Orchestra Week has also become a firm fixture in the station's spring season. Top bands from across the UK join forces to offer a wide range of special concerts and events. Classic FM's National Opera Week takes place every October and sees the Station teaming up with English National Opera, Scottish Opera, Opera North, English Touring Opera and Glyndebourne Touring Opera to stage a host of activities designed to take opera to new audiences.

Classic FM's closest orchestral partnership is with the Royal Liverpool Philharmonic Orchestra. The Liverpool Phil is working with the station to build new audiences of all ages through a Classic FM Concert Series in Liverpool, plus a new Liverpool Music Student Network.

Recent Developments

Year on year, the radio station has built its audience across all ages with those who are tuning in listening for longer. In 2002, Classic FM achieved a record set of listening figures, which include best ever reach, market share and total listening hours.

Despite this success Classic FM has not rested on its laurels. In 2002 Classic FM launched its most significant change in programming output in its ten-year history. New presenters such as ITV newscaster Katie Derham (pictured), along with Mark Goodier (pictured), from BBC Radio 1, have joined the team to help launch a fresh new season of programmes on the station. Stephen Fry's new show 'The Incomplete and Utter History of Classical Music' and 'Chiller Cabinet', a post clubbers overnight show, help complete the new

line-up. The challenge is clear: to encourage younger listeners to tune into the station for longer.

December 2002 also saw the launch of Classic FM TV a free-to-air channel, available 24 hours a day on Sky Digital 464. The station is broadcast to 6.3 million homes. Classic FM TV offers an unrivalled format for music television, the first 24/7 classical music video channel anywhere in the world. Classic FM TV features artists such as Kyung-Wha Chung, Angela Gheorghiu, Kennedy, Izzy, The Opera Babes, Yo-Yo Ma and music from original film soundtracks such as The Lord of the Rings and Star Wars.

Promotion

Classic FM promotion has concentrated on two different target markets in order to grow its audience base. Traditional above-the-line brand advertising using outdoor, cinema, TV and broadsheet press, has been used to talk to a national audience. Along side this, strategic partnerships have been set up with music and art organisations to promote the brand to people at a local level. These partners include festivals such as Mostly Mozart at the Barbican, through to specific productions such as Raymond Gubbay's

Cav and Pag at the Royal Albert Hall. Other partners include Symphony Hall Birmingham, the LSO, the RPO, the Philharmonia, The Welsh Proms, the Canterbury Festival and The Lowry.

Brand Values

Classic FM remains committed to its aim of presenting classical music to an ever-increasing audience by being modern, relevant, involving and accessible. These brand values across the station and its brand extensions, have delivered Classic FM the largest commercial radio audience in the UK. This unique upmarket audience comes to Classic FM because the brand offers them an emotional benefit – an antidote to the stress of modern life.

www.classicfm.com

Market

Coca-Cola is a truly global brand. Not only is it at the top of Interbrand's global brand league and been consistently voted a Superbrand, it is the best selling FMCG brand in Great Britain. Diet Coke too is a major brand in its own right. It is the UK's second most popular soft drink brand and eighth biggest grocery brand.

Coca-Cola aims to refresh consumers with their choice of non-alcoholic ready-to-drink beverages and has a broad range of soft drink brands, including juices, waters and carbonated soft drinks. The Coca-Cola Company's products continue to perform well, displaying steady long term growth and are consumed over one billion times a day in over 200 countries.

While carbonated soft drinks account for over 47% of all UK soft drink sales, GB per capita consumption of soft drinks (194 8oz servings per person per year) is somewhat below other European consumers and significantly below that of US consumers (340 servings). However per capita consumption has grown by 20% in the last seven years (Source: Canadean 2001).

Achievements

'Coca-Cola' is the most recognised trademark in the world, with 94% global recognition. It is also commonly thought that it is the second most widely understood word in the world, after 'OK'.

Beyond doubt Coca-Cola is the most valuable brand on the planet, worth an estimated US$72.5 billion in Interbrand's global brand league. The strength of this global success lies in the relevant local connections that Coca-Cola builds with its consumers every day. In 1982 Coca-Cola launched Diet Coke, which is now the most popular diet soft drink in the world.

All of this has been achieved through an extremely successful combination of global distribution and powerful local marketing. The drink is distributed to more than 200 countries and its strategy is based on the aim that nobody should be more than a few minutes away from an opportunity to buy a Coke. Supporting this, is one of the biggest and most widespread bottling and distribution networks in the world, sending Coca-Cola to all corners of the globe.

Its marketing is legendary, investing in one of the first-ever global advertising campaigns with the 1979 ad 'I'd like to buy the world a Coke'. Sponsorship of major global sporting events such as the Olympic Games and the FIFA World Cup, ensures that the brand not only taps into national passions for sport, but is present when nations come together. The progressive marketing strategy of Coca-Cola is based on a simple message – that it wants to refresh, surprise and inspire everyone who touches the brand.

History

Coca-Cola was invented in 1886 by John Styth Pemberton, a pharmacist in Atlanta, Georgia. He brewed the syrup in a brass pot in his backyard. Even at this early stage, the power of branding was important, with Pemberton's partner, Frank M Robinson, naming the dark brown liquid 'Coca-Cola' because he thought the two Cs would work well in advertising. Having laid the foundations for the product and the brand, the two sold their interests to Atlanta businessman, Asa G Candler in 1888.

The famous signature 'flourish' of Coca-Cola was registered as a trademark in 1893. Candler was a marketing genius and ensured that the Coca-Cola trademark appeared on countless products, from clocks to glass chandeliers. By 1895, thanks to Candler's skill, Coca-Cola was available in every US state.

The design for the famous Coca-Cola glass 'Contour' bottle was created in 1915. It was done to protect the brand from a growing army of imitators, determined to cash in on its success. The company wanted to communicate to consumers that there was only one authentic, Coca-Cola. Designers were given the brief to create a bottle 'which a person will recognise as a Coca-Cola bottle, even if felt in the dark. The bottle should be shaped that, even if broken, a person could tell what it was'.

In 1919 the Candler family sold The Coca-Cola Company to Atlanta banker Ernest Woodruff and a group of

NEW SHARE SIZE COKE

For those who like to share. Coca-Cola

Coca-Cola 'Coke', the design of the 'Coca-Cola' Contour Bottle and the Dynamic Ribbon device are registered trade marks of The Coca-Cola Company.

Photography David Stewart

businessmen. In 1923 Ernest's son Robert Woodruff, elected president of the company, decreed 'Coca-Cola should always be within an arm's reach of desire', setting down a principle which remains central to the company's distribution strategy today.

The distribution expertise of Coca-Cola has been built on the backbone of its bottling operations. The first bottling device was set up by a shopkeeper in 1894, allowing him to trade crates of Coke up and down the Mississippi river. The first major bottling plant was inaugurated soon after, and from 1926 bottling operations spread abroad.

By the outbreak of World War II, the drink was being bottled in over 44 countries. The war helped boost the brand's international distribution

and profile, as US soldiers posted abroad demanded and were sent Coke in vast quantities.

In 1982 Diet Coke was launched. This was the first brand extension of the Coca-Cola trademark and an instant success: by 1984, it was the third biggest soft drink in the US and by 1990 the second biggest soft drink in the UK.

Product

The Coca-Cola product range includes Coca-Cola and Diet Coke along with additional flavour varieties such as Cherry Coke, caffeine-free Diet Coke, Diet Coke with Lemon and, in the US, Vanilla Coke.

As for the formula, there's very little to say. It is one of the most closely guarded secrets in the world.

Recent Developments

Coca-Cola is continuously looking to deliver against consumer needs and uses consumer insights to help shape progressive new solutions to packaging and product offerings. In Great Britain, changing demographics and the growing number of two-person households, drove the 2002 launch of a new sized 1.25 litre bottle for Coca-Cola and Diet Coke.

June 2002 saw the launch of Diet Coke with Lemon. Developed with a taste specially formulated for the British public, it has performed extremely well since launch, already capturing a significant share of the market and showing a very high repeat purchase rate.

Promotion

The first-ever Coca-Cola advertisement was an oil cloth sign, bearing the phrase 'Delicious and Refreshing'. Since then the brand's slogans have developed from 'It's the real thing' in 1942 (used again in 1969) to 'Things go better with Coke' in 1963. There has also been 'Coke adds life' (1976), 'Have a Coke and a smile' (1979), 'Coke is it!' (1982), 'Always Coca-Cola' (1993), 'Coca-Cola Enjoy' (2000) and 'Life Tastes Good' (2001).

The 2002 advertising of Coca-Cola in Great Britain was based on specific British insights and was rated by consumers as some of the most enjoyable yet from the brand. The World Cup ad was an animated 'zero to hero' story of 'Leggsy', a three-legged boy who realises every football fan's dream of scoring the winning goal for England at the World Cup. In the Summer, 'Mower Man' took an optimistic (and humorous) look at one man's spontaneous way of finding his perfect English summer dream.

The authentic Coca-Cola Contour bottle has always been a timeless design classic, but 2002 saw the resurgence of the bottle as a modern icon. In 48 sheet outdoor posters, the Coca-Cola Contour bottle took on a modern, highly sensuous look, with a series of slick images of the bottle's curves juxtaposed with the curves of the human body. Chilled glass bottles of Coke have always had a place in the hands of trendsetters in bars and at events and parties all over the country.

GET YOUR HANDS ON A CONTOUR

win a spending spree of up to £100,000

Diet Coke.

GO FIND YOUR SUMMER

As a leading marketer Coke continues to innovate with impactful promotions on a big scale that engage and appeal with broad consumer audiences. 2001's 'Music4You' was the biggest ever music promotion, run in conjunction with The Sun and News of the World newspapers. This opened up a massive range of music items and money-can't-buy experiences for consumers for which they collected tokens and made online bids.

In 2002, Coca-Cola linked with one of the most credible music magazines in Great Britain, NME, to launch an on-pack promotion offering thousands of gig tickets and 'access all areas' experiences to music fans.

Coke is a brand which also has the ability to work in ways which capture the imagination and bring a progressive feel to its activities. Christmas 2001 saw Coca-Cola unveil the record-breaking World's Biggest Advent Calendar on the side of Birmingham's Town Hall: the huge scale of the 3D calendar gave a sense of festive drama to the city centre, while themed events brought the community together as each window came to life every day with music, fireworks and, on Christmas Eve, Santa appeared with 'real' snow.

The brand used its global link with Warner Brothers' Harry Potter films to 'Bring the magic of reading alive' – a three-year worldwide partnership launched with the opening of 'Harry Potter and the Philosopher's Stone'. As part of this commitment, Coca-Cola in Great Britain pledged to distribute 300,000 books to schools and community libraries.

Coca-Cola has a long-standing heritage of supporting sport and in particular football, where the brand invests at every level of the game – from international tournaments right through to community and grassroots levels. In the global arena, Coca-Cola has sponsored every World Cup tournament since 1978 and has maintained an unbroken presence at every Olympic Games since 1928.

Coca-Cola regularly offers consumers the chance to do things they would never normally be able to: the FIFA World Cup 2002 activation saw Coca-Cola encouraging fans to 'Eat Football, Sleep Football, Drink Coca-Cola' through a multi-faceted programme of innovative marketing activity – including bringing the FIFA World Cup Trophy to England for fans to touch and lift in a whirlwind one-day tour.

In a world first, Coca-Cola invited consumers to design a perimeter board ad to support the football teams out in Japan and Korea. The winning design from England – by a seven year old boy from Huddersfield – featured pitchside at all England's World Cup matches.

2001 saw a further strengthening of support from Coca-Cola of top level English domestic football in the signing of a three year deal to sponsor ITV1's The

Premiership weekly football highlights programme.

With an eye on the future of football, the brand has created a number of major grass roots tournaments which encourage children to get out and enjoy playing the game – including the English Schools Football Association Coca-Cola English Schools Cup – the biggest tournament of its kind open to boys and girls under thirteen – and the Scottish Schools Football Association 'Coca-Cola 7s', an U12s 7-a-side football tournament.

Diet Coke has a sexy heritage built from the 'Diet Coke Break' ads, starting with the hunky window cleaner now developed on to the lighthearted 'Taste the Moment' advertising campaign. Diet Coke in 2002 turned its bottles silver and invited consumers to take a chance at winning a 'Silver Spree' with a £100,000 spending spree up for grabs.

Brand Values

Coca-Cola is renowned for being the world's biggest brand. In Great Britain, on average, it touches consumers over 50 times a day. The brand's personality has the values of an 'optimistic spirit, authenticity, leadership and sociability'. The taste of Coca-Cola, brings 'thirst-quenching and energising refreshment' when served 'ice-cold'.

www.coca-cola.co.uk

Things you didn't know about
Coca-Cola

In 1995 Coca-Cola established The Coca-Cola Youth Foundation. The focus of the charity is to provide a positive contribution to the development of youngsters, helping them to achieve their full potential.

Father Christmas, as we know him with red suit, long beard and jolly face, was first illustrated with those characteristics for a Coca-Cola advert back in the 1930s.

Coca-Cola has been associated with the Special Olympics for over 24 years.

Coca-Cola was a founder member of Tidy Britain Group (now ENCAMS), established in 1965 and had a long association with three key programmes – National Spring Clean; People & Places and Eco-Schools. The current Sweeper Zone programme targets litter at and around major football clubs, with young people from the local community interacting with fans to raise awareness and improve the immediate environment.

Since 1996 Coca-Cola has developed the Coca-Cola Valued Youth programme, a pupil tutoring scheme that meets the needs of secondary school students who need support to keep them in school. The project was expanded to include 3,000 pupils in 2002, and operates in eighteen local education authority areas.

Comfort

Market

The annual number of household washloads in the UK is over seventeen million and it is estimated that 60% of that figure use a fabric conditioner. Fabric care is one of the largest and most competitive in the UK grocery market, with the total UK laundry and fabric conditioner sector now worth some £1.1 billion a year.

There are three distinct product areas within the fabric conditioner market: perfumed – as fragrances are increasingly important, influencing 50% of purchase decisions; skin sensitive – for people with concerns about their family's skin; and added benefits – such as easier ironing and shape retention.

The fabric conditioner market can also be split into two product formats: dilutes, which dominate the rinse conditioner market at 60% of the share and concentrates, which make up the other 40% share of the market.

Comfort currently leads the UK fabric conditioner category with just under 50% share of the market.

Achievements

Comfort was the first fabric conditioner brand to enter the UK market and today remains the number one brand in its 33-year history.

The introduction of Comfort Easy Iron conditioner in 1999 proved to be a phenomenal success and maintains a 10% share in the rinse conditioner market. Comfort Easy Iron was such a success that supermarkets' own brands of Easy Iron conditioners quickly followed suit making up 6% of the market.

A new 'out-of-the-washing-machine' category was created in 2001 with the launch of Comfort Vaporesse, the first mass-market fragranced ironing liquid that is poured directly into the water reservoir of a steam iron to give clothes a 'just washed freshness'. More than one in five of all UK households have purchased Vaporesse (equivalent to more than five million households) and the repeat purchase rate is nearly 50%. To date, over

one million households have bought Vaporesse, purchasing, on average, ten bottles each. Due to Vaporesse's success, the Comfort brand has grown to hit the 50% market share target.

In 2002, Comfort broke new ground in the fabric conditioner market by introducing two new fabric conditioner fragrances – Passion Flower & Ylang Ylang and Mandarin & Green Tea. Comfort collaborated with two designer French fragrance houses to deliver the latest in modern fragrance trends for clothes.

Comfort launched an innovative advertising campaign in 2000 that moved away from the traditional image of the laundry category. The advertisements featured characters (created by Aardman Animations) who lived in Cloth World – a world where everything was made of cloth and where Comfort was used to make life softer. In October 2002, due to an overwhelming number of requests to the Careline about the teen cloth characters Darren and Lisa in the ads, an on-pack promotion to obtain limited edition Darren and Lisa cloth characters was launched. With this, Comfort established a fully integrated communications campaign. Darren and Lisa enabled the brand to enter new territory – into the realms of aspirational teen marketing. See 'Promotion' later.

History

Comfort was launched nationally in the UK in 1969 and was the first fabric conditioner available in the UK market. Lever Brothers was already the leading manufacturer of washing detergent within the UK with the Persil and Surf brands. Market research at this time had shown that although there was no problem getting clothes clean, they returned from the wash feeling scratchy and uncomfortable. Comfort was marketed to 'fight fibre fatigue' by restoring softness and springiness to frequently washed clothes.

The idea was slow to catch on, partly because washing machines didn't have separate compartments for powder and fabric conditioner. Eventually, free samples were given away with new washing machines after manufacturers agreed to install separate compartments.

Fabric conditioners work by lightly lubricating the fibres of the fabric, preventing them becoming tangled. This gives extra bulk to textured fabrics, such as towels, and a smooth feel to flat surfaces.

In the three decades since its launch, Comfort has been continually developed and enhanced to provide the best possible care for clothes, now both in and out of the washing machine.

Product

The Comfort brand is made up of two ranges: the 'in washing machine' range i.e. fabric conditioners and the 'out of washing machine' range i.e. tumble dryer sheets and ironing/freshening products.

The Comfort fabric conditioner range is currently made up of Comfort Blue/Normal, Passion Flower & Ylang Ylang, Mandarin & Green Tea, Silk, Pure, Easy Iron and Comfort Forme.

Whether the aim is to add softness in the washing machine and tumble dryer or add a 'just-washed freshness' to clothes during the ironing process Comfort has a product to suit.

Fourteen years after the launch of Comfort, the brand was relaunched with improved softness benefits on synthetics and a richer creamier appearance. A year later, concentrated Comfort was introduced into the market, which was three times the concentration of regular Comfort. In 1989 a new variant was introduced called Pure Silk Comfort, specialising in silk/delicate fabric washes.

1992 saw a variety of changes to the whole of the Comfort brand. A new single colour logo was launched, the design of the packaging was modernised, Comfort Purely Soft was introduced for consumers with sensitive skin and a clearer distinction was made between the regular and concentrated variants.

The following year in 1993, after consumer market research highlighted that people prefer to have a choice of fragrances, Comfort Island Fresh was launched, later known as Comfort Country Garden.

Between 1997 and 1999 Comfort Purely Soft was relaunched with a new delicate fragrance and hypoallergenic claim, an improved label design and skin care properties. The whole of the Comfort range was given new labels highlighting its 'clothes care' benefits. Country Garden conditioner was replaced with Comfort Easy Iron conditioner, which has become immensely successful.

2001 proved that Comfort is at the forefront of innovation with the introduction of the first mass-market product of its kind, Comfort Vaporesse. As you iron, the Comfort Vaporesse liquid turns to steam and infuses the fibres of your clothes with a delicate fragrance to give them long-lasting freshness.

Recent Development

Comfort's success lies in understanding its consumers and delivering products that meets their needs. Comfort Vaporesse and the two new fragrances are real success stories for the brand.

Comfort's recent launch of Comfort Forme, saw the introduction of the first mass-market product of its kind as it contains Elastra. This is an ingredient similar to that used in the garment industry, to help maintain shape by sustaining the natural body and elasticity of fibres.

Promotion

Since the introduction of Comfort in 1969 there have been three distinct phases of Comfort advertising: Market Education, Market Establishment and Market Commoditisation.

'Market Education' took place between 1969 and 1972 and defined the need for a fabric conditioner within the washing process and explained how Comfort worked and the benefits it provided to fabrics. Advertising focused on 'softness' and 'freshness' benefits.

From 1972-1978 'Establishment' advertising took place, which was a critical brand-building phase in which Comfort's brand values of softness and freshness were established. Comfort moved away from the association with clothes in the drawer, shifting to clothes as they are worn and experienced by the family. The softness that Comfort gives clothes being shown to represent a way of expressing care and love for ones family.

'Commoditisation Advertising' occurred from 1979-1999 due to the lack of volume growth and penetration as the market matured. The opportunity for volume growth was through increased usage as well as the introduction of 'added value' variants such as Easy Iron. This allowed for increased choice within the brand, which led to an increase in penetration.

In November 2000, Comfort launched an innovative advertising campaign that moved away from the traditional staid image of the laundry category. The advertisements feature Darren Denim and Lisa Weaver, teenagers in a first love relationship.

This campaign was created because Comfort wanted to generate a stronger involvement and reinvigorate people's relationship with the brand.

FINE FRAGRANCES FOR YOUR CLOTHES FROM *Comfort*

Lever Faberge Limited 2002

The strength of the brand could be expressed in a simple thought that pulled it apart from the competition – 'when you use Comfort you are caring both for your clothes and the ones you love'. The thought of putting 'caring for clothes' and 'caring for people' together is how the Cloth World was born.

The introduction of this execution marked a turning point in Comfort's advertising. Shortly thereafter the Comfort Careline began to receive

THE CLOTH FAMILY

calls from consumers saying how much they loved them and asking if there were any Lisa and Darren dolls available – some callers even asked if there were any Lisa and Darren figurines to put on top of wedding cakes.

This was proof enough that Lisa and Darren had been taken into consumers' hearts with their teenage romance. By building on the popularity of theses characters, Comfort had the opportunity to build brand awareness as well as drive sales.

The PR strategy aimed to bring to life the characters so that mums, kids and teens would love them while they retained the link to the Comfort brand at all times. This has been done in three ways 1) Solid awareness driving to build their profile; 2) Involving the audience so they have an emotive reason to engage with Darren and Lisa; and finally 3) Creating icons out of them just as the character 'Monkey' was created by ITV Digital.

In a matter of a couple of months awareness for Darren and Lisa, and the Clothworld entity has heightened dramatically. The campaign alone has reached more than eight million people via radio, press and online editorial. Comfort has launched a designated website – www.darrenandlisa.co.uk, which has established a fan base of hundreds of people logging on every day, for example, to download a Darren and Lisa ringtone to their mobiles or get wallpaper for their computer screens, hence directly involving the audience.

Numerous other tactics have been employed, from a celebrated pop hit for the couple – which has been virally marketed to mums and is currently hitting the media – to partnering with the charity Parentalk by joining their 'parenting with inspiration' campaign. Clothworld for Comfort has only just begun and plans are to expand it fully into the realms of family and teen marketing for 2003.

Brand Values

Comfort is a trusted family brand that cares for clothes.

With a heritage of taking care of clothes that spans over three decades, Comfort has and will always care for clothes that people love to wear. With the brand expanding into new areas, Comfort will keep pace with people and their needs to ensure they are never disappointed.

www.darrenandlisa.co.uk

Things you didn't know about **Comfort**

Comfort made enough fabric conditioner in the UK in 2002 to fill 46.4 Olympic sized swimming pools.

If all the Comfort bottles made in the UK in 2002 were lined up, they would stretch from Piccadilly Circus to the Empire State Building and back again.

Comfort Forme found that two thirds of women would rather pay a painful visit to the dentist than have their favourite blouse or much loved dress left shapeless after a washing disaster.

DIRECT LINE ®

Market

There are 35 million private motorists in the UK, all of whom are legally obliged to insure themselves and their cars as well as other people against injury and damage. Most motorists prefer the security of comprehensive cover, rather than a basic Fire and Theft policy. A total of £8 billion is spent annually in the UK on motor insurance with 40% of drivers opting for comprehensive insurance policies (Source: Mintel 2002).

The price war of the 1990s within the industry helped to push premiums down for many motorists but resulted in a battle for supremacy among the growing number of companies in an overcrowded market.

The introduction of direct selling, which cut out the middleman, helped to change the face of the insurance market. Growing use of the internet – by 1999 there were an estimated 12.3 million internet users (Source: National Opinion Poll 1999) – added to changes in the structure of the market.

The approach to selling insurance over the telephone was pioneered by Direct Line. The simplicity of its selling methods modernised the world of motor insurance and revolutionised the insurance market across all sectors from motor to home insurance, pet cover to life assurance. It also raised the expectations of millions of consumers in terms of value for money and customer service.

Today, Direct Line is the UK's leading direct motor insurer and the sixth largest home insurer. The Direct Line Group operates in five geographical territories – the UK, Spain, Italy, Germany and Japan – it employs over 10,000 people and has over ten million policyholders. In 2001, it reported record pre-tax profits of £261 million an increase of 30% on the previous year.

Achievements

Direct Line is renowned for having transformed financial services in the UK following its arrival in the motor insurance market in 1985.

By dealing direct with consumers over the telephone and using sophisticated computer technology to streamline processes, it was able to pass the resulting cost and efficiency benefits on to consumers in the form of cheaper premiums and faster service, delivered at a time to suit customer needs.

Since then the company has gone on to use the same business model in a wide range of other markets – from home, travel, pet and life insurance to mortgages, loans and savings – and has quickly established itself as a leading player in each sector.

The introduction in 1999 of Direct Line's internet site, directline.com enabled the company to capitalise still further on its advanced technological skills while bringing the benefits of one of the fastest and most efficient quote and buy services to millions of UK internet users, 24 hours a day, 365 days a year. Today, the company is the UK's leading internet insurer.

History

Direct Line is a wholly owned subsidiary of the Royal Bank of Scotland. When it launched in 1985, Direct Line was the first insurance company to use the telephone as its only method of selling motor insurance policies direct to customers. Using the advantages afforded by its technological efficiency, it was able to reduce premiums for millions of motorists while offering a faster, more efficient and convenient service than had been available ever before.

Such was its success in the motor insurance sector, that in 1988, Direct Line went on to use the same business model to challenge the grip that mortgage lenders exercised on the home insurance market, introducing buildings and contents insurance as its second core product. During the 1990s, the company added other financial services, including mortgages, loans, pet and travel insurance, to its portfolio of products, quickly establishing itself as a leading player in each new market.

In 1998, Direct Line entered the roadside recovery service, mounting a direct challenge to the traditional motor breakdown companies. Its individual approach enabled it to price 20% lower on average than existing companies and as a result Direct Line Rescue has grown to become the UK's fastest growing breakdown service.

Building on its reputation for providing a fast and efficient service,

Direct Line began operating via the internet in 1999. With the launch of directline.com, it was able to deliver a quote and buy service to customers 24/7 and quickly grew to become the UK's leading internet insurer gaining over 30% of the online insurance market. Key to the success of Direct Line's web operation is its full integration with services offered by telephone, ensuring a seamless customer service.

In July 2000, the company launched www.jamjar.com, a telephone and web-based car retailer providing an online showroom and fully integrated call centre access. Within a year, it had become the leader in its field, with over 40% of the UK online car market.

International expansion has always been one of Direct Line's aims. In 1995, it embarked on its first overseas venture in Spain with Linea Directa which is now that country's largest direct motor

Confidence and Security
DIRECT LINE Motor Insurance

DIRECT LINE Rescue

Automated call handling systems also ensure that the company can quickly and effortlessly re-route its fifteen million customer calls each year between its six call centres around the country. As a result, the length of time customers have to wait to speak to an operator is kept to a minimum.

Recent Developments

Enhancements to its internet site and the launch of 'My Direct Line' in 2001 meant that for the first time, customers could register and monitor the progress of their motor claim online – a service that has since been rolled out across

insurance provider. In March 2001, through a joint venture with Japanese life insurer, Yasuda Life, Direct Line Motor Insurance was launched in Japan – the world's largest single motor insurance market. During that same year, geographical expansion continued in Europe and resulted in the red phone brand being launched in Germany and Italy at the start of 2002.

Product

Each of Direct Line's products is designed with the same basic philosophy – to offer consumers a clear, straightforward, good value alternative to products that are sold through traditional distribution channels. Products are designed to be adapted to the needs of individual customers and customer service

is at the heart of the Direct Line proposition. All staff members are trained in customer care and sales processes are reengineered to cut out complicated forms and jargon. One of Direct Line's earliest revolutionary actions in this respect was to remove the need for motor insurance 'cover notes' by arranging for all documents such as policy schedules and insurance certificates to be laser-printed immediately and forwarded by first class post to customers, usually for delivery the following day.

Innovative technology also helps to keep down costs and reduce premiums. For example, most customers use credit cards or Direct Debits to pay for Direct Line products so that payments can be processed electronically, keeping staffing levels and overheads to a minimum.

other product areas.

In 2002 Direct Line introduced an innovative new service, Direct Line Home Response 24 which provides customers with access to an efficient and reliable 24/7 home emergency service, using Direct Line approved tradesmen to carry work out. The service, which embraces wiring, plumbing and drainage, security and heating, gives customers immediate advice in the event of an emergency. It also organises and pays for emergency assistance, including call out and labour and guarantees all permanent work carried out.

Promotion

When Direct Line Insurance launched in 1985, its aim was to sell cheaper car insurance direct to customers using modern technology to speed up and simplify the sales process while keeping costs down.

The company's first television advertisements appeared during the late 1980s but its branding breakthrough came in 1990 when the first television commercial featuring the distinctive Direct Line red phone on wheels appeared on UK screens.

The Direct Line red phone and its associated jingle, rapidly established high levels of recall among consumers soon after its introduction, helping to heighten awareness ratings to levels normally associated with high profile consumer brands. With a 95% brand awareness level, the red phone icon already has proved a huge success with UK consumers and has come to represent innovation, value for money and leading customer service. It is now also well on the way to achieving similar recognition overseas.

Today, the famous red phone continues to appear in all of Direct Line's advertising and marketing communications and is a constant 'cheeky but likeable' symbol of Direct Line's brand personality. It evokes feelings of friendliness, fun, innovation and the arrival of a rescuer – emotions rarely associated with the dry world of insurance.

Sponsorship continues to be an important promotional tool for Direct Line. In partnership with Victim Support, the national charity for victims of crime, it has helped to fund research into improving the support given to victims of burglary. It also sponsors Brake, a not-for-profit road safety organisation that works to stop death and injury on the roads and cares for people traumatised by crashes.

Brand Values

Direct Line has set itself a mission to succeed. The company as a whole and the individuals it comprises strive to treat customers in a way that is always trustworthy, straightforward, human and challenging. It is customer-focused, innovative and pioneering. Its level of consumer awareness in the UK is high, reflecting the success of the red phone icon. The culture is non-hierarchical and 'can-do', allowing the business to come up with new ideas and translate them into concrete benefits for customers as quickly as possible.

www.directline.com

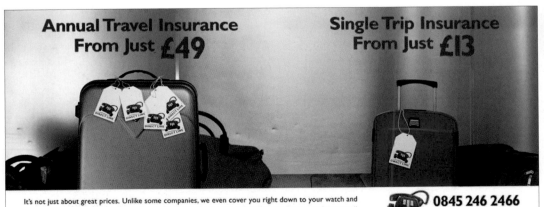

Annual Travel Insurance From Just £49

Single Trip Insurance From Just £13

It's not just about great prices. Unlike some companies, we even cover you right down to your watch and sunglasses - you'd be surprised who doesn't. So for total peace of mind and great value cover, give us a call.

0845 246 2466
call or buy online
DIRECT LINE directline.com

The BrandCouncil

DURACELL®

Market

Originally batteries were simply considered as things that powered electrical gadgets. They were kept under the counter at shops and only those fortunate enough to have such wonderful electrical items that required battery power, would ask to buy them.

The modern world now depends on batteries to power a wide range of items from personal stereos and remote controls, to toys, games and torches. Furthermore, batteries are no longer only of the zinc carbon variety, there is a vast choice of long lasting batteries including alkaline, lithium, lithium ion and nickel metal hydride. In short, batteries are now far superior to their predecessors.

The average household has over twenty battery-operated appliances including remote controls, alarm clocks, radios, smoke alarms, cameras and CD players. However, one third of all appliances lie idle for want of a battery, even though batteries are one of the most widely distributed products. Batteries are available in a vast array of retail outlets from newsagents to chemists and electrical shops to petrol stations.

Achievements

Since its arrival in the UK, Duracell® has made many significant accomplishments.

In the 1970s when Duracell® made its UK debut, many people thought that alkaline batteries wouldn't catch on. Now around 80% of all batteries sold are alkaline, while zinc batteries continue to decline.

By the late 1980s Duracell® had achieved the successful elimination of virtually all mercury from its batteries and in the same and subsequent periods made dramatic improvements to performance. In the three decades of Duracell® history, the life expectancy of an AA cell has increased by nearly 100% while remaining much the same in terms of size and design.

In 1992, Duracell® gained the British Standards Kitemark for product excellence and 1995 saw the introduction of titanium dioxide to its batteries, which acted as a catalyst to make the other ingredients work harder and give more power.

In 1996 the company resolved the previously unanswerable question – 'When is the battery going to run out?' by introducing its Powercheck® battery tester – firstly on-pack then on the battery itself. Duracell® made a further development in monitoring the lifespan of a battery by printing 'best before' dates on all packs and batteries.

At the turn of the new millennium, Duracell® earned the prestigious Gold Lion at the Cannes International Advertising Festival in 2002. The award for 'Best Event' was presented to Duracell® for its spectacular use of the London landmark, Battersea Power Station, when it launched its new range of Duracell® Ultra M3 batteries. The former power station, which overlooks the River Thames, was transformed into four giant replica Duracell® Ultra M3 batteries to celebrate the occasion.

History

The twenty first century marked the 200th birthday of the battery, which was invented in 1800 by Alessandro Volta who described it as a 'construction of an apparatus of unfailing charge, of perpetual power'.

Early batteries were hardly the neat cylinders we know today. The 'Voltaic Pile' battery, based on Volta's design, constructed in 1813 by Sir Humphrey Davy in the cellars of the Royal Institution in London, covered 889 square feet.

The first portable batteries were seen at the turn of the last century where they were used in conjunction with flashlights – so called because the battery power could only sustain an intermittent light. By World War I, batteries were being used extensively in communication equipment and from there technology moved fast, simultaneously reducing the cell size and increasing its capacity.

The story of Duracell® began in the early 1920s with an inventive scientist named Samuel Ruben and an eager manufacturer of tungsten filament wire named Philip Rogers Mallory. Ruben and Mallory united inventive genius with manufacturing muscle, which was the bedrock of Duracell® International, revolutionising battery technology.

In the 1950s, Samuel Ruben went on to improve the alkaline manganese battery, making it more compact, durable, and longer lasting than anything before it. At about the same time, Eastman Kodak introduced cameras with a built-in flash unit that required more power than zinc carbon cells could provide. The cameras needed alkaline manganese cells but in a new size, the AAA – this put alkaline cells on the map – and the Duracell® brand was introduced in 1964. Soon, the consumer market for Duracell® batteries rocketed.

Product

Duracell® is well established as the world's number one battery brand. When it arrived in the UK 30 years ago, it created the first element of competition within the battery market. Consumers began switching to Duracell®'s alkaline batteries, due to the genuine longer lasting qualities.

Duracell® batteries achieved a meteoric growth, which ran hand-in-hand with the development of more complex appliances that ran better on alkaline power than zinc. The personal stereo alone saw the demand for AA alkaline batteries escalate beyond anyone's wildest marketing plans. Without alkaline batteries such as Duracell®, it is questionable whether personal stereos would have caught on, as they required longer battery life to work well.

Duracell® does not just manufacture alkaline batteries. The brand was at the forefront of lithium technology – used primarily for photographic applications – which allowed the surges of instant power required to operate several features simultaneously. Today, well over half of all new battery operated cameras use lithium power.

Recent Developments

In 2001 Duracell® launched Duracell® UltraM3 and Duracell® Plus.

The Duracell® Ultra M3 range – designed specifically for power hungry, 'high-drain' devices offers 'more energy, more efficiency and more power' versus standard Duracell® batteries in 'high-drain' devices.

The Duracell® Plus range complements Duracell® Ultra M3, providing long lasting, dependable power and quality across a wide range of everyday appliances.

Both Duracell® Plus and Duracell® Ultra M3 are available in sizes AA, AAA, C, D and 9V.

2003 sees the relaunch of Duracell® Ultra M3 and Duracell® Plus with improved technology. In addition, Duracell® will be introducing a 'Colour Coding' system to help consumers select battery sizes more easily. A fully co-ordinated launch with new packaging, point-of-sale material, promotions and advertising ensures selecting Duracell® will be easier than ever before.

Promotion

Duracell® has consistently promoted itself as a long lasting battery brand.

The line 'No ordinary battery looks like it or lasts like it' was used in a long running statement in which consumers had great confidence. Now Duracell® simply states 'Duracell® Power. More Life'. However, the overall message remains constant and it is this single-minded proposition used across all advertising, which despite the varied treatments of its campaigns has remained unchanged. Research by Millward Brown has shown that 79% of people consider Duracell® to be the longest lasting battery and 70% said it is 'in a class of its own'.

To mark the launch of Duracell® Ultra M3 in July 2001, Duracell® converted the chimneys of Battersea Power Station into four giant replica batteries. Using one of the UK's most famous 'power' landmarks, the scale of the event was such that

approximately two million people would have seen it over three days – 4,500m² of vinyl was used in the manufacture of the chimney covers, equivalent to an entire football pitch. The Battersea chimneys measured 40 meters high and four cranes were required to position the covers onto them.

Planning for the event did not go exactly according to schedule. The first attempt was halted after a pair of rare peregrine falcons was discovered nesting in one of the towers. Then, after later being given the go-ahead by the Royal Society for the Protection of Birds, the project was threatened with a further delay by freak winds. However, the team worked around the clock to ensure the spectacular event went ahead. The campaign went on to win the prestigious 2001 Cannes Gold Lion award.

Duracell® sponsored the 2002 Fifa World Cup by offering new merchandising material, PR promotions and an on-pack promotion with Duracell® Plus. Consumers could buy two packs of Duracell® Plus AA size batteries and pick up a free Duracell® 'Roaring Mini Football', which created the noise of a crowd each time it was thrown.

In the UK and Europe during autumn, Duracell® announces results of an annual survey of the top ten toys. Voted for by children aged 7-11, it is the only pan-European toy survey of its kind that asks the users of toys – children – to nominate their favourite new toys. This gives the Duracell® brand a valuable association with toys and gadgets, approaching the important Christmas selling period for batteries. This is the year's single biggest battery sales opportunity as by value, over one third of all batteries are sold in the last three months of the year.

Once again Duracell® pledged its support to the Government's on-going fire safety initiative, Fire Action Plan. During September and October 2002, Duracell® worked with brigades and Kidde smoke alarms, to support the important issue of maintaining smoke alarms and checking

and changing their (9V) batteries.

To conjure up associations with the brand other than that of a practical item, Duracell® adopted, over 30 years ago, the endearing 'Duracell Bunny'. The Bunny has prompted 85% recall among consumers, who immediately link the character to Duracell® batteries.

He has been seen drumming, then boxing, canoeing, jetting into space, playing football (in celebration of Duracell®'s involvement with the 1998 and 2002 World Cups) and globetrotting complete with rucksack, heavy duty walking boots and protective peaked cap.

Brand Values

Duracell® is the number one alkaline battery brand in the world. The brand is a pioneer of new battery technology and has many groundbreaking technology launches to its name. The brand strives to ensure that consumers associate it with providing reliable, longer lasting batteries.

www.duracell.com

easyJet.com
the web's favourite airline

Market

easyJet operates in what has become one of the world's most competitive air travel markets; the European short haul, point-to-point sector.

Before 1987, European air travel was effectively carved up by the national flag carriers, who considered air routes between the major European cities to be their own permanent domain. Under the old regime, flying schedules, fares and even the amount of passengers that each national airline could carry were negotiated between governments in uncompetitive 'bilateral' agreements. Competition from other airlines was almost unheard of.

In the face of huge opposition from a number of EU States wanting to protect their own airlines from competition, the European Commission introduced its ten-year reform process in 1987, which was responsible for creating an environment in which low-cost airlines could flourish and prosper.

Since April 1997, any airline holding a valid Air Operators Certificate in the EU can operate on any route within the European Union, including wholly within another country, without restriction on price or capacity. As a result, European air travel has been flooded with an influx of low-cost airlines. Having been the only European budget carrier when easyJet launched in 1995, there are now several low cost operators including Ryanair, Virgin Express, Buzz, bmibaby and a host of others. For the year ending 2001 the low cost airlines had a 7.1% capacity share of intra-European traffic. By June 2002, the airlines had an 8.7% share. (Source: Official Airline Guide).

The European short haul aviation market is in the process of consolidation. Some of the large flagship carriers had been running unprofitable networks in Europe for some time. As they cut their services, easyJet is likely to prove more resilient, able to pick up landing slots and increase its market share.

Achievements

easyJet's biggest achievement has been to change the shape of the European aviation market with its no-frills business model.

easyJet's high frequency, point-to-point services between major European airports meet both business and leisure customers' needs. Many businesses have come to believe that it is a waste of money to spend the large amounts demanded on short haul flights with the flag carriers. easyJet now carries up to 50% business traffic on some of its mature routes and calculates that companies can save up to 89% on their travel budgets by using low cost airlines.

While other operators have gone bust or made heavy losses, easyJet is constantly expanding its operations. easyJet went into profit in its third financial year. The company floated in October 2000, with an Initial Public Offering (IPO) of 310p. In the twelve months to September 30th 2001, the company reported profits of £40.1million – up 82% on the previous year when profits stood at £22.1million. easyJet reported a first half profit before tax (end March 31st 2002) of £1million. This was the first time in the company's history that it had recorded a profit in the first half of the year.

184 weekly flights

Liverpool
London Gatwick
London Luton

from Barcelona • Madrid • Majorca • Malaga

easyJet.com
the web's favourite airline

Awards won by easyJet are numerous and include Best Low Cost Airline (Business Traveller Magazine) 1999 and 2000. In 2001 and 2002 this award was won by Go. easyJet won three Consumer Superbrands awards in 2001 for Best PR work, Most Significant Impact on Market Sector and Most Impressive Brand Developed in the Last Ten Years. Go was awarded Best International short haul airline in 2002 by the readers of Conde Nast Traveller.

History

Stelios Haji-Ioannou, the son of a Greek shipping tycoon, launched easyJet in 1995. Stelios got the idea for easyJet from Southwest Airlines in the US, which has also prospered by introducing a no-frills, low cost service on short haul routes.

With an initial £5 million, the company began with two leased Boeing 737s and a headline grabbing fare of £29 from Luton to Glasgow (seven years on and the lowest fare is actually £12.50 including all taxes and charges which reflects the fierce competition within the market).

easyJet caught the imagination of customers in the late 1990s. It had the feel of a new economy company; low cost, bright and energetic. Additionally, its use of the internet has marked it out as an innovative, dynamic company.

At first easyJet operated without too much competition. However, after only a year of business, British Airways made an attempt to buy the airline. This initially friendly approach soon turned sour when the global giant launched its own budget carrier, Go, in 1998. easyJet accused BA of unfairly cross-subsidising Go and took its case to the High Court in February 1998.

Fast forward to August 1st 2002 and easyJet has completed a deal to buy Go, turning easyJet into the largest low cost airline in Europe, carrying 11,350,350 passengers in the rolling twelve months to September 2002.

The airline is currently based in a bright orange building adjacent to the main taxiway at London Luton Airport. To accommodate the needs of combined easyJet/Go staff, the company will move to a new, larger site in Luton during summer 2003.

Product

easyJet's mission is 'To provide our customers with safe, good value, point-to-point air services. To offer a consistent and reliable product at fares appealing to leisure and business markets on a range of European routes.'

As of the end of September 2002, the new easyJet served 88 routes to 36 airports in 33 cities. easyJet has won plaudits for operating one of the youngest fleets in the airline industry. easyJet currently operates a single fleet of Boeing 737 300s and 700s, all with 149 seats and in a single class. In September 2002, the combined airline had a fleet of 65 aircraft.

In January 2002, easyJet announced that it was in discussions with Boeing and Airbus concerning the possible acquisition of 75 (this figure has, subsequent to the Go deal, risen to 120) additional aircraft and that it was reviewing the benefits of operating a mixed fleet.

On October 14th 2002 easyJet announced that it had selected Airbus as the supplier for

120 A319 aircraft, with a price protected option for a further 120 A319s.

There are no free meals on-board. Eliminating free on-board catering cuts out cost and unnecessary bureaucracy and management. People joke about airline food, so easyJet take the stance 'why provide it if people do not want it?'.

All tickets are booked direct, either on the internet or by telephone. Buying a ticket involves being given a reference number, which is used in place of a ticket. The direct sales approach is a prime example of how easyJet seeks to simplify business processes to maximise efficiency and reduce costs to itself and its customers.

The internet plays a vital role in the easyJet business plan and is critical to its on-going success. As a low cost operation, controlling the cost of doing business is crucial to the airline's ability to offer low fares. The internet provides the most cost effective distribution channel and easyJet has aggressively pursued its strategy of encouraging passengers to book their seats online. A £5 discount for each flight is provided on all internet bookings. Customers can only book seats via the call centre if they are travelling within one month.

Since easyJet started selling seats via the internet in April 1998, the airline has enjoyed dramatic growth in its online sales. The airline reached the one million seat mark in October 1999 and celebrated this important landmark by giving one lucky passenger unlimited free flights for a whole year. Five months later in March 2000, easyJet reached two million seats – it only took another three months after that to reach the three million mark. easyJet now sells over 90% of its seats online, which is a higher percentage than any other airline, reinforcing its position as the 'Web's favourite airline', a slogan approved for usage by the Advertising Standards Authority.

easyJet employs a yield management strategy, meaning that prices are closely linked to demand and the amount of time in advance that the ticket is booked. A ticket booked three months in advance will be significantly cheaper than one booked a week before the flight.

easyJet's product also relies on punctuality. Central to this is the ability to turn the aircraft around quickly on the ground. Compared to the hour and a half that it takes on average to turn a 737 around at Heathrow, easyJet's target time on the ground between flights is just twenty minutes.

In September, easyJet relaunched its uniform for cabin crew and ground staff. With a variety of shirts, trousers, tops and accessories (including deer stalker and beanie hats) to choose from, staff can create their own individual look.

Recent Developments

easyJet completed the deal to buy Go on August 1st 2002 for £374 million. The combination of the two airlines makes easyJet the largest low-cost airline in Europe. The benefits of the merger include the addition of a number of mature routes, which reduce the cost of network development, compared to creating new routes from start up. The acquisition also complements easyJet's infrastructure, systems and people without affecting the planned growth and operating efficiency of its existing operations.

easyJet's new economies of scale bring greater purchasing power for aircraft, fuel, maintenance and marketing expenditure. As a result, the new easyJet will be able to bring more low fares to more people across Europe.

easyJet continues to expand its European network. In 2002, it launched in Paris, and expanded considerably from Gatwick with the introduction of seven new destinations, making it the second largest scheduled airline from the south London airport. In August 2002, the low-cost airline signed an option to acquire Deutsche BA, BA's German subsidiary, and is in the process of turning the German operation into a low-cost airline, whilst deciding whether to purchase the airline outright.

Promotion

easyJet does not use television advertising. Instead it relies heavily on press, outdoor and radio advertising and PR, orchestrated in-house. All advertising is intended to reinforce the easyJet brand values. easyJet has developed its central principle of being 'consumer champion' with its campaigns, which the airline has initiated on behalf of consumers to defend their 'right to affordable air travel'. The company vigorously opposes any activities that might jeopardise this.

All easyJet sales promotions are exclusive to the internet, so customers must go online if they wish to take advantage of promotional fares.

Awareness of easyJet has also been raised by 'Airline' the ITV docu-soap. It is about the life of staff and customers at easyJet in Luton and is ITV's premier docu-soap with audiences of over eight million per episode. Six series of the programme have now been aired.

easyJet also uses its own aircraft as airborne billboards. Following the introduction of several new easyJet routes in Gatwick in Feb 2002, easyJet painted the sides of some of its planes with 'BIG @ Gatwick'.

Brand Values

easyJet's principal brand values are 'good value' and 'fun'. All the advertising seeks to reinforce this message, and was a huge advantage in the mid 1990s when most airlines promoted themselves on quality of service, rather than sense of fun.

In the intervening years, other values have been added to the brand. easyJet balances its cost-cutting image with an emphasis on safety, security, punctuality and in-flight service.

Today, most people would consider the airline to be 'challenging the established order' and a 'consumer champion'. These values have been imparted by a series of high profile campaigns over the past five years.

www.easyJet.com

NEW ROUTE • NEW ROUTE • NEW ROUTE • NEW ROUTE

Oooh la la...

Paris from £17.50 single

easyJet.com the web's favourite airline

Market

Eurostar competes within both the business and leisure travel markets and with competition primarily coming from airlines, Eurostar's point of differentiation is its 'product' position: the seamless train journey from city centre to city centre and a more fluid, relaxed experience.

Market leader on both the London-Brussels and London-Paris routes, these markets are the heartland of the Eurostar business. For the Leisure market in particular, Eurostar is also competing against a much broader range of short break destinations, and a key objective for Eurostar going forward is to communicate that Eurostar also connects with over 100 destinations in Europe (generally via a simple connection on to a partner railway).

Eurostar can justly claim to have revolutionised links between three of the top capitals in the world – London, Paris and Brussels. It can also claim to offer seamless and enjoyable direct links to other destinations on the continent, for example Lille in Northern France, which is two hours away. Eurostar also travels direct daily to the Disneyland Resort Paris and during the winter season, a weekly night as well as daytime train takes skiers and snowboarders direct to the French Alps. In summer 2002 a direct service to Avignon in the south of France was introduced. Covering the 722 miles in just six hours and fifteen minutes, this service was an immediate success with virtually every train running full. The Avignon service is running for an extended season in 2003.

In the UK the service departs from London Waterloo International and Ashford International in Kent, which is one hour closer to the continent.

Achievements

Eurostar's claim to have revolutionised travel between London and the continent is without exaggeration. Before its launch in November 1994 about five million passengers per year were carried by air between London and Paris and London and Brussels, but now Eurostar on its own carries over seven million passengers annually and has a market share in excess of

60% on the Paris route and around 45% on the Brussels route. Indeed, Eurostar doubled the overall market in its first five years of operation.

Eurostar has achieved this leadership by a combination of convenience, speed, comfort, reliability and frequency of service, while striving to provide the best levels of customer service in the industry.

With a wide appeal, Eurostar is used by people from all walks of life, from royalty and senior politicians to 'stars of stage and screen' to families, to the student backpacker. Its passengers come from almost every country in the world and it is an important link in European tours for visitors from such regions as North America and the Far East.

Eurostar has received a long list of awards from a range of organisations including the Royal Institute of British Architects, National Heritage Arts Sponsorship, the Civic Trust, English Tourist Board, Queen Elizabeth's Foundation (for disabled access), French Chamber of Commerce and numerous awards from trade and national press for the quality of the service provided, as well as awards for its online offering, call centre and for best railway operator.

History

Eurostar traces its origins back to 1981, when the British and French governments announced studies for a fixed link under the English Channel. By 1986 the decision in favour of a rail tunnel was taken and planning started on linking the three capitals of London, Paris and Brussels by what was then known as the 'Trans-Manche Super Train'.

Following construction of the Channel Tunnel, the first train arrived in England for tests in June 1993 and commercial service started on November 14th 1994 with just two trains per day each way on each route. However, the timetable was soon expanded; the millionth customer travelled in May 1995, after six months' service, and within twelve months Eurostar carried three million passengers. Subsequent enhancements to the service included: the opening of Ashford International station, Kent, in January 1996; the inauguration of direct trains to Disneyland Paris in June 1996, the introduction of business lounges at terminals and the frequent traveller programme in November 1996. The following year saw the opening of a high speed line in Belgium, reducing London-Brussels journey time from three hours fifteen minutes to two hours 40 minutes, and the start of a through service from London and Ashford to the French Alps.

The UK arm was privatised in 1996 and in 1999 the three operators created Eurostar Group, a centralised company responsible for

determining the commercial direction and development of the Eurostar service. Plans are now in hand for the creation of a single entity, to be called Eurostar International, which will be responsible for running the service and will make its own decisions on the service specification – including investment programmes.

Product

The first customer contact with the Eurostar product could well be its award winning call centre, taking the majority of bookings direct from the public. The internet, relaunched in late 2002, is however growing its share of bookings, true to the consumer trends across the travel industry. Travellers also have the option of booking through travel agents or direct-selling tour operators.

The traveller arriving at any of Eurostar's modern terminals will find Eurostar's service to be relatively 'hassle-free'. Passengers need check in only 30 minutes before departure, or, in the case of those travelling on fully flexible tickets, or Frequent Traveller carte blanche members, just fifteen minutes.

On board, Eurostar offers two classes of accommodation, First and Standard. First class accommodation offers wider seats and an at-seat meal service. On the London-Paris route within First Class, a Premium First service offers a range of additional benefits. All passengers benefit from air conditioned coaches and the articulated design gives an exceptionally smooth ride even at maximum speed. Passengers on fully flexible first class tickets, and Frequent Traveller carte blanche holders, can also access the new lounges. Eurostar's sales and customer service staff are a very visible part of the product. Those in contact with customers speak both English and French and those working on the

Brussels route also speak Dutch. Staff are available at all terminals to help passengers with enquiries and particularly to attend to passengers with special needs. Assistance can be given to wheelchair, blind or elderly passengers as well as those with children.

And then there is the hardware itself. Eurostar trains can be distinguished from other trains by their eye-catching, award winning design and sheer size. The nose cone is a particularly impressive feature (as dramatised in the 2002 TV advertising). Each train is almost 400 metres long (approximately 1/4 mile), travels smoothly at speeds of up to 186 mph, and seats up to 766 passengers –

almost the equivalent of two fully loaded Boeing 747 'Jumbo' jet aircraft. Derived from the basic mechanical features of the highly successful French TGV trains, Eurostar trains can operate from three different electrical supply systems in Britain, France and Belgium.

Eurostar as a brand not only offers train tickets for purchase: its offering extends into the all-inclusive package market (under the guise of 'Eurostar Holidays direct') and through its direct channels, links with partner suppliers also enable its staff to offer customers the chance to purchase insurance, hotel bookings and car-hire as components through Eurostar. This extended product range is an attempt to service all customers travel needs within a 'one stop shop' ideal.

Recent Developments

During 2002, Eurostar embarked on a £35 million programme to renovate all aspects of its product – terminals and train interiors, on-board service and catering, signage, staff uniforms, literature, its website – all points where there is customer interface. The French designer Philippe Starck has been appointed Artistic Director of this project called 'Creating the New Eurostar'. During 2002, there were substantial changes to the terminals at London Waterloo, Paris Gare du Nord and Brussels Midi, with new dedicated business desks and check in points and, most notably, spectacular new business lounges.

The countdown has now started to the next big improvement to the Eurostar service. This will be the opening, in autumn 2003, of the first UK section of the high speed line, which will reduce all journey times from London by twenty minutes. The second stage will take the line to a new London terminal at St Pancras in 2007. When it is completed, the transit times between London St Pancras and Brussels will be just two hours, and two hours twenty minutes between London St Pancras and Paris.

Promotion

In its advertising, Eurostar aims to drive awareness, create a desire to travel by Eurostar and build on its brand values. When targeting business customers directly, product benefits tend to be stressed (eg city centre to city centre, time on board to work and relax), while for leisure customers the emphasis is on the great experience provided by the combination of its journey benefits and passion for and knowledge of its destinations at great prices. Destination marketing is founded on an 'insider' view of destinations. Partnerships with key influencers leverage Eurostar's unrivalled expertise on the destinations it serves.

Eurostar's endline 'J'Aime le Train' aims to further enforce the message that the brand offers a service that customers will 'fall in love with'.

Eurostar uses all available communication

channels – television, press, radio, outdoor, and direct marketing, including the frequent traveller loyalty scheme. Online marketing is increasingly used as a marketing tool, both through online advertising and via Eurostar's redesigned website.

Eurostar has a high public relations profile and is regularly featured in print and broadcast media, whether as part of a travel feature or because it is synonymous with its destinations. Eurostar is frequently used as a tangible visual symbol of links between Britain and Europe.

Brand Values

At the heart of the Eurostar brand is a strong product, linking like-minded people between three of the top capitals of the world.

The functional values of fast, direct, reliable, frequent, comfortable and safe, present the foundations for an experience which is hassle-free, productive, relaxing and special.

Beyond these 'roots' is a personality which embraces a European or French feel, is contemporary, cosmopolitan, passionate, with a good sense of humour, whilst also being professional and trustworthy.

In its short history, Eurostar has succeeded in appealing to a wide range of people, is highly salient, and has established itself as an aspirational brand without being exclusive.

www.eurostar.co.uk

Market

As healthy living and diet assume increasing importance in consumers' lives, the consumption of bottled water, which is seen as synonymous with balance and well-being, is rising exponentially. The bottled water market has grown five-fold in just twelve years, achieving double-digit growth over the past five years. It is a key driver of the total soft drink market and over the past two years accounted for a third of the total soft drink value growth. Still water is more popular than sparkling, and drives 80% of this value growth.

Consumers increasingly reach for bottled water rather than other soft drinks, understanding that not only is it healthy and detoxes the body, but it is the most effective drink for quenching thirst. Bottled water's growing popularity means that consumption for 2003 is expected to break the 1.5 billion litre barrier.

There are more than 50 different bottled water brands in the UK market, and Evian accounts for one in ten bottles of water sold throughout the world. It is the second largest bottled water brand worldwide, and market leader in the UK. Evian's dominant position is driven by its premium and aspirational positioning and constant innovations in packaging and communication.

Achievements

Evian helped to create the UK bottled water market back in the 1980s and has become an increasingly dominant brand leader, despite the plethora of competitive brands and own-label offerings that have entered the market over the past five years.

Heavy investment in marketing and advertising has driven the growth of the brand and raised spontaneous brand awareness to 61% in the UK – significantly above any of its competitors (Source: Millward Brown 2002).

Evian enjoys one of the highest brand penetration levels in the bottled water market and its consumers are increasingly drinking Evian on a daily basis, demonstrating that the brand has become part of their lives (Source: Omnibus 2002 & TGI 2000).

Evian's leadership is also reflected through its high level of loyalty among bottled water brands. In 1999 Evian became the first still water brand to sell 100 million litres in the UK and in 2002, Evian broke a new record by selling a total of 150 million litres.

History

Evian dates back more than 18,000 years. It has its genesis in a vast aquifer of glacial sands deep

within the French Alps. The aquifer was formed in about 16,000 BC and gives Evian its taste and mineral composition. Evian water begins as snow and rain falling on the Alps, which then filters through the aquifer to emerge at the spring – Source Cachat – in the small town of Evian-les-Bains in the foothills of the Alps.

Our Iron Age ancestors living on the shores of Lake Geneva drank Evian as long ago as 10,000 BC. But the mineral water's more recent history began in 1789 at the start of the French Revolution. The Marquis de Lessert, who suffered from kidney stones, 'took the waters' from the fountain of Sainte-Catherine, which was fed by

a spring in a certain Monsieur Cachat's garden. The nobleman swore that the spring's pure, refreshing water cured his ailments and word of the benefits of Evian spread. Specialists analysed the water and testified to its purifying properties and doctors began prescribing the water to their patients. Monsieur Cachat, meanwhile, shrewdly decided to fence in his spring and sell its water.

The first Spas opened in Evian-les-Bains to accommodate those seeking to benefit from the spring in 1824. Two years later, the Duke of Savoy granted the first official authorisation to bottle Evian. In 1878, the French Government first registered water from the Cachat Spring.

Growing demand for Evian prompted a new pump room to be opened at the source in 1956 and a new state-of-the-art bottling facility followed in 1965. The bottling facility is continuously updated and modernised with the world's leading bottling technology. Four million litres of Evian are bottled there every day.

In 1969 Evian's first PVC bottle was launched, the first of a series of packaging innovations culminating most recently in the first compactable

bottle in 1995. Designed to encourage recycling, the sculpted bottle is also designed to evoke the source at Evian-les-Bains.

In 1988, annual worldwide sales of Evian reached one billion litres and in 1984 a hotel, L'Espace Thermal Evian, opened at the source, offering thermal treatments and body conditioning.

In the UK, Evian made its first foray into television advertising in 1994. Adopting an educational stance and showing the generic health benefits of water; the advertising message was: 'Evian. Every day for everybody's wellbeing'.

Consumer attitudes changed in the late 1990s. Previously sceptical about mineral waters, consumers, unhappy with the taste and quality of tap water, turned to the purity and premium quality of bottled water. Evian changed its advertising message accordingly, and its new campaign repositioned bottled water as more humorous and approachable. The message was conveyed initially through posters and then through the successful 'Sugar Daddy' television commercial featuring actor Anthony Zerbe and former boxer Gary Stretch. The strapline for both posters and TV ads was 'Purity. Not just for the innocent'.

As the bottled water market evolved and matured, 'purity' became an entry requirement for the category, and as a brand message was rendered generic to bottled water. Evian sought, therefore, to focus on the physical and emotional benefits of purity in the 'Live Young' message, which extolled the benefits of drinking Evian but also brought to life the individual personality that is Evian. The 'Live Young' message has garnered high recall from consumers as specific to Evian and is differentiated from the plethora of bottled water brands, reinforcing Evian's position as market leader.

Product

The name Evian comes from the Celtic word 'Evua' or 'Ew', meaning water, but it also conveys a sense of life through the transposed letters 'vie' and has associations with Eve (from Adam and Eve).

Evian water comes from rain and snow falling on the Chablais foothills in the northern French Alps. The water is slowly filtered for at least fifteen years through a vast aquifer made of glacial sands, deep within the mountains before emerging at the source Cachat in the town of Evian-les-Bains on the banks of Lake Geneva.

The aquifer, a geological phenomenon formed over several millennia, is what gives Evian water its distinctive mineral balance and pure and

distinct taste. Bottled straight away at its source and untouched by man any moment before it touches your lips, Evian comes to you 'as nature intended'.

Evian acquires its essential minerals by slowly filtering through the glacial sand compacted between two plates of waterproof clay. These plates are several tens of metres thick, and were created by the most recent glaciers on the Northern French Alps.

Containing calcium and magnesium, which are nutritionally valuable, Evian is low in nitrates, sodium and sulphates, making it suitable for salt-free diets, pregnant women and people of all ages, including babies. Because of its relatively low mineral content it is easily absorbed and passed, which makes it particularly suitable for those suffering from kidney stones.

First tested in 1807, the composition of Evian has never changed, nor has the temperature which remains constant at 11.6 degrees centigrade at the source.

In answer to the growing trend for bulk packs, Evian has launched multi packs of its successful 50cl, 1.5 litre and 2 litre bottles and since 1978 it has been available in an atomiser to refresh and cool the face.

Recent Developments

Evian's appeal was broadened in 1995 with the innovative launch of the world's first compactable bottle. The bottle was designed to collapse when empty, to encourage recycling. This concept further aided Evian's number one brand status and was supported with a witty advertising campaign with the line 'gets drunk and collapses.'

Since this, product development has remained key to the Evian brand. To celebrate the start of the new millennium, Evian launched its first millennium glass bottle in winter 1999. Reminiscent of a teardrop in shape, the bottle was designed to symbolise the purity and perfection of water itself.

Other packaging innovations have included 'Evian Action', which was launched in 2001. The product consisted of an innovative 75cl squeezable bottle with dispensing system and ring cap that allows it to be carried by hooking ones finger through the hole in the cap. Technically innovative, the bottle is also attractive to look at. Evian Action meets the needs of the

growing market of consumers who want to drink water on the go.

In September 2002, Evian introduced detachable barcodes on heavy multipacks to save shoppers having to lift the water out of their trolleys at the till – one simply hands the sticker with the barcode to the cashier. This innovation reinforced Evian's innovative leadership in the water category, as well as its understanding of consumer's unmet needs.

Promotion

In the spring of 2001, Evian launched its 'Babies' ballet' TV advertising campaign, featuring babies performing synchronised swimming in a sky-blue swimming pool. With the strapline 'L'Evian live young', the campaign was designed to convey Evian's youth-giving properties – in terms of both mind and body. The ad ran again in 2002, along with a follow-up execution featuring older people and using the same strapline.

In 2001, Evian saved Brockwell Lido in south London from closure by investing in essential maintenance work and refurbishment. Its sponsorship is ongoing and has helped the brand establish a permanent presence in London during the summer months. As well as swimming

new year's solution

Flush out last year's nasties and make a clean start to 2003. Evian Natural Mineral Water is filtered through the French Alps for over 15 years, guaranteeing absolute purity and a unique mineral balance. Detox with Evian, help restore your body and mind.

DÉTOX with evian

and leisure activities, the venue is also an increasingly popular function venue. The Lido, which sports Evian's logo on the base of the pool, was advertised on the London underground and attracted notable media attention.

The following year Kylie Minogue became Evian's first official endorser in the UK and Germany. Kylie embodies Evian's brand values, namely youthful in body and mind, energised and spirited. Furthermore, Kylie claims to drink at least two litres of Evian every day. Her role as Evian brand ambassador lasted until March 2003. Evian sponsored her two-month Fever Tour in May and June 2002 and created 220,000 limited edition Kylie Evian bottles which were handed out to fans outside the concert venues in key cities across the UK. The bottles subsequently changed hands for as much as £30 on ebay.com.

After the tour, Evian produced ten million special 1.5 litre bottles graced with a Kylie image – the first time the brand has used a celebrity on the back of its labels. The bottles were sold through all Evian's usual outlets during the summer of 2002 – traditionally the brand's busiest time of year.

Evian's history in sponsorship has included being the official mineral water of numerous sporting events, including the Stella Artois Tennis

Championship and it also continues to sponsor the 'Evian Masters' women's golf open tournament. This was won in 2002 by the Swede, Carin Koch.

In January 2002, Evian created a precedent within the water category by featuring a special Detox on-pack promotion to tap into the British awareness of detoxing particularly relevant at this time of year.

In 2003, Evian reaffirmed its ownership of the 'after festive season' Detox period. Momentum was strengthened by a heavy and specific TV and press campaign featuring the strapline 'Evian your new year solution', encouraging people to detox with Evian and restore their body's youthfulness.

Brand Values

Evian is the UK's leading premium and aspirational natural mineral water, long favoured by young, fashion conscious and discerning consumers. Its heritage is seen as very important to its consumers, who recognise Evian as being the expert in water, and as such remains the referent of the market.

As the bottled water market becomes more mainstream, Evian intends to continue to operate in the up-market segment, where the reassurance of product quality and innovation in all aspects of the brand remain key to its success in holding consumers trust and loyalty.

www.evian.com

first direct ⬕

Member HSBC Group

Market

firstdirect was the first brand to anticipate the decline of branch banking and the rise of financial services based on telecommunications and mobile technology. It launched its 24-hour telephone banking service in 1989, and since then, an increasing percentage of the UK's 38 million banking customers have joined the 'direct' banking revolution; managing their accounts by land line telephone, mobile phone, internet or even SMS. After years of brusque letters, tense telephone conversations and patronising conversations with traditional bank managers, a new generation of consumers has embraced a bank that thinks and acts like them.

firstdirect has a 2% share of the overall current account market, but more than a 5% share of the entire internet banking market. More than 500,000 firstdirect customers do their banking on the web, and 200,000 have begun using its SMS service. They are also good communicators, a factor that has worked very much in firstdirect's favour, with 30% of new customers joining each year as a result of a personal recommendation.

firstdirect has evolved from simply offering a current account into a fully-fledged financial services proposition. The business has three main areas: banking, smartmortgage (its highly successful offset mortgage proposition) and financial advice. The bank's database shows that its one million-plus customers are young, busy professionals, typically aged between 25-44 and clustered in the south east of England. Furthermore, they are confident users of financial services and early adopters of new ideas and technology and likely to shop around, but are essentially looking for financial brands in which to place their trust. In addition, 90% of them are mobile phone users (against a population average of 70%) and nearly 70% are internet users (compared to a national average of 45-50%).

Achievements

firstdirect now has more than a million customers, an average of around 100,000 new customers joining every year since its launch. And for a bank which lacks the 'human' interface

found in high street branches, it has built up an impressive level of loyalty and customer satisfaction. According to MORI, it has had the most satisfied banking customers in Britain for over a decade, and has been the country's most recommended bank for the same period. Additionally, research conducted by the Institute of Customer Service in 2002, ranked firstdirect second in terms of customer service in a survey of worldwide brands, behind only Singapore Airlines – and ahead of heavyweight brands like Virgin Atlantic and Tesco.

tonight, 'tis the

switching hour

does your bank give you the willies?
Are you fed up with disappearing lunch hours and skeleton staff? Don't stay chained to your old bank. Join **first direct** instead.

We're a bank for free spirits... with free 24 hour banking, a fee-free automatic £500 overdraft and free banking on the internet and your mobile phone. We'll even treat you to a **free £25** when you join. (No tricks.)

So call us at midnight – or any time you like – and switch to **first direct**. It's frightening how easy it is.

£25 free. wicked...

call us any time on
0800 24 24 24 *quoting ref: BD263*
visit us at
firstdirect.com

no more...

eerie silences
free banking – 24 hrs a day

creaky old doors
we have no branches

voices that don't sound human
real people – not robots

creeping bank charges arrggghhh!!!
banking with us is free

we're magic. join us. post to: First Direct, FREEPOST, Leeds LS98 2RF

Mr/Mrs/Miss/Ms	Surname	Forename(s)
UK Address		
Postcode	Telephone	c BD263

To maintain a quality service, calls may be monitored and/or recorded. Applicants must be 18 or over. We reserve the right to decline to open an account for you. Credit facilities are subject to status. Written details, quotations and terms and conditions of our products and services available upon request. The £25 offer is valid for new customers who open a current account, quoting the reference above and have a credit balance within 3 months of this advert. Mobile Phone Banking is only available to **first direct** customers and is subject to terms and conditions. Once your **first direct** Bank Account is up and running, you need to pay in at least £1,000 each month, or maintain a balance greater than £1,000 or other charges and conditions may apply. **first direct** is a division of HSBC Bank plc.

The bank's own report shows that over 80% of firstdirect customers believe that it is better or much better than their previous bank, while 85% are extremely or very satisfied with its service, and 82% of them have recommended it at some point. The average customer on average holds 2.02 products with firstdirect, more than the customers of any other bank in the UK.

In recent years, firstdirect's credentials have been strengthened further by illustrating an

overt link, through its logo, to its parent organisation HSBC (The Hong Kong & Shanghai Banking Corporation). Since Midland Bank evolved to become HSBC in 1999, the parent bank has quickly grown a reputation for excellent service, innovation and reliability. The brand link between HSBC and firstdirect has meant that both brands are benefiting from each other's strengths and the net result is a stronger, more competitive group position.

History

firstdirect was the UK's first 24-hour 'person to person' bank, taking its first calls on October 1st 1989. The brand was established with no branches, no managers, no closing times and with the major benefit of no queues. The traditional banks (with, of course, the notable exception of firstdirect's sister organisation Midland Bank), ridiculed the whole concept, saying people would always want branch contact and face-to-face dialogue. Yet traditional banks were disliked by many customers, who believed they were getting a poor service, both in terms of being treated like a human being and getting value for money.

From the very start, a new type of dialogue was opened up. Staff at firstdirect were chosen for their communication skills, and then went on to be trained in banking. The service they provide on the phone is what gives the brand its unique selling point, especially as it has no retail presence. Although an increasing number of customers are banking via the web, they still need to discuss more complex products and services. Ultimately the brand is all about people – and how customers feel when they have finished a dialogue with a customer service representative.

Product

Apart from the range of financial services listed above, firstdirect's real 'product' is branch-free remote banking. Its fully integrated service allows customers to access their banking when, where and how they want – with free internet, telephone and mobile phone banking services. Phone calls are answered by real people, not automated systems, and transactions can be carried out

seven days a week. The bank is effectively open 24 hours a day, 365 days a year.

Key to firstdirect's proposition is free banking, which means no charges for normal banking transactions within the UK, irrespective of whether the customer is in credit or overdrawn. In addition, all customers can have access to an automatic fee-free overdraft of £500. firstdirect offers very competitive rates to all customers, irrespective of how they choose to do their banking.

Recent Developments

Summer 2000 saw the introduction of a full internet banking service with extremely competitive pricing across branded products. This service has been a huge success and since launch, firstdirect has taken a large chunk of the internet banking sector, with a 5% share of the market and 250,000 internet banking 'log-ons' recorded per week during 2001.

Now its goal is to establish itself in every remote banking sector, beginning with an SMS or text messaging service. This enables customers to receive balances, mini-statements and event alerts straight to their mobiles as and when they require them.

The bank has plans to continue adapting its service to each technological breakthrough. Indeed, WAP next-generation mobile telephone technology services were introduced in December 2000 and other services are planned to give ever increasingly technology literate customers further diversity in the way in which they approach their relationship with their bank in the twenty first century.

The goal is a fully integrated multi-channel banking service, where each channel complements the others. Customers are offered a wide choice of options that allow them to bank when and how they wish, without any hidden charges or conditions.

Promotion

The firstdirect brand has never been about mass targeting and huge media spend. It has focused its advertising and marketing on a core target group of young, smart, busy professionals who want to simplify their lives, and who want to use new technology to do it.

Television campaigns have attracted attention, but to better reach its target group the bank has increasingly begun turning away from traditional marketing and towards the area of interactive media. By the end of 2002 it will have sent out eight million targeted electronic messages, 25 million website sales banners and one million SMS marketing messages. It will back these up with direct mail, targeted press inserts, and prompts by its telephone staff. It says that its goal is to sell 500,000 new products, including three times the number of smartmortgages sold in any previous year.

In the past, the brand has won a number of awards for the effectiveness of its marketing, including a Gold award from the British Television Advertising Awards for the 'Little Fella' campaign during early 2000. This campaign introduced a brand icon who shared the concerns and problems of the bank's customers. 'Little Fella' followed the campaign, featuring the comedian Bob Mortimer. It focused on the absurdities of traditional banking, highlighting the anti-customer stance of banks closing early, forcing people to queue, imposing unfair charges and so on. Different television ads focused on different firstdirect propositions, such as 'no queuing' and 'no closing'.

firstdirect positions itself as the 'independently minded bank for independently minded people'. While peoples' lives become more complex, banking with firstdirect can at least sort out one area of life quickly, easily, without fuss and with personality and friendliness.

The campaign which ran in 2002 featured Bob Mortimer's comedy partner, Vic Reeves. This campaign highlights features of the firstdirect service – such as its personal service. In one execution, Reeves asks diners in a restaurant if they would rather be served by a robot (which in this case looks like it has come straight from a Doctor Who set) or a person (the real waiter at the restaurant).

Brand Values

The idea behind firstdirect remains the same as it did when the bank launched in 1989 – to provide a fully integrated service, enabling customers to access their banking when, where and how they want to. It is a trusted brand which challenges the accepted attitudes to banking and money, and continually innovates to reflect customer needs. Its philosophy is to be on the side of the customer in a complex financial world.

www.firstdirect.com

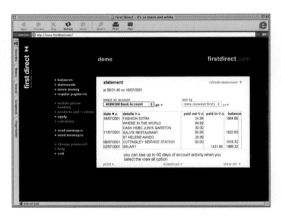

Things you didn't know about
firstdirect

firstdirect handles around 300,000 customer calls per week, with 50% taken outside normal banking hours, including 50,000 calls every weekend.

Over a third of all customers join firstdirect as a result of 'word-of-mouth'.

During the early years of firstdirect, 60% of customers were male, 40% female. The ratio is now 50:50.

firstdirect has never closed.

In January 2002 firstdirect's 500,000th customer registered for its Electronic Banking service.

Market

As the business world faces its worst advertising recession for 30 years, the global threat of terrorism, corporate scandals on a grand scale, turbulent stock market movements and the ensuing loss of business confidence, the demand for independent, authoritative and accurate business and financial news is greater than ever.

Achievements

Whether the FT is targeting its readers, its website users and subscribers or its corporate clients, the FT's reach has never been stronger. The combination of the FT's newspaper circulation, the traffic figures for FT.com, and the number of people viewing FT content via corporate content sales and syndication services, ensures that more people than ever before now rely on the FT brand.

FT.com was named Best Global Markets Site by Barron's magazine, in their annual 'Best of the Web' awards. FT editorial has received many other accolades throughout 2002 including three British Press Awards – Tim Burt was named Business Journalist of the Year, Sathnam Sanghera was named Young Journalist of the Year and Nigel Andrews was named Critic of the Year.

In the Business Journalist of the Year Awards the FT received 'best article' in six categories, namely Communications, Banking, Insurance, Service Industries, Personal Finance and Manufacturing.

Furthermore, the David Watt prize for Political Journalism was awarded to Philip Stephens, editor, UK & Ireland in the same year.

In The State Street Global Advisors Institutional Press Awards, Florian Gimbel was named Best Newcomer and Philip Coggan named Best Fund Management Correspondent for their work on the FT Fund Management supplement.

History

The Financial Times launched in 1888 as the 'friend' of the 'Honest Financier and the

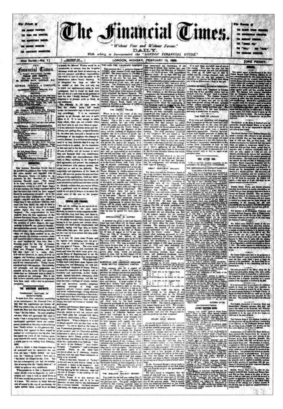

Respectable Broker'. However, it wasn't until 1893 that the FT began printing on pink paper. This was done through a stroke of early marketing genius by Douglas Macrae to distinguish the paper from its rivals.

In 1919, Berry Bros, owners of The Sunday Times, and later The Daily Telegraph, took control of the FT. Developments took place over the course of time, for example in 1935 the 30-share index was introduced to the Financial Times for the first time.

The Financial News, which was established in 1884, finally merged with the FT in 1945 when its chairman Brendan Bracken bought the company. The paper did however retain the name Financial Times as well as its signature pink paper.

In 1953 the 20,000th issue of the FT was celebrated. To reflect the increased scope of the newspaper an arts page was launched and 'Industry' 'Commerce' and 'Public Affairs' were added to the masthead.

Four years later the paper was taken over by Pearson and the business moved in 1959 to Bracken House, Cannon Street. Following this, further improvements were made and in 1960 the Technical page (now Technology), Executive's World page (now Inside Track) and the Saturday paper's 'How To Spend It' page were all introduced. By the following year, average circulation exceeded 132,000. Developments continued, with the European edition being printed in Frankfurt for the first time in 1979.

Circulation of the FT in the UK had increased significantly and in 1986 passed the 250,000 mark with the aid of the 'No FT…No Comment' ad campaign. In the same year, technological advancements also took place when printing processes moved from hot metal to cold set printing.

In 1987, the FT published the first world share

index and, two years later, the FT Group Head Office relocated to Number One Southwark Bridge. Under the new editor, Richard Lambert who joined the company in 1991, several new initiatives were introduced, including the first edition of 'How To Spend It' magazine in 1994. One year later, the international edition was relaunched and FT.com, the Financial Times website, was created.

In 2000, Creative Business was introduced as a supplement with the UK edition and the European edition was relaunched. 2001 saw the launch of Global Investing pages in the US edition, Richard Lambert named Business Journalist of the decade and the FT reach the 500,000 copies mark. Andrew Gowers, former founding editor of Financial Times Deutschland, was appointed editor of the FT.

In 2002 significant events for the paper included the launch of the FT Fund Management supplement as well as the relaunch of FT.com with additional features such as subscription services. Unique monthly users of the site reached 3.2 million and page views exceeded 50 million by December of that year.

In terms of the FT's international development, its first move abroad took place as far back as 1979 when a European edition, printed in Frankfurt, was launched. By the end of 2002, the FT newspaper was being printed in nineteen cities across the world, including New York, Paris, Tokyo, Madrid, Stockholm, Los Angeles, Hong Kong, Milan, Kuala Lumpur and Seoul. Indeed, these operations have been so successful that international circulation sales now exceed that of the UK. International expansion has continued, with the FT now being digitally printed in South Africa.

Product

The FT is firmly established as one of the world's leading business information brands, internationally recognised for its authoritative, accurate, and incisive news, comment and analysis. Whether in print or online, the Financial Times is essential

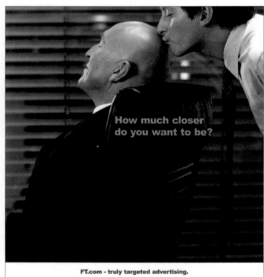

reading for the global business community.

The Financial Times is one of the world's leading English language newspapers. Following the launch of a new digitally printed version in South Africa, and the opening of a new London print site, the newspaper is now printed in nineteen cities across the world. With a daily circulation of over 460,000, the Financial Times has a readership of more than one million people and is available in 140 countries.

FT.com (www.FT.com) is one of the world's leading business information websites, and the internet partner of the Financial Times. The site reflects the values and authority of the Financial Times newspaper, with the immediacy and interactivity of the internet. Since its relaunch in May 2002, the website has continued to be the definitive home for business intelligence on the web, providing an essential source of news, comment, data and analysis for the global business community.

FT.com's 3.2 million unique monthly users generate 50 million monthly page views, delivering a premium audience to advertisers. The website combines agenda-setting editorial content with comment and analysis, financial data, discussion groups, and a range of tools to search the web, manage the working day and seek out leisure opportunities. At the core of the site is authoritative news and analysis, updated throughout the business day by journalists in the Financial Times' integrated newsroom and by the FT's large network of correspondents around the world.

Recent Developments

In May 2002, FT.com was relaunched, with a new design, new content and new subscription services. The new site enables customers – whether they use the free part of the site or the new subscriptions packages – to get the best possible access to global business news, analysis and insight, effectively making FT.com the definitive home for business intelligence on the web.

Subscription services include Lex live, an intra-day email building on the newspaper's famous 'Lex' investment column, an improved Power Search facility with fast, intelligent information retrieval from over 500 worldwide publications, increased company data with the World Company Financials package, the view print edition service enabling readers to view a printable pdf of all editions of the FT newspaper the night prior to publication and Personal Office – a full personal administration system, which includes a reading and sending email facility and calendar tools.

In 2002, FT Fund Management was launched as a weekly supplement. FTfm has the world's largest circulation of any fund management title, and offers one of the most comprehensive pricing services for funds. Covering a variety of industry news, analysis, trends, opinion pieces, fund performance reviews and a full listing of managed funds, FTfm provides essential insight and analysis of the fund management industry and the people behind the scenes.

Creative Business, the FT's weekly supplement on the media, design and communications industries also goes from strength to strength and recently celebrated its second anniversary. The annual 'Creative Business Top 50' profiles the UK's 50 most creative business people, and is now seen as essential reading for Britain's creative community.

The FT's US edition celebrated its fifth anniversary in 2002, publishing a commemorative magazine highlighting the best reporting and commentary from the FT, over the past five years. Since the launch of the US edition in 1997, the FT has become the fastest-growing business newspaper in the US, with a four-fold increase in circulation since 1997. The FT's readership has increased faster than any other nationally distributed US newspaper and the US is on track to become the FT's largest single national market during the next ten years.

Brand Values

The FT aims to be the world's leading business information brand. Its goal is to become essential reading – both in print and online – for business leaders and other decision-makers, through the quality of its editing and reporting. The FT is now a truly global news organisation, seeking to explain how events in one area of the world are likely to have an impact on institutions and economies in other regions, looking for trends and common patterns, context and connections.

The FT is distinct by virtue of its commitment to accurate, impartial and authoritative reporting, which is always of the highest quality.

www.FT.com

Promotion

The launch of FT.com's subscription services was complemented by an extensive marketing campaign, based on the 'go further' premise. The key message is that it is worth 'going further' into the site by paying for certain elements of premium content. The message was echoed in a campaign for the advertising community, highlighting the benefits of the new FT.com site in terms of its facility for greater creativity and more effective targeting. The campaign included press and online advertising, direct mail and a full public relations campaign in the national and trade press.

Gillette®

Market

The male blades and razors category is now worth £177 million in the UK alone, an increase of 28% since 1995, making it is one of the fastest growing sectors within the toiletries market. Furthermore, the male grooming market is predicted to experience even higher growth over the next five years.

The main catalyst for spectacular growth has been a fundamental change in men's attitudes to the grooming process over the last decade. The rise in popularity of 'lad mags' and a defined male culture has evolved into an awareness of health and well being – in this context it is much more acceptable for men to care about their appearance and look good. Today 67% of men use aftershaves and out of the 78% of men who wet shave, 84% are using shaving preps.

This trend has resulted in a massive influx of male grooming products onto store shelves, such as male specific skin care and shower, providing a dramatically increased choice for the male grooming regime. In many households the male bathroom cabinet now rivals the female's, both in size and choice.

Female grooming is also maturing into a very important part of the health and beauty category. It now equates to 19% of the total blades and razors sector and delivers retail sales of more than £42.6 million – up a massive 59% since 1995, driven predominantly by the launch of Gillette for Women Venus in 2001.

Women view the process of hair removal as very important in their beauty routine, with more than 46% removing hair at the slightest re-growth (twice a week or more). Wet shaving continues to be by far the most popular amongst 83% of women – an increase of four million women since 1991.

Achievements

The millennium heralded Gillette's centenary year. Much has changed over this 100 year period. However the passing of time has not changed the 'number one' positioning that Gillette holds in both the male and female grooming markets. While Gillette is synonymous with shaving, it is a global leader in nearly a dozen major consumer product categories. Grooming undoubtedly remains the principal business unit but the company is also a major supplier of toothbrushes and oral care applications under its Oral B and Braun brands, and the number one source of portable power with the Duracell brand.

The core element of the wet shaving category remains blades and razors, of which Gillette has a 78% value share of the male and a 71% value share of the female market. Gillette has a long established position as the most popular brand and is market leader in the two principal wet shaving categories – blades & razors and shave preps.

For men who wet shave, shave preps go hand-in-hand with shaving. While this is secondary to blades and razors in the wet shaving market as a whole, the category is becoming a very significant player. The male shave prep market is worth more than £62 million (up from £53 million in 1995) of which Gillette holds a 55% share. With the growing success of 'own brand' brand labels and

an increase in competition from other brands, Gillette has also aggressively attacked market trends with the launch of a new fragrance line for its series range – Arctic Ice.

The company's strong focus on technological advancement has created new market opportunities. Many of Gillette's pioneering

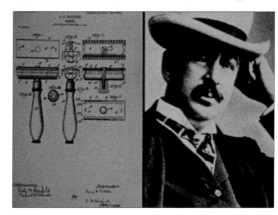

innovations have become patented inventions, accepted as industry standards: from adjustable razors, fully contained cartridges, pivoting heads, lubrastrips flexible microfins and spring mounted twin blades, to the first razor designed specifically for the shaving needs of women.

Venus has driven the female blades and razor market forward and reinforced Gillette for Women as a worldwide leader in the female shaving market. Since the razor's launch, female shaving has become the fastest growing part of the Gillette Grooming portfolio. Venus built on the principles established by the Gillette for Women Sensor – a product 'designed by a woman, for a woman to address the shaving needs of a woman'. The introduction of the three blade Venus has further revolutionised the female market and driven significant growth. Venus has established its role as a favourite with female shavers a fact that has driven year on year growth on Venus replacement blades to over 103%.

Gillette for Women also holds a strong position in the other two areas of the female shaving category: Satin Care holds a 67% value share of

the £9.5 million female shave prep market and Gillette maintain a 38% value share of the £11.2 million female disposables sector.

History

100 years ago, US travelling salesman King C Gillette had the idea of developing a safe and easy to use razor – an idea which was to revolutionise the shaving market. His frustration with traditional cut-throat shaving led him to start work on a model razor, and so the Gillette Company was founded in Boston in 1901.

Gillette's early success was built on strong technological foundations. The 'wafer thin' metal needed to make the razor blade was even dubbed by Thomas Edison to be a 'technical impossibility'. However, Gillette broke new ground with the development of new processes for tempering and hardening mass produced steel. In 1903 the Gillette Safety Razor was finally launched.

In spite of a slow start (only 51 razors and 168 blades sold in the first year) more than 90,000 Americans possessed a safety razor by the end of Gillette's second year of trading. The safety razor had already become a hit. It was deemed to have changed the face of a nation. The rapidly growing company established a factory in South Boston in 1905 under the new name of the Gillette Safety Razor Company.

Strong domestic growth prompted international expansion. Overseas operations commenced in 1905, with a manufacturing plant just outside Paris and a sales office in London. Annual blade sales had risen to more than 40 million units before the outbreak of World War I.

The Great War saw Gillette become the first supplier of razors to the US Army when, in 1918, the US Government decided to issue each of its servicemen with their own shaving equipment. 3.5 million Safety Razors and 36 million blades were duly supplied.

The company has come a long way since its first patent in 1904. Techmatic, the first system razor, was introduced in 1967. Its 'continuous band' meant that consumers would no longer have to touch the blade. This was followed in 1971 by the GII, the world's first twin-bladed system. The first twin bladed disposable razor followed in 1976 and Contour, the first razor with a pivoting head, arrived in 1977.

While developments in the 1960s and 1970s focused mainly on blades, the 1980s and 1990s saw improved features for a smoother, more comfortable shave. The Contour Plus in 1985 heralded the first lubrastrip and 1990 saw the company's first ever Pan-Atlantic launch with the introduction of Sensor in sixteen countries. This razor featured the first spring mounted blades and shell-bearing pivot. Then, three years later, the SensorExcel was launched with soft, flexible microfins. The MACH3 arrived in 1998, introducing the revolutionary triple bladed shaving system, which in January 2002 was given a boost in performance resulting in Gillette's best razor ever – the MACH3 Turbo. Integrated with the completely reformulated new Gillette Series range the MACH3 Turbo is now designed to provide the closest shave, in fewer strokes, with less irritation, even when shaving against the grain.

There had been little development in the female shaving market before the 1990s. Gillette introduced the first ever razor for women called 'Milady Decollete' in 1915 and the first disposable for women called Gillette Daisy in 1975. The ground-breaking Gillette for Women Sensor arrived in 1992, which was then surpassed by the new and very much improved SensorExcel for women.

In 2000 Gillette for Women launched Venus – a unique triple blade razor, designed specifically for how and where women shave. Venus combines pioneering innovation and proven technology to offer a far superior shave, significantly out-performing even SensorExcel for Women by a 3-to-1 margin.

Venus revolutionised the female shaving experience, ensuring skin stays smoother for longer with a single stroke.

Product

The company's biggest technological breakthrough in recent years has also been Gillette's biggest success story to date – the MACH3 shaving system. The creation of MACH3 involved more than a decade of research and development, the involvement of hundreds of Gillette scientists and engineers and financial investment of over £449 million.

The MACH3 Turbo is a new generation razor that builds on the heritage of its predecessor, the MACH3, giving an extra boost in shaving performance.

Four key innovations and improvements have been made to the MACH3 design to produce the MACH3 Turbo.

An enhanced indicator lubrication strip releases more lubrication over a greater number of shaves. New anti-friction blades allow the MACH3 Turbo to glide through beard hair with less resistance for the closest shave, even against the grain. Ten soft and protective microfins – twice as many as the MACH3 – feature to gently smooth down the skin so the blades can shave evenly and effortlessly. Finally the redesigned razor handle with textured rubber grips and metal grooves improve sureness of grip to provide better handling and control throughout the shave.

The New Gillette Series Range has been reformulated to provide a fully integrated grooming solution for men. It now consists of eleven new products from shaving gel and foam, after-shave cooling gel, after-shave balm and splash to anti-perspirants, deodorants and shower gels. Shaving gels and foams have been enhanced with 'anti-friction' lubricants for ultra razor glide and specially formulated with skin comfort ingredients for five different skin care needs – sensitive, moisturising, protection, conditioning and clean skin.

Recent Developments

The MACH3 Turbo is a new generation of razor that will raise the standard in male shaving to the next level. Combining a series of product innovations, the razor boasts the ultimate test of a close shave – performing even when shaving 'against the grain'. In the US, five million men have already upgraded to the MACH3 Turbo 'ultimate shaving experience'.

Consumer testing amongst men established that MACH3 Turbo is the best performing shaving system ever with performance increased further when used in conjunction with the new Gillette Series shave gels and conditioners.

In terms of product innovation within female shaving, nothing can rival Venus: in designing Venus, Gillette for Women 'threw out the book'.

Acknowledging that women weren't completely satisfied with the wet shaving process, Gillette addressed women's complaints that results of shaving are not long-lasting enough, that razors don't really adjust to the curves and contours of female bodies and

the lingering fear that wet shaving causes nicks and cuts – when designing Venus.

Created for women by a woman, the razor features an oval-shaped cartridge with three patented blades, set between soft, protective honeycombed cushions that gently smooth out the skin as a woman shaves.

The handle features an elastomeric grip, finger pad and ball shaped end for improved comfort, control and manoeuvrability and the system includes a shaving compact which is easily mounted on the wall in the shower or bath to conveniently store razors and blades together.

Overall, Venus operates under 50 separate patents combining advances created for MACH3 and Sensor with others unique to Venus. These special features account for the unprecedented consumer test results – 73% of women preferred Venus to any other female razor – for perspective the performance of Venus amongst women is even more dramatic than the performance of MACH3 among men. In Gillette's 100 year history, this is

the strongest performance of a Gillette shaving product in this type of test – Venus sets an entirely new standard in female shaving.

Promotion

Gillette's advertising campaign for the MACH3 Turbo continues with the 'Best A Man Can Get' theme but uses creative imagery of outer space. MACH3 Turbo's advertising has focused on 'turning the shaving world upside down' and draws parallels between the zero-gravity factor in space and the option of using the MACH3 Turbo to shave against the grain.

Sponsorship plays a large part in promoting the brand. In March 2003 the MACH3 Turbo and Gillette Series will be reaching space with the MACH3 Turbo rocket – breaking the 'ultimate performance barrier'. Gillette are once again sponsoring Richard 'Rocket Man' Brown in his latest record-breaking attempt bid to send the first amateur rocket into space. Cutting edge technology, highly innovative style and breaking performance barriers all form strong synergies with the values of the MACH3 Turbo razor.

In 2002 Gillette sponsored the World Cup Championships in Japan and South Korea, backed by a fully integrated marketing campaign.

This football association continues with the sponsorship of premiership football on Sky Sports' 'Gillette Soccer Saturday'. Historically, Gillette has used sport as a major promotional vehicle and embarked on its first sponsorship deal with a radio broadcast of the US World Series back in 1939. There remains a strong association due to the performance focused and highly aspirational nature of sport.

Brand Values

Gillette is dedicated to driving superior technology that will develop and produce hair removal products that deliver a superior shave with superior performance.

Its male image is sporty, masculine, clean and immaculately groomed. The female image is modern, energising and understanding of women's needs. Gillette's success has been its ability to make men and women look and feel their very best by continually developing technologically superior grooming products.

In essence, the Gillette Company celebrates world class products, world class brands and world class people. It is committed to growth through innovation to maintain the company's position as a world leader in the consumer products marketplace.

www.gillette.com

Market

Now it is almost hard to recall that there was a time when by and large ice cream was perceived as a cheap treat, in the main associated with kids and summer.

Häagen-Dazs changed UK consumers' perception of ice cream for good when it created the super premium sector.

Significantly, growth has been measured in value terms with a high increase over the three-year period from 1997, reflecting a consumer trend away from the low-end towards high-value products (Source: Mintel).

The UK ice cream market was valued at £690 million in 2002, an increase of just 0.1% year on year (Source: ACNielsen), this makes it at extremely difficult and competitive market to play in.

In today's ice cream market, adult and children's brands are clearly defined. Noticeable market trends include the introduction of brand extension lines from the confectionery and beverages sectors as well as a swing away from seasonal consumption habits. The popularity of super premium products positioned as indulgence treats is also strong as well as the growing popularity of organic and healthy-eating products.

Häagen-Dazs, Ben & Jerry's and Hill Station all sit within the 'Super Premium' category, this is decided purely on the quality of the product, 'Super Premium' also sits within the 'Premium' category where other brands such as Carte D'or, Mars and Cadbury as well as many own label products are all players.

Achievements

Whilst the UK dairy ice cream market for tub sizes of one litre and under is growing at an annual rate of 15%, the Häagen-Dazs brand is ahead of the market at 34% growth, to make it category leader within entire premium sector.

The brand's outstanding achievement is in having invented the UK super-premium sector through its introduction in 1989. Consumer response was instant and Häagen-Dazs gained an immediate healthy share within the category.

Häagen-Dazs is now a highly visible global brand, selling strongly in Japan, France, Germany, Canada, China, Latin America, North America, Hong Kong, Singapore and many other countries.

The Häagen-Dazs brand has attracted a growing level of competition within the super premium sector, which has directly led to combined premium and luxury product sales now representing over a quarter of total market value (Source: Mintel).

History

Häagen-Dazs traces its origins back to the early 1920s. From the outset, the brand's originator insisted upon using only the finest, purest ingredients to create the product's distinctive flavour and in 1961 took the decision to form a new company dedicated to furthering this individualistic vision.

Having started out with just three flavours: vanilla, chocolate and coffee, Häagen-Dazs's obsession with selecting only the best ingredients took them as far afield as Madagascar and Belgium, further enhancing their products' connotations of the exotic and indulgent.

Initially available only through selected New York gourmet food stores and delis, Häagen-Dazs ice cream rapidly became synonymous with the city's fashionable café culture. The brand developed a powerful word of mouth reputation, creating an enthusiastic following that was being serviced nationwide by 1973 without the benefit of any tangible advertising or promotion.

In the meantime, those original retail outlets led to the development of the first dedicated Häagen-Dazs shop in 1976, the basis on which over 650 Häagen-Dazs cafés are now currently located around the world.

In response to global demand for the product, international distribution of Häagen-Dazs took off in 1982 when it first became available in Canada. Shortly afterwards, the Häagen-Dazs brand was

Fall head over heels in Häagen~Dazs.

Fall deeply in Häagen~Dazs.

It was Häagen~Dazs at first sight.

Fall deeply in Häagen~Dazs.

sold to the Pillsbury Company Limited. Just one year later it began to produce Häagen-Dazs in Japan where it quickly became the best selling premium ice cream brand in the country.

Since 1987, Häagen-Dazs has made in-roads into many other European countries such as France, Germany, Spain and Italy. In January 1989, Pillsbury was acquired by Grand Metropolitan plc and after a series of acquisitions is now owned by The General Mills Company and has many sister brands such as Green Giant, Old El Paso and Betty Crocker.

Product

True to the vision of its originator, Häagen-Dazs ice cream is made from the highest quality natural ingredients: fresh cream and milk, sugar, eggs and natural flavourings, and without the addition of any artificial flavours or colourings.

Only double-pasteurised fresh egg yolk is used in production, and all Häagen-Dazs flavours are marketed as suitable for lacto-ovo vegetarians. In line with the brand's quality control standards, pectin is used as the preferred gelling agent, a natural ingredient that is found in all fruits.

Häagen-Dazs's distinctive texture is achieved by ensuring a high ratio of cream to air, this further differentiates it from less expensive products at the lower end of the category which tend to contain a lot more air, which is why they are softer than Häagen-Dazs. For optimum enjoyment, Häagen-Dazs is best left to temper a little once removed from the freezer.

Top-selling flavours in the UK include Vanilla, Pralines & Cream and Belgian Chocolate. A total of sixteen different flavours are available in the 500ml (pint) tub format including Banoffee, Strawberry Cheesecake, Cookies and Cream, Baileys, Strawberry, Toffee Crème and Vanilla Caramel Brownie.

Many of the 500ml flavours are also available in 100ml (minicups) which are mainly available in cinemas or smaller local stores.

Recent Developments

New product development is fundamental to continuing success within the super-premium category, and Häagen-Dazs is dedicated to constantly innovating its range of flavours, the most recent new entrants being Banoffee, Vanilla Caramel Brownie, Cookie Dough Chip and Tiramisu. 2002 was a busy year for Häagen-Dazs, they also launched the new 'Minissime' in both Chocolate Cookie and Vanilla Macadamia Nut flavours, these are miniature (45ml) stickbars that are an everyday treat. They also updated their minicup multipacks (4x100ml tubs) to show the differentiation between the two packs 'True Classics' being smooth flavours (Vanilla, Baileys, Toffee Crème and Belgian Chocolate) and 'Pure Pleasures' being the more indulgent flavours that have bits in (Vanilla Caramel Brownie, Pralines & Cream, Cookies and Cream and Strawberry Cheesecake).

A new refurbished flagship Häagen-Dazs Café opened its doors in London's Leicester Square in June of 2000, with customers encouraged to experiment with different flavour combinations by visiting a purpose-built scooping and serving area. A characteristically opulent interior décor scheme underlines the brand's association with intimacy and indulgence. Häagen-Dazs has a total of 70 Cafes throughout the UK at present.

August 2000 saw the launch of the Häagen-Dazs website, welcoming online visitors to 'the source for pure pleasure' with reminders of the product's insistence upon natural ingredients serving to further instil an overriding impression of self-gratification. The site offered recipes for 'nights in' and also included details of indulgent offers and competitions such as shopping-trips to New York, designed to appeal to the lifestyle of the Häagen-Dazs consumer.

Promotion

The company started stealthily and did not advertise; instead it made sure that the product was distributed in upmarket outlets such as Harrods and began a 'whispering campaign' about this new, incredibly creamy ice cream from the US. The campaign then went one step further with PR activity and sampling of the 'Häagen-Dazs experience' in stores, at college freshers' balls, at celebrity parties and film premières.

Full scale press advertising began in 1991 and presented the brand as an adult pleasure through images of couples enjoying the product together. After this, the brand built on its seductive credential with a US$30 million European marketing package to take the strategy one step further. The 'Dedicated to Pleasure' campaign in 1988 saw full-page ads incorporating sensuous pictures of couples in provocative embraces in up-market magazines such as Vogue and Harpers & Queen.

in a series of romantically cast advertisements, with couples variously described as 'falling head over heels in Häagen-Dazs', or blinded by 'Häagen-Dazs at first sight'.

In a move away from previous campaigns, humour was used in the '100% Perfect' creative campaign; one of its memorable characterisations being the old man with a beautiful young wife, sadly unable to remember where he lives – a tongue-in-cheek reminder that 'in this uncertain world only Häagen-Dazs is 100% perfect'.

In the wake of a brand relaunch three years later, Häagen-Dazs launched the light-hearted 'Pleasure is the Path to Joy' campaign which parodied a faddish new age interest in self-awareness programmes and pleasure retreat workshops.

In 2002 TBWA were the third appointed UK agency to take on this advertising legacy and the product's affinity with the silver screen was again firmly established in its 'Made for Movies' campaign, a campaign that linked film with Häagen-Dazs by film title links. One of Häagen-Dazs's first fully multi-media campaigns included TV, where the ads depicted two mates eating and hiding a flatmates tub of Häagen-Dazs 'Usual Suspects', or else appealed to a single indulger 'Home Alone'. Outdoor poster displays in major cities nationwide also linked the product with iconic movies such as 'Vertigo' and 'Point Blank'.

Regular spots appeared on the Sky movie channels to promote 'Friday nights with Häagen-Dazs', again linking the Häagen-Dazs tub with

1995 saw the launch of the 'Heat' campaign, in its day the ultimate in risqué advertising, and establishing the product's continuing association with television and the cinema. Viewers were just able to make out the bodies of a man and a woman, who were sensuously covering one another with Häagen-Dazs.

Häagen-Dazs started the new millennium by substituting the brand name for the word 'love'

film titles such as the shark's fin circling the tub before pulling it under the water for 'Jaws'.

A key feature of the campaign was to tie-in product sales with rentals of the Nick Hornby book turned movie 'About a Boy' via 650 Blockbuster Video outlets. Consumers were encouraged to buy a 500ml tub and get a little one (i.e. 100ml mini-tub) free. The promotion also found its way into 'the world's smallest cinema' on the concourse at London's Victoria Station.

In addition to radio drive-time slots and regional press ads, the 'Made for Movies' campaign also extended online (madeformovies.co.uk) with co-promotions linked to www.amazon.co.uk and the 'La-Z-Boy e-cliner' chair manufacturer.

Häagen-Dazs also continued to sponsor Sky Movies on Friday nights throughout the year.

An immediate success notched up as a direct result of its exposure during the campaign was the elevation of the newly launched 'Banoffee' flavour.

Brand Values

Häagen-Dazs is universally recognised as a high quality luxury brand. The product's consumers are defined as being worldly, intelligent, highly discerning and intent upon the pursuit of pure pleasure.

www.haagen-dazs.co.uk

Things you didn't know about Häagen-Dazs

Häagen-Dazs Baileys ice cream and stick bars do contain real alcohol – but less than 0.5% per 100ml of actual product.

Although initially packaged as an American dessert, the very first 'Banoffi Pie' was devised by Ian Dowding and Nigel Mackenzie of the 'Hungry Monk Pub' near Eastbourne in Britain.

The perfect temperature for eating Häagen-Dazs is -15°c, which usually means leaving it to stand in room temperature for ten minutes or so, it is worth the wait as during this time the bits in the ice-cream are actually blending with the product, making it taste mouthwateringly delicious.

Market

Heinz is a leading global food company which encompasses over 5,700 varieties of products around the world, representing sales of more than US$8 billion.

In the UK the highly successful Heinz brand is visible in many markets from Baked Beans to Tomato Ketchup to Frozen meals.

UK retail sales of soups are now worth an estimated £462 million and UK retail sales of baby food and drink is worth an estimated £381.8 million (Source: Mintel).

By focusing on its power brands, Heinz aims to achieve growth and drive the future dominance of the company around the globe.

Heinz sets itself apart as the 'PREMIER' food company in Europe by delivering greater earnings and sales value to shareholders, whilst that same determined focus and drive provides a programme of innovation and development of 'food solutions' that meet consumer demands for quality, taste and convenience.

Achievements

Heinz has always been at the forefront of advertising, with famous campaigns including 'Beanz Meanz Heinz' and 'Toast To Life'. In June 2002, Heinz featured two new TV commercials for Heinz Tomato Ketchup emphatically enforcing the message, 'you can't eat without it'.

Furthermore, the 'Ice Station' and 'Granny' adverts assert Heinz's position as the 'definitive' ketchup. The adverts not only celebrate the brand's personality, but also emphasise the message that Heinz Tomato Ketchup needs to be present to 'complete all meals'. To support this campaign, 35 million bottles had a special edition message label that contains the strapline, 'you can't eat without it' within the keystone (Heinz distinctive label shape).

History

The Heinz brand has been in existence for over 130 years and still takes into account the attributes of its founder.

H J Heinz, the brand's energetic founder, had a passion for good food and applied standards that were, at the time, unheard of. H J Heinz believed that one should 'always look for a little extra improvement in everything you do'.

H J Heinz's achievements,

and those of his successors, are such that today, Heinz is still a very strong brand with literally 96% of British households choosing Heinz products (Source: TNS Superpanel MAT October 2002).

He was born in 1844, in a small village outside Pittsburgh, then a powerhouse of the US economy, which boasted US industry titans such as Carnegie and Westinghouse. Entrepreneurial spirit ran in the water and this, coupled with an upbringing which was rooted in high moral principles, religion and a steely work ethic, proved a formidable combination.

At the age of eight, Henry started work in his parents' brickyard. By ten, he was tending a smallholding and growing his first vegetables and later selling those vegetables, delivering direct to local shopkeepers by horse and cart. Henry quickly worked out that the route to success was not cheap produce, but better produce.

His horseradish, for example, was made only from the cultivated roots of one year's growth. He scrubbed each and every one individually. So while his competitors sold their horseradish in dark coloured glass jars to hide the cheap fillers they contained, Heinz chose to package his in clear glass.

At the time this was seen as an extraordinary step, and an eloquent statement of confidence. Transparency in every sense was to be the cornerstone of Heinz as a company.

From his earliest days in business, he developed a keen understanding for the traditional homemaker feeding her family, and what she wanted. Similarly, he understood the needs of the farmers who grew his food, and the grocers who sold it.

Throughout his life, this driven man found energy and enthusiasm which others envied. On his 71st birthday, someone asked how he was feeling. In reply, the Founder got to his feet and jumped over a chair.

Product

Heinz iconic brands feature in our daily lives. Almost every household in the UK will have in its kitchen cupboards one of its famous products – possibly a can of Heinz Baked Beans or a bottle of Heinz Tomato Ketchup, not to mention Heinz or Farley's Babyfood for the new addition to the family. Additionally, a much expanded range from Heinz in the freezer these days.

Since acquiring UB Frozen & Chilled in 1999 H J Heinz Company Ltd has developed ranges

of ready meals and desserts under the Heinz brand as well as developing the more established Linda McCartney label. Recent launches include the Linda McCartney 'Kitchen Garden' meal varieties, including Cannelloni filled with Spinach & Mushroom, which won a Silver award for the Best New Pizza/Pasta Product from the British Frozen Food Federation in 2002.

The more established Weight Watchers from Heinz frozen products goes from strength to strength, establishing itself as a number one brand in the growing Healthy Meals sector (Source: IRI November 2002). The range is complimented by varieties across ready meals, pizzas and desserts.

Under the Heinz name, Deeply Delicious is a range of cheesecakes. The range comprises of Blackcurrant Swirl, Raspberry Swirl, Strawberry and for chocoholics Deeply Delicious Chocolate Cheesecake. A simple but effective packaging concept means that each cheesecake comes packed in a lightweight transparent plastic pot that can be easily pushed through the base.

Continuing the innovation in sauces since the launch of the popular children's Heinz Green Sauce, a new range of sauces specifically developed for young children includes four varieties from Choppin' Sweet 'n Sour' to Supersonic Pizza Flavour. The bottles have been designed for little hands to easily grasp and be creative with the sauces on their foods.

In December 2000, Heinz acquired the food division of the Dutch group CSM BV, operating in Northern Europe. The goal of the integration of Anco (Belgium) and Honig, HAK and KDR (Holland) was to create an entirely new Heinz organisation in the Netherlands and Belgium.

The huge operation integrated over eight companies, eleven sites and over 2,000 employees and was delivered over a period of five months from March to July 2001.

Heinz acquired the leading seafood brand John West from Unilever in 1997. This enabled John West to take advantage of Heinz's vast expertise and resources, including the latest developments in food technology as well as its marketing resources. John West has seen many product innovations, including fish in sauces, All Day Light Meals, Lunch Kits and value-added products. In total, the John West range comprises over 60 different products

Celebrating the Golden Jubilee in 2002, Heinz launched a celebration of the 'Best of British' recipe book with British celebrities offering their own recipes involving Heinz products.

Some of the UK's most popular famous faces, such as Chris Tarrant and Joanna Lumley, revealed what they enjoyed cooking in the kitchen. The book, also containing 50 easy and simple ideas on how to use products was offered at a special purchase price on promotional four-packs of Baked Beans. For every book sold, a donation of 50p was given to ICAN, a national educational charity for children with speech and language difficulties.

Heinz Salad Cream became relevant to a whole new generation of consumers following its relaunch in March 2000. A range of quirky 30-second TV commercials was created in spring 2001 to support Heinz Salad Cream, in which Heinz is depicted as the gold standard in salad creams in a humorous way – "There is only one salad cream worth tasting and that's Heinz Salad Cream Vintage 1914!".

A new microsite was also created to complement the brand's repositioning in addition to TV advertisements. This provided a mix of communication routes to cement the brand's message.

The Heinz baby food brand first went online in September 2001 with the launch of www.tinytums.co.uk, fulfilling an online need for

babyfoods, www.tinytums.co.uk contains an extensive collection of recipes for every stage of weaning for mothers to make at home. In bigtums, there is a healthy, yet realistic, eating plan for pregnancy where mum-to-be can find out what to feed her bump, what to avoid, and how to accommodate these changes effortlessly into her daily routine.

With an ever-increasing number of parents using the internet as an information resource, www.tinytums.co.uk provides an interactive, interesting and efficient communication tool for the Heinz Baby Food brand.

whose ingredients are sourced from around the world. For its famous 'Bear' TV ad the brand won a raft of awards including the 'ITV Best Television Commercial of the Year' award in 2001 and a Cannes Lions Gold award in the same year. John West has followed this success with an equally impressive and humorous 'Shark' TV ad.

Recent Developments

H J Heinz Ltd established its Wigan manufacturing base in 1959 and it has played a vital role in the local economy ever since. Today Europe's largest food manufacturing plant can be found at Kitt Green, Wigan where 1500 people are employed working on seventeen manufacturing lines, producing 377 products.

The continued success and growth of the company combined with changes in the grocery retailing industry recently created the need for a national distribution centre.

A site at Martland Park, Wigan was chosen. The decision to locate it in Wigan was seen as a sign of the company's continuing investment and commitment to the area. The proximity of Martland Park to the national motorway network and the valuable support from the local authority and other decision makers were significant factors as was the availability of a local skilled workforce.

The national distribution centre occupies 38 acres of land and utilises the latest materials handling technology to cope with 83 million cases of food each year. The centre operates 24/7, employing a further 160 people.

Promotion

Heinz has a long history in adverting, from its first black & white TV ad for beans in the 1950s, to the classic 'Beanz meanz Heinz' ad campaign which ran for the best part of two decades from the 1970s. Heinz Soup advertising remains one of the most memorable, from Granddad entertaining his grandson with stories of 'When I was a lad' to 'Your dinner's in the dog' campaign for Farmhouse soup in the 1980s and the risqué Microwaveable soup campaign of 2002.

a definitive baby feeding guide, with tips, product information and nutritional expertise for babies up to eighteen months old. The addition of a month-by-month guide to pregnancy also reflected Heinz's awareness of the need to engage with mums-to-be and develop an on-going, interactive relationship with them throughout their pregnancy and after the birth of their baby.

In 2003, two new microsites – the 'tinytums club' for mums and the 'bigtums club' for mums-to-be – will be launched. The sites reflect the Heinz babyfood brand positioning of 'Real Food for Real Lives' with engaging images of happy, smiling (and mucky) babies enjoying mealtime.

In order to create an interactive online community, both microsites provide mothers with the chance to contribute to product reviews, top tips and discussion topics. They also contain informative guides on topics such as childcare options and maternity rights, and also feature a medical diary that follows one mum through pregnancy and her baby's first eighteen months.

Acknowledging that most mums 'dual feed', i.e. use both home-made and pre-prepared

Brand Values

Heinz is a trusted and familiar brand conveying quality and reassurance whilst providing tasty and nutritious meal solutions that meet with ever-changing consumer needs and demands.

It is a brand that has a role to play in feeding babies to teens to adults – the majority of which have grown up with the products as well as the brand's advertising surrounding them.

Heinz continues to build on the strengths of its brands through innovation and quality, focusing on the needs of the consumer and continually developing and refreshing the extensive ranges on offer.

Further to being an iconic brand in the UK, Heinz is a global player and maintains the same ethos of consumer and brand focus across the world markets.

www.heinz.co.uk

Market

The international car rental market is a tale of two halves. On one side there are many small companies serving local markets, and then there are global brands, of which Hertz is the biggest, which serve both the local and international markets.

Active in over 150 countries and with approximately 7000 rental locations, Hertz is a recognised leader in the vehicle rental market for providing a high level of service, and offering competitive rates on a wide range of vehicles.

Worth over £3 billion per year in Europe alone, the vehicle rental sector is highly competitive. Leading players compete on the reach of their networks and the variety of vehicles they offer, however Hertz also focuses on offering customers the best service possible.

the Hertz Idea

has become the Hertz Habit

Here and now...Hertz has the new 1959 Chevrolet!

Many of the innovations in this market are in the area of service, ensuring customers can quickly rent the right car with the options they want, at a convenient location, wherever they are in the world.

Achievements

Hertz has built one of the most extensive vehicle rental networks in the world, in the process creating a brand that has become synonymous with its product. Its instantly recognisable yellow and black logo is never more than a few paces away in most of the worlds' major airports and European cities, furthermore Hertz offers good quality both in terms of its fleet, and the level of service which it offers. Indeed, as Interbrand says, "Hertz makes the point that branding applies as much to service as it does to products." According to Interbrand's annual league, Hertz is number 71 in the top 100, with a brand value of US$3.6 billion. That makes the Hertz brand bigger than giants such as BP, Shell and Fedex, and the only travel company to feature in the list.

History

Hertz has had a variety of owners and ownership structures during its long history, but has never changed from its core values or goals.

The Hertz business began in 1918 when Walter L Jacobs opened a car rental operation in Chicago, USA. Within five years Jacobs, who maintained his own fleet of twelve model T Fords, grew his business to annual revenues of around US$1 million.

In 1923 the business was bought by John Hertz, president of the Yellow Cab and Yellow Truck and Coach Manufacturing Company who retained Jacobs as his top executive.

Three years later Hertz 'Drive-Ur-Self' system, as it was called, was acquired by

Hertz Rent a Cat

Hertz Prestige Collection

General Motors Corporation when they bought Yellow Truck in 1926.

Hertz stayed with GMC for 27 years until it passed to the Omnibus Corporation in 1953 who then sold the bus interests and focused on car and truck renting and leasing. In 1954, as The Hertz Corporation, it became a publicly traded company listed on the New York Stock Exchange.

In 1967 Hertz was bought out by RCA until 1985 when it was bought by United Airlines.

Since 1987 the Ford Motor Company has had a major financial interest in Hertz, and in 2001 bought the public share of Hertz and the corporation became a wholly owned subsidiary of Ford.

Hertz began its European operations in France during the 1950s, with 50 cars in one location in Paris. This was the first European location opened by a US car rental firm.

Product

Hertz now operates throughout central and eastern Europe, Middle East and Africa, with over 7000 locations globally. In addition to its comprehensive international franchise network, The Hertz Corporation is also represented through corporately run operations in Australia, Brazil, Canada and New Zealand.

Hertz is well known throughout the world as a brand that offers competitive rates on a wide variety of cars. Whether a renter wants a single day, a weekend away or longer, Hertz prides itself on being able to meet their requirements with a vehicle to suit. Its extensive fleet ranges from 'runaround' vehicles to luxury touring cars, or sporty convertibles.

As well as the basic car rental service, Hertz adds value for its customers by offering the very highest level of customer service and efficiency. Schemes such as the Hertz #1 Club, a time-saving, paperless service for frequent travellers, products like the on-board navigation system 'Neverlost', a user friendly GPS-based route-guidance system which provides turn-by-turn driving directions to virtually any destination, and the convenience of online booking, all play a significant part in giving customers the very best car rental experience.

Hertz #1 Club Gold is a premium, time-saving enrolment service which has been designed to give customers both the level of service they expect and the convenience they demand. Removing the need to complete and sign a new rental agreement every time they rent a vehicle speeds up the entire car rental process for frequent travellers.

The customer simply completes a one-off master rental agreement which applies worldwide, providing all the information needed for the rental. When a booking is made, the only information required is the #1 Club Gold membership number along with when and where a car is desired.

Customers who have access to the internet can make booking easier and more convenient by logging onto www.hertz.com. The website contains all the relevant information on helping the renter make their booking, including photographs of the cars on fleet to aid accurate selection.

Hertz was the first car rental firm to launch a website in five different languages including English, French, German Italian and Spanish. Non-English speakers are able to access any Hertz website and then switch to their preferred language.

Many of Europe's reservations and customer relations are handled at the Hertz Reservation Centre in Dublin. Opened in 1996, the centre serves nine European markets and employs over 1000 staff. It has one of the fastest service levels in the industry, aiming to answer 90% of calls within twenty seconds.

Recent Developments

Hertz recently launched the 'Hertz Prestige Collection' in Europe, offering a new level of premium car rental service which combines a range of high quality vehicles with Hertz' exclusive customer services.

The European launch of the Hertz Prestige Collection follows a successful launch in North America in 2001, which was further expanded in 2002 and is now available in 31 North American Hertz locations.

The new European collection has been introduced

with the discerning renter in mind, who wants the very highest level of service and a car to match.

Available at key locations in the UK, France and Germany from June 2002 the range features vehicles including the Mercedes CLK Convertible, Mercedes E and S Class, BMW 5 and 7 Series, the Jaguar S Type, and the Volvo S80 and V70, all of which can be reserved by model. The service is already operating in the US and has proved extremely popular.

Another important development was Hertz's recent expansion into China. Hertz is the first global car rental company to operate in China, opening several locations in Beijing, Shanghai and Guangzhou. Hertz signed an agreement with China National Automobile Anhua (Tianjin) International Trade Company (CNAA) which is Hertz' licensee in China and will operate under the trade name Hertz China.

Constantly improving its product, Hertz recently redesigned its European websites to expedite the reservation process and provide browsers and customers with more content to enhance the overall car rental experience.

The new sites include an all-new 'While You're There' section which provides

Like to know where you are...

...Love Hertz

Hertz Neverlost our remarkable satellite navigation system for North America.

Hertz rents Fords and other fine cars.

08708 48 48 48
www.hertz.co.uk

Hertz Neverlost is our advanced in-car GPS satellite navigation system which can be requested when you book your Hertz car for a nominal additional daily charge and offers clear maps and voice prompts to thousands of hotels, airports, attractions and even individual addresses in North America.

So now you can drive with confidence, no matter where you are going. No more fumbling with maps, hunting for street signs or having to ask for directions.

more travel destination information, in the form of road maps, point to point driving directions, recommended safety tips and weather information.

They also provide easy access to more pre-reservation information, under the heading 'Before You Rent'.

Another development by Hertz in 2002 was to introduce services for disabled customers, to offer vehicles fitted with hand-controls from many of its corporately owned key locations in Europe, at no additional charge.

These vehicles are suitable for customers that have a lower limb disability, but, full use of the upper body. The service is available from major gateways in France, Belgium, Luxembourg, Germany, Italy, Netherlands and Spain, with no minimum keep, and from more remote locations, on rentals booked for five days or more.

Promotion

As befits the world's number one car rental company, Hertz invests significant marketing budgets above and below-the-line in support of the multiple channels for car rental services. These comprise communications to consumers, travel trade and tour operators, partners, associations, wholesalers and corporate accounts.

Hertz works with a variety of partners and associations, including major hotel groups and almost all of the major airlines, which it recognises are a key part of the marketing and distribution mix.

Hertz has also helped pioneer the phenomenal growth in online travel bookings and has for many years offered multi-lingual Hertz websites with online booking capability in all major markets. These are important promotional tools in their own right.

Hertz maintains a global brand guardian to ensure that every piece of Hertz communication reflects the core values of the world's number one car rental company.

Brand Values

The Hertz brand values remain consistent. From the early days when John Hertz himself said, "We are going to create this business on the proper foundation – on a foundation where everybody connected with us is going to believe in us."

For almost 80 years the Hertz brand has meant trust, reliability, confidence and the very highest standards of customer service. Quality is the cornerstone of every aspect of Hertz operations.

www.hertz.co.uk

Introducing the Hertz Prestige Collection

Luxury cars, personal service.

A range of luxury vehicles, including the Mercedes SL500, which are reservable by specific model and come with personal service as streamlined as the vehicles themselves.

Recently launched at selected locations in the United Kingdom, France and Germany, the Hertz Prestige Collection offers vehicles designed and engineered for the pure pleasure of driving.

To reserve your Prestige Collection vehicle please call your local Hertz Reservation Office.

We look forward to welcoming you soon.

United Kingdom:	0870 600 1614	Heathrow - Gatwick - Marble Arch
France:	0825 00 11 55	Charles de Gaulle - Nice Airport
Germany:	01803 000 794	Frankfurt - Munich - Düsseldorf

Hertz rents Fords and other fine cars.

Hertz
Prestige Collection

Market

The UK market for pre-recorded music at the end of 2001 was worth an estimated £2 billion (Source: BPI). Of that, around a tenth was accounted for by sales of singles, with albums responsible for 90% of all purchases. Compact disc was by far the dominant format, accounting for 97% of all sales, with cassette and vinyl accounting for just 3% between them.

After a particularly buoyant period in the mid 1990s, when sales were boosted by Brit Pop and Girl Power, annual rates of increase levelled off in the late 1990s. However, stimulated by new artists and strong product releases, sales are again showing signs of growth.

Music retail is becoming increasingly competitive, with specialist chains such as HMV offering value through new products, range, knowledge and service. In HMV's other major markets, UK video sales – boosted massively by the arrival of DVD – are now worth in excess of £1 billon. The computer games market, in which the company also specialises, has also passed through the £1 billion barrier on the back of the launch of Sony's PlayStation 2, Nintendo's GameCube and Microsoft's Xbox gaming platforms.

Achievements

HMV is the UK's leading specialist retailer of music, video and computer games with a 25% share of UK music sales (Source: Chart Track – based on unit sales), and around 20% and 10% of the video and computer games markets respectively. With 150 stores nationwide, the chain operates in all major centres around the country with flagship stores in London's Oxford Street and regional superstores in Glasgow, Edinburgh, Newcastle, Leeds, Liverpool, Manchester, Birmingham, Reading and Southampton.

In 1996 HMV celebrated its 75th anniversary, and another landmark was achieved a year later with the opening, by Robbie Williams, of its 100th store at Birmingham's Fort Shopping Park. Since

then the company has continued to grow rapidly, both in the UK – where it recently reached its landmark of 150 stores, with a new outlet in Truro – and internationally where it operates some 300 stores across nine countries in Europe, North America and Asia Pacific.

Since its very first store was opened in 1921, HMV has always sought to offer the widest possible access to music, and to play a pioneering role in the way it is sold and promoted.

History

On July 20th 1921 Sir Edward Elgar, the celebrated British composer, opened a new record store in London's Oxford Street. It was to prove a transforming moment in popular culture, as HMV's new store was the first to tap the burgeoning demand for recorded music and effectively established a template for record retailing as we know it today.

The store's many innovations, including listening booths and self-service record counters, combined with its range of titles, dedicated customer service and striking interiors were all key factors in laying the foundation of HMV's rich heritage.

Such brand values were to become symbolised in one of the world's most enduring and compelling images: the picture of a Jack Russell Fox Terrier, head slightly cocked, ears pricked up, listening to an old gramophone with a brass horn. Instantly recognisable as the trademark of 'His Master's Voice', the dog's name was Nipper and the artist who painted the famous image in 1898 was Francis Barraud. The painting initially featured a phonograph, but a year later this was replaced by a gramophone after The Gramophone Company, later to become EMI, paid the sum of £100 to acquire the painting and copyright. Today the Nipper trademark still adorns the modern face of HMV stores.

From the company's earliest days, EMI had franchised HMV products exclusively to just one store in major towns around the UK but this system was abandoned in the mid 1950s when HMV goods were made available to all dealers. HMV Oxford Street was now free to stock the products of EMI's rivals – thus paving the way for real high street competition.

The move came just in time for the rock 'n' roll explosion of the 1960s. Indeed, one meeting, in February 1962, played a decisive role in shaping the very direction of popular music. At that time the store had a small recording studio, and a Liverpool entrepreneur, Brian Epstein, paid a visit to cut demo discs in his bid to secure a record deal for a band he was managing called The Beatles. The store loved what they heard and, through publishers Ardmore & Beechwood, who were based in the building, put him in touch with Parlophone's George Martin. Just four months later the band were recording at Abbey Road studios.

In the years that followed, HMV took advantage of a buoyant market to expand from its Oxford Street base. Initially taking sites around London, by the 1970s HMV had opened stores in Manchester, Glasgow, Birmingham, Leeds and Bristol. Towards the end of the decade the number had risen to 30, and HMV could stake its claim as the UK's first chain of specialist record stores. With the 1980s came Live Aid, a new wave of recording artists and, most crucially, the compact disc – all of which helped maintain HMV's momentum. In October 1986 it opened the world's largest record store, again located in Oxford Street, and a year later the midlands-based Revolver Records was acquired to boost the overall store number to 50.

Expansion continued throughout the 1990s, significantly raising HMV brand awareness and also underlining HMV's position as the UK's dominant specialist retailer of music, video and games. During this time HMV opened its 100th store, launched a transactional website and celebrated its 75th anniversary. In March 1998 HMV was acquired along with the Waterstone's book chain to form a new company – the HMV Media Group. In 2002 the company was listed on the London Stock Exchange under the new trading name of HMV Group plc.

Product

Through its range, knowledge and customer service, HMV aims to provide the widest possible access to music, DVD/video and games. Although consumers can increasingly access music through other channels, such as the internet, and indeed HMV's own hmv.co.uk website, the retailer remains firmly convinced that the vast majority of consumers will continue to make their purchases through high street stores for the foreseeable future.

HMV stores carry the widest selection of music titles across all genres, and unique among music retailers, they also stock three own label series: HMV Classics, HMV Jazz and HMV Easy. The chain is also a committed specialist retailer of video and DVD and computer games software, while all stores carry an extensive selection of related products, including t-shirts, music, books and accessories.

In addition to weekly chart releases, HMV seeks to give added-value to its customers through monthly sales campaigns, which often follow the 'multi-buy' format that the company developed in the 1990's i.e. 'Buy 2 CDs for £22 or 'Buy 3 Videos for £15'.

Recent Developments

To mark the new millennium HMV looked to its original brand values. In April 2000 the famous HMV store at 363 Oxford Street was closed to make way for a much larger replacement at 360 Oxford Street, which was officially opened by Ronan Keating in May 2000. The store reflects both the heritage of its predecessor while also embracing new technology to offer a glimpse of the future.

HMV's website, www.hmv.co.uk, which was launched in 1997, is now one of the UK's most successful online music stores, breaking even and generating a profit in 2001. A year later, in 2002 it teamed up with digital content provider, OD2, to make available more than 100,000 titles for download.

In 1998 HMV relaunched the HMV Classics own label series, adding HMV Jazz and HMV Easy just one year later to offer a wide range of budget priced titles. During this time HMV also launched its own free, consumer publication, HMV Choice to further support its specialist music credentials. HMV is passionately committed to supporting New Music and accordingly in 2002 launched its 'Playlist' sampler CD. This showcases new artists and is given away with purchases of HMV NEW MUSIC titles.

Promotion

HMV at 363 Oxford Street virtually invented the idea of record store promotion. As early as the 1920s and 1930s it staged personal appearances by leading artists of the day, and this still remains a fundamental part of today's public relations strategy. Around 200 are staged each year, both to launch new stores and promote new releases. Over the past ten years those making special appearances at HMV have included Sir Paul McCartney, The Spice Girls, Blur, Robbie Williams, Prince and Tony Bennett. More recently HMV has played host to Dido, Westlife, Blue, Craig David and David Bowie. Stores also regularly stage midnight openings and other events to launch cult releases such as Star Wars or new products like PlayStation. Capitalising on the appeal of its brand, HMV has held nationwide searches, often in conjunction with a media partner, to find real-life Nipper look-a-likes to attend events and perform other promotional duties. In recent years major coverage has been secured on the 'That's Life' and 'This Morning' television programmes. Taken as a whole, HMV's promotional activity not only seeks to create media opportunities, but also to support HMV brand values of range and authority in order to raise corporate profile and differentiate it from its rivals.

Marketing activity is fundamental in reaching the core market HMV operates in, and this is usually achieved in partnership with suppliers. This generally involves co-operatively funded advertisements across a range of media – most commonly press and posters, but also television and radio during key trading periods. These are often tied to in-store merchandising and window campaigns, while customer listening posts, radio broadcasts and video screens provide further means of in-store support.

Promotions play a key role in attracting customers, and key target groups, such as students, to stores and in raising their spend levels. HMV, therefore run numerous third party promotions each year in partnership with other leading brands with the basic aim of raising brand profile and generating increased sales.

Brand Values

Famously symbolised by its 'dog & trumpet' trademark, HMV's core brand values are based firmly on key customer service requirements of outstanding product range and staff knowledge. Such values help underline HMV's authority as a specialist retailer, and also support its trading ethos of giving customers the widest possible access to music, video or games.

HMV's authority and position as the UK's leading specialist retailer is further reinforced by the company's current advertising strapline 'Top

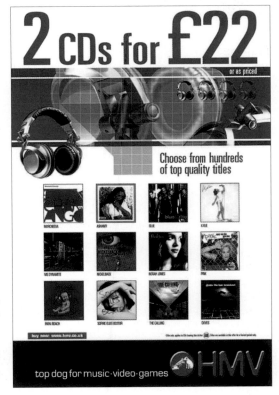

Dog for music, video and games'. This play on a popular expression is simple but direct, and is used by HMV in all its advertising and promotion.

www.hmv.co.uk

Market

This isn't news to parents but to those who have not had the pleasure of a baby it is difficult to imagine just how many nappies one little person can go through. On average a baby will be changed five times a day. Multiply this by the number of babies in the UK and this adds up to a lot of nappies.

A total of 2.9 billion nappies are bought in the UK each year in a market worth approximately £465 million. This highly competitive marketplace is dominated by two major players – Kimberly-Clark's Huggies and Pampers from Proctor & Gamble.

Category originators Pampers are the market leaders with 53.6% market share however in a relatively short space of time and in a market which enjoys strong consumer loyalty, Huggies has achieved a significant hold with 30.4% market share and a strong growth of 35% over the past two and a half years.

Achievements

Huggies are designed and produced using the very latest nappy technology. The research and development team at Huggies have spent years studying the technical aspects of nappies and their impact on dryness, comfort and skin health. This has resulted in the current Huggies range being the best performing Huggies to date.

The brand's nappies have been awarded a number of prestigious awards including Mother & Baby Magazine's Gold Award for best disposable nappy for an unprecedented third consecutive year. The 'Adventurers' nappy picked up the flagship award for 'Best Disposable Nappy' 2001/02 and the 'Beginnings' nappy was voted 'Best Buy for Newborns' from Practical Parenting.

In addition, Huggies Club, one of the UK's largest parenting clubs has won a number of prestigious awards including Marketing Week's silver award for relationship marketing.

Huggies Adventurers Gold Award Winner

Huggies is a highly successful global brand occupying the number one or two positions in every market in which it operates. In 2000 Huggies was recorded as the UK's 4th fastest growing grocery brand (Source: ACNielsen 2001) and was rated 33rd in ACNielsen's survey of the top 50 brands in the UK.

History

Huggies launched in the UK in 1993 and quickly began to take market share from Pampers. It has maintained a competitive edge with innovative developments such as the addition of adhesive stretch ears in 1995 and the introduction of a breathable outer cover in 1998 – a market first.

Further product innovations over the next three years including improved fastening, increased absorbency and a more breathable outer cover have helped to build the Huggies brand.

With breathable technology, Huggies was the first nappy clinically proven to protect against nappy rash furthermore, its research into keeping babies skin naturally healthy is supported by the British Skin Foundation.

A big development on the Huggies brand occurred in 2001 when the 'Challenger Brand' strategy was adopted in order to revitalise the brand. This led to the positioning 'Huggies gives your child the freedom to develop and thrive' and a brand architecture that segmented the range into three sub-brands, namely Beginnings, Freedom and Adventurers each with different product specifications to reflect the needs of babies at different stages of their development.

The trade response to this category innovation was considerable. The relaunch was hailed as the single biggest event in the nappy category since Huggies were first launched in the UK. Its success was also reflected in the strong launch support it received from leading grocery retailers.

By July 2001, six months post-launch, Huggies volume share had grown from 28.8% to 32.7% with July setting a new record volume for Huggies in the UK. Value share also increased from 28.8% to 33.6%. Pampers' volume and value shares declined in the same period from 51.5% to 48.9% and 53.5% to 49.9% respectively (Source: IRI Market Research).

The recent relaunch of Adventurers – which has been proven to be the most flexible nappy ever developed – was supported with a significant above and below-the-line campaign. It is the latest in a succession of real product innovations which have maintained Huggies strong competitive edge.

Further product launches and upgrades to the existing range are currently in development.

Product

At the centre of the Huggies brand is its understanding of the varying needs of babies at different stages of their development.

Huggies Beginnings is for new babies and is all about providing maximum comfort. They are made from soft materials and have a dermatologically tested liner, proven to protect delicate skin. Beginnings' absorbent system draws wetness away from the skin and keeps it locked away, helping to maintain smooth and dry skin.

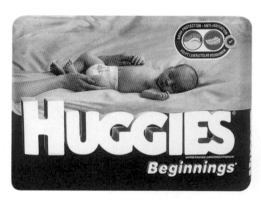

Specially designed for growing babies, Huggies Freedom nappies lock away wetness and enable babies to stay dry and comfortable. They are also clinically proven to help protect against nappy rash and help keep delicate skin healthy.

Huggies Adventurers, feature Winnie the Pooh and Tigger characters and are designed with active toddlers in mind. Every component of the nappy has been re-worked to deliver improved fit and comfort, resulting in a product that is like no other in the market. The nappy also features an innovative flexible-fit waistband, a stretchable outer cover and a slimline cut.

New Huggies Cotton-Touch wipes are stretchy, thick, soft and strong, alcohol-free and pH-balanced. Unlike other brands of baby wipes, they have a quilted texture which cleans well and leaves skin fresh and smooth. The product is available mildly fragranced or fragrance-free, which is regarded as the best choice for newborns. Another distinctive feature of Huggies Cotton-Touch wipes is its resealable, 'quickzip' packaging. This provides the moisture retention of a tub which prevents the wipes from drying out, whilst making them easy to carry around and reseal. Furthermore, its pop-up hygienic dispensing system has an inner section which is spacious enough to hold a nappy, keeping all essential changing items conveniently together.

Recent Developments

In 1998 Huggies launched its parent and baby club – Huggies Club – which has quickly grown to become one of the UK's most successful parenting clubs with 40% of all women giving birth registering as members.

Following extensive consumer insight studies, Huggies recognised the value of creating an ongoing dialogue and sense of support between Huggies and the millions of mums who use Huggies products. As a result, the brand relaunched its already successful Huggies Club in 2002. A new 'visual and verbal language' was developed to reflect the brand's 'Freedom to thrive' positioning. It aims to speak from adult-to-adult, treating mothers as women, parents and people.

Huggies Club is positioned as being positive, cheerful, colourful and fun and realises both the pleasures and problems of parenthood and responds appropriately – offering, amongst other things, sympathy and humour to mums.

Membership of Huggies Club is free and benefits include informative guides on pregnancy and parenting, product samples and coupons from Huggies and the Club's marketing partners Persil, KLEENEX®, Andrex®, Tomy, Tommee Tippee and Sudocrem. The club also produces a changing bag packed with luxurious mother and baby products, available with proof of purchase of Huggies Beginnings.

The Huggies Club can also be accessed online at www.huggiesclub.com and has sections relevant to babies of different ages and information for women at various stages of pregnancy. The site contains additional features such as lists of child-friendly places to visit by postcode area and chat rooms where mums can share experiences and childcare tips.

Another major strength of Huggies Club is Rewards – Huggies loyalty scheme – which gives mums the opportunity to redeem tokens from packs of Huggies nappies and wipes against hundreds of gifts in the Huggies Club Rewards guide. Over 2500 Huggies Club Rewards gifts were redeemed in the first three months of its introduction. This ground-breaking initiative is a first for the industry and was welcomed by the Parenting Press as having real 'mum appeal'. Furthermore, it has been short listed for 2002/03 Mother & Baby Awards for Most Innovative New Product.

Promotion

Huggies is promoted as being modern, innovative and focused on babies' needs. Huggies marketing campaigns focus on delivering a synergistic message and building upon its positioning and personality. The brand identity, packaging design

and exploitation of the visual equities have been at the core of this.

Huggies packaging has recently been redesigned to communicate the notion that Huggies allows one's child the freedom to develop and thrive. The packs are produced in vibrant colours and have a distinct look and feel which aims to capture the image of a child engrossed in their own world.

This is reflected throughout the Huggies range, so that mums will make the connection between their own baby and the babies featured on-pack through the photography that captures a real baby doing real things. Whilst a mother's presence is not overt in the design it aims to clearly reflect that she is there.

The new identity and packaging design has been incorporated into all other elements of the marketing mix. It has inspired the look, feel and tone-of-voice of all Huggies communication including the highly successful press/poster 'Icons' campaign and the advertising campaign which features children playing in the 'hyper-reality' Huggies World.

'Great Performance' – Huggies advertisement to launch super flexible Adventurers – is based on the idea of road testing a nappy. It took its inspiration from car advertising and this analogy is carried through to the music, reminiscent of a Formula One build up, the powerful voice over read by David Suchet, and the endline 'The Ultimate Toddling Experience'.

Huggies altered consumers' value perceptions within the nappy category with the launch of 'Extra Free' promotional packs in 1999. This created new excitement in the category and the mechanic was quickly adopted by its main competitor.

Huggies packaging also played a major role in raising consumer awareness of Huggies Club Rewards. UK specific gift-wrapped packaging, Many Happy Rewards was developed across Beginnings and Freedom nappies. Economy packs contained the Huggies Club Rewards Guide and a free pack of Huggies wipes – fragrance-free on their newborn range and fragranced on the Freedom range.

In addition, special bonus packs of Beginnings and Freedom (convenience and economy) contained double Huggies points redeemable against hundreds of items in the Rewards guide.

Every parent knows that, to a child, often the best part of any present is perceived to be the box. Based on this insight, Huggies created a

'fun box' – the first interactive nappy packaging. Designed to achieve impact on shelf, the box can be used for storage or wherever the child's imagination takes him.

Brand Values

Huggies brand values have been based on consumer insights. It was found that mums are intuitively aware of how babies discover, explore, experiment and learn to deal with the world. The majority of mums also believe that babies should be 'free' to pursue life's adventure.

Huggies look to share parents' sense of amazement at how their child develops and encourages this. It understands that babies can be messy, noisy, bewildering and a little disruptive at times as well as being truly amazing. In recognising this, Huggies products aim to facilitate babies' individuality at each stage of its development. They hope to allow babies to 'forget' that they are wearing nappies – helping give them the freedom to explore.

www.huggiesclub.com

Do it in Huggies. The new Huggies® nappy range is tailored for each stage of your baby's development. This means that new Huggies are so soft, dry and comfortable that your baby probably won't even notice them, and can concentrate on the new and exciting things in life.

www.huggiesclub.com

Market

Despite the fact that its main product is smaller than a human thumbnail, Intel has been one of the main drivers of a revolution that has fundamentally changed our society. The company is the world's largest manufacturer of computer chips, and paradoxically also one of its best-known consumer brands. Today, chips can be found in cars, toys, mobile phones and even alarm clocks. In fact we now have access on a daily basis to computer technology more powerful than NASA had when it first sent man to the moon.

Due to an increase in consumers knowledge of technology teamed with a successful marketing strategy, many purchasers of computer equipment now demand to know whether the computer that they are considering purchasing has 'Intel Inside®'. Analysts' estimates of Intel's market share range from 79% to as much as 90%.

But Intel is not just a component maker – it is providing the means to create ever more powerful communications tools, whether these are desktop PCs or wireless devices. Its stated goal is to be the pre-eminent supplier to the internet economy.

Achievements

When Intel was founded in 1968, it had twelve employees, operated out of a leased building in a quiet corner of California, and earned revenues in its first year of US$2,672. In 2001, it announced net revenues of US$26.5 billion. Third quarter net income in 2002 was US$686 million, up 54% sequentially and 547% year on year.

Intel's market dominance can be ascribed to a series of scientific breakthroughs and well-timed alliances. It came up with the first microprocessor, the 4004, in 1971, after being approached by a Japanese calculator manufacturer. Ten years later, IBM chose the company's 8088 processor for use in the first ever PC.

By 1993 Intel had introduced its first Pentium processor. Since then, the company has continued to render its own products obsolete almost every year – a strategy unheard of in any other business. As founder Gordon Moore comments; 'If the auto industry advanced as rapidly as the semiconductor industry, a Rolls-Royce would get half a million miles per gallon, and it would be cheaper to throw it away than to park it.'

History

In 1968, computer boffins Robert Noyce and Gordon Moore created Intel. At the time, Moore stated; 'We are the true revolutionaries.' But it was to be another 30 years before his words rang true. In the meantime, Moore and Noyce had set out to create a more efficient computer memory, based on semiconductor technology. They came up with the 1103 in 1970, and it became the world's biggest-selling semiconductor device.

However, their most significant breakthrough came when a Japanese company called Busicom asked them to design twelve chips for a range of calculators. At the time, each electronic product required its own individually tailored chip. But Intel engineer Ted Hoff felt that it might be possible to create a single chip capable of carrying out a wide range of different functions – an advanced computer 'brain'.

The invention worked, and Intel realised that it had created a product with almost limitless applications. There was a problem, however – under the terms of the original contract, Busicom held the rights to the product. This Japanese company was also in some financial difficulties at this point, so Moore and Noyce negotiated the purchase of the rights to the chip for just US$60,000.

Originally known as a 'microcomputer', Intel's first microprocessor – the 4004 – went on the market in 1971. By the time the company introduced the 8008, a few years later, its early predictions had begun to materialise: the chip revolutionised supermarket cash registers, traffic lights, petrol pumps, airline reservation systems and arcade games to name but a few applications. As fast as its chips were installed, Intel created smaller and more powerful versions.

In the early 1980s, IBM began tentative talks with Intel over the possibility of using its 8088 processor for an undisclosed new product. Since IBM had never before used an outside supplier, the details were shrouded in secrecy. Only when the deal was finally struck did Intel realise it was providing the brain of the first PC – although at the time, neither of the two companies realised how big the home computing market would become.

Intel continued to develop ever more efficient microprocessors, including the Pentium® processor in 1993, which became its most famous brand name. Intel is now the best known manufacturer of microprocessors and dominates the market. Its Pentium 4 processor is more powerful than Robert Noyce and Gordon Moore could ever have imagined. The company recently announced plans to introduce an even more powerful 3.06 GHz Pentium 4 processor, which will bring Hyper-Threading Technology to the desktop for the first time. Invented by Intel, HT Technology allows software to run as if a system has two processors, improving performance by as much as 30%.

Product

Intel produces the chips, boards, systems, software and communication equipment that make up the architecture of the high-tech world. But through its 'Intel Inside®' campaign, it is primarily known for producing microprocessors.

Microprocessors are the tiny brains that control the central processing of data in personal computers, servers, workstations and a myriad of other electronic devices. Intel designs processors for a number of different markets and applications, from the high-end Pentium 4 processor to the Intel® Celeron™ processor for 'value' PC and mobile systems. It also produces a chip called StrongARM, for portable applications.

Intel spent US$3.8 billion on research and development in 2001 and is moving into an increasing number of new business areas, including web hosting and data centre services, design and manufacturing services for optical component makers, and custom chip design. The company is heavily committed to the internet, and now handles practically all its business online. Currently, 85% of customer orders are processed electronically.

Recent Developments

Although Intel has been affected by the recent downturn in the dotcom economy, as have other technology brands, revenues remain strong and it continues to introduce new products. It recently began customer sampling of a new mobile product that will connect easily with wireless networks, in offices, homes and public 'hot spots' such as airports, hotels and restaurants.

The company has also launched various products that are designed to bring the richness of desktop PC applications to handheld devices. Its Xscale wireless technology has been adopted in more than 25 handheld devices, including palmtops from Acer, Fujitsu Siemens, HP, Hitachi, Sharp and Toshiba.

In 2002 Intel introduced a new family of microprocessors specifically designed to bring high performance and long battery life to wireless communications devices. This allows makers of wireless communications devices to take the next step in high-performance and low-power wireless handheld computing technology.

The new processors are based on the Intel® XScale™ technology and has the capability to power multimedia mobile phones, handheld computers, in-vehicle (telematics) systems and other wireless internet products.

To increase multimedia efficiency and performance, Intel also created Intel® Media Processing Technology. It is designed to work specifically with the device's audio, video and gaming applications to increase the number of frames per second in videos, improve sound quality and give advanced graphical effects.

Promotion

Not so long ago, if you mentioned the word 'microprocessor' to a consumer, you would most likely get a blank look. But these days, many personal computer users care about the specification and speed of the processor in their machines, just as car owners care about engine power. The awareness of the Intel brand has grown alongside awareness of chips themselves, and the brand has become associated with technological leadership, quality and reliability.

This situation has come about thanks to the Intel Inside® programme. Launched in 1991, it was the first attempt by a component manufacturer to directly target consumers, rather than the computer industry. Today Intel is one of

the best-known brands in the world, in a class with Coke and McDonald's, according to analysts such as Interbrand.

There was a considerable amount of media scepticism about the campaign when it began, as it was doubted that a pure technology company could ever achieve the same level of awareness as a typical consumer brand. The main challenge was the fact that Intel was not a standalone product – it was a component, buried deep inside another device. As part of its research, the company studied successful consumer marketing techniques used by other companies supplying an ingredient of a finished product, such as NutraSweet, Teflon and Dolby. Its advertising agency Dahlin, Smith and White came up with part of the solution – the slogan 'Intel. The computer inside.' This was later contracted into the famous 'Intel Inside®'.

At the same time, Intel began approaching computer manufacturers with the idea of a co-operative marketing programme whereby Intel would share the cost of any ads that showed its logo. In the first year, 300 companies took it up on the offer. Meanwhile, in 1995, Intel embarked on TV ads promoting its product. These included

an animated logo and the now familiar five-note melody.

Together with the high-profile launches of the Pentium and PentiumPro processors, the campaign achieved strong results. According to research carried out by Intel in 1991, only 24% of European PC buyers were familiar with its logo. One year later that figure had risen to 80%, and by 1995 it had reached 94%. The success was sealed in 1997 when Intel launched its 'bunny people' TV campaign in the middle of the US SuperBowl broadcast. The ads featured dancers dressed in multicoloured versions of the protective 'bunny suits' technicians wear during the manufacturing process.

Now more than 2,500 computer manufacturers are licensed to use the Intel logo. It is expanding its advertising onto the web and continuing to run its own TV campaigns alongside co-branded spots. But this success has a price – Intel says that since 1991, it has spent over US$7 billion convincing consumers that the best technology has 'Intel Inside'.

Brand Values

Intel's external brand values are evident from its advertising, which emphasises groundbreaking technology, quality and reliability. Intel also aims to be open, egalitarian and disciplined. When Robert Noyce and Gordon Moore were building Intel, they were keen to banish hierarchies within the organisation and did not want to look at the company structure and see a complex set of hurdles. They preferred a company with no social hierarchy, no executive suites, no pinstriped suits and no reserved parking spaces. Among its six guiding principles, which include customer orientation, quality, risk-taking and results, Intel also sets itself the goal of being 'a great place to work'. In this way, it aims to keep the spirit of its founders alive.

www.intel.com

Market

Between 1997 and 2001 consumption of blended whiskies fell by 7%, from 35%-28% of adults, while consumption of premium malts fell by 3% from 21%-18% of adults (Source: TGI BMRB 1997, 1999 and 2001 Mintel). Consumption of imported whiskies (such as Jack Daniel's), meanwhile, has remained constant at 11% over the past four years.

The recent buoyant sales of imported whiskies have been largely spurred by the success of brands like Jack Daniel's and its appeal to younger drinkers.

Achievements

Jack Daniel's Old No. 7 Tennessee sour mash whiskey, owned by the American company Brown-Forman, is the leading imported whiskey brand in the UK, both in terms of volume and value. Made in Lynchburg Tennessee since 1863, the brand's authentic heritage and iconic status appeals to a wide range of consumers, many of whom prefer to call themselves Jack Daniel's drinkers rather than whiskey drinkers, seeing themselves as far removed from the traditional drinkers of dark spirits.

The Jack Daniel's Distillery in Tennessee is the oldest registered distillery in the US and a National Historic Site. First registered in 1866, the distillery continues to craft old-time Tennessee whiskey the way Mr Jack did 140 years ago and remains true to its founder's straightforward motto – 'Each day we make it, we will make it the best we can.'

Jack Daniel's has won a raft of awards, including seven international gold medals – the first awarded to Jack Daniel in person at the St Louis Exposition and World's Fair in 1904, when Jack Daniel's was honoured as 'the world's best whiskey'.

History

Born in 1850, the tenth of thirteen children, Jack Daniel left home at the age of six and went to live and work with a neighbour, Dan Call, a Lutheran minister and owner of a whiskey still. At the age of thirteen Daniel bought the distillery from Call, and the distillery became the first to

MR. JACK DANIEL WAS NO SAINT.
BUT HE DID START SOMETHING OF A RELIGION.

Our drinkers are a loyal bunch, and if you know where to look, some of them are pretty easy to spot. We think Mr. Jack would be gratified to know his Tennessee sippin' whiskey still attracts zealous devotees. And that the folks in Lynchburg who produce his whiskey today, are equally passionate about making it his oldtime way.

 JACK DANIEL'S TENNESSEE WHISKEY

be registered with the US Government in 1866.

Just 5'2" tall, Daniel's stature as a distiller grew rapidly. To mark his 21st birthday he went on a shopping spree and returned dressed in the formal knee-length frock coat and broad-brimmed planter's hat that was to be his daily uniform for the rest of his life. His friends' claimed, "once he got something the way he liked it he never changed it". This was also reflected in his approach to whiskey making.

In 1905 'Mr Jack' as he became known, kicked the safe in his office in a fit of temper because he couldn't remember the combination. He broke his toe, infection set in, and he finally died of blood poisoning in 1911.

He passed the distillery on to his nephew Lem Motlow, who saw it through Prohibition. Between 1910 and 1937 the distillery was prohibited by law from producing spirits in Tennessee.

Between 1942 and 1947 the Lynchburg distillery was temporarily converted to producing industrial grade alcohol for the war effort. The Government lifted the restriction in 1946 but would only allow inferior grades of grain to be used. Because Motlow wouldn't compromise the quality of the whiskey, Jack Daniel's wasn't produced again until the restriction was lifted.

In 1947 Motlow died, passing the distillery on to his four sons, who sold it to Brown-Forman in 1956.

Product

Jack Daniel's is a Tennessee whiskey, not a bourbon. It is made from corn, rye, barley malt and iron-free water from the limestone cave spring at the distillery. After distillation Jack Daniel's is mellowed through ten feet of charcoal made from hard sugar

IN ANY BAR IN THE U.K.
YOU KNOW SOMEONE BY NAME.

JACK DANIEL'S TENNESSEE WHISKEY

IF BURNING CHARCOAL TO MELLOW JACK DANIEL'S
SOUNDS EXTRAVAGANT,

WELL, IT IS.

JACK DANIEL'S TENNESSEE WHISKEY

Your friends at Jack Daniel's remind you to drink responsibly.
www.jackdaniels.com
JACK DANIEL'S and OLD NO. 7 are registered trademarks of Jack Daniel's. © 2002.

EVERYTHING YOU NEED TO KNOW ABOUT OUR WHISKEY IS HERE
IN BLACK AND WHITE.

JACK DANIEL'S TENNESSEE WHISKEY

Your friends at Jack Daniel's remind you to drink responsibly.
www.jackdaniels.com
JACK DANIEL'S and OLD NO. 7 are registered trademarks of Jack Daniel's. © 2003.

maple in a process known as charcoal mellowing – a crucial step that gives Jack Daniel's its distinctive taste. The whiskey is then aged in charred new oak barrels for at least four years, resulting in a rich brew which is 40% alcohol.

The distinctive square bottle with its black and white label is as much a part of Jack Daniel's as the whiskey itself, and was embraced by 'Mr Jack' as a fittingly unusual container for his product.

Recent Developments
Jack Daniel's can be drunk either neat, with ice, or with a mixer such as coke, lemonade or ginger ale.

Promotion
Since 1955 Jack Daniel's promotional strategy has been to 'tell not sell' and not to appear to be trying too hard. The first black and white ad appeared in the October 18th edition of Time in 1954. The quirky, under-stated but eye-catching approach continues to draw people to the brand nearly 50 years on.

The essence of the strategy is to communicate that Jack Daniel's is about style rather than fashion. Typical press executions include a simple picture of the distinctive bottle, with the caption underneath reading 'In any bar in the UK you know someone by name' or 'Mr Jack Daniel was no saint but he did start something of a religion'. Meanwhile a typical London Underground poster depicts two men in the distillery with the caption: 'It takes one man to plug a leaky barrel of Jack Daniel's and a second to keep him from getting any ideas'.

Today the typical Jack Daniel's drinker is a man in his mid twenties, and the company targets 18-24 year old male students and young workers. This highly social group expect a lot from life and have a 'live for today' attitude. The brand is also redoubling its efforts to retain 25-44 year olds. Jack Daniel's is advertised year round in magazines read by the brand's target market as well as on radio and in the cinema.

A tremendous amount of promotional activity takes place in September – the month Jack Daniel was born – with teasers in August. For example, in 2002 poster ads variously proclaimed: 'Jack's Birthday Celebrations: starting 1st of the month, 7pm till late (late September that is)';

'Jack's birthday parties go on for days (30 to be precise)'; and 'Nobody knows the exact day Jack Daniel was born. September should cover it.'

Brand Values
Jack Daniel's core essence is that of an authentic, respected American product. It is an extremely masculine product, with 70% of its consumers being male.

www.jackdaniels.co.uk

Things you didn't know about
Jack Daniel's

The White House played an important part in Jack Daniel's rise to prominence. During Prohibition, President Franklin D Roosevelt's vice-president, John Garner, was said to gather his political friends every day and 'strike a blow for liberty' by raising and drinking a glass of Jack Daniel's.

Jack Daniel's whiskey barrels are not held together with nails, screws or glue, but hand-fashioned from 30 wooden staves, six metal hoops and two wooden heads, one for each end.

Because of its distinctive charcoal mellowing process, the US Government accorded Jack Daniel's the distinction of a category all of its own – Tennessee Whiskey – to differentiate it from Bourbon, Canadian and Rye. Jack Daniel's follows all requirements to be named a bourbon but takes an extra step called 'charcoal mellowing', which Jack believed gave the product a more rounded taste.

Mr Jack didn't use paper labels until after 1895, and used quite a number of different designs and colours until the start of prohibition. The black label did not become the 'standard' until after the repeal of prohibition, and it has continued to be modified only slightly through the years.

JAGUAR

Market

Jaguar competes solely in the premium (otherwise known as luxury) car market, which is predominantly associated with prestige European manufacturers. In 2001, this market accounted for about 10% of the UK's total new car sales. With increasing levels of affluence and wider product choice, this percentage has steadily increased in recent years as consumers have traded up from volume into premium branded products.

Total new car registrations in the UK reached 2.45 million in 2001 and premium sales in the sectors of the market in which Jaguar competes were approaching 240,000. Jaguar sales for the year were an all-time record at just over 22,000, which represented almost a 10% share of the market and double the volume achieved only four years previously.

Up until 1999, Jaguar was a niche manufacturer competing only in the Large Premium Saloon and Sports sectors with the XJ and XK Series respectively. Its growth as a company has come primarily with the recent addition of new model lines – the S-TYPE and X-TYPE – which allow Jaguar to compete in the higher-volume Medium and Compact sectors.

In the UK, company car drivers in particular are tending to downsize in their choice of vehicles to lessen the tax burden based on carbon dioxide emissions. But their choice is also product-led because manufacturers generally are naturally focusing new model development on the most rapidly expanding areas of the market. The introduction of the Jaguar X-TYPE for example, is one of the main reasons for the major growth of the Compact Premium sector over the last two years.

Achievements

Jaguar has won numerous awards worldwide in recent years across each of the model lines. In 2002 the new XJ was voted 'Best in Show' by Autoweek at the Paris Salon, further to the X-TYPE being awarded 'Most Beautiful Car of the Year' (Large Premium Saloon/High Class saloons Segment) by 'L'Automobile più Bella del Mondo' in Italy in 2001. The S-TYPE won 'Best Imported Car of the Year' (Upper Class Category) in 2001 from Auto Motor und Sport of Germany. In the US, Automobile Magazine ranked the XK Series 'Best Luxury Coupe' in 1998.

Jaguar has also won prestigious industry awards for vehicle design and manufacturing best practice. In 2002 it received a Commendation for Commitment to the Environment in the BCE Awards. Furthermore, in 2001 the brand won the Autocar Design Award for R-COUPE concept which went to Ian Callum (Jaguar Design Director) and Julian Thompson (Jaguar Advanced Design Studio Chief). In the same year, Jaguar received the Green Apple Award for Environmental Best Practice for its water monitoring system at the Browns Lane Plant, Coventry.

History

The current Jaguar range has a heritage which includes some of the most famous cars in motoring history. Designs like the XK120, the E-TYPE and the Mark 11 saloon established a reputation for power and performance but, above all, it is their sensuous styling which has set Jaguar's cars apart.

Always long, low and elegant to emphasise their sporting character, this design philosophy remains essential to the marque.

It was established very early on by Jaguar's founder, William Lyons. Knighted in 1956 for his services to the automotive industry, he led the company for almost 50 years. Sir William is the most important figure in Jaguar's history and his legacy is still felt profoundly today.

In 1922, William Lyons started the Swallow Sidecar Company in Blackpool, Lancashire with his friend, William Walmsley. They were both motorcycle enthusiasts and as soon as Lyons had reached his 21st birthday, the partners borrowed £1000 from their parents to rent a small factory. They were soon producing distinctive aluminium sidecars for a booming market.

From the start, Lyons showed his flair for line and style and by 1927 he had moved on to motor cars; designing his own coachwork for an existing chassis. The Austin Seven Swallow – a two-seater sports car – was soon followed by designs based on cars by other manufacturers. The business grew quickly and in 1928 it relocated to Coventry; the heartland of the British motor industry. Jaguar's headquarters is still in the city today.

In 1931, Swallow Sidecars introduced its first car under the SS brand name and soon Lyons was producing a whole range of new models. In a country gripped by economic depression, the cars were very popular because as well as being stylish and fast, they also represented exceptional value for money.

The SS Jaguar of 1935 was the first to bear the name that the company would use exclusively after World War II. As well as being a skilled stylist, Lyons was highly aware of the power of advertising and publicity. He chose 'Jaguar' because it represented power and grace and in the 1930s, he entered cars in international rallies to ensure the company had a high profile. This thinking was continued after the war when XK120's, followed by C-TYPE's and D-TYPE's, dominated sports car racing. Jaguar won the Le Mans 24-hour endurance race five times in the 1950s.

William Walmsley left the company in 1935 and from then until the 1960s, Lyons remained at the helm. In the post-war years, Jaguar became a major UK exporter – especially to the all-important North American market – and it acquired an increasingly glamorous image as the so-called 'car of the stars'. Clark Gable, Tony Curtis and Frank Sinatra became enthusiasts of the marque, together with many of their Hollywood contemporaries.

By the 1960s, however, Sir William had decided that Jaguar would be too small a company to survive in an industry becoming increasingly dominated by the large mass producers. He took Jaguar into a merger with the British Motor Corporation which subsequently became British Leyland.

The XJ6 saloon introduced in 1968 was Lyons' crowning achievement but Jaguar's reputation suffered under British Leyland and it wasn't until 1984 that the company regained its independence. Even then, there were successive fuel crises to contend with and Jaguar needed the protection offered by

the Ford Motor Company when it acquired the marque in 1989.

Considerable investment in capital equipment and the adoption of new working practices saw quality and productivity improve markedly in the early 1990s. This paved the way for the current Jaguar range, starting with a new XJ saloon and then the introduction of the XK sports car. In 1999, Jaguar launched its first entirely new model line for three decades – the S-TYPE medium-sized sporting saloon – and this was followed in 2001 by the addition of the X-TYPE compact saloon range. Jaguar is now once again a major force in the premium car market.

Product

Jaguar competes across the premium saloon and sports car markets with a four car line-up. All models feature an Advanced Jaguar (AJ) engine in a V6 or V8 configuration.

The flagship of the range is the XJ saloon and from 2003, it is an all-new, all-aluminium design. William Lyons' first sidecar used the same material and for the same reason – its exceptional lightness and strength. The elegant styling is distinctively Jaguar and 'under the skin', the car benefits from a new air suspension system and new technological features to enhance safety, convenience and enjoyment. It also receives new engines, ranging from a 3.0 litre V6 up to a 4.2 litre, supercharged V8.

The S-TYPE medium-sized sports saloon has an engine line-up which extends from a 2.5 litre V6 up to the V8. Jaguar pioneered this type of car with the Mark II in the 1960s and the S-TYPE echoes aspects of its styling in a very contemporary way.

The X-TYPE compact saloon joined the range in 2001, initially with 2.5 and 3.0 litre V6 engines and standard Jaguar Traction ④, full-time, all-wheel drive. A 2 litre V6 model was added in 2002.

The XK Series sports car was first launched in 1996 and revised in 2002. It has become Jaguar's best-selling sports car ever and is available in coupe and convertible form with either a naturally aspirated or supercharged 4.2 litre V8 engine.

company in the 1980s meant that investment in new product and facilities became increasingly difficult. But Jaguar retained the sense of pride, passion and aspiration which has always been attached to its name and this was recognised and respected by the Ford Motor Company. Survival, though, was still an issue because in the early 1990s annual worldwide sales had fallen to around 20,000, which was well behind the main competition.

As a measure of how far the brand has come in the past decade, annual worldwide sales in 2001 set a new all-time record for Jaguar breaking through the 100,000 barrier for the first time in the company's 80 year history. Crucially, a commitment to the constant improvement of engineering and

manufacturing processes has also seen customer satisfaction levels improve sharply. Confidence in the product can now be set alongside traditional Jaguar virtues like styling and performance.

As a member of the Ford Motor Company's Premier Automotive Group – which also includes Land Rover, Aston Martin and Volvo – Jaguar is now looking confidently to the future.

Promotion

In television and press advertising, the Jaguar logo is always linked to the line, 'The Art of Performance', which encapsulates the essence of the brand – sporting character and totally distinctive styling.

It was the desirability of the cars and the loyalty of customers which kept Jaguar alive during difficult times in its history but in the 1990s, the company set about building more solid foundations for the future. In design and manufacture, what are called the 'rational reasons for purchase' – like durability, quality and reliability – became the priority. Today, Jaguar can justly claim to be totally competitive on this basis, whilst retaining its emotional appeal.

TV campaigns are used selectively to promote brand awareness, particularly when a new model is launched. Press advertising features on a more sustained basis, balancing the desirability of Jaguar cars with the rational reasons that justify their purchase.

As database technology becomes more developed, increasing use is also being made of Direct Marketing and CRM. A more precise

form of marketing, it allows the right people to be approached at the right time. Jaguar also enhances the ownership experience by inviting customers to a wide variety of events in line with their interests.

Brand Values

'The Art of Performance' echoes the template for the marque set down by Jaguar's founder, Sir William – 'Grace, Space and Pace'. He also positioned Jaguar as a brand that people could genuinely aspire to own.

Distinctive styling and refined, powerful performance lie at the heart of the brand's appeal. The famous leaping Jaguar symbol expresses these dynamic qualities together with a sense of assured agility and control.

The use of wood and leather to create contemporary, luxurious interior designs is another Jaguar trademark. Traditional craft skills feature alongside the relevant modern technology that enhances driving safety and enjoyment. Most importantly, today's Jaguars also enjoy an excellent reputation for product quality.

www.jaguar.com

Recent Developments

The last ten years have seen a complete transformation of the Jaguar marque. Its status as a relatively small, independent

Johnnie Walker

Market

The world has a taste for Scotch whisky. Despite the economic downturn and competition from white spirits like vodka, tequila and white rum, 2001 was a strong year for the Scotch whisky industry with record exports of more than one billion bottles (Source: Scotch Whisky Association 2002).

Johnnie Walker is the biggest brand within this market; its annual sales are running at 10.5 million nine litre cases worldwide. In Europe the Greeks, whose national spirit is ouzo, are the second biggest drinkers per capita, not only of Scotch but Johnnie Walker in particular. The French consume more whisky in a month than cognac in a year, while fun-loving Brazilians appear to have abandoned their national drink, caipirinha, in favour of Scotch. Given its international strength, it's hardly surprising the UK isn't in the brand's top ten markets but the nation's drinkers still have an affection for Scotch. In a Mintel study in 2002, lager followed by wine and beer ranked as the top three alcoholic drinks respectively, with Scotch in fourth place.

The continuing popularity of the spirit is due largely to Scotch whisky distillers actively repositioning their products to appeal to a new generation of drinkers. On a global scale industry consolidation will undoubtedly help Scotch maintain its position.

In 2001 the Seagram Spirits & Wine business was split between Diageo (United Kingdom), parent of Johnnie Walker and Pernod Ricard (France) leaving the market, with three major players – the third one being Allied Domecq. Not only do these three players now account for 57% of global sales but they also possess the financial power and distribution outlets to allow them to develop markets, which should keep Scotch in a strong position in the international drinks league.

Achievements

By 1920, its centenary year, Johnnie Walker was established as one of the first truly global brands, sold in more than 120 countries. Thirteen years later, the company was granted a royal warrant, which it still retains, to supply whisky to King George V. In 1937, Walker's acquired a seven acre site in Kilmarnock for warehousing. The new premises were completed by October 1939, however, Walker's gave occupation of the premises to the Government for the duration of World War II. The new blending and bottling premises

were not opened until 1956. In 1966, to keep pace with demand, Walker's acquired a 32 acre site at Barleith, near its Kilmarnock birthplace, leaving Hill Street entirely devoted to bottling and Barleith to blending. Johnnie Walker celebrated its 150th anniversary in 1970 and opened a new blending and bottling complex in Glasgow nine years later. The brand has been preferred by generations of Scotch drinkers and is acknowledged by experts and whisky 'evangelists' as the finest blended whisky. The brand received its first recorded award for excellence at the 1879 International Exhibition in Sydney and since then, has won countless medals and awards all over the world, including the prestigious International Wine and Spirit Competition and Monde Selection. In 1966 Johnnie Walker won its first Queens Award for export and has since received further accolades and recognition.

Today, more than 120 million bottles of Johnnie Walker are sold annually in more than 200 countries.

History

Brand originator John Walker was born at Todriggs Farm in Ayrshire, Scotland in 1805. John was too young to take over the farm when his father died in 1819 so, the following year the income from its sale was used to start a Kilmarnock grocer's shop for the fifteen year old and his mother. Kilmarnock flourished and so did the business. John began stocking casks of malt whisky but found the flavour was heavy and inconsistent. To overcome this, he started blending malt whiskies and found he could create a product with a consistent flavour which exceeded any competition. Customers started demanding 'Mr Walker's' whisky – and as such, the brand was born.

By the time of John's death in 1857, his blends were so well known in the west of Scotland that he had laid the foundations for an

empire. Alexander Walker inherited the family business aged twenty and created 'Old Highland Whisky', the precursor to Johnnie Walker Black Label. The blend had a significant advantage. In 1860, a law was passed allowing grain whisky to be blended with malt, which in turn enabled Alexander to create an even smoother, more enjoyable blend. He copyrighted the now familiar slanting label in 1867, demonstrating an appreciation of marketing way ahead of his time by creating an instantly recognisable brand identity. The distinctive square bottle followed and was soon being exported as far as Australia where, in 1887, a distributor wrote to Alexander advising him to drop the price because of an influx of cheaper and inferior whisky. Alexander replied: "We are determined to make our whisky, so far as quality is concerned, of such a standard that nothing in the market shall come before it." It was a policy which his sons George and Alexander rigidly adhered to and 'Old Highland' increased in popularity overseas, especially among large communities of Scot expatriates, who thirsted after a taste of their native land. The far-sighted duo realised they would have to create new brands to meet changing tastes as well as securing a reliable supply. In 1893 they bought the Cardhu distillery, whose malt whisky became the cornerstone of their blends. In 1909 Old Highland and Extra Old Highland were enhanced and rebranded as Red Label and Black Label. The 'twelve-year-old' statement was added to Black Label, making it one of the first Scotch to carry an age guarantee. Johnnie Walker's popularity soared and in 1925 it amalgamated with Buchanan-Dewar to become part of the Distillers Co Ltd, initially created in 1877. Alexander Walker Jnr continued to blend whiskies into old age and, in 1932, in response to demand on international luxury liners, created Johnnie Walker Swing.

Over the decades Distillers grew the brand and the company which, in 1986, became United

Deep gold in colour, it is blended from over 40 whiskies. At the heart of Black Label is a twelve-year-old Cardhu, an outstanding malt from the Speyside distillery the family acquired in 1893. Blue Label was created in the style of John Walker's nineteenth century blends. The whisky is a blend of the rarest whiskies in Scotland and has an intense character, combining rich peatiness and deep smoke with traces of spice. Gold Label, a superior deluxe eighteen year old blend, is made from a selection of approximately fifteen aged whiskies, which deliver an exceptionally smooth taste with a richness of character. Taking into account the growing fashion for malt whisky, the brand introduced Pure Malt, a fifteen year old whisky made from selected Highland malts. It has successfully brought a new dimension to the market appealing to both deluxe and malt whisky aficionados.

Recent Developments

In 2001, Johnnie Walker ONE was added to the portfolio and was initially launched in Thailand. This long, slightly carbonated, ready mixed drink has an alcohol strength of 5%. It is aimed at young adults and bottled such that it can compete with other ready to drink products that are drunk from the bottle, such as premium lagers.

footballer Roberto Baggio have appeared in a series of commercials which encouraged people to 'Keep Walking' to fulfil their dreams. To date the advertising has been seen in 210 countries. The brand began a global association with the CNN and Discovery television networks sponsoring a series of programmes broadcast to more than 150 million homes, which showed 'ordinary people on extraordinary journeys'. In 2001 it launched 'The Keep Walking Fund', an initiative designed to support individuals to fulfil their dreams. The Fund has given thousands of pounds to individuals to allow them to fulfil their dreams. These dreams cover all types of achievements from setting up a business to organising community programmes. The brand's website, www.johnniewalker.com, espouses the message of personal progress through effort, which is also reflected in Asia Pacific's premier golf event 'The Johnnie Walker Classic' which was launched thirteen years ago.

Brand Values

It was John Walker's vision that revolutionised the liquor industry by blending whiskies to create a superior product. The story of the Johnnie Walker brand is one of success and leadership founded on elements as simple and

Distillers following its acquisition by brewing giant Guinness. Eleven years later, Guinness combined with food and drinks group Grand Metropolitan to form Diageo. Thanks to the ambitious plans and inspiration of John Walker, the brand is now in a position to create blends he can only have dreamt of.

Product

The basic principle of whisky making is relatively straightforward. A brew is made similar to beer – water, cereals, and yeast – then distilled to extract high-alcohol spirit. While beer is ready in a matter of days, whisky is a time consuming process. The spirit or new make whisky, collected after the long distillation process cannot yet be called Scotch whisky. Nor would it be pleasant to drink. The liquor has to be matured in oak barrels, in Scotland for a minimum of three years before it can be sold as Scotch. In practice, the whiskies selected for Johnnie Walker blends are matured for much longer – eight, ten, twelve, fifteen, eighteen years. In fact, some of the whiskies that are used in Johnnie Walker Blue Label can be up to 60 years old. Once sufficiently matured the whiskies are blended. Each Johnnie Walker blend has its own distinctive taste and consistency. Red Label is reddish gold in colour and blended with 35 different whiskies, making it a substantial and characterful Scotch. It has an exuberant, sweet yet smokey taste. Black Label is a deep, complex Scotch that is silky and rich.

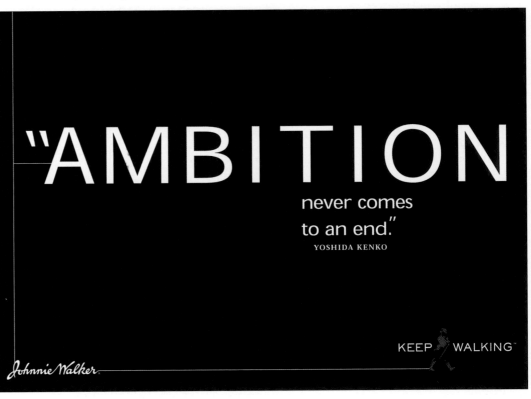

"AMBITION never comes to an end."
YOSHIDA KENKO

KEEP WALKING

Johnnie Walker

Promotion

When George and Alexander Walker launched Johnnie Walker Black & Red Label in 1909 they were determined to instil the brands with a new personality. They eventually sought the help of famous cartoonist Tom Browne who, over a legendary lunch, sketched the 'Striding Man' on the back of a menu. George Walker added the words, 'Born 1820 – Still Going Strong' and the figure rapidly became one of the first globally recognised advertising icons. The Striding Man has remained central to the brand's communication strategy. The first truly global 'Keep Walking' campaign was launched in 1999 with an initial investment of £100 million. The campaign builds on the pioneering and courageous heritage of the Walker family and the perseverance that made Johnnie Walker one of the first global brands. International names like film director Martin Scorsese, actor Harvey Keitel and

natural as the ingredients in the original blend. Hard work, honesty, a relentless pursuit of excellence in all aspects of the business, and the willingness to take risks in pursuit of clearly held objectives are the values which underpin the brand.

www.johnniewalker.com

Kellogg's CORN FLAKES

Market

Many people view breakfast as the most important meal of the day. Research shows that 96% of the UK population eat or drink something for breakfast and 49% start the day with breakfast cereals.

This signifies a huge change in UK breakfast eating habits over the last twenty years. In 1968 approximately half the population tucked into a cooked breakfast on a regular basis, but by 1990 this had dropped to around 10%.

This change can be attributed to increasingly busy lifestyles and an awareness of the importance of healthy eating. However, hectic lifestyles can mean breakfast is often sacrificed to keeping to a tight timetable. The major challenge facing cereal companies today is to persuade people that eating cereals is both convenient and beneficial both at breakfast time and at any time of the day.

In terms of volume, the UK is the largest consumer of breakfast cereals in Europe. In 1999, the market was valued at £944 million. Per capita consumption has risen in the last decade by almost 10% and currently stands at 5.9 kilos, with over 35's eating more per head than anyone else.

Achievements

The Kellogg Company takes advantage of this opportunity firstly by continuing to be committed to leading the food industry in research and development. Its WK Kellogg Institute for Food and Nutrition Research, which opened in 1997 in Battle Creek, Michigan is among the world's most advanced food development facilities. At the WK Kellogg Institute, nearly 300 Kellogg professionals from throughout the world are developing the foods of the future.

Secondly, the company is committed to providing people of all ages with great tasting foods that are good for you, more tasty, more convenient and more fun.

Almost half of the UK's population start their day with a bowl of 'breakfast cereal' and along with Ireland, the UK has the highest capita consumption levels of breakfast cereals in the world. Kellogg's commands a 39% volume share of the UK market, supplying eleven out of the nations top twenty brands – with 78% of households having a pack of Kellogg's breakfast cereals in their homes. Today in the UK more than 1.6 billion bowlfuls of Kellogg's Corn Flakes are eaten every year, making it the most popular single breakfast cereal brand on the market.

Recent years have seen Kellogg's build on the success of its core cereal business and move into

new areas with groundbreaking new product development. For example in the UK, Cereal and Milk bars, Nutri-Grain bars as well as fruit snacks such as Real Fruit Winders have been introduced.

Through this innovation Kellogg's continues to meet changing consumer needs and offer new and relevant breakfast and good food 'on the go' solutions.

History

Kellogg's Corn Flakes were discovered by a quirk of fate. Back in 1884, Dr John Harvey Kellogg, superintendent of the internationally famous Battle Creek sanatarium, in collaboration with his business manager brother, Will Keith (WK) Kellogg, developed a nutritious cereal food for his patients.

One day a laboratory accident exposed cooked wheat to the open air for over a day. The Kellogg brothers then processed the wheat through rollers, ensuring an even distribution of moisture – resulting in wheat flakes.

The patients loved this new flaky cereal product and demanded supplies even after leaving the sanitarium. As a result WK Kellogg set up the Battle Creek Toasted Corn Flake Company.

The success of the sanitarium's flake foods quickly spawned 42 imitations from local rivals. To counter this, WK had his name and signature scripted on each individual package of Kellogg's Corn Flakes.

WK quickly realised the benefits of advertising and demand was soon exceeding expectations. By 1909, more than a million cases of Kellogg's Corn Flakes had been sold across the US. A variant, Kellogg's Bran Flakes, was introduced in 1915. Coco Pops, Frosties and Special K are amongst many others that have been added to Kellogg's repertoire in subsequent years. With the introduction of other brands, international expansion became inevitable. Kellogg's Corn Flakes was first introduced into the UK in 1924 and in 1938 a new factory was opened in Trafford Park, Manchester.

Manufacturing plants were also built in Canada and Australia. Today, Kellogg's operates plants around the globe, marketing its products in more than 160 countries worldwide.

Product

A strong commitment to health has consistently been the cornerstone on which Kellogg's success has been based. From the early days of the pioneering work of the Kellogg brothers to now, the emphasis on the valuable role that breakfast

cereals plays in the diet has been constant.

It is also significant that health and nutrition agencies around the world are recommending that people modify their diets to increase fibre and decrease fat in the foods they choose. Many health conscious people have already increased their consumption of grain based foods. These foods satisfy hunger at a reasonable cost while providing essential nutrients and convenience.

Kellogg's Corn Flakes does just that – the golden flakes of toasted corn provide 25% of the recommended daily allowance of essential vitamins such as thiamin, riboflavin and iron. Added to this, they are very low in fat.

Recent Developments

Kellogg's Corn Flakes has undergone a comprehensive makeover with an improved taste and stunning new look, designed to meet the ever-changing consumer tastes of the twenty first century. Over 100 years on from the discovery of the Corn Flake, Kellogg's has set about making developments to the 'original and best'. The new modifications to the food itself and the packaging are undoubtedly the first significant changes to one of the world's biggest brands since that date.

The path to Superbrand status has not always been a smooth one for Kellogg's Corn Flakes, particularly in the early years. When the Company was formed in the UK in 1924, it imported Corn Flakes from Canada. However, to a nation used to eating eggs, bacon and porridge every morning, the concept of simply shaking ready-cooked food from a packet, adding milk and sugar and then calling it breakfast was completely alien and treated with considerable suspicion by the great British housewife. Like their American counterparts a generation earlier, the majority of women believed in sending their husbands and children out with hearty – and hot – meals inside them. However, Kellogg's set out to challenge this belief and backed by massive and sustained advertising, headline grabbing promotions and, above all, a sincere belief and passion in the quality and value of their products, they succeeded in changing the eating habits of a nation.

Promotion

Kellogg's Corn Flakes has always been a well-supported brand from the outset. WK Kellogg realised that promotion was vital to growing his first brand. In 1906, he placed a full-page advert in the Ladies Home Journal which helped catapult sales from 33 cases per day to 2900. Spurred on by this success, he embarked on a series of

promotions offering free samples of the 'Original and Best' Kellogg's Corn Flakes, including the 'Give the Grocer a Wink' campaign and a book, in 1910, the 'Jungleland Funny Moving Pictures'.

Free product sampling also played a big part in the growth of Corn Flakes in the UK in the 1920s and 1930s. Outside the larger towns and cities, retail trading was largely based upon thousands of small, independent stores, or corner shops (which were often little more than the converted front room of a terraced house). It was a fearsomely complicated system served by an equally complex web of wholesalers and distributors, with intense competition and rampant price-cutting. Undeterred, Kellogg's pioneer salesmen managed to talk Corn Flakes onto the shelves and window displays of this myriad of stores, giving away millions of sample packets as they went, to a rapidly converting public.

Such was the success of these early campaigns, that in 1938, a new UK factory was opened in Stretford, Manchester – just in time to help feed the country during the ensuing War. It was also well placed to meet the growing demands of the new post-war consumer society in the 1950s, fuelled by a new phenomenon that was to have far-reaching consequences for Kellogg's; Britain's first supermarket, which opened in London in 1951. With the advent of TV, branding really came into its own and Kellogg's Corn Flakes has gone from strength to strength, despite the increasing challenges to its number one position. Based on the core nutritional values, but also with an increasingly sophisticated mix of advertising and promotions, Kellogg's support for the brand has continued to grow. Some memorable on-pack promotions include the 25 Ford Escorts given away in 1974 and more recently, a massive prize of £100,000 per year for life to celebrate the 100th anniversary of the brand in 1999. Some may remember the effective campaign from the late 1980s with the theme, 'Have you forgotten how good they taste'. With the proliferation of new breakfast cereals on the market, many people obviously had but were enticed back to the brand by this campaign.

Brand Values

Today's theme for the brand is 'Wake Up', with Kellogg's promoting Corn Flakes as the best way to wake up in the morning. This has been communicated through metaphors for waking up, such as the Dawn of Man campaign, where early man evolves into modern man, thanks to

his bowl of Kellogg's Corn Flakes.

TV certainly encouraged the use of brand characters, or icons, and, in keeping with many of its other brands, in 1958, Kellogg's introduced an icon for its number one cereal. First introduced in the US, Cornelius the Cockerel appeared on UK packs in 1963 and has been omnipresent on packaging ever since. Synonymous with breakfast time and waking up (or being woken up), the cockerel was an obvious icon for the brand. Cornelius dominates the new packaging, as if to deliver a 'loud and proud' 'Wake up' call to existing and new consumers.

The bold new iconic pack design, is just part of the intended added value of the brand to consumers in 2003. For the first time since their introduction, the Corn Flakes themselves have a new look, a new freshness and a new taste, with crispier flakes and a new texture. What's more, in another first for the category, the larger size packets of Corn Flakes will come foil wrapped to seal in this new freshness. These changes will ensure Kellogg's Corn Flakes remain 'the original and best' and synonymous with breakfast.

Kellogg's Corn Flakes have enjoyed a long history of popularity based on offering a quality product with appetising taste and high nutritional value. The brand has been driven by a belief first perpetuated by its founder, WK Kellogg, that cereals can provide an integral part of our diet as a high carbohydrate, low fat food.

www.kelloggs.co.uk

Things you didn't know about Kellogg's

Over four million bowlfuls of Kellogg's Corn Flakes are eaten every day in the UK.

It takes 140 days of sunshine to grow the corn that makes them.

The total number of Kellogg's cereals sold since 1906 would reach the moon and back 160 times.

The official mascot of Kellogg's Corn flakes is Cornelius Cockerel.

Kellogg's makes 240 million boxes of Corn Flakes per year.

Celebrity fans of Kellogg's include Victoria Beckham, Liz Hurley, Robbie Williams and Anna Friel. Emma Buton loves making chocolate crunchies from Kellogg's Corn Flakes.

Market

Facial tissues are commonly associated as essential allies in the war against colds, flu and hayfever, but they were originally positioned as cold cream and make-up removers.

The facial tissue market has increased in value by over 60% since 1994, driven by product innovations that bring new consumers to the category. For example, the launch of KLEENEX® UltraSoft in 1994 created the super premium sector of the tissue market, which now accounts for approximately a quarter of the total category value. (Source: ACNielsen)

Achievements

KLEENEX® is arguably the world's most famous tissue brand and largely pioneered the disposable tissue market. The brand has remained the market leader since production began in 1924. KLEENEX® has constantly stayed ahead of the market and has sustained a reputation for quality and reliability as well as having a 'warm' image. In 1996 KLEENEX® facial tissue was named as the fastest growing brand in the UK (Source: ACNielsen) and sits in the top 50 of all UK grocery brands (Source: ACNielsen 2002). In 2002 the KLEENEX® market value share has averaged almost 50% and has doubled in size since 1994. KLEENEX® is also one of only 43 brands worldwide with sales in excess of US$1 billion (Source: ACNielsen).

History

It was wartime ingenuity that led to the development of the company's first consumer product. The cellulose wadding tissue, trademarked Cellucotton by Kimberly-Clark, was first developed in 1914 and became an essential medical item during World War I. It was used in wartime hospitals and first aid stations where it often stood as an ideal substitute for surgical dressing when cotton was scarce. Army nurses adapted this wadding for menstrual uses and soon after, in 1920, Kimberly-Clark began producing Kotex® feminine pads for the public. This then led to the company developing the KLEENEX® facial tissue.

KLEENEX® tissue was first presented in response to the rash of cosmetics and cold creams then launched in the market as a cold cream remover. KLEENEX® tissue was positioned as a disposable substitute for facial towels. In those distant days, a pack of 100 sheets retailed at 65 cents in the US.

In 1929, the patented familiar interfold method used in the KLEENEX® tissue Pop-Up box was added to the range of KLEENEX® tissues. At the same time, coloured tissues were introduced. Through extending choice to the consumer, KLEENEX® tissue steadily gained users. However, it was still regarded somewhat, as a luxury item. Its primary usage was divulged through a consumer test in 1930, which clearly demonstrated that over 60% of KLEENEX® tissue consumers used the tissues as a disposable handkerchief, as opposed to its original intended use as a cold cream remover. As a consequence, Kimberly-Clark swung the positioning of its product towards this section of the market, and pioneered its usage as a handy

disposable tissue suited for use on the move. Advertising enforced this usage and sales promptly soared.

KLEENEX® tissue was unavailable for civilian use during World War II. However, production of the base product – the wadding – continued but was diverted once again to the war effort and adapted for industrial uses; such as insulation. Once the war was over, tissue production resumed and production facilities increased to meet growing demand. In 1967, Kimberly-Clark introduced KLEENEX® Boutique tissues in a new attractive upright packaging and the first sub-brand was born.

KLEENEX® for Men has now been the brand leader for over 40 years and it is therefore not surprising that this drives the image of KLEENEX® in the UK.

In 1983 KLEENEX® Travel tissues were launched in a flexible pack for out of home use. The next major innovation saw the introduction of the first dry-to-the-touch lotion treated tissues in 1994 – KLEENEX® Ultra (later rebranded in 1996 as KLEENEX® UltraSoft). Over 20% of buyers of

KLEENEX® UltraSoft at launch were new buyers to the facial tissue category (Source: ACNielsen).

In 1996 KLEENEX® UltraBalm tissues were launched. These were the first tissues to leave behind a unique and clinically proven protective balm, containing calendula, to help prevent the nose from becoming red and sore. The launch of KLEENEX® UltraBalm tissues resulted in KLEENEX® facial tissues being named as the fastest growing brand in the UK (Source: ACNielsen 1996). KLEENEX® UltraBalm was rebranded as KLEENEX® Balsam in 1998 and continues its rapid growth, reaching value shares of 12% during peak periods (Source: ACNielsen). In 2000 the KLEENEX® brand celebrated 75 years of being in business.

Product

The basic ingredient of KLEENEX® tissue is high quality cellulose fibre, which is obtained principally from wood pulp that is processed into creped wadding. To ensure a ready supply, Kimberly-Clark conducts a forest management and reforestation programme that ensures a supply of pulpwood for present and future needs. The ideal 'KLEENEX®' tissue fibre is derived from selected tree species, which include spruce, fir and some hardwoods. These thin wood fibres contribute to the desirable characteristics of softness, absorbency and strength in the KLEENEX® tissue.

Throughout the manufacturing process, Kimberly-Clark looks for ways to reduce the amount of energy used per unit of production. In accordance with this policy, the company has embarked on an ambitious energy reduction programme. In fact, over the past five years a 12% energy efficiency improvement has been achieved. The company now uses recycled materials in about half of its total European production.

Before KLEENEX® tissues leave the mill, they are subjected to a series of quality and performance checks. These include tests for softness, absorbency, strength, size and colour. Random samples are sent to Kimberly-Clark's Quality Assurance Laboratory to ensure there is a uniformity of manufacturing standard and product quality among all plants.

KLEENEX® facial tissue products are relaunched on a regular basis and always feature

The KLEENEX® trademark was first registered with the US Patent Office in 1924 to cover 'absorbent pads or sheets for removing cold cream'. This mark has now been registered in over 150 countries.

KLEENEX® Boutique tissues, introduced in 1967, also became a federally registered trademark. As did the quadrant design adopted as a prominent feature of KLEENEX® tissue packaging in 1938 (although not formally registered until 1965). This, in fact, has been one of the few federal trademark registrations ever granted on overall packaging design. The interfold method that typifies the KLEENEX® tissue Pop-Up box has also been patented.

KLEENEX® tissue has always been heavily promoted through magazine, newspaper, and TV advertising. As KLEENEX® facial tissue started life chiefly as a cold cream remover, magazine and newspaper advertising of the time associated the brand with the famous Hollywood actors and actresses of the day. Initial advertising copy stated: "Actresses, screen stars – whose complexions

real tangible product improvements, i.e. softer, thicker and stronger. The KLEENEX® name will only be applied to products that are demonstrably the best in their category.

In the UK the KLEENEX® facial brand equity revolves heavily around the biggest KLEENEX® brand, KLEENEX® for Men. Indeed, Kimberly-Clark research has found that when consumers are asked about the KLEENEX® brand, the first connection they make is with this product.

Recent Developments

Kimberly-Clark is one of the largest tissue manufacturers in the world and has been one of the Fortune magazines 'Most Admired' companies since 1983. In 2002 it came 89th in The Times survey of the Top 100 companies to work for.

KLEENEX® has driven many innovations in the facial tissue market, such as KLEENEX® Travelers which were launched in July 2001. The product consists of a slim pack of tissues with a side opening, specifically designed for use in a car as they fit well in a car door pocket or glove compartment.

Christmas 2001 saw the launch of the KLEENEX® Christmas cube in the UK, as a seasonal product in holographic packaging in bright Christmas colours.

In 2002 KLEENEX® Cosmetic tissues were launched. This soft, white un-fragranced tissue is intended specifically to use with a cleanser for the removal of make-up. The box has a shimmering finish and is available in three designs. The product is intended primarily for use in the bedroom or bathroom.

Promotion

The trademark 'Kleenex' was adopted by Kimberly-Clark back in 1924. It was originally promoted as a cleansing tissue and this is likely to be the origins of the brand name, in as much as it could be shortened to 'cleen'.
The distinctive capital "K" and "ex" ending were probably derived from its predecessor "Kotex", a fellow consumer product trademark in the Kimberly-Clark stable.

Not everything fits in your car like **KLEENEX® TRAVELERS** TISSUES

Thank goodness for Kleenex

are always under scrutiny – use KLEENEX®, the sanitary, velvety-soft tissue to remove their make-up". The Hollywood make-up studios formed a glamorous backdrop to the brand, and hailed KLEENEX® as the new 'scientific way to remove cold cream'. Soon after, advertisements for the KLEENEX® brand began featuring endorsements from the famous Hollywood faces of the day, such as Helen Hayes, Ronald Colman, Gertrude Lawrence and Elsie Janis.

Over the last three decades KLEENEX® facial tissue has enjoyed a continuous advertising presence and in most of these years has enjoyed 100% share of voice – as the only company advertising facial tissues. TV advertisements featuring the 'three girls' have been some of the most successful ever and rank in the top 5% of all UK advertisements for awareness and correct brand recall.

The multitude of other purposes KLEENEX® can be used for has become increasingly apparent and advertising has been expanded to feature the everyday needs of the average consumer. The focus is on moments in daily family lives when KLEENEX® tissues come into their own. In 2001 the 'Thank Goodness for KLEENEX®' campaign was launched with both TV and print. The print campaign was a first for KLEENEX®, focusing on the unexpected moments in life when KLEENEX® tissues are of use.

Radio advertising is used to highlight key promotional activities such as the KLEENEX® Hayfever and Winter Survival Promotions. The KLEENEX® Winter and Hayfever Survival kits provide products to help offer relief from hayfever, colds and flu. The Hayfever promotion was launched in 1991 and so far has collected nine Institute of Sales Promotion Awards, including the Grand Prix Award for the best UK and European promotions of 1991.

In 2000 KLEENEX® launched www.kleenex.co.uk and two microsites www.wintersurvival.co.uk and www.hayfeversurvival.co.uk were later added with information on how to combat colds, flu and hayfever. KLEENEX® also exclusively sponsors the National Cold and Flu Monitor, which is released as a map reflecting the cold and flu situation in the UK throughout the autumn and winter seasons.

Brand Values

Throughout the world, the KLEENEX® brand name stands for quality and softness. The brand also aims to communicate the role KLEENEX® can play in everyday life with the 'Thank Goodness for KLEENEX®' vision. This builds on the presence that KLEENEX® already has in the everyday lives of many people and conveys the message that KLEENEX® can be relied upon not only when suffering from colds and flu but on many other, often unexpected, occasions.

www.kleenex.co.uk

...thank goodness for

Kodak

Market

The UK photography market in general is buoyant, according to Mintel, mainly due to an increase in the number of Britons taking holidays abroad. Foreign holidays now account for 38% of the total, compared to 29% in 1996. Demographic changes to the population, which is generally becoming older and richer, have also boosted camera sales.

The photography market itself is divided into a number of different sectors. Disposable cameras are the most popular among young consumers, as they can be used in places where one wouldn't take an expensive camera, such as pubs and nightclubs. APS cameras – with their choice of portrait, panoramic or group settings – are also popular with younger buyers. Mature users, on the whole, prefer manual or semi-automatic SLR cameras, while those looking for a professional effect without the fuss tend to buy point-and-shoot 35mm compact cameras.

The growth in popularity of digital photography, which has gone hand-in-hand with an increase in the number of home computers, has taken the market by storm. Mintel has found that the digital sector was the largest value segment in 2002, with sales of £250 million. This was followed by £110 million for disposable cameras, £70 million for 35mm compact, £60 million for APS, £21 million for instant and £14 million for 35mm SLR.

Kodak has a key advantage in the market in that it is one of the strongest brand names in photography in terms of producing film as well as making cameras. Its 35mm films are among the most popular in the world, it is highly present in the disposable or single use camera (SUC) market, and led the Advanced Photo System, producing the Advantix film which is the first choice of many APS enthusiasts. It has also moved swiftly into the digital market with its EasyShare range of digital camera solutions, acknowledged as the digital industry standard for ease-of-use.

Achievements

Eastman Kodak Company is based in the US and in 2001 showed profits of US$4.5 billion on net sales of just over US$13.2 billion. As well as being a leading brand in consumer photography (both in the US and in the UK) in which it has interests in cameras,

accessories, film manufacture and developing – Eastman Kodak Company also provides film for the movie industry, makes printers and scanners for business use, and provides complex medical equipment such as laser imagers and radiography materials.

The brand is run on a regional basis, and its UK arm – Kodak Limited – is one of its most successful worldwide, as well as the oldest. As a whole, Eastman Kodak Company has come a long way since its American founder George Eastman arrived in London in 1879 to obtain a patent for his new plate-coating machine. At the time, 'plate' photography was the only technology available to those who wanted to transfer real images to paper, and London was the centre of the nascent industry.

Eastman was not happy with cumbersome plate cameras however, and began a series of experiments, which culminated in the first rolls of film. With a camera he called the Kodak, launched in 1888, he laid the foundations for consumer photography. The Kodak camera was priced at US$25 and could be loaded with enough film for 100 exposures. Users had to return the whole camera to Eastman's base in Rochester, New York, where the film was developed, prints were made and a new film was inserted for US$10.

The product was a runaway success and after a few years it became clear that the Rochester headquarters had more business than it could handle. New production and distribution outlets were needed. The London office came first, in 1889, swiftly followed by a factory in Harrow. By 1900, branches had been established in France, Germany and Italy, and a Japanese outlet was under construction. Today, the company has manufacturing operations in Canada, Mexico, Brazil, the UK, France, Germany, Australia and the US and Kodak products are marketed to people in more than 150 countries.

Over the past decade, the company has been far from complacent. Kodak's 35mm films regularly scoop awards as the first choice among amateurs and professionals alike – but that did not stop the company working alongside other manufacturers to develop the Advanced Photo System. This offers users a choice of formats and easy-to-load film. Kodak Advantix cameras are now the brand leaders in the APS market in the UK.

Kodak has also responded effectively to the growth of the digital market, releasing an increasingly affordable highly acclaimed portfolio of digital cameras, the Kodak EasyShare range, as well as market-leading EasyShare software that helps users share, print and organise their digital pictures.

History

With the slogan 'You push the button, we do the rest', George Eastman put the first simple camera into the hands of the world's consumers in 1888. Eastman was a high school drop-out, but his disinterest in academic matters hid an inventive mind and an entrepreneurial streak. Even as he patented his plate-coating machine, he was looking for a way to make plate photography obsolete.

Eastman announced the invention of film rolls in 1883, and his Kodak camera came onto the market five years later. By 1892 his business was established as the Eastman Kodak Company. Having brought photography to the masses, he went on to make cheaper and more accessible products. He reasoned that the creation of ingenious tools and processes for manufacturing film would enable the company to turn out high-quality merchandise at affordable prices.

In 1886, the 100,000th Kodak camera was manufactured, and film and photographic paper were being made at a rate of about 400 miles a month. At that time, a Kodak camera sold for US$5. Typically, Eastman worked towards a camera that could operate cheaply and efficiently and sell for US$1. The result of this effort was the introduction, in 1900, of the first Brownie camera.

In 1919, Eastman gave one-third of his company holdings, then worth about US$10 million, back to his employees. He was a pioneer in the field of workers' rights, introducing retirement plans, disability benefits and bonuses. He also supported the arts and music and donated large sums to charity, as well as grants to the Massachusetts Institute of Technology. He remained at the helm of his company until 1932 when he committed suicide – depressed by a spinal disease that had drained his previously boundless energy.

The company continued with Eastman's main aim in mind – to make home photography not only cheaper, but better. Kodak launched the legendary Kodachrome transparency film in 1937 and the world's first true colour negative film by 1942. By the 1970's, the easy loading Kodak instamatic camera had become a byword for family photography.

In the 1990s it improved its emulsions – the light-sensitive coating that is the magic behind negatives – to such an extent that its Kodak Gold film was said to offer the best combination of accuracy, colour and sharpness ever available in a consumer film. The Advanced Photo System, launched in 1996, provided consumers with a more convenient way to capture great pictures consistently. Only a year earlier, Kodak had launched the first digital camera to sell for under US$1,000. And in 1998, its Picture Maker Kiosks began to appear in stores. Based on computer technology, these allow customers to remove red-eye, do simple colour corrections, and zoom-in and crop pictures before printing them.

Product

Kodak is a leading brand in both the film and camera markets. In the consumer market alone, it offers a wide range of point-and-shoot 35mm film and digital cameras, as well as its Kodak's APS models. It is also a leading name in the growing disposable camera market, having produced its first Fun Saver camera in the mid 1990s.

In the film segment, it manufacturers a full range of slide, black and white, Advantix (APS) and colour films. Its best-known brands in the latter area are Kodak Gold film, which provides high quality colour and Kodak Ultra Max film, which offers versatility in varying lights and speeds. The company also offers a range of batteries, as well as photo CDs and software. Kodak also makes business imaging equipment – such as scanners and printers – and provides film and technology to the healthcare and film industries.

In the past decade, Kodak has developed best-selling digital cameras for the professional photography market, for whom it also provides specialist films and papers. The company is at the forefront of the world's graphic industry too, following the formation in 1988 of Kodak Polychrome Graphics, a joint venture with Sun chemical.

Recent Developments

In 2001 Kodak launched its EasyShare cameras – essentially a collection of user-friendly digital compacts with the added benefit of a computer docking station, which, together with EasyShare software, enables users to easily transfer pictures to their computers. Images can then be emailed, printed at home (on Kodak inkjet paper), or sent away to be printed by a professional.

More recently, the company has been moving into the new wireless mobile imagery market, providing its dealers with technology that enables them to scan films – or grab existing digital images – and send customers' pictures to image-compatible mobile phones.

Yet despite its enthusiasm about digital technology, Kodak has no intention of abandoning its APS format, having recently released a new range of cameras, which are even more affordable and compact than their predecessors.

Promotion

Ever since the days of its founder George Eastman, who coined the name Kodak, the brand has been conscious of the importance of good marketing. Just as it once plastered Grand Central Station in New York with giant colour photographs to prove the effectiveness of the medium, it recently teamed up with the British Airports Authority (BAA) and Disney World Resorts to stage a major poster campaign, designed to drive sales at Gatwick, Heathrow and other major UK airports.

Around 50 million passengers pass through these outlets annually and from July 10th until the end of September 2002 giant posters headlined 'Picture the Fun' invited them to visit BAA shops for the chance to win Disney holidays, Kodak Advantix cameras and thousands of processing vouchers and single-use cameras. By spending £10 or more on any product, passengers were able to enter a Kodak prize draw and instant win promotion. To further raise awareness, millions of information leaflets were distributed by hand to passengers at all participating airports.

Kodak continues to be committed to high profile advertising and for Christmas 2002 invested £2.5 million in a national TV campaign featuring the Kodak Advantix T700 camera model and new gift pack. Each gift pack contained the camera, film, photo frame, case, strap and batteries, plus a demo disc and free trial voucher for a Kodak Picture CD to show consumers how easy it is to be creative with pictures. The Kodak EasyShare advertisement was also rolled out in November, in the run-up to the crucial Christmas sales season.

Kodak also got involved for the launch of the James Bond film, Die Another Day, in autumn 2002. The 20th Bond film was shot on Kodak stock and included the company's cameras as part of the action. Kodak subsidiary Cinesite (Europe) Ltd was also responsible for many of the special effects featured in the movie. Consumers were invited to 'Win a 007 Experience' by entering a competition after the purchase of Kodak films or single-use cameras. The 'experiences' on

offer included a trip to Iceland, tank driving, a flight in a Tiger Moth plane, and a spa break. Vin Diesel also benefited from using a Kodak EasyShare LS420 digital camera, in his first foray as Xander Cage, in the first xXx movie.

Brand Values

George Eastman had four basic principles for his business: mass production at low cost, international distribution, extensive advertising, and a focus on the customer. Eastman saw that all these principles interlinked. Mass production could not be justified without wide distribution which, in turn, needed the support of strong advertising. From the beginning, he imbued the company with the conviction that fulfilling customer needs and desires was the only road to corporate success. To his basic principles of business, he added these policies: foster growth and development through continuing research, treat employees in a fair, self-respecting way, and reinvest profits to build and extend the business.

The ongoing stance of Eastman Kodak Company remains in line with these basic principles and policies.

www.kodak.co.uk

Things you didn't know about Kodak

The name Kodak does not mean anything – founder George Eastman thought the letter 'K' was a 'strong, incisive letter' and wanted a brand name that began and ended with it. He simply played around with letter combinations until he came up with one that he liked.

The first pocket Kodak camera was launched as early as 1895. It used roll-film and incorporated a small window through which users could read positioning numbers for each exposure.

In 1950 the company unveiled the first in its long-running Kodak Colorama displays at Grand Central Station in New York. These eighteen feet high and 60ft wide transparencies were viewed by an estimated 650,000 people a day. The exhibit was dismantled in 1989 as part of Grand Central's restoration. Images from Kodak now feature in a dynamic display in the city's Times Square.

Kodak received an Oscar in 1952 for the development of Eastman colour negative and colour print films, which were introduced two years earlier and which boosted the production of colour motion pictures.

Market

The UK car market totalled 2.458 million units in 2001, an increase of 2.2% from the 2.221 million in 2000 (Source: SMMT). The 4x4 market accounted for 137,000 units in 2001 (equivalent to 5.6% of the total industry volume (TIV)). This includes around 15,700 light utility/commercial 4x4's not included in the car TIV figures. This is up dramatically from 46,000 at the start of the 1990s (2.3% of TIV) and reflects a growing trend out of normal 4x2 saloons and estates and into 4x4 products to pursue outdoor activities, for towing, or simply for the secure and safe feeling they provide to owners and their families. The UK is the worlds third largest 4x4 market behind the US and Japan.

Achievements

Land Rover is one of the most famous car brands in the world – originated and manufactured in Britain but recognised worldwide as the four wheel drive vehicle of choice by individuals, companies, aid agencies and military forces alike. It is said that in some parts of the world, a Land Rover was the first car that people had ever seen.

Now in its 55th year, Land Rover has succeeded in creating not one but two distinctive sectors in the car market. With the original Land Rover (now Defender), it developed the market for a 'go anywhere' utility vehicle suitable for use in construction, forestry and agriculture – the original 'farmer's friend'.

The second was in 1970 with the launch of Range Rover. This original bridge between a car and a Land Rover rapidly developed the market for upmarket four wheel drive vehicles and today Range Rover is still arguably the world's only true luxury 4x4. An all new model was introduced in early 2002 to great acclaim.

In 2001 Land Rover sold a record 178,000 units worldwide, double the 90,000 unit volume of the mid 1990s. Central to this increase was the addition of a new smaller model, Freelander, and the latest generation of the Discovery. In the UK sales reached a record 45,000 in 2001, a 37% share of all 4x4 sales and 1.83% of all car sales in the UK – a great achievement for a manufacturer that makes only 4x4s.

A survey in 1999 by Interbrand and CitiBank created a league table of the most valuable British brands. The factors they measured included

economic profit, future earnings and other performance indicators. Land Rover appeared in tenth position, the only automotive brand in the top ten, providing conclusive proof that the Land Rover brand was an enormous asset. In June 2000 Ford Motor Company made this value tangible by paying BMW US$3 billion to acquire the Land Rover business.

History

Land Rover was created after World War II as the Directors of the Rover Car Company sought to develop new products to assist in the business's recovery and expansion. The Wilks brothers, Maurice and Spencer, the Engineering and Managing Directors respectively, hit on the idea of manufacturing a light four wheel drive utility vehicle. This would use many existing Rover car components but with a separate chassis, permanent four wheel drive, dual range transmission and a simple bodywork made from aluminium to get around the problem of steel rationing.

Launched at the Amsterdam Motor Show in April 1948 the Land Rover, as it was named, quickly became a huge success and production rapidly increased. The original open topped, utility vehicle featured a centre steering wheel but this was changed as additional models were added. Longer wheel bases, new engines and different styles, including station wagon versions were launched, and by 1966, 500,000 Land Rovers had been built.

By the mid 1960s Land Rover were also pursuing ideas for new models and in June 1970 the Range Rover was launched. It was fitted with Rover's 3.5 litre V8 Petrol engine, and long travel coil springs in place of the Land Rovers conventional leaf springs. While being just as rugged and capable off-road as its sister, the Range Rover also offered comfortable, high performance on-road motoring. It quickly became the undisputed king of the four wheel drive market, setting a trend towards more luxurious vehicles in this market sector.

1989 saw the introduction of the Land Rover Discovery, Land Rover's response to the growing number of Japanese four wheel drives now being bought for leisure usages. It was an enormous success, immediately becoming the UK's best selling 4x4. The latest addition to the family, Freelander, was launched in 1997 and became Europe's best selling 4x4 in its first full year of sales.

In 1978 Land Rover Limited was established as a separate autonomous subsidiary company within the nationalised British Leyland (BL) conglomerate. In 1982 Land Rover took over the whole of the Solihull Site in the West Midlands when Rover Car production moved to Cowley, Oxfordshire.

By the mid 1980s the British Government was anxious to complete the privatisation of BL. In 1986 it proposed to sell Land Rover to the American GM Group but this was to be abandoned in the face of massive public and parliamentary protests.

Finally British Aerospace bought the company, by then a closely integrated part of Rover Group in 1988. When BMW bought Rover Group from BAe in 1994, Land Rover was recognised as their main interest, widely regarded as 'The Jewel in the Crown' of the Rover Group. Ford subsequently paid BMW US$3 billion for Land Rover in June 2000. Land Rover joined Ford's Premier Automotive Group of prestige brands including Jaguar, Aston Martin and Volvo. Land Rovers are sold in 160 countries worldwide.

Product

Most car brands are one-dimensional. Customer choice is limited to a linear choice – same type of product, differing mainly in size and features – to move up the range as one's career/family develops, and possibly down again after retirement.

By contrast, Land Rover is a cluster brand, offering products for separate areas of the 4x4 market with deliberate concept differentiation and communication focus for each.

Land Rover's Brand Icon is Defender, an off-road vehicle designed primarily for functional and utility uses and providing extreme capability. It is trusted implicitly to perform in the world's toughest conditions.

The flagship of the brand is Range Rover. Peerless in its integration of comfort and capability, it epitomises 'tough luxury'.

At the centre of the brand is Discovery,

FREELANDER

a multi-use, seven seat product that combines outstanding design with new technology.

The volume product, Freelander, has attracted a whole new group of customers to the brand and to the Land Rover Experience. A modern 4x4 designed for the current demands of four wheel drive (4WD) leisure vehicles, Freelander was the best selling 4x4 in the UK and the whole of Europe in 2001.

All of Land Rovers products carry a number of common strengths and capabilities. In contrast to most competitor manufacturers, which are equipped with manually selected 4WD, all Land Rover products have permanent four wheel drive and have done so since 1984. This means that optimum control is always available in constantly changing surface conditions. Furthermore, all Land Rovers retain a command driving position, providing good forward vision and adding to the feeling of safety and security. Aluminium panel usage throughout Land Rover's development history has added to Land Rovers reputation for durability and longevity.

Land Rover has also been responsible for a number of significant innovations in 4WD technology as the brand continues to lead the market and stretch the envelope of on-road dynamics combined with off-road capability. Electronic air suspension now interconnected with new Range Rover, four channel ABS, twin airbags, four wheel Electronic Traction Control (ETC), Hill Descent Control (HDC), Active Cornering Enhancement (ACE) are all firsts which Land Rover have introduced into the four wheel drive sector or into the car market as a whole.

Recent Developments

In March 2002 an all new Range Rover was launched. Part of a £1 billion investment, this new vehicle was universally acclaimed by both customers and press alike, and was immediately voted Top Gear magazine's car of the year. All new from ground up, this vehicle combines the latest in on and off-road technology in a body shell reminiscent of the original Range Rover classic and the interior has rightly been praised by many as the finest in the automotive world. Range Rover's position as the 'best 4x4 bar none', and one of the world's great luxury cars was reasserted.

In September 2000 the Freelander range was expanded with the additional of a larger, more powerful 2.5 litre V6 engine, a new common rail 2.0 litre diesel engine and the availability of an

automatic transmission with (unique to sector) steptronic mode.

At the end of 1998 the Series II Discovery was launched, featuring an all new five cylinder 2.5 litre diesel engine and a number of new features. These include innovative folding, forward facing rear seats with three point belts for every passenger. This sophisticated four wheel drive product added new lamps and a new interior treatment in 2002 to keep it fresh.

The introduction of the five cylinder 2.5 litre direct injection diesel to Defender in 1999 added to its capability, while the addition of a one ten double cab version and several limited editions including a 'Tomb Raider' version, gave it new street cred.

There have also been extensive developments in the retail environment. The Land Rover Dealer network, one of the strongest in the industry, has invested over £120 million since 1997 in new or expanded facilities. This was needed to cope with the increased volumes which Freelander has brought, but also to create a 'Land Rover Retail Experience'. Extensive planting, rock features and use of other natural materials were used to 'bring the outdoors in'. Many centres also incorporate off-road demonstration areas.

Promotion

Through the 1990s with volumes increasing with the introduction of Discovery and Freelander, Land Rover has become much more of a mainstream car brand. Television advertising has featured more extensively in the mix, including the award winning Discovery launch ad 'Followers' and the Freelander 'Born Free' commercial. Rainey Kelly Campbell Roalfe/Y&R, the brand's agency since 2000, has also provided award winning work for Land Rover including 'Hippos'; a Freelander ad which won gold medals in the 'Campaign' Press and Poster Awards.

Long standing relationship marketing partners, Craik Jones, have worked with Land Rover for twelve years and their work on the brand has received many DMA and international awards. This direct customer contact and relationship building programme has been a valuable feature of Land Rover promotion and continues to be at the forefront of its communications.

Another key promotional tool is the Driving Experience. As well as a world renowned off-road track at its Solihull Factory, there is now a series of nine franchised operations throughout the country, offering different levels of off-road and driving tuition. Everyone who purchases a new vehicle receives a complimentary introductory off-road driving course at one of the centres.

As the brand has continued to develop, its reach has been extended to encompass 'Land Rover Gear', a range of clothing and merchandise sold in dealerships and selected high street stores. Land Rover's 'Adventure Zones' are highly visible off-road demonstration tracks which provide fun drives in a themed environment. The first of these was opened at the Bluewater retail park in June 2002.

Since 2001 the advertising strapline has been 'The Land Rover Experience'. This replaced the line 'The Best 4x4xFar' which had been used since 1985. This symbolises a new maturity for the Land Rover brand as it moves from simply selling products to providing life experiences for its owners.

Brand Values

From designing a product right through to the customer experience at a Land Rover Centre, the brand has a long-standing combination of values that it associates itself with. Namely authenticity, supremacy, sense of adventure and guts blended with rational factors such as 4x4 engineering, capability and heritage to create a powerful, distinctive personality.

Land Rover plans to increasingly develop the theme of 'Life's Greatest Outdoor Adventure' spanning the retail experience, staff knowledge and passion, communications materials, the driving experience, as well as the product expression.

www.landrover.com

lastminute.com

Market

The e-commerce retail market is fiercely competitive especially the travel and leisure sector where lastminute.com has successfully asserted its brand presence. It is Europe's leading independent travel company and 95% of its turnover by value derives from airline ticket sales, package holidays, hotel reservations and car hire.

Domestic breaks accounted for more than half of the 12.7 million holidays taken by UK consumers in 2001, but the number is forecast to rise to 15.6 million by 2006 (Source: Mintel 2002). At the same time seven out of ten people in the UK who browsed online, later went on to buy something in the third quarter of 2002 giving the market the highest buying to conversion rate in Europe (Source: Nielsen/Net Ratings). The most popular online purchases were flights, holiday accommodation and event tickets. Good news for lastminute.com one of the pioneers of e-commerce which is in a position to benefit from the nation's love of online shopping and leisure. When the brand launched in 1998 industry estimates suggested that a mere 7.5 million people had accessed the internet in the previous six months. By 2002 the number of adults accessing the web at least one a month had risen to 22.5 million adults or 48% of the population (Source: Forrester Research).

A mere four years after its inception lastminute.com is justly regarded as an established online travel and leisure provider and is well positioned to exploit the market further.

Achievements

Following the success of the UK website (www.lastminute.com) localised versions were launched in France, Germany, Italy, Sweden, Spain, The Netherlands, Australia, South Africa and Japan. This immense expansion has been reflected in figures that speak for themselves. By September 2002 the number of subscribers had reached 6.4 million, representing a 53% growth on the previous year and the brand had established 14,500 supplier relationships with companies such as Lufthansa, Air France, bmi british midland, United Airlines, Virgin Atlantic Airways, Starwood Hotels and Resorts Worldwide, Kempinski Hotels, Sol Melia, Six Continents, JMC, Disneyland Paris, English National Ballet, The Royal Albert Hall, Conran Restaurants and The Way Ahead Box Office. lastminute.com is the leading independent European travel and leisure site across six countries (Source: NetValue September 2002) and according to researcher BRMB the brand is the second most recognised e-commerce retailer in the UK. lastminute.com has slashed the cost of acquiring customers – a major financial headache for any brand – from £24 per customer in 2001 to just over £6 in 2002. The brand has won a string of plaudits which would be the envy of more established and traditional operations. They range from a Millennium Product award backed by the Design Council to an industry citation for the best use of new media for e-commerce in 2000. lastminute.com has established itself as a major international lifestyle e-commerce retailer with a formidable brand operating in twelve countries forecasting revenues of £500 million in 2003.

anytime, **anyplace, anywhere**

name the airport and we'll get you there

flight solutions at europe's most visited travel and leisure website*

*NetValue June 2002

do something
lastminute.com

History

Brent Hoberman co-founded lastminute.com with Martha Lane Fox in 1998. Brent had previously been a strategic consultant at Spectrum Strategy Consultants, where Martha also worked, and he was part of the team which founded QXL, the online auction site. The initial concept was to sell last minute holidays, restaurant bookings and gifts – hence the name – at the click of a mouse. The site, which formally launched in October 1998, was an immediate success. By the end of March 1999 over 90,000 people had registered with lastminute.com and more than 200 suppliers were offering their products and services through the site. Since then the company has witnessed tremendous growth.

Product

lastminute.com's strategic objective is to provide inspiration and solutions at the last minute. Having established a reputation as the home of last minute deals online, the brand is building its core proposition, developing into new areas and specialising in offering products and services which may be unavailable elsewhere. By leveraging existing technologies and capabilities lastminute.com has developed a framework for rapid expansion. Each local site benefits from shared supply, technology infrastructure, product development and marketing expenditure across borders. This global network enables lastminute.com to quickly establish mutually beneficial multinational supplier relationships.

do something to shOUT about

do something INspirational

Each regional site adds local character whilst strengthening and developing the global brand. It believes that alternative distribution platforms such as interactive digital television, mobile telephony and personal digital assistants are ideally suited to offer last minute deals. Consequently the brand has signed deals with a raft of companies – BskyB, Telewest, Vodafone, T-mobile, Orange and O2– to offer content using these channels. The brand intends to grow by introducing new products and services, expanding its network of suppliers and strategic partners and enhancing its technology. One example was a world first with the launch of a transactional voice recognition service in May 2002. The system allows people who are on the move but do not have access to the internet to book selected lastminute.com hotels by phone. Another is the interactive TV launch of its services on Sky Active, taking the brand into more than six million UK homes in 2003.

Recent Developments

The e-commerce market has changed and lastminute.com has also evolved. Most expansion has been through strategic acquisition and investment. The year 2002 witnessed considerable activity on all fronts. In January it announced the introduction of a new lastminute.com joint venture business in Japan, the world's second largest internet market where the travel market alone is worth £98.5 billion annually. The site, with two of the market's largest travel operators Kinki Nippon Tourist, the Nippon Travel Agency as main partners, went live in June. Its offerings include an extensive flight inventory supplied by more than 30 airlines, online access to more than 4,000 hotels and inns nationwide and 100 Tokyo restaurants. Within three months the site had attracted 65,000 subscribers. The brand's Australian joint venture partner began trading in New Zealand thereby extending reach to twelve countries. Elsewhere the brand consolidated its position as the leading European online travel and leisure solutions provider through a number of moves. In the UK it completed the acquisition of Travelselect.com in April for £9 million tripling flights volume and producing a further 27 key

airline relationships. The £12 million purchase of Destination Holdings Group in June 2002 enabled the brand to strengthen its product portfolio through tailor made city break and long haul holidays. The deal accelerated the group's delivery of 'dynamic packaging' which allows customers to tailor their own holiday using a select menu of hotels and flights. Simultaneously it formed a strategic alliance with Germany's LCC24.com the online vehicle for Lufthansa City Center. The site went live in October providing access to four million customers in 300 German cities. The following month the group bought e-tailer Travelprice.com for £32 million. Additionally in November it acquired eXhilaration, a UK-based experience provider, through a £1 million share-swap. Just four years after its launch the brand had undoubtedly become one of the standard bearers and an important barometer for the internet economy. This was reflected in November 2002 when lastminute.com announced its first modest profits.

Promotion

lastminute.com uses online and offline marketing to promote itself but, as with most brands, marketing expenditure was reduced (to around £22 million) in 2002 representing a 19% reduction from the previous year's figure of just over £27 million. The agreement with Sky Active, however, will enable the brand to target a far wider demographic than its traditional consumer, the affluent 25-44 year old urban professional. The interactive television deal meant the brand could offer virtually the entire online inventory. The deal helped underline lastminute.com's shift from awareness raising – it is one of the UK's most recognised dotcoms – to direct response selling. The lastminute.com newsletter remains central to the brand's promotional activities. The weekly bulletin is emailed to the site's 6.4 million subscribers worldwide. The newsletter, which has become a key marketing tool, reflects the brand's character and bulletins are customised to reflect the buying habits and interests of individual purchasers using sophisticated segmentation technology. This further enables lastminute.com to strengthen the emotional bond with the consumer.

Brand Values

For the consumer the company has developed a distinctive profile. The brand seeks to satisfy customers by providing great value, inspiration and solutions which is encapsulated by the mission statement "to become the number one European e-commerce lifestyle player". For the supplier lastminute.com carries almost no inventory risk, selling perishable inventory of its suppliers, in some instances protecting their brand names even after purchase.

www.lastminute.com

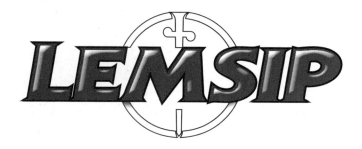

Market

Sore throat, cough, headache, runny nose – we all know and loathe the symptoms of the common cold. In the winter, 15% of the population is suffering from a cold during any week – a statistic which not only means a lot of sneezing, but also makes a major impact on the economy. It is estimated that seven million working days are lost in the UK every year because of colds and flu, with up to 70% of adults taking sick days (Source: U & A Project Deep December 1999).

So, it is not surprising that the market treating this condition is correspondingly large and highly competitive. The cold treatments market is worth £100 million in annual sales, the sore throat treatment sector constitutes another £90 million and we spend a further £94 million on cough treatments and £61 million on oral and nasal decongestants (Source: IR Data All Outlets Value Sales 52 w/e October 6th 2002).

Lemsip is a major player in this market, indeed it is the UK's number one selling cold and flu brand with a 36.8% market share (Source: IR Data All Outlets Value Sales 52 w/e October 6th 2002).

This is a fast-changing and innovation-led market, as more medicines are becoming consumer accessible. The main factor driving this is the increase in over the counter pharmaceutical sales, now accounting for £1.72 billion of sales per year. This trend towards self-medication means consumers are more aware than ever of over the counter (OTC) brands and are looking for products designed to alleviate symptoms quickly and conveniently. This is accentuated by a growing feeling amongst consumers that they must 'keep going' when they have a cold and that taking time off work is unacceptable.

These factors have influenced a lot of new product developments in the cold and flu treatment market, such as the introduction of Lemsip in capsules and an extra strength format. Being successful in this category means having a high brand awareness, combined with the ability to provide consumers with the means to treat symptoms whenever and however is most convenient.

Achievements

Not only has Reckitt Benckiser built Lemsip into the UK's biggest selling cold and flu brand, it leads a highly competitive pack by some distance. Beechams, the second largest brand, is nearly ten percentage points behind Lemsip's share of the market, with 27.2%. Lemsip is growing at a rate of 1.7% year on year and achieving its highest ever market share, while the cold treatments category is in decline by 3% year on year (Source: IR Data All Outlets Value Sales 52 w/e October 6th 2002).

So, not only is Lemsip increasing brand presence, but also stealing share from its closest rivals, cold and flu, which are all in decline.

The brand's success can be partly attributed to adroitly developing products to match emerging consumer needs. For example, the launch of Lemsip Cold + Flu Max Strength in 1995, perfectly fitted the trend for people who wanted to get back to work as quickly as possible. The maximum strength formulation was positioned as a way to 'keep

going', or to minimise the level of debilitation by a cold. The result of this is that Max Strength is now the biggest selling cold and flu winter range and continues to drive the brand's growth six years after its launch. It is now worth over 50% of all Lemsip sales in pharmacy and grocery (Source: IR Data All Outlets Value Sales 52 w/e October 6th 2002) is the fastest selling range in the market and has greatly increased overall loyalty to the Lemsip brand.

Excellence in marketing has also helped keep Lemsip ahead. For example, the poster campaign for Lemsip Cold + Flu Max Strength Capsules won three bronze awards at the 2000 HAAG Awards. And its outdoor advertising campaign in winter 2001-2002 was shortlisted for Response-Driven Campaign of the Year in the 2002 Media Week Awards. Working with the media agency, OMD, Reckitt Benckiser's marketing team developed a

model which could forecast peaks in cold and flu incidence at 95% accuracy. Usually able to predict incidence with eight weeks notice, the media strategy could be planned for when it would have maximum impact. The strategy is thought to have helped the brand achieve a 3% gain in the 2001/02 season, equating to £3 million in additional sales (Source: IR Data All Outlets Value Sales 52 w/e October 6th 2002).

History

Lemsip was launched by Reckitt Benckiser (then Reckitt & Colman) in 1969. At the time, it was the UK's first medicated hot drink, specially formulated to relieve the symptoms of cold and flu. The brand was designed to compete with the market leader at the time, Beechams Powders, which had been on the market since the 1930s. LEM-SIP, as it was then known, offered a new alternative as an effective treatment, based on a real medicine, but in a tasty drink.

By 1975, thanks to its clearly differentiated position, Lemsip had grown rapidly and commanded a 29% value-share of the UK cold market. The growth was also bolstered by Lemsip's highly creative advertising, which differed significantly from the style of Reckitt Benckiser's competitors. Beechams then countered with Hot Blackcurrant and Hot Lemon drinks in the early 1970s. In turn, Reckitt Benckiser (RB) responded by changing the name of its product from LEM-SIP to Lemsip and redesigned the packaging to feature the ingredients as well as the famous 'sword in a glass' logo. It also introduced Junior Lemsip; in 1972.

In the 1980s, Lemsip responded to consumer demand for more varied cold and flu remedies by launching new products, such as blackcurrant Lemsip, and the Lemsip cough range. It also unveiled a new better-tasting Lemsip lemon formulation advertised as Lemsip Best Ever.

The 1990s proved vitally important in the development of the brand. A key factor was the launch, in 1991, of Lemsip Cold Relief Capsules. Capsules and tablets were dominant in the US cold relief market and there was a clear opportunity in the UK. However, Lemsip was so associated with hot drinks that RB feared consumers would not accept the brand extending into solid dose formats. The move did however prove to be a success.

RB also learned from the US that there was consumer demand for more flu-specific remedies, with more powerful analgesics to combat symptoms. As a result, RB launched Lemsip Flu Strength Pseudoephedrine Formula in the year of the flu epidemic, 1993 and indeed the 1993 flu epidemic saw Lemsip's sales reach a peak, at £16.7 million.

Research in the 1990s showed that Lemsip needed a change in positioning; from a benign friendly comforter (likened to a 'hug in a mug'), to an effective, fast-working medicine (likened to an 'empathetic expert'). The launches of Lemsip Pharmacy Power + Rapid Ibuprofen and Lemsip Cold + Flu Max Strength were the first manifestation of this thinking. Lemsip Power + was withdrawn after a year, but Lemsip Cold + Flu Max Strength was a runaway success. One of the keys to Max Strength's success was its focus on the grocery distribution channel, allowing consumers to 'self-select' the product. As a pharmacy-only brand, Power + was seen as too inaccessible.

Continuous improvement to the range in the late 1990s saw further modifications to the pack design and more extensions, such as the launch of Max Strength Capsules in 1998.

1999 marked an important milestone in the company's history, as RB was officially formed following the merger of Reckitt & Colman plc

and Benckiser NV to become the world's largest household cleaning company, with sales in 180 countries and a powerful portfolio of leading brands, including Lemsip.

Product

Over the years, the Lemsip range has evolved to provide consumers with the full range of cold and flu treatments. It is available in enough varied forms to suit different ages and for maximum convenience in order to fit in with people's busy, varied lives. Whether it's as a hot drink, a capsule, an elixir or even a non-medicine patch, Lemsip has a product to fit the requirement.

Overall, the Lemsip range is now split into Children's, Pharmacy Only, General Sales (Max and Original), Sore Throat, Cough and Sinus.

Lemsip Cold + Flu Original Lemon remains a key part of the range, but the hot drink is also available in blackcurrant, in a special Lemsip Cold + Flu Breathe Easy formulation and in the Max Strength variant. The capsules range encompasses Max Strength and Lemsip Pharmacy Powercaps.

There are also two Lemsip Sore Throat Anti-bacterial Lozenges (contains hexylresorcinol), Lemsip Pharmacy Flu Strength hot drink sachets for sale in pharmacies and two liquid cough formulations, Lemsip Cough + Cold Chesty Cough Medicine (contains guaifenesin) and Dry Cough Medicine. New Vapo Patches, a non-medicine product, are designed to stick to children's pyjamas, releasing vapours of menthol and camphor.

Recent Developments

Lemsip continues to expand and improve its range, most recently entering the decongestant/sinus relief category with Lemsip Max Strength Sinus Relief Capsules. The over the counter (OTC) product was launched in September 2002 and is positioned

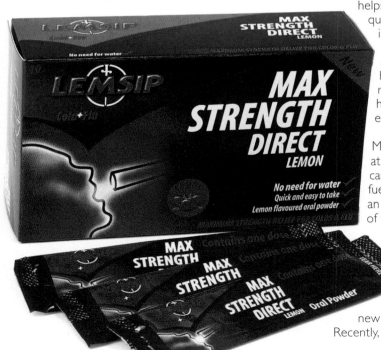

as a direct competitor to Sudafed Dual Relief.

Another important new launch is Lemsip Cold + Flu Max Strength Direct Lemon. This is designed to match consumers' need for more convenient formats to suit their busy lifestyles. It also reflects that 79% of cold and flu remedy purchases are made when ill (Source: U & A Project Deep December 1999). Often they are a 'distress' purchase and need to be in a format that the consumer can take straight away.

In a hi-tech development which is the ultimate in convenience, the lemon-tasting micro granules of Cold + Flu Max Strength Direct can be poured directly onto the tongue and are designed not to be taken with water. Having performed extremely well in consumer tests, particularly for its taste and convenience, Cold + Flu Max Strength Direct was launched in November 2002 (always read the label).

Promotion

Lemsip has a long and illustrious history of marketing, the success of which has set the brand apart from the competition. Over the years, the emphasis of the brand's marketing has evolved.

At first, it was an ingredient-focused theme, lasting from 1969 to 1976, with the famous 'Brain' TV commercial, which associated relief of each cold symptom with a relevant Lemsip ingredient. The tagline of the time was 'Lemsip – for your head, nose and throat'.

The strategy then switched to Lemsip's comforting and soothing qualities, such as the 1980s ad 'Armchair' in which an armchair is seen to get bigger, providing more comfort, after a Lemsip is taken.

More recently, the message has switched to position Lemsip as a powerful medicine which helps you get back to normal life quicker. With consumers increasingly feeling that taking days off for a cold is seen as shirking by colleagues, Lemsip has positioned itself as the remedy for 'Hard-working heroes' who want to keep going, even if they are suffering a cold.

The commercials for Lemsip Max Strength show this concept at work, especially the 2000 TV campaign featuring a testosterone-fuelled duel between two men in an office. Thanks to Lemsip, one of the men had managed to clinch a vital deal, even though he was recovering from the flu. The tagline, 'Hard working medicine – because life doesn't stop', summarises the new 'get on with it' positioning. Recently, the launches of Lemsip Cold +

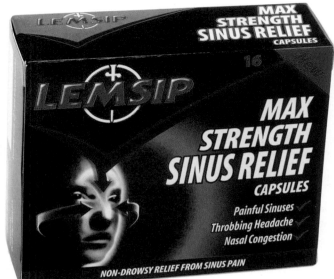

Flu Max Strength Direct Lemon and Lemsip Max Strength Sinus Relief Capsules have been supported with major advertising campaigns, each entailing an investment of £1.75 million. The Lemsip Cold + Flu Max Strength Direct Lemon outdoor and TV advertising campaign is called 'Just Swallow', while the ads promoting Lemsip Max Strength Sinus Relief Capsules feature an 'Iron Mask' theme. Both campaigns ran between November 2002 and February 2003.

Brand Values

Lemsip's personality is based on the fact that it really works and, by that rational, is a totally credible expert that keeps you going when you need it most. Lemsip's 'Hug in a Mug', soothing and reliable positioning first introduced in 1969 still reflects the Original range today. However, the brand has been developed to include the Max Strength range which is described as 'Hard Working Medicine'. This aims to reflect Lemsip's understanding of the pressures of modern lives and that people now need to 'keep going' when they are ill.

Key to the Lemsip brand is its provision of an efficacious solution to illness, delivered in a variety of innovative and convenient formats.

www.lemsip.com

The **BrandCouncil**

Market

The British have a passion for chocolate. We eat 181g per head a week which puts us second only to Germany in terms of consumption. The UK confectionery market is worth an estimated £5.18 billion and sales of chocolate account for £3.49 billion, equivalent to 554,000 tonnes (Source: Mintel 2002).

Over the years, the chocolate confectionery sector has significantly changed. The war time notion that chocolate was a luxury product has been gradually replaced by the idea that it is an everyday treat. It satisfies a number of needs ranging from being comforting to producing energy. Busy lifestyles and an increasing need for on-the-go consumption has driven producers to create new formats and chocolate brands have extended into non-confectionery sectors such as bakery and ice-cream. Maltesers is no exception in its determination to satisfy demand, so it is hardly surprising that this traditional brand remains a firm favourite with chocolate lovers.

Maltesers is part of Masterfoods, a division of the US$13 billion company owned and controlled by the Mars family. It became the new trading identity when Mars Confectionery and Masterfoods merged in January 2002.

Achievements

Maltesers biggest achievement is its domination of the UK bitesize market. Worth £503 million, of which the brand owner of Maltesers, Masterfoods, enjoys a 52% market share. Maltesers is the number one bitesize brand worth £125 million and the nearest competitor is worth £42.7 million. However that competitor is Galaxy Minstrels, another Masterfoods brand. Thus Maltesers continued success is a driving force in the growth of the sector.

History

Maltesers has been a firm favourite with the British public since MARS bar creator, Forrest E

Mars, launched the crunchy malt-centred chocolate covered balls in 1936. This young American, who had established a factory in Slough four years earlier, decided the brand's strapline should be 'the dri-drink' which was further described as 'all the fun and frothiness of a malt drink but encased in chocolate'. Since then its 'light' characteristic has been played upon and the brand has been positioned as a light, indulgent product for women. Maltesers, like its sister brand MARS bar, was an instant hit with British consumers who, at the time, were unused to such innovative products – most chocolate was only available in simple blocks.

Production was discontinued during World War II due to wartime rationing, however the brand reappeared on the shelves in 1951.

Maltesers was then launched in Ireland in 1959 and used the strapline 'Chocolates with the less fattening centre'.

Interestingly, three years later, Mintesers was introduced. This was a very early product extension – like Maltesers but mint flavoured. The product didn't however take off at the time and were discontinued in 1964.

Over the years the brand has been successfully introduced to a number of markets, namely Canada, China, Hong Kong, The Netherlands, France, Denmark, Poland, Germany, Italy, New Zealand, Taiwan and Korea. In 1997 it was the Swedish public's turn to decide whether they should crunch Maltesers or suck the chocolate off first.

In 1999 the brand's commitment to corporate social responsibility was reflected through its support for Comic Relief. As a result the brand was given an award for excellence.

Product

Maltesers are bitesize portions of smooth chocolate with a light textured malt centre sold in one portion size bags. This formula has, over the brands long history, been the foundation for new product development. One very successful innovation is the 'family bag', launched in 1983. The success of this format led to an even larger bag being introduced a year later. Aware that social gatherings are an ideal occasion for chocolate sharing and consumption, the Maltesers box format was first introduced in 1985. Ten years later the larger 275g box was added to the range.

A further development was seen in 1987 when the Maltesers Easter egg was introduced to coincide with the brand's 50th birthday.

More recently, reflecting the renaissance of cinema going and the idea of 'togetherness' when watching a film, whether on the big screen or at home on television, the Maltesers tub was introduced in theatres and video outlets in 2000. The paperboard pots, made to resemble ice cream tubs, have a resealable plastic lid which helps to keep product fresh. Furthermore, in order to exploit the brand's popularity, various special edition packs have also been introduced.

Recent Developments

One of Maltesers' strengths has been an awareness that it is viewed by many as a comforting product.

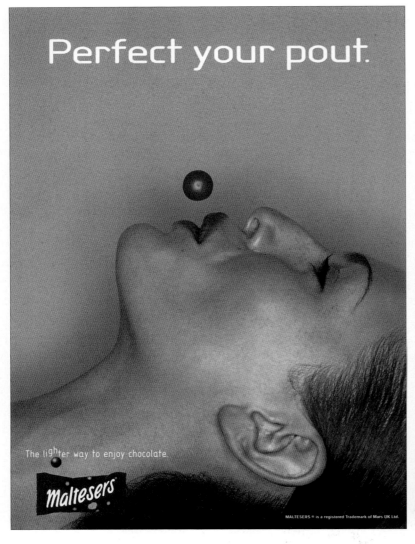

Perfect your pout.

The lighter way to enjoy chocolate.

Maltesers

MALTESERS ® is a registered Trademark of Mars UK Ltd.

Accentuate your cheekbones.

The lighter way to enjoy chocolate.

Maltesers

MALTESERS ® is a registered Trademark of Mars UK Ltd.

Therefore, a natural progression was to make the brand available as a beverage. Maltesers hot chocolate malt drink was launched in 2001, enabling women (who form Maltesers target market) to enjoy the confectionery that they know and are fond of, in the form of a drink. Once again the product has implied connotations of sharing the drink as a social activity.

The brand has also reflected the need to satisfy children who, despite growing levels of sophistication, still rank chocolates and sweets second only to toys as their most important purchases. In 2002 Easter eggs with Maltesers pips in the shell were launched. The same year witnessed the introduction of Maltesers ice cream in tubs, primarily for use in the home or on sticks (which are more versatile as they can be eaten on the move). Reflecting changes in consumer lifestyle, the formats were specifically designed to appeal to more leisurely, sharing moments or, as a quick, convenient snack at home or on the go.

Promotion

Chocolate sales are mainly dependant on impulse purchases and consumers usually buy a brand that is at the forefront of their mind. Consequently, almost 75% of ad spend within the sector (which totalled £93.2 million in 2001) is broadcast during peak viewing times. Maltesers is the second biggest sector advertiser, spending more than £2.1 million in 2001 and £5.1 million in 2002 reflecting its importance in the market (Source: Mintel 2002).

Maltesers first strapline, 'the dri-drink' appeared in 1936, although the brand did not use television until 1963. The notion that Maltesers was a light, enjoyable snack product has been

a key feature of its advertising ever since. In 1967 the strapline 'Chocolates with the lightweight centres' was devised and by 1977 copywriters perfected the famous 'It's the honeycomb middle that weighs so little'. This was followed in 1982 by the similarly memorable, 'The lighter way to enjoy chocolate' strapline and in 1988 by 'The light fantastic'.

The celebrated and much loved 'Wide Mouthed Frog' animated commercial made its debut in 1991 and a new generation of humorous ads (namely, 'Feed Me', 'Roller' and 'UFO'), made their debut in 1999. 'UFO' featured a child's toy floating a Malteser on it which, in a light-hearted way, enhanced the brand's 'light' credentials. Today's commercials also take the humour route, often using bizarre situations, but conveying the message that Maltesers is a fun product that can be enjoyed anytime. 'Balance' features two workmates trying to do just that with two of the malt-honeycomb covered balls. 'Straw' features a young man attempting to pass a Malteser to his girlfriend with a straw while they watch television. While 'Cruncher or Sucker?' is set in an office kitchen where two women are discussing the merits of crunching through the chocolate ball, or allowing it to dissolve on the

tongue. 'Camping', which started airing in 2002, has featured a series of scenarios with three young women in a tent. Despite typically awful British weather the trio find fun ways of eating Maltesers to pass the time and lift their spirits, as well as showing Maltesers as a comforting product.

Maltesers took the same humorous route in its ads for Maltesers ice cream in summer 2002 which showed a woman taking an enormous bite of her friend's ice cream.

The new wave of comedy orientated advertising encouraged the brand to sponsor The Comedy Awards to continue their emphasis that the brand is a fun, enjoyable product. Additionally it sponsored Maltesers Movie Nights on television film channel Sky Premiere during the European Cup football championships. The idents featured two Maltesers sitting in the cinema discussing the end-of-film credits. A Maltesers website (www.drinkmaltesers.com) is in development.

Brand Values

Maltesers' personality is to be approachable, light-hearted and empathetic. The brand has three basic attributes. It aims to be at the centre of women's light-hearted moments. It is the lighter way to enjoy chocolate and finally it is a comfort brand for 'sharing good times'.

www.maltesers.com

The BrandCouncil

MARKS & SPENCER

Market

For its population size, the UK has an unusually large number of department and variety stores in contrast to most other sectors of the British retail market with sales in excess of £200 million (Source: Mintel 2002). These cover many different types of retailers from the full range department stores to fashion focused department stores, general stores, catalogue showrooms and finally, price-led generalists.

Marks & Spencer falls into the general store category and operates across a wide range of retail markets; from clothing, accessories and footwear to food, homeware and financial services. It therefore faces competition from a vast array of players within each area.

a local wholesaler, Isaac Dewhirst, to enable him to buy fresh stock and set up a stall in Leeds market. His first advertising slogan was straight to the point, it stated 'Don't ask the price – it's a penny.'

Less than ten years on, Marks was operating a chain of stalls across the north east. He formed a partnership with Tom Spencer, a cashier at the IJ Dewhurst wholesale company, which accelerated the growth of the business. The family's involvement in the company continued when Michael's son, Simon Marks, was named as a director in 1911 and became chairman during World War I. During this period the Marks & Spencer penny price point disappeared. In 1917 Simon Marks was joined on the board by his friend and brother-in-law Israel

Boulevard Haussmann in Paris (which has recently been sold to Group Galeries Lafayette). In the UK, further expansion in the 1980s led to the opening of the first Marks & Spencer edge-of-town store at the Metro Centre, Gateshead. The establishment of Marks & Spencer Financial Services led to the launch of the Marks & Spencer Chargecard in 1985. The company continued to expand internationally, until in March 2001 it announced its intention to focus on the UK retail market and to sell its stores in continental Europe and Brooks Brothers and Kings Supermarkets in the US.

Marks & Spencer retains a presence overseas through its stores in the Republic of Ireland and Hong Kong, and has 130 franchises in around 30 countries across the world. In the UK,

Achievements

Over the course of several decades Marks & Spencer built a reputation for being the store of choice for the British middle classes to purchase items ranging from underwear to shoes and sandwiches to gifts. Marks & Spencer also has a long-established reputation as a British institution, relied upon for quality, value and service. However, over the last five years it has battled with major challenges to reaffirm its position as one of the UK's premier high street brands.

A recent readjustment of its business strategy, while continuing to focus on its core values, has rejuvenated the brand. Indeed, in November 2002 the company posted a 7.9% jump in overall sales and a 41.1% rise in operating profit. Chairman Luc Vandevelde said that the company had "moved from securing to sustaining the recovery".

History

Marks & Spencer was founded by a young Russian refugee, Michael Marks, who arrived in England in the early 1880s. He started out selling haberdashery from a tray in the villages close to the industrial centre of Leeds. However, he had ambitious plans and borrowed £5 from

Sieff. Together they were to chart the next stage in Marks & Spencer's history. Both became chairman of the company at different stages and were later granted peerages.

During the 1920s, the company introduced the revolutionary practice of buying stock direct from manufacturers, thereby forming long-lasting, close relationships with suppliers, several of which have continued into the present day. Many of the ground rules, which have been key to the company's success, were initiated at this time by Marks and Sieff. In 1928 the company registered the St Michael trademark which distinguished all Marks & Spencer goods. The introduction of retail branding reassured consumers that Marks & Spencer products had a specific quality guarantee. The company grew at a rapid rate, opening its flagship Marble Arch store in Oxford Street, London, in 1930.

One of the aims of Marks & Spencer was to take care of its staff as well as its customers. As a result it set up an in-company Welfare Department in the early 1930s. After World War II – during which over a hundred stores were damaged – the company underwent a period of rapid expansion.

In 1975 it opened its first European store on,

the company employs 60,000 people.

At the end of the 1990s, changing shopping trends and increasing competition began to challenge sales at Marks & Spencer. For the first time, a brand that had previously been able to attract customers with little or no advertising began to feel the pressure of intensifying competition.

The company reacted and in January 2000 brought in new Chairman Luc Vandevelde who had built up the successful French supermarket chain Promodes – to stop the slide and take Marks & Spencer back to the top. Two years later, he had succeeded in sustaining the company's recovery and in 2002 was named Business Leader of the Year in the first National Business Awards and received The Sunday Telegraph's Corporate Giant Award.

Vandevelde's strategy had operated on a number of different fronts. At a corporate level, the company sold its loss-making operations in Europe as well as its Brooks Brothers brand in the US. A restructured balance sheet enabled it to return £2 billion to shareholders, while laying the groundwork for future growth.

Things have also been changing in the stores. After working with a number of fashion designers over the years, Marks & Spencer turned to George

Davies, the man behind Next, to tempt younger customers with his per una range. Yasmin Yusuf was also recruited from Warehouse to become Head of Clothing Design, concentrating on the look, style and appeal of womenswear. Marks & Spencer was once again a strong player in the mid-market style arena.

Another important aspect of the turnaround was the 'Perfect' campaign, which promoted the chain's high-quality, everyday wardrobe staples – from a white blouse to a black roll-neck sweater – while stressing their affordability. The company also worked on improving the fit of its clothing, based on a comprehensive survey of 2,500 female customers. Menswear and lingerie were equally transformed.

At the same time, the brand began to renew or 'refresh' its stores, presenting a more contemporary face to customers. This included improved visual merchandising, the use of dressed mannequins, clearer product segmentation, better lighting and devoting more space to the brand's Home and Beauty concepts. Importantly, more Café Revives were introduced into stores – at the beginning of 2001 there were 94 in-store cafés serving 500,000 customers a week. The company expects this to grow to more than 150 cafés before the end of 2003.

In addition, the website has been updated and expanded, with the result that it is now one of the top three retail sites in the UK.

Marks & Spencer also offers formal wear, View From performance sports wear and the Autograph range for men. The recent introduction of an 'urban survival' suit – crease-free and designed for everyday comfort – has proved as popular with male customers as the innovative machine-washable suits introduced a few seasons ago.

Children's clothes are also in the process of being revamped thanks to the Zip project – a joint venture with long-standing supplier Desmond & Sons. This created a single organisation to design and produce the brand's children's wear, bringing clothes into stores faster and reducing costs, thus improving prices for the customers and margins for the company. In addition, the boy's wear range was given a boost in September 2002 with the launch of DB07, the David Beckham range, which the football hero helps design and promote.

In food, Marks & Spencer launches 1,000 new lines each year – about 30% of the products it sells. It recently celebrated 21 years in the sandwich business with its Chef Specials, a gourmet range developed by six of the UK's top chefs. Marks & Spencer also leads other retailers in food integrity by reducing the use of pesticides and by using only free-range eggs in its products. Marks & Spencer recently won the British Sandwich Retailer of the Year award from The British Sandwich Association and was named Compassionate Supermarket of the Year 2002 by the animal welfare group Compassion in World Farming.

Ronnie Barker, Sean Bean, David Beckham, Cat Deeley, Graham Norton and Hermione Norris. The company also ran a food campaign to remind consumers about the premium quality of its produce, meat and fish. High-profile launches of new clothing ranges have also kept the Marks & Spencer brand in the public eye.

On a different note, Marks & Spencer has been quietly attracting plaudits with its focus on environmental performance, social responsibility and sustainability. The company is the highest ranked general retailer in the Business in the Environment FTSE 300 Index and is due to publish a wide-ranging CSR report in the summer of 2003. Featured initiatives include the company's involvement in the Prince's Trust – which enables managers to develop new skills while working for charity – and work placements for homeless people, helping them to re-establish themselves in society. The company donates unsold food to a wide range of charities and is a member of the PerCent club, under which it contributes at least 1% of its annual pre-tax profits to community investment.

Brand Values

Marks & Spencer's long-established brand values date back to the time of Simon Marks and Israel Sieff, and are summed up quite simply as 'quality, value, service, innovation and trust'.

www.marksandspencer.com

All this activity has renewed faith in Marks & Spencer and brought lapsed customers back; as well as generating a raft of positive press coverage.

Product

Marks & Spencer's cornerstones have always been quality and affordability, blended with a distinctive look that is stylish, modern but also timeless. It remains a clear market leader in lingerie and in adult clothing as a result of an injection of extra flair into its clothing lines. While designers such as Betty Jackson, Sonja Nuttall and Anthony Symonds are contributing to the brand's success through the Autograph sub-brand, George Davies' per una has proved popular with younger, fashion conscious customers. Women have additionally benefited from the launch of Shapewear, lingerie which improves and controls body shape and the designer ranges of Salon Rose (designed by Agent Provocateur) and Wild Heart (designed by Colette Dinnigan).

Meanwhile, the brand has introduced a new range of casual wear for men, Blue Harbour. This combines classic 'New England' style with Marks & Spencer quality in the shape of merchandise including polo and rugby shirts and cotton knitwear.

Recent Developments

As well as improving its core business, Marks & Spencer has developed new product areas. In autumn 2001 it trialled five 'Classic Collection' shops in its stores with such success that another 170 will be introduced in 2003. The Classic Collection is aimed at women who are looking for a traditional, timeless look.

The company has also piloted a new style of high street food store, Simply Food. This format has been created to take Marks & Spencer's quality food offer to locations which are more convenient for their customers. The first two opened in Surbiton and Twickenham in July 2001, followed by three outlets at mainline railway stations in a joint venture with the Compass Group. There are now plans to open 150 Simply Food outlets in railway and High Street locations across the country over the next three years.

Promotion

While Marks & Spencer is a household name, it has recently been making sure that consumers do not take it for granted. The 2002 Christmas advertising campaign featured celebrities who are fans of the brand, such as Denise Van Outen,

Market

The chocolate confectionery market in the UK is very mature and in recent years has developed into an increasingly competitive sector. The past few decades have seen the introduction of a plethora of products suited to everyday consumer purchases resulting in category developments such as eat now, take home, family sharing and gifts. The UK confectionery market is worth over £3.5 billion a year. Whilst sugar confectionery has grown faster than chocolate in recent years, chocolate still accounts for around £2 billion of confectionery sales.

The MARS bar is the pioneer of chocolate bars and remains one of Britain's biggest brands. It's the UK's number one selling single chocolate bar and has been since records began. The diversity of formats and pack sizes and continuing product development ensures that MARS keeps pace with changing consumer need in this market.

In April 2002, in the face of growing competition and a mature market, the MARS bar relaunched with a new look and new strapline 'Pleasure You Can't Measure'. This was created to reflect the 'indescribable' taste and enjoyment that people often attribute to eating a MARS bar. It was recognised that people's needs have changed and there was a need to move the MARS bar away from its traditional hefty image of a sustenance product to that of one of life's little treats. A fresh approach was required to take the brand forward to a wider audience through more emotional territory. The new development makes the MARS bar more contemporary, appealing to both men and women, while still retaining its loyal fans.

Achievements

By far, the MARS bar's biggest achievement in the UK is that it has an enduring quality and remains the best selling single chocolate bar ever since its launch in 1932. The MARS bar has reached iconic status over the last seven decades in Britain. Today over 95% of the UK population has eaten a MARS bar and UK production stands at three million bars a day.

History

When the MARS bar was first introduced to the British public, it was a chocolate recipe never seen before in the UK. At that time most chocolate was produced as simple solid blocks.

The MARS bar however combined for the first time layers of nougat, caramel and thick milk chocolate.

In May 1932, a young American, Forrest E Mars arrived in the UK with a recipe for a new chocolate bar – the MARS bar. He rented a small factory in Slough and registered the new company as Mars Confections Ltd.

In June of that year, the now famous MARS bar trademark was registered and within months the factory was fully operational.

The first MARS bar was made by hand on August Bank Holiday Monday 1932. By December, just four months after opening, there were over one hundred people working for Mars. The first year saw over two million MARS bars made in Slough.

The first MARS bar sold for 2d and the current price of 29p is roughly the same in real terms. In fact, an article in the Financial Times in 1981 entitled 'How MARS bar Defeats Inflation' described the bar as 'a currency of our time' and since then

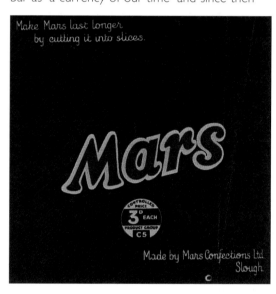

the MARS bar has been used as an indicator of the true value of the pound. It has also been used for price comparisons by organisations ranging from investment companies to the British Antique Collector's Club.

During World War II, production was maintained and MARS bars were supplied to the Allied armed forces. Wartime rationing brought moderate changes to the recipe. Concerned

about customers' views on this recipe change, Mars commissioned a survey in the early 1940s and was delighted that the general public was more than happy with the MARS bar.

The survey also revealed that people cut their MARS bar into little pieces to make it last longer. This led to the introduction of the MARS FUN SIZE bars years later.

In 1941 there was a shortage of gold ink for wrappers and thus the gold disappeared temporarily from the logo.

In the late 1940s Mars introduced the first 'self-service display', making confectionery more accessible, thus unlocking the 'impulse' market. However, rationing was still in effect in the UK in the early 1950s. By 1953 the end of rationing was officially announced and one man was so delighted, that he announced to the world that he would eat a MARS bar 'morning, noon and night', which he did – until his wartime supply dried up.

1953 saw the Coronation and the MARS bar was ready. Mars was the only confectioner to take advertising space to coincide with the big day. These ads gave the MARS bar a massive 50% increase in sales which, for the first time, passed the £10 million mark.

During the 1960s Mars introduced one of the most famous slogans in TV advertising history – 'A MARS a Day Helps You Work, Rest and Play', this captured the public's imagination well into the 1970s and 1980s.

In 1982 the MARS bar celebrated its Golden Jubilee and a special logo was introduced on pack – it became the first confectionery brand to achieve sales of more than £100 million.

During the 1990s the MARS bar was also associated with key sporting events through the sponsorship of the British team at the Barcelona Olympics in 1992 and the Football World Cup in the US in 1994.

Product

Over the years, to complement the original bar, various additions have been developed. In 1972 the MARS FUN SIZE was introduced and in 1985 came MARS King Size, with MARS SNACK SIZE following in 1988.

In the late 1980s Mars introduced MARS bar flavoured milk drinks and ice cream; a MARS bar dessert is

also now available. The MARS bar is also included in the CELEBRATIONS range of boxed chocolates, which includes other miniature chocolates, such as SNICKERS and BOUNTY bars.

The MARS Easter egg is produced on a seasonal basis and is currently one of the top five Easter Eggs on the market. Limited edition bars have also become a regular addition to the MARS range e.g. Dark & Gold.

The hugely popular MARS King Size also saw a change at the end of 2000, relaunching as MARS Big One.

Recent Developments

In 2002 the MARS bar relaunch saw a small technical change in the way the product is manufactured and although the ingredients remain the same the

By 1945, Mars introduced the slogan 'MARS are Marvellous' with a shift in emphasis to the taste.

When commercial television arrived in 1955, Mars was one of the first companies to take advantage of the new medium. Petula Clark, Bob Monkhouse and Richard Murdoch took part in the 'Stars Love MARS' advertisements.

In 1959 came the use of the now famous slogan 'A MARS a Day, Helps You Work, Rest and Play'. At the time the Account Manager at Mars' advertising agency was Formula One racing commentator, Murray Walker and he is often credited with inventing this strapline. However it was actually penned by a team of copywriters and has since become known worldwide.

1969 saw the first colour MARS bar commercial, and in 1973 the introduction of a 'jingle' to go

dedicated to driving home the new MARS bar strapline 'Pleasure You Can't Measure'. This slogan suggests that the MARS bar is one of life's 'simple everyday pleasures' and can be likened to popping bubble wrap or receiving a text message. Moments that are not necessarily life changing, but are simply enjoyable. TV, poster, and press advertising executions focused on communicating everyday simple pleasures were developed. The campaign was further supported by an extensive sales promotion and public relations programme. This relaunch of one of the biggest UK brands was a big news story and generated substantial print and broadcast coverage. Sales figures and consumer research following the relaunch demonstrate that the new look MARS bar has been well received by consumers around the country.

trademark nougat is now whipped more to increase the feeling of lightness. This was in recognition of the fact that now people eat chocolate for enjoyment more than for sustenance. Although the familiar MARS red, gold and black remained the packaging was also contemporised to feature a more flowing modern looking logo.

The recent relaunch demonstrates the MARS bar's ability to move with the times and continue to adapt to meet consumer demand and appeal to British chocolate lovers.

Promotion

The MARS bar first advertised in print in the late 1930s, in an advertisement which reflected its nutritional values. Slogans included 'Packed with Nourishment', 'MARS for Energy' and 'Grand Food – Grand Flavour'.

with the MARS advertising slogans. But throughout, it was the family values and 'wholesome goodness' of the MARS bar ingredients that were the focus in the advertising campaigns.

In the 1980s, however, there was a shift from family values to the bar's values. The 'Biggest MARS bar ever' campaign ran with the 69g Jubilee bar, and advertising made announcements, such as 'In any job, whatever its size, you'll find the Biggest MARS bar ever comes in handy'.

One of the most successful promotional campaigns produced by Mars was the 1999 'MARS – Make It Happen' campaign. This made 140 'dreams come true' for winning consumers, generated £4 million of media coverage and created high levels of consumer awareness of the MARS bar.

The 2002 MARS bar relaunch and repositioning was backed by a £7.5 million advertising campaign

Brand Values

MARS bar is associated with the tangible assets of being of high quality as well as good value for money, which are as important to the product today as it was in 1932.

The brand has however also built more intangible assets to assert a more emotionally based link with consumers. These personality traits include spontaneity, unpretentiousness and generosity.

www.mars.com

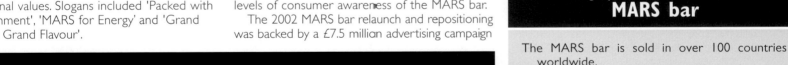

Things you didn't know about MARS bar

The MARS bar is sold in over 100 countries worldwide.

The total number of MARS bars sold in the last 70 years is estimated at 60 billion.

It takes fifteen helium balloons to lift a MARS bar (standard size 62.5g).

Pensioner Mary Scarfe, from Bournemouth, who turned 101 years old in 2002, claims to have eaten a MARS bar every day of her life since 1932.

Paul Tucker a former army major from Mersea Island crossed the English Channel in a pedalo in May 2002 surviving only on MARS bars and water.

It would take the Slough factory only 4.5 days to produce sufficient MARS bars to stretch end to end from Lands End to John 'O' Groats.

Market

In the UK alone McDonald's competes with an ever increasing range of quick service restaurants, including rival burger chains, traditional fish and chips, fried chicken, pizza, Chinese, Indian and the notorious post-pub kebab to the increasing number of sandwich, salad and even soup outlets available. But through a combination of quality, fast and friendly service, clean and pleasant surroundings, canny marketing and high-street profile, McDonald's continues to have a strong presence in the market.

By the end of 2002, McDonald's had 1231 restaurants and directly employed 44,229 restaurant staff in the UK as well as another 25,000 employed by McDonald's franchisees. The chain provides food and drink to around three million Britons per day, and spends about £416 million annually in the UK on ingredients. Its UK turnover is well in excess of £1.6 billion a year. Despite global economic challenges, the McDonald's brand continues to innovate and expand.

in People accreditation, the company was re-recognised in 2000 and 2002. In 2002, McDonald's was named as one of the UK's leading employers in The Times Top 100 Graduate Employers, achieving position 33.

Alongside its successes as a business, McDonald's contributes much to the local communities it belongs to. In the US it established its worldwide Ronald McDonald House Charities (RHCC) in 1984, in memory of company founder Ray Kroc. The organisation's main aims are to keep families together by providing accommodation to the parents and siblings of seriously ill children – through its Ronald McDonald Houses and Family Rooms at children's hospitals and hospices – and to provide grants to charities, schools and hospitals that will benefit children. To date, RMHC's has awarded US$300 million in grants worldwide, and in the UK the independent charity Ronald McDonald Children's Charities has raised more than £18 million.

Aside from all this, the real achievement of McDonald's is self-evident. No matter how unfamiliar your surroundings, there is always a McDonald's nearby.

History

McDonald's was founded by two brothers called Dick and Mac McDonald. But the real driving force behind the chain's expansion was a visionary salesman called Ray Kroc, who started out supplying milkshake mixers to the brothers' restaurant in San Bernadino, California, in the 1950s. Kroc worked out that they were selling one fifteen cent hamburger with fries and a shake every fifteen seconds – which meant over 2000 milkshakes a month. The entrepreneur saw the potential of the business and decided to get involved, buying a franchise from the brothers and setting up his own McDonald's restaurant in Des Plaines, a Chicago suburb, in April 1955.

It was an instant hit, and more branches of McDonald's rapidly followed. The chain had already

Achievements

McDonald's is the largest food service company in the world, with more than 30,000 restaurants serving 46 million people each day in 121 countries and territories, from Andorra to Yugoslavia. The strength of the brand and the quality of its offering are recognised every year by journalists, marketers and analysts. In 1996 it was rated as "the world's greatest brand" by the consultancy Interbrand. More recently it was named one of the best global companies by Global Finance magazine, while Fortune ranked it number one in the social responsibility category of its Most Admired Companies listing.

The company is committed to customer satisfaction that competitors are unable to match and recognises that well trained and motivated staff are key, the development of all employees at every level of the organisation is a high priority. Training is a continuous process, and employees attend courses in the restaurants as well as at the company's six Management Training Centres. When they complete their initial training, all employees are eligible to receive an independently validated Basic Certificate in Food Hygiene, and successful completion of the Management Training programme can lead to a Diploma in Restaurant Management – a nationally recognised qualification accredited by Nottingham Trent University.

McDonald's commitment to the development of its employees was nationally recognised in 1998 when the company achieved the Investor

In addition to these activities, McDonald's in the UK has been involved in a range of good causes from fund-raising work with local schools, youth groups and hospitals to supporting the Child Accident Prevention Trust and Tidy Britain Group's 'Just Bin It' campaign. It has also demonstrated a strong commitment to education – among other initiatives, its 'Write Away' short story competition, in partnership with the Times Educational Supplement and the National Association of Teachers of English, is in its fifth year.

sold 100 million hamburgers in its first three years of trading, and the 100th branch opened in 1959. Two years later, the ever-enterprising Kroc paid US$2.7 million to buy out the McDonald brother's interests, and in 1963 the billionth McDonald's hamburger was served live on primetime television. The McDonald's Corporation went public in 1965 and was listed on the New York stock exchange the following year. In 1967 the first restaurants outside of the US were launched in Canada and Puerto Rico, and the McDonald's formula travelled successfully. The first branch in the UK was opened in Woolwich, south east London, in 1974. Three years later the 5,000th restaurant opened in Kanagawa, Japan. It is possible to buy a McDonald's hamburger in almost any city around the world.

Product

McDonald's observes that its five main ingredients are beef, chicken, bread, potatoes and milk. But to its customers worldwide, the brand is most strongly associated with hamburgers and fries, which remain the mainstay of its business.

However, one of the company's strengths is its flexibility, especially in its ability to adapt to – and often predict – customer demand. The Filet-O-Fish, for example, was developed by Cincinatti-based franchisee Lou Groen, whose restaurant was based in a predominantly Catholic area. Groen had noticed that takings were considerably lower on Fridays, and realised it was because many Catholics traditionally abstain

from eating red meat on that day of the week. He gave them an alternative, which proved so popular that it appeared on international menus in 1963. In 1968 a franchisee from Pittsburgh – Jim Deligatti – also created the Big Mac, it became the chain's most successful menu item ever

McDonald's has also demonstrated an ability to adapt to local cultures, rather than taking a 'cookie cutter' approach to growth. A character from the film Pulp Fiction famously pointed out that beer is served in McDonald's in France – it is also worth noting that restaurants there serve a spin on the French croque monsieur snack, as well as croissants and pains au chocolate.

Perhaps the best example of local adaptation is to be found in India, where the cow is a sacred animal. So in 1996 McDonald's opened its first restaurant that did not sell beef. Instead, mutton is used and the Big Mac is known as the 'Maharaja Mac'.

McDonald's has always been quick to adapt. The first drive-thru restaurant was created in 1975 to serve soldiers from an army base in Sierra Vista, Arizona, who were forbidden to leave their cars while in uniform.

McDonald's is committed to providing its customers with food of the highest quality. This is achieved by using the best quality raw ingredients sourced from approved local suppliers and ensuring that food is prepared to a consistently high standard. The menu is continually reviewed and enhanced to ensure that it meets – and wherever possible – exceeds expectations. To help customers make informed decisions about their whole diet, McDonald's was the first quick service restaurant to provide a complete ingredient listing and detailed nutritional analysis of all its products.

Recent Developments

The past couple of years have seen further innovation, expansion and promotion. The highlight of 2000 in the latter category was undoubtedly its sponsorship of the Olympic Games in Sydney, Australia. But the brand did not lose sight of its main goal of providing high-quality food – in the US that same year it introduced its New Tastes menu, featuring a rotating selection of new products.

In 2001 a country led approach resulted in the exciting and innovative development of the two Golden Arch hotels, in Switzerland. The business also acquired a minority interest in the popular UK sandwich chain Pret A Manger – a brand which shares its enthusiasm for quality products and unmatched customer service.

Promotion

The McDonald's brand is extremely high profile and its advertising expenditure corresponds. Its warm, human campaigns focus on family values and an entertaining restaurant experience. Ray Kroc once commented: "There is something just as basic to our success as the hamburger. That something is marketing the McDonald's style. It's bigger than any product or person bearing the McDonald's name."

Worldwide, McDonald's has demonstrated a strong commitment to sports sponsorship. Nowhere is this more evident than in the UK where it has successfully linked the brand with football – one of the nation's favourite sports. Sponsorships have included the World Cup since 1994 and the Champions League between 1996 and 2000. McDonald's was one of the official sponsors of Korea/Japan 2002 and ran a series of TV commercials starring famous UK footballers

Teddy Sheringham and Rio Ferdinand as part of its World Cup campaign in the UK.

Meanwhile, in August 2002, the company announced a new four-year community partnership with the English, Scottish, Welsh and Irish Football Associations to develop football at a grass roots level. The scheme will create 10,000 new community-based coaches for young players and spearhead the drive to increase football volunteering.

McDonald's actively encourages its restaurant managers to put time and resources back into the local community. Supporting kid's football teams has proved an effective way to do this. Hundreds of local youth teams play in kit donated by McDonald's across the country, taking the brand into the heart of everyday British life. Throughout the UK, over 300 youth teams and 500 restaurants are involved in McDonald's sponsored leagues.

Of course, marketing is not all about big sponsorship deals. Local restaurants devote time to developing links with their customers. This can range from free coffee mornings for senior citizens, organising children's parties, or fund-raising work with local schools, youth groups and hospitals.

Brand Values

Ray Kroc developed his brand vision for McDonald's around a simple but effective consumer-driven premise: quality, service, cleanliness and value (QSC&V). These values remain the cornerstone of the company and, as a result, McDonald's has become known as a trustworthy brand that puts its customers first.

Around the world, the key to the company's success has been its capacity to touch universal human needs with such consistency that the essence of the brand has always been relevant to the local culture, no matter how different that culture is from the origins of McDonald's.

www.mcdonalds.co.uk

Market

Throughout the twentieth century our lives were changed beyond recognition by the advent of modern transport using pneumatic tyres – cars, coaches, aircraft and underground systems. Wheeled agricultural and earthmoving equipment also evolved to keep pace with the needs of the farming and construction industries. Alongside this development has been the monumental growth of the world's tyre industry – now valued at £43.9 billion.

The world's three largest suppliers – Michelin (France), Goodyear (US) and Bridgestone (Japan) – account for almost 57% of the total world market (Source: European Rubber Journal October 2002). Each group has great strength in its domestic market but also has significant influence throughout the world. As vehicle manufacturers seek to grow the automotive industry in South American and Asian countries, China and India for example, the tyre producers seek new ventures in those countries either by acquisition, partnership or new build.

Achievements

The Michelin Group is the world's leading tyre manufacturer with almost a 20% share of the market and a consolidated turnover of £10 billion in 2001. Michelin is based at Clermont-Ferrand in France, but operates 80 manufacturing plants in nineteen countries, six rubber plantations in Africa and South America and research, development and testing facilities in North America, Europe and Japan. The company operates a comprehensive sales network throughout some 170 countries.

Michelin has pursued an effective and consistent marketing strategy, capitalising on its corporate symbol 'Bibendum', otherwise known as the Michelin Man. He was voted the world's best logo by an international jury brought together by the Financial Times and the Canadian magazine Report on Business in 2000.

The company has consolidated its status through pioneering new tyre products which set standards for the entire industry. There are many examples which demonstrate this, one of the most recent being the revolutionary NZG tyre which was an essential factor in enabling Concorde to return to the skies after the Paris accident.

History

Until 1889, the Michelin factory at Clermont-Ferrand produced rubber products such as hoses and general farming implements. But a beleaguered cyclist with both tyres punctured changed all that when he arrived at the factory in an ox cart one day.

André and Edouard Michelin, the brothers who controlled Michelin, spent many hours repairing the tyres which soon punctured again. This was because, at that time, tyres were bandaged and stuck to wheels. Waiting for the glue to harden while repairing a simple puncture was therefore laborious – it could take up to ten hours.

So Edouard Michelin devised a solution – a detachable pneumatic tyre which could be removed, repaired and replaced in just fifteen minutes. His development was set to revolutionise the world's transport industry.

Having patented their detachable pneumatic tyre, in 1891, the Michelin brothers sponsored a well-known French cyclist, Charles Terront, to enter a bicycle race from Paris to Brest. Using their tyres Terront went on to win the race by a full eight hours because he found it easier than his competitors to repair his punctures.

Michelin then organised a bicycle race from Paris to Clermont-Ferrand, secretly depositing nail booby-traps en route to deliberately cause punctures. It gave them 240 opportunities to prove how easy it was to repair a puncture with the new design. A year later, over 100,000 cyclists were using Michelin tyres.

Michelin first used the Michelin Man as a marketing device in 1898. A series of posters

was produced which showed the character drinking nails and broken bottles and claiming 'Nunc est Bibendum' – Latin for 'Now is the time to drink' – to emphasise that Michelin tyres could 'swallow' obstacles without puncturing.

Although it was the bicycle which launched Michelin into tyres, its great breakthrough was with the motor car. The very first cars, produced towards the end of the nineteenth century, used solid tyres. The Michelin brothers were convinced that pneumatics were the way forward and took an opportunity to prove it. They entered a vehicle in a motor race from Paris to Bordeaux in 1895. It was an Edouard Michelin creation comprising mostly Peugeot parts, a Daimler engine and Michelin pneumatics. The steering mechanism was somewhat unstable, hence the vehicle's nickname 'l'éclair' (lightning) reflecting its zig-zag motion under speed. Although they came last in the race, they had proved that a heavy vehicle could ride on pneumatics, a result which prompted André to say; "in ten years all vehicles will be fitted with pneumatic tyres".

His prediction was well founded; such was the demand for the new tyres that by 1905 a Michelin agency had been set up in London, a second factory was built in Italy a year later and a US plant opened in Milltown in 1908.

Michelin launched various innovations as the decades passed up until World War II, notably the concept of twinning rear tyres on trucks and the creation of tyres for 'Micheline' railcars on the railway network.

World War II brought tyre development to a halt until 1946, when Michelin registered the world's first production radial tyre – known as the Michelin 'X' – the prototype of the broad-based pneumatic tyre we use today. This was a moment of enormous importance for the tyre industry and Michelin was soon kick-started into massive expansion to meet demand. It entailed a move into the US market in 1950 with the founding of the Michelin Tire Corporation, based in New York. In 1966, Michelin made its ultimate breakthrough in the US market when Ford decided to launch its new model, the Lincoln Continental III car, complete with Michelin's radial tyres.

Throughout the 1960s, the radial concept had begun to dominate the tyre market. During the 1970s, Michelin experienced huge growth – 23 new plants to manufacture solely radial tyres.

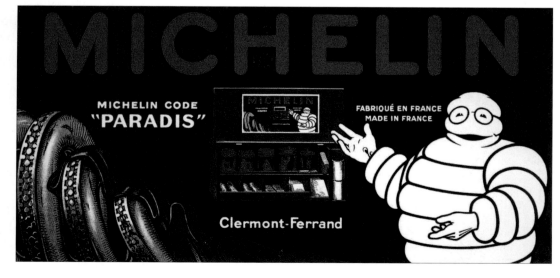

In the US, still regarded then as the prize market for car manufacturing, Michelin became a leading tyre supplier. Fortunately, despite the ensuing worldwide recession, Michelin achieved steady growth, culminating in the acquisition of the American Uniroyal Goodrich Tire Company which secured the Michelin Group's position as a world leader in the long-term.

Product

Michelin's portfolio of brands adds up to a catalogue of 36,200 products marketed today. The company makes tyres for virtually all types of vehicle including bicycles, motorcycles, cars, buses, trucks, tractors, earthmoving machines, aircraft, underground trains, the US Space Shuttle and even the latest human transportation machine, the Segway™ (a two wheeled scooter).

The product can be small, as with a wheelbarrow or a moped tyre weighing a couple of kilogrammes, or it can be very large, as with a gigantic earthmoving machine tyre which is over four metres in diameter and weighs 5.3 tonnes.

Whatever a tyre's size, it has to satisfy the customer's needs in terms of price, quality and performance. And it is in performance that Michelin's products are truly world-class. Tested rigorously in the company's laboratories and on its test-tracks, many tyre designs are ultimately put through their paces on the race circuit. Michelin has a major presence in both two wheel and four wheel motorsports such as Formula One, World Rallying and Superbikes. Its record of World Championship titles is impressive in its industry.

Michelin pursued brand extension before the term was coined. André Michelin, whose first job after graduation was as a junior manager at the French Ministry of the Interior's Map Department, saw the benefits of providing travel information to people in those early days of motoring. The first edition of the now famous Michelin Guide was launched in 1900, with the words 'Offert gracieusement aux Chauffeurs' (free for motorists) on its cover. Other products followed: a route information service (1908), road maps (1910) and regional guides (1926).

Recent Developments

Michelin strives to anticipate customers' expectations in its quest to facilitate mobility. Many issues arise with this objective in mind; for example tyre safety, life and handling. One concern which has become of greater interest in the general public's mind in more recent years is that of the environment. What is involved with producing tyres and the materials used in them, how efficiently do they perform in service and what can be done with used tyres? In striving to be a responsible member of the business community, Michelin, through various industry associations (and at times in conjunction with its competitors) has paid particular attention to such matters.

In 1992, the company invented the 'Green Tyre' which promotes better fuel economy. This tyre has a reduced rolling resistance, thus saving fuel, leading to less pollution. A range of 'Green X' energy-saving car tyres, branded Energy, was subsequently launched. In 1995, this was followed by an Energy truck tyre range, promising a 20% reduction in rolling resistance – the equivalent of a 6% saving in fuel.

Regarding the disposal of tyres which are at the end of their life, Michelin has been involved in a number of initiatives, most recently in partnership with companies involved in the use of tyres as a fuel in cement kilns. Michelin continues to participate in projects which help to solve the issue of waste tyres.

In 1998, Michelin commercialised its PAX System, a revolutionary concept which offers motorists greater security and performance with a tyre which has a run-flat capability. In the event of a loss of pressure, the PAX System tyre continues to handle without compromise and under zero-pressure conditions will not come off the rim. The motorist has complete mobility for 125 miles at speeds of up to 50mph.

Concorde was back in service in 2002 thanks to Michelin's NZG tyre. This tyre uses an innovative high-modulus reinforcement material developed by the company. It represents a whole new technological generation of radial tyres which have reduced weight, a better control of structural deformation and a higher resistance to damage.

On the travel front, Michelin launched a new web-based digital travel service in 2001. www.viaMichelin.com provides a great deal of the company's long-established hotel, restaurant and tourism data in an electronic format and which is being used in partnership with others for in-car navigation systems.

Promotion

The Michelin Man, who has been present in Michelin's advertising for over 100 years, continues to appear in poster and TV campaigns. He features on all the company's travel publications, on the website and can also be found on promotional material such as keyrings, clothing, toys and even hot-air balloons.

The idea of the Michelin Man was conceived by Edouard Michelin at an exhibition in Lyon in 1894, when a stack of tyres struck him as almost lifelike. His brother André, with the poster artist Marius Rossillon, invented the Michelin Man and he was given the nickname 'Bibendum' by Léon Théry, a famous racing driver.

Early posters depicted Bibendum in various roles. An early O'Galop illustration showed him as a wrestler, flippantly kicking the dangers of the road into touch. Another artist, Léo Hindre,

depicted Bibendum saving a young woman from the entreaties of her unwanted suitor.

Bibendum has taken on many guises during his long life – a film star, a mime artist, a politician, a sailor – and he continues to evolve with changing times. He stopped smoking in the 1930s and he has always reflected the basic format of the tyres of the day; from the large diameter, thin section variety at the start of the twentieth century, to smaller diameter, wide section format at the end. Today his figure comprises 26 tyres – in 1905 it was 56.

He is often seen in motorsport victory advertising as the Pilot, reflecting the name of Michelin's range of ultra-high performance tyres and promoting the company's strong associations with rallying, touring car and motorcycle racing.

To celebrate his centenary, an exhibition entitled '1898-1998 – The Michelin Man' toured the world. It illustrated the role played by Michelin in the development of the transport and travel industries. Also to coincide with the anniversary, three books were published.

Brand Values

Michelin is a truly international brand with an impressive heritage. It is renowned for its ground-breaking achievements in the tyre industry which have been achieved through understanding and anticipating customers' needs. Consumers have come to expect consistently high quality and reliability from Michelin.

In brief, the company has but one mission: to facilitate mobility.

www.michelin.com
www.viaMichelin.com

Market

The cake market can be confusing due to the significant overlaps that now occur between sectors. This is a result of recent product developments; such as cake bars, allowing cakes to be eaten on the move, as a snack. However, the cake market can be broadly segmented into wrapped and unwrapped. The wrapped cakes sector, in which Mr Kipling operates, comprises individual cakes, whole cakes, chilled and occasion cakes. Alongside Mr Kipling, Cadbury Cakes and Lyon's Cakes are the leaders of this sector (Source: Mintel 2002).

Britons eat a lot of cake – and are consuming more each year. The market is currently valued at £1.3 billion (up from £1.2 billion in 2001, according to recent Taylor Nelson Sofres (TNS) data w/e August 18th 2002). In fact, the sector is growing at roughly 7% annually, stealing a march on its competitors in the 'sweet treats' category – with biscuits only managing a 3.7% growth, and chocolate biscuit bars actually falling by 1.3% (Source: TNS date w/e August 18th 2002).

The growth is partly being driven by an evolution in cake marketing as well as the effects of product development. While cakes used to be associated with home-baked products that were consumed over a long period of time, brands like Mr Kipling have extended its range of cakes to include 'eat now' products – satisfying snacks that can be eaten on the move. Recent research by Manor Bakeries suggests that 40% of all cake is purchased on impulse and eaten almost straight away. Much of the remaining percentage is used for packed lunches.

Mr Kipling's ability to identify new eating occasions has undoubtedly been of benefit to the brand's development. It has an 11.8% slice of the market, making it by far the biggest branded player – and thanks to heavyweight marketing its share is increasing annually.

Achievements

Mr Kipling and his 'exceedingly good cakes' have commanded respect and affection since the 1970s. Launched in 1967, the brand was a market leader in less than ten years, having achieved an awareness of 89%. But while it remained popular in the 1990s, by the beginning of the twenty first century the cake category was in decline and changing eating habits were beginning to take their toll.

Research by owner Manor Bakeries showed that supermarket own brands had become a formidable player within the cake category by offering a cheaper alternative. On top of this, qualitative research hinted that Mr Kipling's image might be a little old-fashioned. The brand and its advertising agency Saatchi & Saatchi decided to rejuvenate Mr Kipling and give consumers a reason to have more of an emotional bond with him. The resulting ads showed Mr Kipling gouging wads of turf out of the golf course with his errant club, causing chaos at a picnic, and provoking a stampede of horses on a school trip. But everyone forgives him – as he does make 'exceedingly good cakes'.

The strategy worked. The brand's research reaffirmed their position of quality and since its

relaunch in 2001, Mr Kipling's market share has been growing steadily. The value of the brand has increased to over £110 million since April 2000. The number of packs sold has risen from 85.8 million to 100.9 million. Furthermore the average number of packs that customers buy each year has risen from 6.8 to eight. The brand has helped to increase growth of the category as a whole.

Perhaps even more importantly, given the objective of the relaunch, brand loyalty is up from 32% to 49% and more customers believe that Mr Kipling cakes are relevant to today's lifestyle.

History

In the mid 1960s traditional corner shops and village bakeries were in decline, gradually being replaced with supermarkets and grocery stores. Packaged cakes were certainly available, but research showed that they were considered unappetising and mass-produced. And yet the market was still worth around £150 million.

In 1965, work began on a brand new range of cakes which was completely different from existing product offerings. Mr Kipling's brand new range of cakes was created to give consumers choice and quality in a market previously dominated by bland and unappealing products. Rank Hovis McDougall's (RHM) modern plants were used to ensure the quality of Mr Kipling's range, and care was taken to ensure that the packaging was more colourful and tempting than had been seen before.

Mr Kipling's range was launched in 1967 and quickly became the most popular brand on the market. The initial range of twenty products was based on the traditional baker's shop and packed in colourful, premium boxes with handles for carrying home. The image of the handled box became the familiar Mr Kipling logo and acted as a mark of expertise on the range. Products like French Fancies, Jam Tarts, Battenberg and Almond Slices were among the brand's earliest successes and remain part of the range today. In addition, roughly fifteen seasonal products and limited editions are launched every year, ensuring that new favourites take their place alongside traditional products.

Product

From the very beginning, Mr Kipling focused on making high-quality small cakes. When the brand was created, small cakes accounted for 30% of the market, but there were practically no high-quality packaged products. Mr Kipling was able to quickly dominate the sector by providing products that were easy to consume, while being difficult to reproduce at home. Meanwhile, the top quality recipes and colourful, convenient packaging allowed Mr Kipling to hone the image of a master baker, providing nothing but the best.

This general theme remains true today. Consumers are prepared to pay a little more for the superior quality of Mr Kipling's cakes, and the packaging has maintained its qualities of being bright, attractive and easy to use, with a process of continued evolution keeping it fresh and modern. The sense of personal service is still very much apparent too, in the form of the Mr Kipling vans that can be seen delivering cakes to stores all over the UK.

Of course, as well as small cakes, the range also embraces slices, fruit pies, teatime cakes and cake bars with a total product range of 60 items.

Recent Developments

As part of the brand's 2001 relaunch, Mr Kipling products got a new look. The packaging was redesigned, providing improved stand-out on shelves while encapsulating the brand values of warmth and freshness. The logo was also redesigned but did continue to incorporate its well-known phrase 'exceedingly good'.

Meanwhile, in response to increasing 'on the move' snacking, the packaging of Mr Kipling's popular fruit pies was completely transformed. The old style packs were jettisoned in favour of an upright pack of plastic pods – each containing individually wrapped pies – complete with carrying handle. Furthermore, the most popular Mr Kipling products have been introduced in twin pack formats and distributed to smaller independent retailers and forecourts so consumers can have their favourite Mr Kipling cakes wherever they may be. Qualitative research revealed that they quickly became a lunchtime and football-match staple. The bold move also immediately distanced Mr Kipling from the own label products that had imitated its fruit pies for a long time.

Promotion

Advertising and promotion for the Mr Kipling brand has been planned as a totally integrated concept ever since its launch. The original objective of expressing the personality of the brand not only through the products themselves, but also via the brand name, packaging, pricing, advertising, display and merchandising, still remains today.

Television was chosen as the primary launch medium, partly for its impact and immediacy, and partly for its ability to express the warmth and friendliness of Mr Kipling. Television has continued

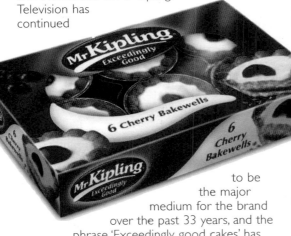

to be the major medium for the brand over the past 33 years, and the phrase 'Exceedingly good cakes' has become one of the best known and most frequently quoted slogans in advertising. Mr Kipling has generated affection amongst consumers as a kindly, very British, old gentleman. Most importantly, he is recognised as a master baker and craftsman.

Recent research also shows that more people believe in Mr Kipling than Santa Claus, emphasising the emotional bond between Mr Kipling and consumers.

As part of its relaunch in 2001, a great deal of the promotional budget was channelled into its sponsorship of Comic Relief. This capitalised on the association between a Cherry Bakewell and Red Nose Day, and used the good cause to help convey the brand's sense of fun.

By the time the event was over, a total of £250,000 had been donated to Comic Relief from the sale of Red Nose Cakes, and staff at eight sites gave an average of £12.50 each to raise a further £48,000 from fundraising activities. This activity contributed to a record 16.6% share of the ambient packaged cake market (by spend) in the period immediately following the promotion.

Other recent activities have maintained the humorous tone.

To support a TV commercial in the 'forgiveness' series – this time featuring a bouncy castle that floats away – Mr Kipling launched an on-pack offer giving consumers the chance to win a bouncy castle for a day. There were also 1,000 mini bouncy castles on offer. This activity was backed up by a Mr Kipling Big Bounce tour, covering 30 UK stores, and a PR campaign featuring a bouncing celebrity. Millward Brown promotional recall research reveals that the Big Bounce campaign had a recall of fifteen compared to an average of eight for grocery promotions.

The results showed increased sales, higher visibility, and the reinforcement of the idea behind the TV ad. The public relations support generated extensive radio and press coverage, with an estimated total audience reach of nearly 18.4 million consumers.

Brand Values

Mr Kipling cakes are crafted by traditional methods to modern standards. They contain superlative quality ingredients creating the right total recipe.

This translates into a concept whose basic appeal is adult self-indulgence – a treat rather than an essential food – that makes you smile and generates a feeling of happiness from a brand that is warm, friendly and personable. The brand values have evolved to reflect a product that can be eaten any time, any place, with modern convenient packaging to appeal to today's consumer.

www.mrkipling.co.uk

Things you didn't know about Mr Kipling

More than 64 million Mr Kipling Apple Pies are sold each year.

In 2000 Mr Kipling made over 41 million Mini Battenberg cakes. If you put these end to end they would go round the M25 nine times.

In the four weeks of the Red Nose campaign 2001 the British public ate their way through 21 million Red Nose Cakes.

Nearly one in three housewives always have cake available at home, with one in four keeping cake in the house in case friends or family drop by (Source: Mintel 2002).

Market

Over the last few years, a combination of key factors, including a rise in the number of people living alone, increased interest in healthy eating and greater demand for convenience have all played key roles in the growth of chilled pot desserts. Yogurts, traditional desserts and fromage frais – now referred to as SLDP's (short life dairy products) – hit all the right buttons for today's busy consumer, who seeks increasing variety and innovation. As lifestyles become more hectic, snacking forms an integral part of the modern diet and chilled yogurts and desserts offer consumers everything from health to indulgence in a convenient format.

One of the main growth areas in the UK is the use of yogurt as a breakfast food, moving on from its traditional purpose as a dessert. Yogurt has been eaten as a breakfast staple for many years in continental countries, for example, in Germany twice the amount of yogurt is eaten and in France two and half times as much yogurt is eaten than in the UK.

While other top grocery sectors are either static or in decline, SLDP's continue to buck the trend and are a key driver of grocery sales. Penetration rose to a record level of 94.5% in 2001, as consumers were given a variety of new reasons to buy into the category.

With UK consumers last year spooning their way through a record two billion pots of yogurt – enough to fill over 200 Olympic size swimming pools – it is no surprise that yogurt is the key driver of the SLDP market, holding the biggest share. Sales leapt £36 million to £698 million in 2001, making it one of the fastest growing food sectors (Source: ACNielsen).

Müller, the 3rd largest grocery brand in the UK (Source: ACNielsen), has played a key role in the development of the SLDP market. Its commitment to quality, value and innovation has driven the category and helped differentiate it from the competition, reinforcing its position as the UK's principal SLDP manufacturer.

Achievements

Müller now holds a 40% share of the yogurt market and 27% of the total SLDP market, with retail sales in excess of £300 million. Since its introduction as an unknown brand to the UK in 1987, Müller has become the UK's third largest grocery and

the second largest food brand, with seventeen different product lines and 65 product variants.

The key to Müller's success has been the launch of innovative, high quality products. Müller Corner for instance, is now the UK's best selling yogurt. There are over twenty varieties in the Corner range. 2002 saw further product development with the launch of Müller Corner Squeezers, a handheld, squeezable tube containing yogurt and fruit sauce. Müllerlight is the second best selling yogurt as well as the UK's favourite virtually fat free yogurt and fruit sauce. Müllerice, which created a completely new sector when it was introduced to the UK, is now the UK's top selling pot dessert, helping to make rice the fastest growing sector in chilled desserts.

In 2001 Müller invested £55 million in a state-of-the-art extension to its Market Drayton factory in Shropshire to double production capacity to more than two billion pots a year.

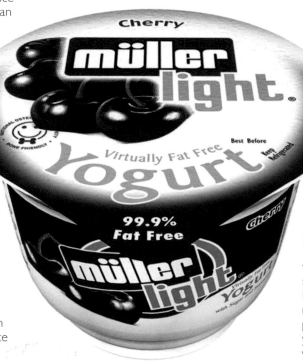

In one record day in 2001, the brand sold 4.7 million pots of yogurt – exactly equal to its first full year's sales fourteen years ago. In addition, managing director Ken Wood was judged to be the Marketer of the Year, by The Marketing Society, in recognition of the strengths and commitment he has shown to the Müller brand since launch.

History

In 1896, Ludwig Müller founded a small village dairy in the Bavarian region of Germany. 74 years later, in 1970, his grandson Theo Müller took the helm and broadened the company's horizons. He recognised that the success of his dairy's products as popular regional brands could be transformed into national successes if he improved the recipes and gave the products some heavyweight marketing support.

The first product he launched was buttermilk. It proved to be a great success and from here the company began to grow rapidly. In 1980 an innovative product, which had both fruit sauce and dairy rice in the same container, was successfully brought onto the market. This led to the development of Müller's now famous twin pot concept.

In 1987, recognising the possibilities of taking the brand into the rest of Europe, Theo Müller started his British company by test marketing Fruit Corner and Crunch Corner in the Borders region. Due to the success of the trials, Müller products were launched nationwide the following year. The brand revolutionised the yogurt sector with its modern, fun image and continued to steadily increase its presence in the market.

In 1990, the company launched the virtually fat-free yogurt, Müllerlight and the rice based snack Müllerice, with Müller Thick & Creamy following two years later.

Five years after its UK launch, the brand had become the yogurt market leader, overtaking long-established British brands. Since then the company's philosophy has been one of continuous innovation, with the introduction of new products and range extensions such as Müllerlight Mousse, being paramount.

Product

Early in his career Müller managing director Ken Wood saw many excellent product ideas in many dairy companies let down by cost cutting and the lesson stuck. One of his key beliefs is that consumers respect quality. He therefore strives to set a new quality 'gold standard' for the market. The company's commitment to quality extends from the products themselves back through the company's modern production

facility to its relationships with its suppliers. Every step of the process is meticulously monitored to ensure that every pot leaving the dairy is in perfect condition.

Recent Developments

In keeping with the brand's innovation philosophy, Müller brought a number of new products onto the market in 2002. In February, it extended its probiotic range, launching Müller Vitality Drink, the UK's first probiotic yogurt drink with added vitamins. The low fat drink is aimed at busy health-conscious people who realise the importance of a balanced diet, but require the benefits in a convenient format.

In May that year Müller added a new variant to its Müller Breakfast Corners with the Kellogg's Cereals range. Developed to be a quick one-stop breakfast solution for time poor parents and their children, Müller Corner with Kellogg's Rice Krispies joined the Coco Pops and Frosties varieties. This addition to the range aimed to strengthen the rapidly expanding 'on the go' children's breakfast market. This market has substantial growth potential, as over 20% of children in the target audience of 6-10 year olds regularly skip breakfast.

Yogurt is growing rapidly as a breakfast staple amongst UK consumers as they become more aware of its convenience and health benefits.

Also in May 2002, the brand successfully relaunched its Müllerice and Müllerice 99% Fat Free brands with new packaging and four new flavours: chocolate, original, toffee and apple. It was found that only a quarter of consumers were aware that Müllerice can be served hot as well as cold, so a microwave symbol has been added to the lid to reinforce the range's versatility, and this message has been emphasised through advertising.

In July 2002, the Müller Corner range was refreshed with a new look and three new flavours: pink grapefruit, strawberry cheesecake and lemon cheesecake to strengthen Müller's indulgent dessert selection.

Müller Corner Squeezers, the revolutionary new twin tube format containing Müller Corner yogurt and fruit sauce, launched in September 2002. It is aimed at children and teenagers and allows the product to be eaten on the move. These developments have all played a key role in extending usage into new areas and switching new consumer groups onto the Müller brand.

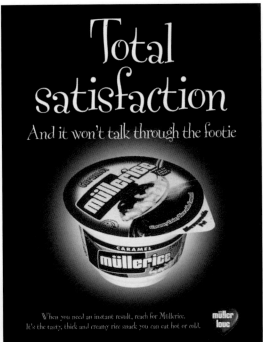

Fruity Russian seeks mixing and fun times together

Would you go through hoops for a sweetie like me?

Juicy twosome seek one more to mix with

Choose me I'll go all red and crumble for you

With 20 deliciously different varieties to choose from, there's a new love around every Müller Corner.

product while capitalising on the fun and irreverent values of the brand itself. This theme is used across all marketing disciplines, lending itself to new product launches as well as tactical promotions across the range. A good example is Müller's first ever digitally-led multi-media campaign which ran over Valentine's Day 2001 and incorporated a 'Müllerlove Matchmaker' website, an SMS campaign, plus Frank Sinatra and Barry Manilow look and sound-a-likes serenading commuters on Victoria station, in London.

The 'Müllerlove' campaign continued throughout 2002 with a budget of £12 million. The brand spent a further £1.9 million on Corner specific press, radio, sampling and PR, all focusing on consumer product news and communicating the different sub-brand propositions.

Brand Values

Müller's mission is to provide innovative products for its diverse range of customers. The three cornerstones of the company's success are its commitment to quality, relentless innovation and robust market support for its product range. While engaged in the serious business of producing healthy snacks it has extended the fun and irreverence exemplified in the innovative split pot through its marketing communications.

www.muller.co.uk

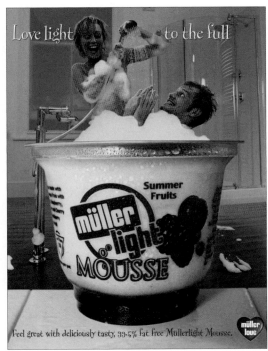

Love light to the full

Feel great with deliciously tasty, 99.5% fat free Müllerlight Mousse.

Promotion

As a major advertiser, Müller's aggressive sales and marketing activity has allowed it to establish lines before other manufacturers have the chance to react. Consistent price promotions and on-going product innovation have also helped drive the brand forward.

Müller's most successful long term marketing activity has been the '3 for 99p' promotional mechanic. Introduced in 2000, it instantly revolutionised volumes, by increasing weight & frequency of purchase and brand penetration in one move.

The brand has used several straplines in its advertising campaigns for individual products over the years including 'Pure and sinful' for Fruit Corners, 'So much pleasure – where's the pain?' for Müllerlight and 'Life would be duller without Müller' as part of a corporate campaign. However, in 2001 the brand took a new approach to its marketing and promotion, launching 'Müllerlove', its first umbrella campaign to support the growing portfolio of Müller products. It taps into consumers' 'love' for the

NIVEA

Market

It's easy to see why skin care is a huge business with more and more people – men and women alike – wanting to stay looking and feeling healthy and young for as long as possible. Skin care products now offer something for everyone: from moisturising, deodorising, cleansing and revitalising to combating visible signs of ageing and offering protection from the sun. The rise of male grooming is simultaneously also a massive consumer trend, opening up a multitude of new product opportunities and brand extensions.

As the leading and one of the most trusted skin care brands in Europe, NIVEA has a 13% share of the enormous £850 million UK market. The largest and fastest growing segment in the market is facial skin care, where product sales total £263 million, increasing by 14% year on year. The next largest is deodorants at £244 million (Source: IRI 2002).

The value and importance of 'skin caring' brands is clear to see. For example, the growing number of men taking better care of their skin has translated into a huge growth in NIVEA FOR MEN sales of shaving, after shave conditioning and male facial products in recent years, giving NIVEA nearly a 20% share of a £80 million category. And, in the deodorant category sales of effective products such as NIVEA are seeing strong growth.

In all, the penetration of NIVEA's products has grown by 22.5% in the last year, which means over thirteen million people in the UK have bought a NIVEA product in 2002.

The health and beauty market is being driven by technology. Consumers are eager to try new, advanced formulas while demand for the next great innovation places enormous pressure on those companies active in this sector. Manufacturers at every level must maintain a frenetic programme of new product development in order to keep up with their competitors. The self-select skin care market is dominated by a small number of large brands, as only those manufacturers with significant research budgets can hope to compete in such a technology-focused arena. Foremost among these is Beiersdorf, manufacturer of NIVEA: the largest skin care brand in the world.

Achievements

Present in over 160 countries, NIVEA is the world's largest skin care brand. It has built an enviable reputation being ranked the most trusted skin care brand in sixteen European countries. This unprecedented level of trust is built on its long history. When NIVEA was launched in 1911 it was the world's first stable oil in water emulsion moisturising cream, and, as such, is considered to be the beginning of modern skin care.

Nowadays, NIVEA's name is synonymous with quality skin care on a global level. Its strong heritage as a brand that soothes, nurtures and protects allows it to command a strong position across the worlds' skin care market. On this solid foundation the brand's owner, Beiersdorf, has

successfully extended NIVEA to meet all skin needs, such as anti-ageing moisturisers, lip balms, deodorants, hand creams, sun lotions, shaving and shower products.

NIVEA has always been strong on innovation, and, with the launch of NIVEA FOR MEN in 1998, is credited with founding the mass market for male-specific skin care products.

Further evidence of NIVEA's popularity with consumers can be seen in the many awards it has won, such as 19 magazine's 'Can't Live Without' award for Best Skin care Brand for NIVEA Visage and Now magazine's '50 best all time beauty products' for NIVEA Body Firming Q10. In addition, the NIVEA FOR MEN range won the FHM Grooming Award 2002, and again for 2003.

History

NIVEA traces its roots back to 1911, when Dr Oscar Troplowitz, a medical researcher and owner of the Beiersdorf Company in Hamburg, turned his experience of making medical ointments to developing a new kind of cosmetic cream.

The key to his plan was a 'secret ingredient' called Eucerit, used to form a new oil in water emulsion which encouraged the skin to repair

itself, making it an ideal base for skin emollients. This formula was also remarkable for its stability, meaning that it could be stored for a long time without separating. This made it ideal for commercial use, as it could be packaged, shipped and marketed on a global scale without losing product quality.

Dr Troplowitz joined forces with Eucerit's creator, Dr Isaac Lifchütz, and dermatologist Professor Paul Gerson Unna to conceive, develop and market a new cream blending this formula with glycerine, citric acid, rose oil and lily of the valley. The team were so impressed by the cream's brilliant pure whiteness, they named it NIVEA, a name derived from the Latin expression 'Nix Nivis', meaning 'snow white'.

The brand quickly took off on a global scale, reaching the UK and the US in 1922 and South

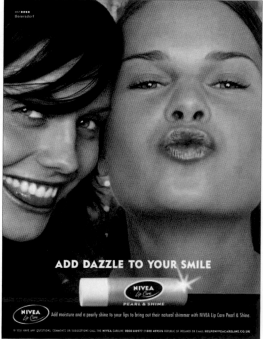

America in 1926. Over the next 50 years, NIVEA Creme's reputation as a soothing and effective skin moisturiser was cemented. Then, in the 1970s, NIVEA began to spread its wings, driven by advances in technology and changes in consumer demand. This expansion of the portfolio set the brand on the road to where it is today: a trusted brand with a comprehensive range of skin care products.

Product

While NIVEA Creme remains the brand's signature product, the range now encompasses a wide portfolio of products addressing specific skin care needs.

NIVEA Creme minimises moisture loss, replenishes lipids and supports the skin's natural protective barrier. It has been found to be suitable for soothing irritated skin conditions like eczema, as well as minor sunburn and nappy rash. It is also available in a variant designed for younger people, NIVEA Soft.

NIVEA Visage is a complete range of products specifically developed to care for the face, offering cleansing, moisturising and anti-ageing formulas for women of all ages. The NIVEA Visage Q10+

collection has a specially developed anti-ageing formula, using the natural coenzyme Q10 to stimulate the skin's natural regeneration.

NIVEA Sun offers a complete range of caring products for the whole family, from sun sprays to children's protection and sunless tanning products. The brand is also committed to broadening people's knowledge of how to help protect from the sun's harmful rays and keep skin healthy. NIVEA Sun grew by almost 50% in 2001 and outperformed its rivals with the largest growth in value and units sold in 2001.

The Nivea Body range provides body moisturisers to meet the needs of all skin types below the neckline. The wide product choice includes a moisturising Body Spray, an exfoliating Body Scrub, Q10 Skin Firming Complex and Satin Sheen Moisturiser for, what NIVEA describes as, a 'wonderfully warm glow'.

The NIVEA Hand range comprises caring nourishing formulas to help hands remain soft, supple and young looking.

NIVEA FOR MEN has proved to be a particularly successful part of the range. Men's skin, which tends to be thicker and oilier than women's, is treated most effectively with specific products. NIVEA FOR MEN's comprehensive range of reliable, quality face care products contains cleansing, shaving, after-shave and face care products to suit every skin type.

Recent Developments

NIVEA has seen many innovations in 2002, with the launch of a raft of new products. A significant development was the launch of NIVEA Deodorant in the UK market; a range of eight products offering effective protection and care. The range includes a conventional roll-on and modern aerosol in male and female variants, and a real innovation in the form of a convenient pocket size Compact, which lasts as long as a standard 150ml aerosol. All these offer effective 24-hour antiperspirant protection and are alcohol, colour and preservative free. Also available are NIVEA Deodorant Wipes in individual sachets, which cleanse, refresh and provide odour protection when and where it's needed.

In addition, 2002 saw the launch of Nivea Visage Anti-Shadow Eye Creme – a soothing and cooling eye product that reduces puffiness and diminishes the appearance of under eye shadows. NIVEA Visage Soft Facial Cleansing Wipes have also recently been relaunched into two skin types, a Dry/Sensitive and Normal/Combination variety.

Another major new product launch is NIVEA Lip Care Pearl and Shine, a daily use lip care product designed to keep lips feeling and looking soft

and smooth. It also responds to the trend towards shimmering face and body products by giving lips a pearly shine.

Furthermore, the NIVEA Sun range has been enhanced with the addition of several new products, including Firming Sun Lotions, Anti-Ageing Sun Creams and Children's Coloured Sun Spray.

Promotion

Nivea has a strong marketing heritage, with campaigns as far back as the 1920s focusing on many of the benefits and values that the brand still stands for today.

Nowadays, each section of the brand portfolio is supported by a fully integrated multi-media strategy, encompassing above and below-the-line advertising, sampling, direct marketing and ambient media.

Education goes hand in hand with many campaigns, as NIVEA sees it as its responsibility to promote skin protection and the association between healthy skin, general fitness and well-being. This strategy of educating the consumer through promotion has helped NIVEA build new markets, such as the male skin care segment. Whilst this may prove costly in the short term, long-term investment in the skin care sector serves to consolidate NIVEA's position as a leading skin care manufacturer and a source of valuable advice that inspires consumer trust and loyalty. Sampling is an extremely important aspect of NIVEA's strategy for introducing new products. For example, the launch of NIVEA Visage Anti-Shadow Eye Creme involved a press sampling campaign to over two million women – part of a £9 million integrated marketing campaign behind

the NIVEA Visage brand. TV and press advertising, advertorials and public relations are also extensively used in the NIVEA marketing arsenal.

Brand Values

The emotional values associated with the NIVEA brand have changed little in the last 90 years. 'NIVEA Cares for Your Skin' is the current strapline used to communicate NIVEA's brand values. These values are communicated via clean, fresh, healthy and positive imagery in all NIVEA's promotional material and advertisements. NIVEA is dedicated to protecting the skin of the entire family; therefore family values form an important aspect of its brand character. NIVEA, however, is also stylish, contemporary and fashion conscious, creating products that fit in with the latest cosmetic trends, such as the 'Pearl and Shine' NIVEA Lip Care balm. It is a tribute to the strength in depth, and years of experience, of the NIVEA brand that it can appeal to consumers on so many levels.

www.nivea.com

GLOWS ON BEAUTIFULLY

NIVEA SATIN SHEEN BODY MOISTURISER.

CHIEF SUN PROTECTION

NUROFEN®

Market

Market research indicates that people today are more interested in maintaining their own health than ever before. Recent years have seen a trend towards self-medication, with sales of over the counter (OTC) medicines reaching £1.79 billion in the UK alone (Source: IMS Health 2002). Worth in excess of £349 million (Source: ACNielsen 2002) the size of the UK's painkiller market indicates that relief from pain rates highly in our healthcare priorities. As we continue to seek to prevent everyday ailments from interfering with the pace of modern life, the pain relief market is poised for further growth.

Within the market, today's consumers are more likely to buy a repertoire of products to suit different types of pain. A vast range of modern analgesics is now available OTC, differentiated not only by their active ingredients but also by their formats. Ibuprofen continues to be the primary driver of growth in the analgesics market, however paracetamol and aspirin remain popular (Source: ACNielsen and internal estimates June 2002). Industry innovation is continuing to provide more targeted and effective solutions, while the recent explosion of information on health matters and an increased awareness of safety amongst consumers has led to greater confidence in self-medication.

Achievements

Nurofen was the first brand of its kind in the UK, creating the OTC market's Ibuprofen sector and dominating it ever since. It is currently sold in 53 countries worldwide, and is the number one selling analgesic brand in the UK.

Since its launch in 1983, Nurofen has been instrumental in building the pharmacy analgesics category. Changes in legislation during the 1990s saw the brand extend its distribution into the grocery healthcare market, and its impact in this sector has proved equally phenomenal. Recent product launches and distribution gains have grown Nurofen's share of the adult analgesics market in UK grocery to around 25%; higher than any other brand (Source: ACNielsen 2002).

Nurofen's dedication to developing its brand through advertising has been recognised in recent years as the winner of the OTC Consumer Marketing Award 2002. This is reinforced through the acknowledgement that Nurofen has the highest advertising awareness of brand in its category (Source: Millward Brown 2002). In addition, Nurofen was voted 'Best Product' in Top Sante healthcare magazine in 2002.

Contains Ibuprofen. Always read the label.

www.nurofen.co.uk

NUROFEN KNOWS CHILDREN

History

Nurofen is one of the healthcare brands managed by Crookes Healthcare Ltd, the UK subsidiary of Boots Healthcare International. The Boots Company, whose healthcare heritage spans over 120 years, developed Nurofen's active ingredient Ibuprofen in the 1960s. Initially a prescription only product, Ibuprofen quickly established a worldwide reputation. In 1983, approval was given to switch Ibuprofen from a prescription only medicine to being available OTC, based upon its excellent efficacy and tolerability record. Nurofen was subsequently launched as a multi-indication analgesic across Europe.

Nurofen went on to establish itself as a leading OTC brand, maximising its market position by ongoing product innovation. Indeed, Nurofen Plus proved to be one of the UK's most successful OTC launches of the year when it came to market during the 1990s. In 1996, the regulatory status of Ibuprofen (200mg) changed from 'Pharmacy only,' leading to Nurofen Tablets being awarded General Sales List (GSL) status. This allowed the brand to extend distribution beyond its pharmacy heartland into supermarkets and other convenience channels. It is now possible for consumers to buy Nurofen products from a variety of outlets, including vending machines, garage forecourts and even over the internet.

The growth of the Own Label proposition during the 1990s saw many consumers moving from branded goods to retailers' own lines, including own label healthcare products. By continuing to provide solutions to consumers' needs and by demonstrating its relevance to its target audience, Nurofen has proved sufficiently powerful to repel threats from both low priced own label products and strongly promoted branded competitors.

Nurofen is now the UK's number one selling analgesics brand (Source: ACNielsen 2002) as well as the number one OTC brand (Source: Information Resources 2002), continuing to grow in both market share and reputation. A recent audit actually found its total market value share to be 21.5% (Source: ACNielsen 2002).

Product

Since the launch of Nurofen Tablets in 1983 the brand has evolved into a portfolio of ten UK variants. The range encompasses not only adult oral painkillers, but also topical, cold and flu, and paediatric pain relief products.

The familiar sugar-coated tablet was joined in 1995 by an easy-to-swallow torpedo-shaped format: Nurofen Caplets. More recently, two further GSL-licensed oral formats have been added to the range: innovative Nurofen Liquid Capsules, and dissolve-in-the-mouth Nurofen Meltlets.

Nurofen's remaining adult oral products are designed to deliver specific types of pain relief, and are only available from pharmacies. Powerful Nurofen Plus provides relief for stronger pain through the dual action of Ibuprofen and codeine while Nurofen Long Lasting uses sustained release capsules to provide up to twelve hours of pain relief.

Nurofen extended its expertise into other sectors of the adult pain relief market in the 1990s with the launches of Nurofen Cold & Flu

Contains ibuprofen. Always read the label.

NUROFEN

TARGETED RELIEF FOR PAIN.

www.nurofen.co.uk

and Nurofen Muscular Pain Relief Gel. In the paediatrics market, Nurofen for Children (launched in 1998) is continuing to build both its reputation and brand share.

In 2002, due to outstanding growth in 2001/02 (48% in pharmacy against a category growth of 3.6%), the Nurofen for Children core range of 100/150ml bottles has been extended to include a GSL offering in paediatric analgesics with Nurofen for Children Singles (sachets 5ml). They are available in packs of eight and sixteen and allow parents the convenience of a mess free sachet.

Recent Developments

In recent years, Nurofen has undertaken a variety of innovative new product launches. In 1999, Nurofen Liquid Capsules were the first gelatine capsules of their kind to be launched in the UK. Absorbed more quickly by the body than ordinary tablets, the format has already acquired a loyal consumer following.

In April 2000 Nurofen grew the analgesics market further with the launch of Nurofen Meltlets, a revolutionary new kind of tablet which is designed to comfortably dissolve in the mouth. Since they can be taken without water, Nurofen Meltlets can be taken anywhere, providing convenient pain relief for people on the go – as well as for those who have difficulty in swallowing conventional tablets.

Nurofen has also led the way in packaging innovation in the analgesic market with the introduction of a matt, silver plastic click-top container for packs of Nurofen twelve tablets. The new Nurofen 'Mobile' pack is designed to make battered boxes at the bottom of bags or even single tablets rolling loose a thing of the past. The new pack slips easily into a bag or pocket, looks good and ensures the product is kept in pristine condition, ready for use.

Promotion

Nurofen's familiar target logo, symbolising its ability to target pain, has been a consistent feature of its advertising since its launch in 1983. Indeed, reinforcing Nurofen's targeted strength remains a pillar of the brand's advertising strategy. Today, its growth and expansion into 53 countries worldwide has given Nurofen a wider stage for its brand communications. It is therefore no surprise that like many other Superbrands, the dominant objective of Nurofen's advertising strategy is to create a global brand which acts in a consistent way.

Throughout the brand's history Nurofen has used television as a promotional vehicle in the UK and other key markets. In addition to the numerous commercials designed to raise awareness of new launches, broad brand-building campaigns have been used to promote Nurofen's values and establish its relevance to its target audience. The recent 'Bodymaps' brand creative

Vvvrrroooooom!

TARGETS PAIN FAST.

CONTAINS IBUPROFEN. ALWAYS READ THE LABEL.

PLAY AT www.nurofen.co.uk/reliefracer

proved to be one of the analgesics industry's most successful campaigns to date. Featuring a Nurofen target travelling through the pathways of the body to the site of pain, the advert reinforces Nurofen's efficacy credentials and visually communicates 'Targeted Relief from Pain' to consumers.

In recent years, many of Nurofen's promotional activities have been focused around its new product launches. The launch of Nurofen Liquid Capsules in 1999 was supported by attention-grabbing colour advertisements in daily press, followed by bursts of awareness-building television activity.

Nurofen has also experimented with more innovative consumer media in recent years. It was the first analgesic in the UK to use backlit pharmacy signs, depicting the familiar Green Cross and with the Nurofen target and 'Targeted Relief for Pain'. The Nurofen global website, which provides information on products and pain relief, was launched in 1998 (www.nurofen.com) with satellite sites providing regional information. The website was then relaunched in 2001 and was redesigned to reflect Nurofen brand values.

It offers various pieces of information and advice about pain and how to treat it and information is included about Nurofen products, as well as an area especially dedicated to Nurofen for Children, containing specific information about childhood illnesses. Furthermore, the website contains a link to the Liquid Capsules interactive Relief Racer game. The brand also sponsors an impartial internet site providing information and advice on pain and remedies (www.painforum.com), and has engaged in partnerships with online health portals.

In addition to its consumer marketing, Nurofen has continued to support its pharmacy and health professional heritage. Its ongoing UK pharmacy programme – Nurofen Pharmacy Solutions – provides an accredited pain training programme for pharmacy assistants. Similarly, the brand has worked with external organisations such as the charity Backcare to promote better pain management. The brand has also brought its expertise on pain relief to various industry events including Dental 2002 and the British Pharmaceutical Conference 2002, where Crookes Healthcare was one of the key sponsors.

Brand Values

Nurofen has a brand heritage which delivers substantial consumer trust. It is regarded by consumers, healthcare professionals and retailers as an effective product with considerable experience in the OTC market. Nurofen's expertise and continued new product development have allowed it to achieve its 'number one selling analgesic brand' status in the market, and helped it to accumulate a valuable loyal-user group. An innovative brand with a clear focus on providing effective relief from pain around the globe, it continues to attract consumers and healthcare experts worldwide.

www.nurofen.co.uk

Nurofen, Nurofen Caplets, Nurofen for Children, Nurofen for Children Singles, Nurofen Long Lasting and Nurofen Liquid Capsules contain Ibuprofen. Always read the label.

Oxfam

Market

The charity sector may deal in compassion but it is no less competitive than the commercial world. Oxfam, the international humanitarian concern, was the UK's fourth largest charity in 2000 (Source: Charities Aid Foundation 2002). The sector, however, is vast. Oxfam is one of more than 162,000 registered charities in England and Wales competing for donations as well as for people's time. Like other aid agencies, Oxfam seeks volunteers to staff its charity shops and run local campaign events to raise public awareness and money for its work.

Fortunately the British are a nation of givers and donated nearly £5.6 billion to the 500 largest charities in 2000 representing a 6.7% growth in real terms from the previous year. Broadly speaking, donations and grants accounted for 50% of the sector's income with legacies contributing another 28%. The combined efforts of charity shops and fund-raising brought in another 15% with the remainder coming from covenants, gifts in kind and community funding.

International agencies, like Oxfam, were the most popular causes, although cancer and medical charities have benefited from increased public concern about health. Animal charities, often used to illustrate the eccentric nature of British philanthropy, were the third biggest sector ahead of children's charities which ranked fourth.

Contrary to talk of compassion fatigue, research indicates that people do care and want to help. Events have shown that, in times of disaster or public grief, people turn to philanthropy as a way of expressing their feelings. People attach a strong social value to charity and all the indications are

that this giving attitude will continue. The challenge for charities such as Oxfam is to capture it.

Achievements

Oxfam is one of the world's best known charitable brands. Its main achievement has been to change the concept of charity from institutional benevolence to one of mutual self help. In doing so it has successfully married the concepts of emergency relief and rehabilitation by lobbying for change. Along the way it has raised and distributed hundreds of millions of pounds in aid throughout the world.

As a relief agency Oxfam played a central role in the United Nations Freedom from Hunger campaign in the 1960s. A decade later it stepped up its activities when it became obvious that major poverty and famine related problems could only be relieved by concerted global action. In 1979 it successfully appealed for help in Cambodia to tackle the aftermath of the murderous Pol Pot regime and has addressed humanitarian problems caused by conflicts ranging from sub-Saharan Africa to Kosovo and Afghanistan. It has helped those affected by natural disasters whether they were the Indian famines of the 1950s and early 1960s or more recent flooding in Bangladesh. And it has continued to develop its expertise working in collaboration with poor communities in more than 80 countries.

Oxfam has won countless accolades in recognition of its work. In 1992 it was nominated for the Nobel Peace Prize and a decade later it received the Seoul Peace Prize.

History

It is just over 60 years since The Oxford Committee for Famine Relief was formed with the specific aim of providing aid to starving civilians in German-occupied Greece during World War II. The newly launched charity's first fund-raising week in 1943 raised £12,700 for the Greek Red Cross. Four years later the Committee opened the UK's first

Street children have names too

charity shop in Oxford and celebrated by sending a shipment of clothes and supplies to refugees in the Middle East. The shop in Broad Street is still open today and nationwide nearly 23,000 volunteers now work in hundreds of Oxfam shops.

In 1948 Oxfam extended its aims to include 'the relief of suffering arising as a result of wars or other causes in any other part of the world'. Throughout the 1950s the charity responded to the aftermath of natural and man-made crises in India, Korea and elsewhere in the world until, by the end of the decade, it had been transformed from a small UK charity to one with international status. In 1963 the charity opened its first overseas office in Canada and two years later formally adopted Oxfam as its name. By 1971 Oxfam had eleven expatriate staff working overseas managing 800 community projects in nineteen countries. Today's headcount is nearly 4,000.

Oxfam continued to make the headlines with its innovative fund-raising campaigns and work on behalf of poor people around the world. Oxfam faced its biggest ever humanitarian response in 1994 when the genocide of an estimated 800,000 people in Rwanda prompted an exodus of more than 1.7 million refugees. At around this time, it joined with nine other relief and development agencies in North America, Australasia and Europe to form Oxfam International. In 1999 Oxfam International launched Education Now, a campaign for universal primary education.

Product

The Oxfam product, in as much as there is one, is the work it does to overcome poverty and suffering around the world. It is a big task. A quarter of the world's population live in dire poverty with at least twelve million children under five dying from poverty-related diseases annually. About 1.5 billion people are without clean water or basic sanitation. In a world where one in five adults is illiterate, Oxfam focuses on

creating an environment in which every individual is safe, healthy, skilled, heard and equal. Oxfam acknowledges the problem cannot be solved by one agency, hence it recognises the need to work with local people, non-governmental organisations, governments and international bodies to secure its aims. Oxfam makes a tremendous difference to the lives of individuals through its work in more than 80 developing countries. It aims to help millions more by changing policies which maintain a status quo where the rich get richer and the poor become poorer.

Recent Developments

As a campaigner Oxfam worked successfully with other agencies to end the controversial voucher system and other discriminatory practices against asylum seekers in the UK. The scheme was dropped in 2002.

Oxfam has worked with the UK Working Group on Arms for the introduction of legislation relating to arms exports. In collaboration with other humanitarian and aid organisations it devised The Sphere Humanitarian Charter, which sets guidelines for the basic humanitarian assistance that should be available to disaster victims. Oxfam International launched the global Make Trade Fair campaign to fight for improvements in international trade rules and workers conditions in developing countries. The campaign has highlighted concerns that trade barriers cost developing countries US$1 billion a year, twice the amount they receive in aid. Collectively the world's richest countries spend US$1 billion a day on farming subsidies which puts farmers in poorer countries out of business. Recently the campaign has focused on

the coffee industry where low global prices have devastated the lives of 25 million coffee farmers. It helped develop the Fair Trade retail brand and goods like Cafédirect which ensure that growers in developing countries get a fair deal for their product. Oxfam has worked with the commercial sector in other areas too. It introduced the Oxfam Visa Card which raises more than £250,000 annually. Friends Provident gives £80 to Oxfam for each new policy it sells to a charity supporter. In 2001 Oxfam recruited its half-millionth regular donor and a year later the number of people who give regularly to Oxfam had risen to nearly 650,000. Such generosity contributed to help Oxfam raise £189.4 million in the financial year 2001/02.

Promotion

Oxfam was the UK's best known charity brand in a survey of the sector by the Future Foundation. Arguably the brand does not need to promote its name, but needs to promote its work. Oxfam considers every contact with the public as a promotional opportunity usually through its shops which are the brand's public face.

One third of the UK population visits an Oxfam shop at least once a year. The outlets are gradually being refurbished to build the brand and present a clean, modern image to attract more customers. The 'One off' poster campaign has helped to celebrate the individuality of items available in shops. Light-hearted straplines included 'Now in stock until we sell it' and 'It's a limited edition. Unless someone else brings it in'.

Reporting to donors is essential as it is the main way they connect with the work they are funding. Apart from media coverage regular methods of reporting include mailings, newsletters (Oxfam Reports, Oxfam News, Oxfam Campaigner), and its Annual Report and Annual Review. The Oxfam website (www.oxfam.org.uk) has also been used as a promotional vehicle and as a means of building relationships with supporters. The organisation employs an email marketing tool to send newsletters and action updates to over 10,000 regular subscribers and to communicate with 50,000 general supporters.

Viral email campaigns and multi-media are used to recruit supporters and generate action.

Oxfam has used direct response TV since 1994 as one of its core methods for attracting new donors who make a commitment to give at least £2 a month. The current emotive commercial, 'Dream', encourages viewers to call an 0800 number and pledge their support.

Brand Values

The Oxfam brand has four core values. It is an authoritative brand and an acknowledged expert in its field, which means it is listened to by influential individuals. Simultaneously it listens to those without a voice. It fosters a culture of empowerment so that everyone understands they can make a positive difference. Oxfam promotes the notion of inclusiveness. It was founded on partnership and equality and believes in collaboration. Above all it is an ingenious brand. It is inspired, creative and passionate about the way its resources are used to achieve the greatest effect. The creative approach to the brand's identity aims to communicate the reality of its work in simple and innovative ways.

www.oxfam.org.uk

Things you didn't know about Oxfam

- Oxfam was originally the organisation's telex address.

- Legacy gifts to Oxfam have included a dentist's chair and a pack of racing greyhounds.

- Oxfam receives royalty payments from Dr Finlay's Casebook, plays, books and television series.

- The 1979 Blue Peter Appeal for Oxfam's work in Cambodia raised £3.5 million; the largest ever appeal by the popular children's television programme.

- An Oxfam designed water bucket for use in emergencies won a Millennium Product Award.

Market

In recent years eating patterns in the UK have shifted, there has been an increase in the number of single person households and individual family members eating at different times as well as an increasing prevalence of TV dinners. However, despite these factors, more than half of fathers and mothers think that it is still important to have at least one family meal a day (Source: NOP/Mintel).

Mothers in particular are very likely to insist that main meals in their household are eaten at the table; six in ten do so and half of all mothers, whatever the age of their children, state that the whole family eats at the same time (Source: NOP/Mintel).

writing to Liebig asking for the extract, but he found it increasingly difficult to meet this escalating demand. To combat the problem he decided to take advantage of the huge surplus of meat in South America where cattle were slain purely for their hides, then discarded. In 1861 a young engineer called George Christian Giebert read of Liebig's work and wrote to him suggesting that they should meet to discuss a manufacturing plant in Uruguay. A factory was built in the South American country in a town called Fray Bentos. The product then became known as Extractum Carnis Liebig.

Liebig's extract first came to England in 1865 and was marketed throughout the country as being 'invaluable not only in the sickroom but also in the

distinguish it from other cargo. Oxo was registered as a trademark in 1899 everywhere in Europe, though not until June 1900 in the UK.

In the early 1900s there was a certain amount of anxiety about the quality of the product, caused by the unappetising sediment left in the bottom of the cup or bowl. Chemists were set to work on the problem and they came up with the idea of selling Oxo in capsules. Liebig's chief chemist was given absolute control to pursue a 'penny product' and by feeding beef essence and beef fibrine into a Swiss cube-making machine the Oxo cube was born. The poor took the cube to their hearts and their stomachs, making a meal of it with a hunk of bread.

The move away from traditional family meals has hit the stock cube market. In addition, it is suffering the effects of younger consumers, who are cooking less traditional meals which don't involve stock. A further general decline in culinary skills means that young consumers are not familiar with how to use stock.

The stock cube market is worth £62 million (Source: IRI 2002) and Oxo accounts for over half of this market. Oxo did not have any significant competition until the launches of Bovril and Knorr cubes in the 1970s, but have managed to maintain the position of market leader.

Achievements

Oxo cubes are the UK's largest stock cube brand. Some 75% of UK households have Oxo cubes in their cupboard and over two million Oxo cubes are used every day. Since its creation Oxo has been endorsed by a wide range of diverse characters such as Florence Nightingale, the second Duke of Wellington and Captain Scott of the Antarctic who took a supply of Oxo on his South Pole mission.

History

Oxo was originally launched in 1847 as a fluid beef concentrate dietary supplement for invalids and explorers, under the name 'Liebig's Meat Extract'. It was created by the chemist Justus Liebig, the son of a German paint and colour manufacturer. The product was so successful that doctors started

kitchen'. Liebig's Extract became Oxo in 1899. Surprisingly, nobody knows exactly how the name came about. One unsubstantiated legend is that while a crate of the extract was at the docks, a keen docker chalked O-X-O on the side to

There were no major changes to the product until the launch of the Golden Oxo (later called Chicken Oxo) in the 1960s, to coincide with Oxo's Golden Jubilee, and in 1968, the parent company merged with Brooke Bond.

Oxo was one of the first to advertise on television in the 1950s and thanks to highly successful long-running campaigns starring the likes of 'Katie' and the 'Oxo family' the brand has continued to stay close to the hearts of the British public.

Product

The product has come a long way from its creation as a dietary supplement for invalids and explorers; from its initial liquid format to being foil wrapped in the well known cube format.

As well as being available in the distinctive original beef flavour, Oxo cubes are available in chicken, vegetable and lamb flavours. In more recent years the brand has been extended to include a range of Oxo gravy granules, which are available in beef, chicken, onion and vegetable flavours.

Oxo has recently launched a range of 'special occasion' gravies. The 'With a Hint Of' range has been designed to respond to the growth in modern British food. There are four varieties, Chicken with a Hint of Sage and Onion, Lamb with a Hint of Mint and Beef with a Hint of Mustard. Another brand initiative currently underway is the relaunch of the Oxo Herbs and Spices range. Each cube is blended to help cooks recreate dishes with flavours from different parts of the world. The ranges include four varieties namely Italian, Indian, Chinese and Mexican.

Recent Developments

In May 2001, the Oxo brand and its trademark in Europe were acquired by the Campbell Soup Company. On acquiring the brand, the Campbell's business re-evaluated the brand, including its properties. As part of that review, its communication strategy, namely the move away from the traditional Oxo Family, was evaluated. Research indicated that although family mealtimes were in decline, the majority of consumers aspired to the idea of having a traditional family meal. It was also found that this desire was felt equally by those who were yet to start their families, as by those who were in a firmly established family unit. The brand team therefore decided to re-introduce the device of the Oxo family.

A number of initiatives have recently been conducted to capitalise on the brand's iconic status. This included the Oxo Food Book and a number of sampling roadshows. Each initiative is intended to draw on the brand's warmth whilst driving its relevance in an ever-changing and complex market.

Promotion

As soon as Oxo was introduced to the UK market

in the early 1900s it was advertised in a number of women's magazines.

In 1902 the first Oxo promotional gift was given away, this was a baby's rattle with a handle that spelt Oxo. It was offered in exchange for one bottle wrapper. Oxo also made itself synonymous with health, strength and endurance by the simple device of sponsoring athletics events, such as the London to Brighton walk. The company was not only official caterers to the 1908 London Olympics, sustaining the runners in the marathon with drinks of Oxo, but also managed to persuade the entire British team of athletes

to recommend the product. By the mid 1950s the television commercial had arrived. One of the first television adverts for the product starred the popular glove puppet Sooty. As the 1950s drew to a close, Oxo created one of the most successful characters ever to appear in a television commercial – 'Katie'. By the dawn of the early 1960s she was established as believable, attractive and interesting. Her trials and tribulations became so real to the nation that people wrote to her in their thousands. The advert was so famous that it became part of the fabric of the social life of the 1960s and 1970s. Some eighteen years after her television debut, Oxo felt that Katie had become rather dated. Her 'Gives a meal man appeal' slogan stayed, but the new symbol of the product was a pair of fingers doing the 'Oxo crumble' – used in poster campaigns.

The first famous on screen face to replace Katie was Dennis Waterman of 'Sweeney' fame. Despite the popularity of these new advertisements the ghost of Katie still hung around. She was finally reincarnated with the introduction of Lynda Bellingham and the 'Oxo family'.

The Oxo family presented common ups and downs of family life. The children shouted and squabbled and the parents rowed and sometimes were not even on speaking terms. They would however, occasionally share a sexy memory or two over the supper table. After the popular family had spent almost two highly successful decades on the nation's television screens, the lead up to the millennium saw Oxo adopt a new advertising approach. This major packaging redesign and new television campaign also coincided with Oxo's 100th birthday. The new advertisements portrayed 'families of the new millennium' and gave clear instructions on how and why to use an Oxo cube when preparing a mince meal. The voiceover explains how adding Oxo will add depth to such a meal. The households featured in the ads were designed to give the impression of being genuine. The style of the new adverts was a complete departure from the previous advertisements in order to establish a more contemporary and functional image for Oxo, whilst maintaining the emotional 'warmth' and

'care' associated with previous Oxo campaigns.

Promotions were run to help younger consumers learn how to use Oxo cubes through recipes attached to packets of meat. The new pack design also features an updated version of the Oxo logo. In addition to this eye-catching design element, simple instructions with usage suggestions can be found on the packs. Oxo also launched a website that contains the history of the product and provides modern recipe ideas (www.oxo.co.uk).

Brand Values

Oxo's brand values haven't really changed since its introduction in 1899.

Oxo has always stood for nutrition, flavour, and nurturing in the consumers minds. Its quirky name and instantly recognisable packaging have given Oxo a fun and wholesome brand identity. It is a familiar, trusted brand that conjures images of bringing families together at the dinner table. The heritage of the brand is also endearing, with much of its early advertising merchandise highly sought after by collectors today.

www.oxo.co.uk

Things you didn't know about Oxo

During one of the early years of commercial television, 52 Sooty commercials were produced so a different one could be shown every week.

In what was seen as a revolutionary move at the time, Oxo began employing female labour in 1902. However, to avoid unseemly liaisons with male members of staff the ladies were located in a separate department with a different entrance to the men.

In 1903 the name Oxo was beamed from an electric sign in the Strand.

During World War II the Nazis confiscated all wireless sets in the Channel Islands. An ingenious pair of mechanics called Harold Rive and Louis Roche, manufactured over 2000 miniature sets, so small that they were concealed in Oxo tins, making it possible for the Islanders to hear Winston Churchill's speeches.

Persil

Market

Every day seventeen million washes are carried out in the UK – that is almost seven wash loads per week for the average UK household. With annual sales in the UK of 300 million packs of detergent to facilitate this number of washes, the laundry market is worth more than one billion pounds in the UK.

The laundry detergents market in the UK is one of the most competitive in Europe, and successful products rely on continuous innovation to maintain their competitive advantage. There are four distinct product areas within this market: biological products for tough cleaning, non-biological products for people with concerns about their family's skin, colour care products, which keep coloured items looking vibrant and new for longer and special care products for delicate fabrics such as silk and wool.

The detergent market can also be split into four product formats: powders, tablets, liquids and capsules. Persil was the first to bring tablets onto the market and now leads the sector. Persil Capsules, which was actually third to market, is leading the capsules sector; selling over £28.1 million in the first eight months of launch. After the first year, one in five people in the UK had bought Persil Capsules, with the product outselling its nearest competitor two to one.

Persil is the UK's number one laundry brand with nearly 30% share of the market. Persil Non-Bio is the original non-bio brand and together with new Persil Aloe Vera has 45% share of this sector of the market.

Achievements

Persil was the foremost brand in this competitive market for almost the whole of the twentieth century and now, well into the new millennium, the brand remains the UK's number one detergent brand. Its place in the country's cupboards has been maintained by continuous innovation of the brand throughout its 93-year history. Persil has always been at the leading edge of new technology and is consequently seen as both reliable – by virtue of its heritage and product performance – and innovative.

In May 2002, Persil launched Persil Aloe Vera, the first main stream washing detergent to contain extracts of aloe vera. One in four people believe they have sensitive skin and the product was introduced to meet these consumers' need for a washing powder which was kind to skin. Persil spent five years researching just what it is that makes a detergent 'kinder on skin' and, for added reassurance, this research is supported by the British Skin Foundation (BSF).

Persil Aloe Vera is a non-biological detergent that has been dermatologically tested. The product has met Lever Fabergé's ambitious targets, securing a 4% share of the washing detergent market within six months of launch.

Persil has been voted the UK's most trusted washing detergent. Reader's Digest conducted a European-wide survey, which resulted in Persil topping the detergent charts as well as being recognised for meeting consumers' needs.

Persil is foremost a caring brand and in 1984, recognising that consumers were becoming increasingly concerned about caring for their skin, Persil introduced the first non-biological format onto the marketplace.

To strengthen their long-term commitment to skin research, Persil works alongside the BSF and the National Eczema Society to provide consumers with information and reassurance on skin-related issues. Persil also works closely with the National Childbirth Trust (NCT) with a relationship going back over five years.

History

Persil was launched in 1909, as the 'Amazing Oxygen Washer'. Originally developed by two Stuttgart professors – Professor Hermann Gessler and Dr Hermann Bauer, the brand was owned by Crosfield until 1919, when it was acquired by Lever Brothers.

Before the launch of Persil, soap bars were used to wash clothes. Persil was introduced as a soap-based powder which was combined with an oxygen bleaching agent to remove staining in the wash. Persil functioned rather differently from the traditional bar soaps – it had to be stirred into a paste before being added to the water. The brand was therefore advertised as soap powder that would do away with the dolly rub, the washboard and the labour of rubbing clothes. Persil made the washing process much easier, simplifying it to 'soaking, boiling and rinsing'. Initially, the conservative housewife

was a little reluctant to desert her established cleaning methods. However, Persil's convenience and the whitening power that it offered combined to gradually win over British housewives.

The 1950s saw the next dramatic change in clothes washing habits, brought about by the introduction of the first reasonably priced washing machine to the UK. As machines became more sophisticated, a low lather washing powder was required to prevent excess foam interfering with the spin drying and rinsing process or causing overflowing. At the same time, other trends were affecting people's requirements for washing powders – coloured fabrics were becoming more common, synthetic fibres were replacing natural fibres, and before long high temperature washing was superseded by the low-temperature wash.

Persil responded to these changes with a continuous programme of product innovation and improvement. In 1968, once the early twin-tub machines had given way to the more advanced automatic front-loading drum machines, Persil launched Persil Automatic. The name identified the newly created detergent technology with the new machine technology.

Persil has always been in step with changing lifestyles in the UK: for example, Persil made its detergents biodegradable well ahead of legislation. During the 1980s stain removal was enhanced with energy-efficient ingredients such as enzymes and offered greater convenience with the launch of detergent liquids.

All these innovations mirrored technological development in washing machines, the change in washing load and an increased concern about the environment. Indeed, environmental concerns were further alleviated with Persil's revolutionary innovation of 1998 – laundry tablets. Unit dosing minimised product wastage previously caused by consumers using too much powder, thus addressing environmental concerns about washing and washing powders.

The start of the new millennium saw the

launch of Persil Capsules and Persil Aloe Vera – two products from Lever Fabergé which again won the hearts and minds of UK consumers.

Product

The name Persil is derived from 'Per' and 'Sil' – two of the product's original ingredients – perborate and silicate, both registered in 1906. Persil prides itself on being able to meet any type of washing needs by always having a product in the Persil range to suit.

Within each of the four product formats – powders, tablets, liquids and capsules – Persil has a range of different formulations. Persil Performance is a biological product containing enzymes formulated for tough cleaning to help break down stubborn stains at low temperatures. People with concerns about their family's skin often prefer non-biological formulations without cleaning enzymes. Persil also has a range of products specifically developed for coloured clothes – Persil Colour Care. This does not contain any bleach or optical brighteners and so helps to keep coloured items looking vibrant and new. Finally, Persil Silk and Wool containing neither enzymes nor bleach making it ideal for use on delicate fabrics.

Recent Developments

In September 2002, Persil unveiled the world's largest picture mosaic to mark the start of its 'Get Creative' initiative. 15,000 pictures of mums – created at school desks and kitchen tables all over the country, were arranged into one giant image of a mother. The mosaic was the culmination of a three-month long drawing programme in schools and playgroups led by Persil.

The spectacular work of art, called 'Big Mummy', covered 625 square metres, big enough to cover two and a half tennis courts. Big Mummy even caught the eye of the Guinness Book of Records and they have officially declared Persil's Mosaic as the biggest of its kind in the world.

In 2002 Persil also launched the 'Get Creative' arts scheme. This is designed to encourage children's creativity and learning through play by providing much-needed resources for pre-school and primary children. By collecting 'Persil Stars', parents can help their child's class or school get their share of at least £7 million worth of

free art and craft classroom kits. To put that figure into context, it will more than double art spending in schools. It therefore comes as no surprise that over half of all primary schools have registered to date.

The scheme is completely scaleable, with realistic and achievable collection targets for over 40 different art and craft classroom kits. So it is not just the larger schools that can benefit from the scheme – even remote village playgroups with small class numbers can also 'Get Creative'.

The scheme has been specifically designed to make a real difference to schools with the minimum effort from parents and teachers. The initiative is supported by the Prince of Wales' Arts and Kids Foundation, a nationwide campaign to promote the positive impact that the arts can have on young people.

Excludes ROI

Free art and craft materials for schools

Get creative with Persil

www.persil.com/getcreative

Promotion

Persil has always taken a progressive approach to advertising. It was the first detergent to be advertised in the press in 1910 and was also the first detergent to be advertised on television in 1955. Persil was also the first washing powder to show a man doing the washing in a television advertisement.

Persil has taken numerous approaches in its advertising campaigns across the years.

During World War II, it emphasised the whitening benefit of the brand, often through comparisons with inferior brands, using the slogan 'Persil washes whiter'. This style of advertising was perpetuated into the 'TV age'. And it worked. The consistency of the message and familiar packaging built a huge brand loyalty that has been sustained over many decades.

Persil continues to explore new ways to communicate with consumers. For example, to encourage the association between Persil Aloe Vera and skin kindness, an unlikely sports team benefited from Persil sponsorship. Persil Aloe Vera sponsored and supplied branded

sports kit to the British Naturist Petanque Team, who took part in the International Petanque Championships in August 2002.

The 'kit' consisted of branded caps, sweat bands, socks and mini towels for wiping boules clean. The sponsorship was extensively covered in international media – press and broadcast.

Persil also believes strongly in the power of building relationships and is in regular direct contact with a group of mums who are the most important consumer for Persil. These mums are contacted regularly as part of the company's 'Messing About With Persil' programme. This is an initiative which provides mums with offers and ideas for having fun with their families – both outdoors and at home.

Brand Values

Historically, Persil has been regarded as a trusted family brand with a strong heritage. The launch of Persil Tablets in 1998 also attracted younger people to the Persil brand, creating a brand with a contemporary, progressive feel whilst retaining its family values.

Persil is a brand which combines great cleaning with genuine care, indeed the heart of the brand's philosophy is getting dirty clothes clean in a caring way.

In its communication, Persil strives to demonstrate both its cleaning credentials and its care.

At the same time, the brand has been a key partner of Comic Relief in both 1999 and 2001. This is set to continue in 2003, with Persil pledging £400,000 to Comic Relief's good causes.

www.persil.com

Market

Tea is Britain's national drink. The nation loves it – so much so that we drink an estimated 150 million cups of tea every day. This equates to an average daily consumption per person of 2.5 cups, 365 days a year. Or, to put it another way; tea accounts for 36% of all liquid drunk. It is therefore hardly surprising that tea outstrips its nearest rival, coffee (18%), in the UK hot beverages market and continues to be the nation's favourite drink as soft drinks currently account for 26%. Annual tea sales amount to £650 million. Tea has always been an important part of the UK grocery trade and remains so today.

Achievements

Brooke Bond is the UK's number one tea company. Its flagship tea brand is PG Tips. For more than 40 years, PG Tips has been one of the UK's favourite tea brands and currently holds a market value share of 24.7% (Source: Nielsen MAT September 2002). Furthermore, it is ahead in one particular sector, packet tea, with a 40.4% value share (Source: Nielsen MAT September 2002).

Founded over 125 years ago, Brooke Bond has an established heritage in tea which has contributed to the strong reputation and trust of PG Tips. Awareness of the brand amongst the British public is extremely high and has grown steadily since the TV campaign featuring the PG Tips chimpanzees began in 1956. This proved to be one of the longest running and most successful TV advertising campaigns of all time. The high awareness has continued with the recent introduction of the T-Birds campaign.

History

Although it is now a major UK company, Brooke Bond came from humble beginnings – as a small high street shop in Manchester. It was founded by the son of a wholesale tea merchant, Arthur Brooke, who was born in 1845 above his father's shop in Ashton-under-Lyne, Lancashire.

At nineteen, young Arthur joined the Liverpool branch of a wholesale tea company. He then transferred to the company's head office in London but eventually left to join his father in business. The pair opened new branches throughout Lancashire, enabling Arthur to save around £400 – enough to set up in business on his own.

In 1869, Arthur Brooke opened his own shop in Manchester's Market Street, selling tea, coffee and sugar. It was a shrewd move as the location was opposite the Royal Exchange in a street always busy with housewives. In a break with convention, Arthur didn't accept credit, trading only in hard cash for his goods. An ambitious man, Arthur mixed his own teas, formulating specialised 'Quality blends' and selling them in half pound and one pound paper bags. His teas became an immediate success. Customers liked them so much that rival grocers were forced to sit up and take note. Following this, other retailers began to ask if they could buy his tea at wholesale rates and sell it from their shops.

Arthur needed to brand his teas and settled on the name Brooke, Bond & Co – the name of his business.

Oddly, there never was a Mr Bond, to work alongside Mr Brooke, but the name had a certain ring to it, "it seemed to him to sound well", a contemporary observed.

Brooke, Bond & Co was soon printed on every bag in its founder's distinctive copperplate script. Before long, customers associated the Brooke, Bond & Co logo with top quality teas they could rely on.

Arthur Brooke was soon able to open more shops and started advertising the teas which had made his name. His tea, however, eventually earned itself a brand name all of its own. At first it was known as Pre-Gestee, which means 'to aid digestion'. A change in the law, however, outlawed the description of tea as medicinal so the name was shortened to PG Tips. The tips reference referring to the top two leaves and bud on the tea plant which provides the finest tea.

Arthur Brooke prospered and eventually opened shops throughout the UK. By the turn of the century, Brooke Bond and Company Ltd had become primarily wholesale, built on three principles – intelligent buying of tea, sensible blending to satisfy the market and clever advertising. Inspired by a trip to the US, Arthur championed novelty and modern methods of

salesmanship. Tin advertising plates were soon fixed to corner shops throughout the north of England promoting Brooke Bond teas.

In the 1930s, the Co-Operative Wholesale society was the giant of the tea trade in Britain.

During the depression, a so called 'divi' (or dividend) system was created. The manager of Brooke Bond's Manchester shop produced an economical tea blend to be marketed with special packaging and promotion involving a 'dividend card' comprising 60 perforated and gummed squares. Customers could save the stamps – each valued at an old penny – and hand in completed cards to grocers in exchange for five shillings. 'Dividend' tea was launched in November 1935 and became a bestseller.

Since then, Brooke Bond has continued to place high value on the qualities that helped Arthur Brooke's teas lead the market. Skilful marketing has been the enduring strength of the PG Tips brand. Considerable effort is taken to ensure that the quality of teas used and the blending process behind PG Tips remain of high standard.

Product

Today all Brooke Bond's tea is blended and packed at the company's high-tech factory at Trafford Park, Manchester. The tea comes from plantations in South East Asia, India and Africa, either direct from tea gardens or from auctions.

The Brooke Bond blending plant was built as part of a £20 million investment programme and is computer-controlled. It is one of the most advanced of its kind in Europe. The plant was first built in 1921 to produce tea for Scotland and northern England. It now has the capacity to serve the whole of the UK as well as Brooke Bond's overseas market, and produces around seven billion tea bags a year.

PG Tips is a blend of 28 teas. It is available in tea bags, the most popular format of tea accounting for 90% of all tea sold today, or loose. Originally, all tea was bought loose in packets or caddies but in the 1950s, tea bags arrived in the UK. It did however take some time for them to catch on. Technical developments – such as a special paper bag which wouldn't break up in boiling water – aided the growth in the public's trust of the tea bag.

Further innovations in the tea market included the launch in the 1980s of single-serve tea bags which enable a quick, easy brew made in the cup. PG Tips One Cup was the first single serve tea bag to add a tag and string to the bag for easier handling and a twin pouch for faster infusion.

In 1991, PG Tips was the first brand to launch instant tea granules as PG Instant Tea.

Recent Developments

In 1996, PG Tips celebrated the 40th anniversary of its chimps advertising campaign. The celebrations were accompanied by a new TV advertisement featuring a compilation of key moments from the chimps campaign, starting from the earliest black and white executions (when chimps drank packet tea).

The brand also ran an intensive programme of on-pack offers as a reward to consumers who had remained loyal to the brand and helped maintain its leading position since the 1950s. PG Tips' new generation Pyramid tea bags were also unveiled in 1996. The pyramid-shaped (or tetrahedral) tea bags took four years to develop and marked a major advancement in tea bag technology. The bags promising a brew closer in flavour and quality to loose-leaf tea than any before.

The innovation has proven to be a tremendous success for PG Tips – it has helped grow the brand's volume share by an estimated 30%. Much of this has not only been due to improved taste and the new, robust 'caddy pack' packaging but also the innovative way in which the bag was launched. A record £25 million was invested in advertising and promotional activity. A totally integrated approach was taken which encompassed traditional media including TV, press and posters as well as bus ticket advertising, strategically placed post-it notes, bus-sides and regionally focused door to door sampling which used characters from the adverts and PG's own 'rocket men'.

The success of the pyramid bag has been transferred to the Out of Home (OOH) market where PG Tips pyramid bags have been successfully introduced into the catering market.

Promotion

The hot beverages market is a highly competitive business. To keep ahead of its competitors, PG Tips relies on a top quality product and memorable advertising. The idea for a family of chimps to endorse the taste of PG Tips tea was conceived in 1956 shortly after the launch of commercial television. The campaign was inspired by news at the time of chimps' tea parties at London's Regents Park Zoo.

The first advert showed the chimps enjoying a party in an elegant country mansion, drinking tea from silver tea pots and bone china tea-cups. The commercial was a huge success. It led to a further 100 TV commercials which were to prove enduringly popular. Subsequent executions covered a range of

Need a PG moment?

chimps in unusual situations, such as workmen digging the Channel Tunnel; cyclists in the Tour de France race; racing car drivers and mechanics.

The Tipps family (who were chimps living in suburban Britain) were introduced in 1992. These ads featured parents Geoff and Shirley Tipps with their children Samantha and Kevin. The common thread running throughout was that of a cuppa as the ultimate reward (or consolation) after a busy day.

The chimps campaign coined a number of memorable catch phrases, such as: "Avez vous un cuppa?" and "It's the taste". Celebrity voices used to support the cast of chimps have included Russ Abbott, Griff Rhys-Jones, Cilla Black, Bruce Forsyth, Peter Sellers, Stanley Baxter, Kenneth Connor, Pat Coombs, Arthur Lowe, Irene Handl, Bob Monkhouse and Kenneth Williams. In 1998 the chimps were rested to allow the comedienne Caroline Aherne to promote the brand for a time.

The new millennium brought the end of the Chimps, who had served the brand for over 45 years. Market research indicated that PG Tips needed to attract a new younger generation of tea drinkers and that new advertising needed something fresh and up-to-date. The company and its advertising agency worked with Aardman Animations to create the T-Birds; four twenty-something 'claymation' characters who live together in a houseshare. The characters are Pete – a starling, Maggie – a pigeon,

Tom – an owl and Holly – a blue tit. The advertising depicts the trials and tribulations of domestic life soothed by PG Tips. The T-Birds commercials sum up the benefit of drinking PG with the end line "We all need a PG moment". As you would expect from PG Tips, the new advertising is highly enjoyable and entertaining just as the chimps were and the advertising has been successful in making the brand up-to-date and more appealing to the young.

PG Tips has also contributed to high profile charity campaigns, including Comic Relief where almost £1 million has been raised.

Another popular charity with which the brand has long been associated is the World Wide Fund for Nature (WWF). PG Tips has featured WWF in on-pack promotions and has contributed significant funding towards WWF conservation projects.

Strong packaging design has also played an important role in PG Tips' marketing strategy, contributing to its distinctive brand identity. PG Tips packs are well-known for their familiar red, green and white livery and the tea-picker logo. The brand's tea bags also bear a watermark motif, depicting a tea leaf overlain by the PG logo. This has been further strengthened by the introduction of the robust 'caddy pack'.

Brand Values

PG Tips enjoys a strong brand heritage and reputation for top quality tea. Research has shown that the British public associate PG Tips with a sense of security, comfort and continuity – values also associated with drinking a cup of tea. Some of the brand's most recognisable advertising straplines sum up how the brand looks to represent itself: 'Britain's best-loved tea'; 'The unbeatable taste of PG'; 'Everything we love in a cup of tea'; 'It's the taste' and 'We all need a PG moment'.

www.pgmoment.com

PHILIPS

Market

The small electrical appliance market is fiercely competitive with brands such as Braun, Remington, Russell Hobbs, Tefal, Kenwood, Rowenta and Philips battling for market share. Philips is a leader in this market in terms of innovation, influence, design and technological advances and every year markets in the region of 130 products. It operates in four distinct product categories – Male Shaving and Grooming, Body Beauty, Food & Beverage and Home Environment Care.

The small electrical appliance market is now worth over £848 million (excluding vacuum cleaners & oral care) (Source: GFK) and is showing a year on year growth of about 12%. Philips share of this market is estimated at 13% (Source: GFK).

The market for men's electric shavers in the UK is worth nearly £85 million a year. This figure accounts for sales of over 1.6 million models a year – battery, mains and rechargeables. Philishave is the number one electrical shaver in the UK and indeed the world. In 2002 Philips celebrated the production of its 400 millionth shaver, having sold an average of 700 an hour since production started in 1939.

Within the Philips portfolio of products, Ladyshave commands a 66% share of the market (in value), while Philips Epilators have an 82% share of the Epilator market (value). Within men's shavers, Philishave enjoys a market share of 58% (in value) (Source: GFK).

Achievements

Philips has a history of consistently winning awards, accolades, commendations and industry recognition.

Its success in the marketing of technologically advanced, well designed products manifests itself in the creativity of its advertising, print and promotional activity, which has been widely acknowledged.

The influence of the media on the success achieved within each product sector in Philips DAP's portfolio has been considerable. In the men's grooming category, magazines like Esquire, Maxim, Front and FHM have consistently given Philishave accolades for their particular models.

In the Food and Beverage and Home Environment Care sectors, where the women's press is an important element of all PR, such magazines as Good Housekeeping, BBC Good Food, Woman, Bella, Essentials, Family Circle etc have nominated Philips food preparation products as 'best buy', 'editors choice', 'product of the year' and 'gadget of the month'. In a similar vein, Philips beauty products are also consistently highly rated.

History

In 1891 Gerard Philips established a company in Eindhoven, The Netherlands, to manufacture incandescent lamps and other electrical products.

Developments in new lighting technologies fuelled a steady programme of expansion, and in 1914 he established a research laboratory to study physical and chemical phenomena, so as to further stimulate product innovation.

In 1920 Philips began to protect its innovations with patents, for areas taking in X-ray radiation and radio reception. This marked the beginning of the diversification of its product range. Having introduced a medical X-ray tube in 1918, Philips became involved in the first experiments in television in 1925. It began producing radios in 1927 and had sold one million by 1932. One year later, it produced its 100 millionth radio valve, and also started production of medical X-ray equipment in the US.

Philips' first electric shaver was launched in 1939, at which time the company employed 45,000 people worldwide and had sales of 152 million Dutch guilders.

Science and technology underwent tremendous development in the 1940s and 1950s, with Philips Research inventing the rotary heads which led to the development of the Philishave electric shaver, and laid down the basis for later ground-breaking work on transistors and integrated circuits. In the 1960s, this resulted in important discoveries such as CCDs (charge-coupled devices) and LOCOS (local oxidation of silicon).

Philips also made major contributions in the development of the recording, transmission and reproduction of television pictures. Its research work leading to the development of the Plumbicon TV camera tube and improved phosphors for better picture quality.

It introduced the Compact Audio Cassette in 1963 and produced its first integrated circuits in 1965.

The flow of innovative new products and ideas continued throughout the 1970s. The Compact Disc was launched in 1983, while other landmarks were the production of Philips' 100-millionth TV set in 1984 and 400-millionth Philishave electric shaver in 2002.

Product

Philips markets a wide and hugely diverse range of domestic and personal care products.

These include men's shavers, irons and steam generators, a wide range of kitchen products including toasters, kettles, blenders, food processors, coffee makers, juicers, ice cream makers, health grills and handmixers. It also has a conspicuous presence in ladies shavers, epilators, solaria and haircare products.

The strength of Philishave comes from a combination of precision engineering, continual research and development, performance, style and marketing. Over one in two of all men's electric shavers sold in the UK is a Philishave. For over 60 years Philishave has been one of the most important products in the Philips portfolio. Developments to the product have included the 1980 introduction of the 'lift & cut' shaving system, the 1996 introduction of the Reflex

Action series and the launch of the Philishave Cool Skin in 1998, which simulates a wet-shave experience. It is also waterproof and dispenses NIVEA FOR MEN moisturising emulsion or fresh gel, which help to condition the skin and give the user a close and comfortable shave.

Philips 'cube' kettle and toaster set, designed by Oscar Pena was inspired by the notion of an 'ice-cube at melting point'. Each product has aesthetically pleasing soft and slightly rounded corners, produced in a high gloss polished chrome with ceramic white accents.

In 2002 Philips developed three labour saving, highly sophisticated 'smart' food preparation products for its Essence Range.

There are two Philips Essence Food Processors and an Essence Blender in the range of 'smart' products. The secret of their success is the 'Smart Control' system which uses a set of fully pre-programmed tasks with different speed profiles. Smart Control helps users select the best process and speed profile for each food processing job.

Other appliances in the Essence range include a Toaster, a Coffee Maker, two Bar Blenders and a set of Kitchen Scales.

In coffee makers, the Philips Cucina Café Term is Philip's latest innovation. This one litre stainless steel coffee maker has a Thermos jug with a double

walled vacuum, designed for keeping coffee piping hot and fresh. The Thermos jug is unbreakable due to the strength of the stainless steel. The machine can be switched off directly after brewing, and the coffee will be kept fresh and hot due to the vacuum double wall Thermos construction.

Philips Health Grill meets the increasing need for healthy methods of cooking as the fat from the meat is drained away during grilling.

Philips Juice & Co combines a juice extractor and blender in one appliance. Features include a 1.2 litre pulp container and a 700ml jug in which the juice can be stored.

Philips has a significant influence in the iron market. The Azur 4000 range features a soleplate coated with 'Careeza'. This is a multi-layer material developed by Philips which easily smoothes out creases and makes it quicker to iron a garment. The Philips Elance 3000 irons are also highly specified. They can cope equally well with a pair of jeans as a fragile silk scarf.

Steam generators are taking ironing into a new era. It is now the fastest growing sector of the irons market with a year on year increase of 70% (2001-2002) (Source: GFK).

Philips has two models in its ProVapor 6000 series that significantly reduces the time spent on ironing.

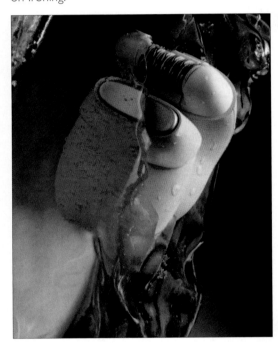

Philips specialist range of three cylinder vacuum cleaners provides a carefully tailored solution for most cleaning problems. The specialist Hygiene model offers full HEPA filtration (a system which is of particular benefit for allergy sufferers) and a special dustbag.

Philips beauty products cover hair, skin and body care. Ladyshave is the number one ladies shaver in the UK and has been responsible for building the electric hair removal market. The waterproof Philips Ladyshave Skin Comfort has the added benefit of NIVEA Body Shaving Emulsion cartridges which fit into the back of the shaver releasing cream during use.

The Ladyshave Soft Select range of shavers is another innovate product. It features a '3 Zone Softselector™' – giving separate settings for legs, bikini area and underarms. Its 24ct gold plated foil aids a close, comfortable shave.

Philips 'Satinelle Super Sensitive Epilator' lifts and removes hairs as short as 0.5mm with 21 rotating discs. By gently stretching the skin with rapid massaging movements, the body's nerve transmitters are 'distracted', minimising pain.

Satin Ice Epilators features a small detachable skin cooler, which when placed into a freezer for two hours before use, numbs skin whilst using the epilator.

The Philips beauty Geometricks is a six-in-one hair styler and is the best selling multi-styler in the UK. Geometricks has an ergonomic handle

in which to plug a crimper, spiral tongs, brush, straightener and two curling tongs.

Philips also leads the market in tanning products, such as Full Body Solaria and a Facial Solarium.

Recent Developments

Philips now markets a treatment for Winter Blues, which is a mild form of SAD (Seasonal Affective Disorder) suffered by

a growing number of consumers. It is called Bright Light and when used every day from October – March the debilitating symptoms of depression, tiredness, eating and sleeping problems are reduced, if not completely eliminated.

A significant development in 2002 for Philishave was the introduction of Sensotec, an advanced shaving system designed to give a personalised, close shave with unsurpassed skin comfort. Sensotec features a 'Personal Comfort Control' with nine settings which allows the shaver to adjust to the skin type of the user. Sensotec was featured in the recent James Bond film 'Die Another Day'.

Promotion

Philips has invested massively and consistently in TV, radio, press advertising, point of sale and promotional activity. It also sponsors strong and

brand building PR programmes that surround each product with highly newsworthy and influential events and people.

When the Cool Skin shaver was launched, tongue in cheek cinema and TV ads devised by the photographer Helmut Newton were used to capture the interest of young shavers.

In 2002, for the first time ever, two Philishave models appeared in the same TV commercial. The Philishave 'Quadra Action Man' was seen

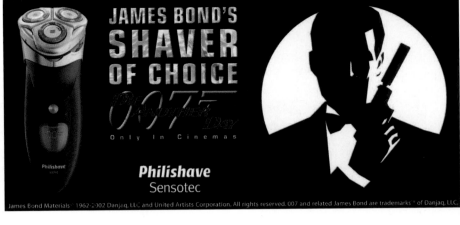

shaving in the bathroom in front of a mirror, while the Philishave 'Cool Skin Man' was filmed shaving in the shower. The World Cup provided Philishave Hair Clippers with a good opportunity to link hair cutting with famous footballers.

A two week promotion on Talk Sport featured the best and worst footballers' haircuts and was running at the time when Beckham's haircuts were front page news. Sales of Philishave cutters increased dramatically. In addition, Philishave advertorials were run in men's magazines including FHM, Loaded, Maxium, Men's Health and Front. At the same time, a month long promotion of Philips beauty products was running on 'Sun-On-line'. It was aimed at 'World Cup Widows' and the pampering opportunities provided by Philips beauty products. Prizes were offered by Philips every week during the month.

Celebrity cook Tony Tobin endorsed Philips products at the BBC Good Food Show and two advertorials in the BBC Good Food Magazine introduced readers to the new Philips 'Smart' products.

Recent PR activity included a Hole in One Golf competition for Philishave, Wakeboarding for Cool Skin, A Man's Guide to Ironing and a Christmas in June Press Bonanza for all Philips products. The latest PR coup is the association Philips beauty has with the national team of UK Cheerleaders, who appear at sporting and charity events all over the country. From summer 2002, the British team adopted the name Philips Team Britain.

Brand Values

The Philips' brand name is the company's most important asset. Together with the 'Let's Make Things Better' theme, which was launched in 1995 and represents the direction chosen and the activities undertaken by the company from the earliest research and development to the final product. Since 1995 the company has invested heavily in supporting and promoting the Philips brand.

Philips has earned its reputation as a creative, innovative designer of high quality, technologically advanced, small electrical appliances. It has a great heritage and at every stage of its business lives up to its core values.

www.philips.co.uk

Things you didn't know about
Philips

Philips' first electric shaver was launched in 1939.

The concept of the Philishave was produced out of the experience gained from the manufacture of the bicycle dynamo and the material 'Philite' originally intended for radio cabinets.

New Philishave models are tested in a Marathon Shaving Salon in which 24 men at a time can shave, recording their findings directly onto computer.

★ PRET A MANGER ★

Market

The humble sandwich is the most popular fast food in Britain, with over 8.5 billion eaten every year. The prepared sandwich market in this country is currently worth over £3.5 billion, equivalent to every man, woman and child eating an average of 37 a year (Source: BBC Food in Focus). Prepared sandwiches account for 41% of fast-food sales; bigger than pizzas, fish & chips and burgers combined (Source: British Meat Education Service). Brits are seven times more likely to choose a sandwich over a Chinese takeaway. Unsurprisingly, all this makes us the highest per capita consumption of sandwiches in the world.

Chief among sandwich consumers in the UK are office workers who – with the average lunch 'hour' having dropped by nine minutes to a record low of 27 minutes (Source: Eurest national survey 2002) – are constantly on the lookout for a quick, handy, relatively inexpensive bite at lunchtime. It was in locations populated by office workers such as these, that sandwich bar chain Pret A Manger initially flourished.

Achievements

Since it was established in 1986, Pret A Manger has revolutionised its chosen market. From the outset the company has used nothing but fresh, natural ingredients in its sandwiches, which are served – invariably with a genuine smile – by friendly, helpful staff in a clean, modern environment. Others have attempted to replicate the Pret 'formula', but Pret's relentless innovation, attention to detail and unwillingness to compromise has kept it ahead.

Over the last decade, Pret A Manger's growth has been rapid. The number of shops had reached 50 by 1997, and 100 by the end of 2000. At the end of 2002, that number stood at 145. Now, as well as prime sites in over fifteen UK cities – including Birmingham, Brighton, Cambridge, Edinburgh, Glasgow, Leeds, Manchester and Oxford – Pret A Manger has gone international with a fast programme of shop openings in Hong Kong, New York and Tokyo. Today the company employs more than 2500 staff and has an annual turnover of more than £130 million.

The first Pret A Manger shop had its own kitchen where fresh ingredients were delivered first thing in the morning, and food was prepared on site throughout the day. Every Pret shop opened since has followed this model, with team members still making all the sandwiches, wraps and baguettes they sell in each shop, every day.

The company's mission statement, displayed prominently in each shop, sums up its approach: "Pret creates handmade natural food avoiding the chemicals, additives and preservatives commonly found in much prepared and fast food". Everything on the Pret menu – whether a special fish sushi, the traditional egg & cress sandwich, freshly-pressed carrot juice or the indulgent chocolate brownie – complies with these principles. Pret pays painstaking attention to the way it sources ingredients, regularly auditing suppliers and reviewing the effectiveness of its supply-chain procedures and in-shop systems to ensure the ingredients used are as fresh as possible. For example, each shop bakes their own supply of baguettes and croissants and toasts almonds and pine-nuts every day.

History

Pret A Manger was founded by entrepreneurs Julian Metcalfe and Sinclair Beecham, who quit their City jobs after reasoning they could do a better job than the many and varied sandwich bars lining the streets of the capital. Their first shop, on Victoria Street in London, built its reputation on being 'passionate about food' and uncompromising on freshness. The concept took off and within a year the shop was serving more than 7,000 customers a week.

In 1998, Andrew Rolfe joined Pret as Chairman & Chief Executive and has been instrumental in steering the company's current expansion. In January 2001 the McDonald's Corporation bought a minority stake in Pret A Manger. Although they have no direct influence over what is sold, or how it is sold, it is their international influence and expertise in property, construction and business systems which has helped to enable Pret to recently expand further beyond the UK.

As well as delicious fresh food, Pret has a strong reputation for efficient, friendly service. A company standard is that customers should be able to 'pay without delay', meaning no-one should have to queue for more than 90 seconds before being served. Even a cappuccino will be freshly made and served within 60 seconds. Pret's team members are not constrained by any kind of prescriptive customer service training; instead they are encouraged to bring their own personalities to work. Basically, Pret says, it strives to recruit and retain individuals who like dealing with people. As a result of this, the company has developed a loyal and vocal following. Customers' views are actively solicited, via informal comment cards in the shops (the text of which contains a pledge from the shop manager: "My team and I meet every morning. We will discuss the points you've raised…the good, the bad and the ugly"), by printing contact details on every piece of packaging, and through a feedback section on website www.pret.com.

Pret's innovative recruitment and incentive programmes have won a number of industry awards. Recent accolades include being rated one of the top ten companies to work for in Europe by Fortune magazine (February 2002) and for the second year running being named one of the top 50 best places to work in the UK by The Sunday Times (March 2002).

In 2002, a new stand-alone recruitment centre was opened in Victoria train station. This year alone, it expects to receive over 70,000 enquiries from prospective job candidates. Of these, only 6% are likely to be accepted for interview, with less than half of those going on to receive job offers. The unconventional interview process consists of candidates being interviewed firstly by the recruitment centre team (all of whom used to work in the shops themselves), then by a Pret manager. If things look good so far, the candidate gets invited along for a 'Pret Experience Day' which involves working a full day in the shop (including the 6:30am start in the kitchen). At the end of the day, the shop team – each of whom will have spent some time with the candidate – get to vote on whether they feel he or she has the necessarily skills, enthusiasm and attitude to join their team. Only if the team vote for the person, do they receive a job offer. Those who are taken on then go through an intensive ongoing training plan, beginning with a highly-structured ten day induction period.

Pret's internal communication style has always been open, honest and two-way. In each shop, the day begins with a team brief where company news and any other relevant information is shared. A daily news email keeps everyone informed of events likely to affect business during the next 24 hours. Once every three months, all shop managers and head office staff get together to review the company's recent performance and flag forthcoming initiatives. Staff magazine 'The Pret Star' is produced by Pret's full-time journalist, and is uncensored in any way by Senior management. Staff attitudes are also captured once a year through a company-wide opinion survey.

Another Pret innovation is the 'Buddy Scheme' where each member of the office team is 'paired up' with one of the shops. Everyone based in the office therefore spends at least one day a quarter in their Buddy shop, making sandwiches and coffees and serving customers. This is a way of ensuring they keep in touch with customers and life in the shops generally, and can witness first-hand how their own work contributes to the company's success.

Product

The core product range comprises twenty different granary sandwiches, up to six baguettes and four tortilla wraps. Sidelines include cakes, danishes, crisps, salads made in-store, and hot and cold drinks. To keep the menu exciting and innovative, new products and flavours are constantly being introduced (even though probably only one idea in every twenty makes it through the testing process). Over the past year, a new product has gone on sale, on average, every four days.

At the end of each day, any sandwiches, baguettes or wraps that haven't been sold are offered to charity to help feed the homeless. In the UK, Pret's work in this area has been predominantly with the London-based organisation, Crisis. Already in New York and Hong Kong, Pret has forged strong links with City Harvest and St James' respectively.

Pret's innovations extend beyond sandwiches.

It was the first retailer to put sushi on to the high street, among the first to make all products GM-free, and the first major coffee retailer to introduce organic milk.

Recent Developments

In the past year Pret has launched a new half fat mayo range of sandwiches and baguettes, wheat-free open sandwiches, a range of new made-in-shop seasonal salads, mini-doughnuts, a daily changing menu of hot soups, and a range of food for kids.

In its new markets, Pret's menu has so far featured a mix of the company's 'classic' recipes, such as the Big BLT and Chicken Avocado, as well as new ideas and combinations specifically geared to local tastes.

In 2001 Pret launched its internet-based delivery service, 'Pret Delivery', providing breakfast and lunchtime food for businesses. With a million pound investment and a dedicated management and customer service team, delivery sales are scheduled to take a bigger slice of Pret's overall business.

Promotion

Pret A Manger has rarely used conventional advertising nor promotional activities. Its reputation has grown organically through word of mouth recommendations from customers and through press endorsement, in recognition of its high-quality products and service.

Pret does however, do small-scale tactical promotions. For example, as part of its advertising-free launch in Scotland, complimentary sandwiches were delivered to offices in the area. Such initiatives are largely confined to new shop openings. Pret is very confident about its food and believes that the most effective marketing is for people to taste the difference themselves.

The look and feel of the shops is distinctive: stainless steel interiors and bright colours give a sense of vibrancy and create an expectation of cleanliness and pace. Customers experience the 'passion' through the quality of the food, the attitude and service of the staff and the messages on the packaging and the walls of the shops. The mission statement is displayed prominently in every outlet, and the walls are adorned with 'Pret Passion Facts' – a selection of stories about the lengths Pret goes to, to find the right ingredients and suppliers to guarantee delicious fresh products.

Brand Values

Though Pret has rarely carried out conventional brand or product advertising, recent focus groups have proven that customers have a strong clear image of the brand personality and style. Key words used to describe the brand have been 'cosmopolitan', 'young', 'discerning', 'principled', 'obsessive', 'conscientious' and 'passionate'. The personality and style are underpinned by Pret's core values: passion (for food, enthusiasm and belief, a love of life and others), integrity (honesty, principled with the courage of their convictions), uncompromising (striving for perfection, the best taste and quality, driven yet respectful of others and approachable), and commitment to constant innovation.

www.pret.com

Things you didn't know about Pret A Manger

Each week, every Pret A Manger shop is 'Mystery Shopped' through an independent company. The mystery shoppers focus on key Pret standards, and team members' weekly bonuses are linked to how well their shop performs.

Any member of staff mentioned by name in a letter from a customer for good service gets a silver star made exclusively by Tiffany the jeweller.

Pret throws huge summer and Christmas parties for all its staff and suppliers, with all food, drink and entertainment laid on for free. Radio 1 even flagged the Pret Summer party one year as worthy of gatecrashing.

Staff magazine 'The Pret Star' was crowned the best staff magazine in the UK at Total Publishing's Corporate Communications Awards in 2000.

The Pret brownie is currently in its 33rd incarnation, with each change to the recipe reckoned to have improved on the previous one.

Market

When people think oats many think of Quaker. The brand is synonymous with hearty breakfasts and enjoyed by many people all year round. However, as a traditional winter warmer, porridge comes into its own when the 'clocks go back' and the weather gets colder.

Porridge has been a staple of the Scottish diet since the Middle Ages and brand sales in Scotland continue to be stronger than those seen in the rest of the UK with Scott's Porage Oats (also owned by Quaker) taking the highest brand share (Source: Mintel 2002). The main competitors to Quaker brands in the UK hot cereals sector are Ready Brek and supermarkets' own-label product (Source: ACNielsen).

More and more people in Britain are adopting a positive approach to their health and diet. Quaker Oats is the market leader with 13.3% of the total hot cereals market and is introducing new consumers to the taste and proven health benefits

heart disease". This provides consumers with on-pack, positive health information.

Achievements

Quaker Oats is no stranger to recognition both at home and abroad. In 1950 Quaker Oats Ltd received the Royal Warrant and this commitment to quality is still evident today. The mill at Cupar, Scotland is the company's main centre of oat milling excellence in Europe, and is fully accredited to the most exacting worldwide quality standards (including ISO9002).

In 2001 the US magazine Business Ethics named the Quaker Oats Company as one of the '100 Best Corporate Citizens'. The magazine ranks public companies based on corporate service to various stakeholder groups, including employees, customers, the community, shareholders and the environment. Quaker ranked 51st and has also featured in previous years.

'Bottom line' achievements are no less

sold in open barrels at general stores. When these independent companies combined they brought together the top oat milling expertise in the US.

The founders adopted the Quaker symbol to represent the purity of living, honesty and strength of character epitomised by the Quaker movement – qualities they wanted to emulate in their new venture. The original trademark depicted a man in full Quaker outfit carrying a scroll bearing the word 'pure'. When it was registered at the United States Patent Office in 1877, it was the first trademark to be registered for a breakfast cereal. In later years, the character evolved to become more robust and cheerful while sustaining the image of tradition and honesty.

In 1899 Quaker Oats Ltd was formed in the UK. Initially it imported products from Quaker mills in Canada and the US, but demand grew steadily and in 1936 a manufacturing site was built at Southall in Middlesex to process grain in this country.

of porridge. Though women over 45 make up 37% of the market for Quaker Oats, the brand enjoys a younger consumer profile than for porridge generally, with children and young adults being significant consumers.

Quaker has found that product innovation and marketing are the key factors in attracting new consumers. Quaker Oatso Simple – single serve microwaveable portions in different flavours – amount to 20% of the market in value terms. Backed up by television advertising in the winter months, Oatso Simple is the fastest growing brand in the hot cereal market.

People have trusted the health benefits of oats for many years and Quaker Oats has worked hard to cement the link in consumers' minds between its product – pure and natural oats – and maintaining a healthy heart. In 1997, the US Food and Drug Administration (FDA) approved the first food-specific health claim. The claim, which can be used on oatmeal and oat rich products, reads "soluble fibre from oatmeal, as part of a low saturated fat, low cholesterol diet, may reduce the risk for

impressive, with Quaker the only UK cereal company to enjoy two years of continuous value growth (Source: ACNielsen 2002).

History

The word porridge is believed to have its origins in the old French word potage meaning soup or stew. In the middle ages, oats played a vital role in the European peasant's diet and old Scottish crofter cottages often had a 'porridge drawer' into which porridge was poured, cooled and cut into slices.

The origins of the Quaker Company started in 1850 when one John Stuart left the Highlands of Scotland for Canada where he acquired an old oat mill that produced 25 barrels of oatmeal a day. He and his son Robert later moved to Cedar Rapids, Iowa, where they built a new mill and, in association with other creative and progressive people in the industry, built up a substantial business. The three founding companies began to process and sell high quality oats for consumers, giving families in the US a superior product than that

In 1982 Quaker Oats Ltd bought A & R Scott (maker of Scott's Porage Oats) and in 1989 the company announced that the oat mill at Cupar in Fife was to become the main centre of Quaker's oat milling in Europe. The mill was extensively expanded to become one of the largest oat mills in Western Europe and its products are sold in Scandinavia, France, Africa and the Middle East as well as the UK.

The original Cedar Rapids mill has now grown to become the largest plant of its kind in the world, employing around 1400 people. It is one of more than 30 factory sites manufacturing Quaker cereal products around the globe, the others being in Argentina, Brazil, Britain, US, Canada, Colombia, Italy, The Netherlands and Venezuela.

Product

Porridge is not short of attributes. It is easily digestible, provides long-lasting energy and contains more nutritional value than any other cereal. A good source of energy-giving fats and carbohydrates, oats also contain protein for growth and the repair of

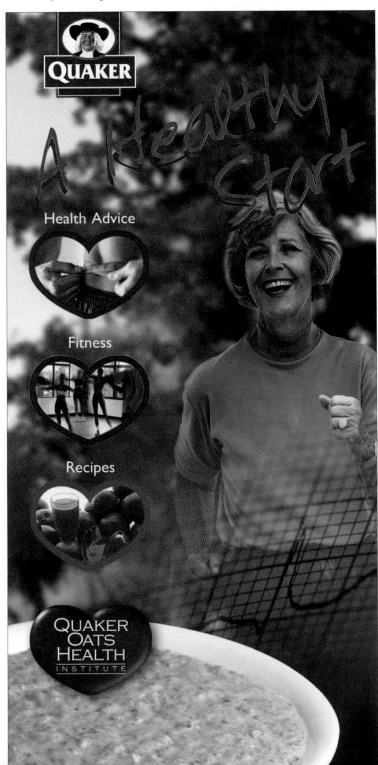

body tissues, iron for the blood and a range of vitamins, including Vitamin B1. Quaker Oats are rich in soluble fibre, called beta-glucan, which acts as a series of tiny sponges that soak up fatty deposits during digestion, therefore helping to reduce excess cholesterol levels in the blood, particularly if eaten as part of a low fat diet.

Quaker Oats use only the best oats and, on arrival at the mill in Cupar, testing by the Quality Assurance department ensures they meet stringent quality standards. The oats are stored in a 9000-ton capacity storage area before being transported to an initial processing area where all the agricultural

impurities are removed. Then the husk is removed from the 'groat' – the kernel of the grain – and the groats are cleaned further before being processed in kilns to achieve their flavour. A special granulating machine then cuts the oats into three, each of which will eventually become an oat flake.

The groats are partially pre-cooked by high capacity steamers and are then passed through heavy rollers that turn them into flakes. These flakes are then rolled to a specific thickness. Careful control is required, because this thickness determines the texture of the finished flake and therefore the time it will take to cook. Quaker Oats is a 100% natural cereal with no artificial additives.

Quaker is not afraid to add to its traditional recipes to appeal to a younger market. Quaker Oatso Simple uses taste and convenience to capture a new audience. Single-serve portions of Quaker Oats Oatso Simple come in five popular flavours including Original and can be microwaved once milk is added. Oatso Simple has proved a popular choice among people who appreciate the benefits of a warm and healthy breakfast but didn't think they had the time to enjoy it.

Quaker Oats are also a popular and versatile ingredient. They can be added to soups or stews to give extra flavour and body, substituted for some flour in baking, or blended with egg white to make a crisp coating for meat, chicken or fish, as well as many other culinary uses.

Recent Developments

After 100 years as a publicly traded company, Quaker merged with PepsiCo in 2001. The combined entity is the fifth largest consumer goods company in the world.

Also in 2001, Quaker launched Scott's So Easy in Scotland. Scott's So Easy is a hot cereal in portion-controlled packs. The base is the original Scott's Porage Oats, offering a more textured porridge than Oatso Simple to cater for the differing tastes of the strong Scottish market.

Promotion

Quaker has always been extremely conscious of the benefits of motivating and compelling communications. To promote the energy benefits and health-giving properties of porridge, one of the ads from the 1930s featured the fresh-faced film star and dancer Jessie Matthews. The vitamins contained in oats were heralded as a tonic to prevent 'nerviness'. The ad read: 'Nerves have never troubled Jessie, temperament and temper are unknown to her. Her girlhood growth was

healthy and normal, and her energy is proverbial. She's seen to it that her daily food includes the vital tonic Vitamin B – she's stuck to the golden rule of her childhood, porridge oats for breakfast from Quaker Oats.' Movie star Shirley Temple and cricketer Jack Hobbs were among the other celebrities enlisted to promote Quaker Oats.

In recent years, Quaker Oats has capitalised on the public's growing concerns about maintaining a healthy diet. Its communications highlight the links with maintaining a healthy heart and eating Quaker Oats as part of a balanced, nutritious diet. An important element of the brand's communications is informative guides on keeping healthy produced by the Quaker Oats Health Institute. The Institute provides material for health professionals and their patients in surgeries and health centres across the UK.

As a family favourite on cold mornings it makes sense for Quaker Oats to sponsor GMTV weather. The sponsorship communicates the warm properties of the product during the winter season.

Brand Values

Quaker Oats continues to sustain its heritage of providing traditional and natural goodness combined with quality and trustworthiness. The product is warming, filling and satisfying and offers significant health benefits. In short it is natural, simple and good for you.

www.quakeroats.com

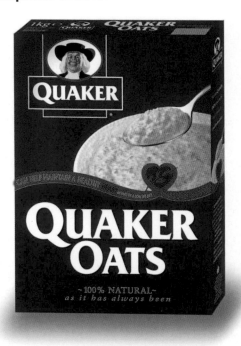

Market

It's a fact of life that most cars will break down at one time or another. New cars are increasingly reliable, but the incidence of simple faults like flat batteries and flat tyres remains stubbornly high; supplemented by electronic-related failures. For most of us, the answer to these problems is to request assistance from a breakdown recovery organisation. There are 27.5 million cars on the road in the UK and 30.6 million licensed drivers, 75% of which have membership of a motoring organisation, either individually or as part of a corporate scheme. RAC's share of the market is approximately 30%.

Achievements

RAC has been meeting the needs of motorists since the beginning of motoring itself. The core of RAC's offering is its roadside breakdown service, which today is enjoyed by 6.5 million motorists – two million individuals and 4.5 million corporate members. Currently, half of all new subscribers to breakdown services join RAC. RAC cover is included when you purchase a new car from a number of leading manufacturers: over 45% of new cars carry RAC cover, the largest market share of any breakdown supplier in the UK.

In 1986 RAC revolutionised its breakdown recovery provision with the introduction of CARS – Computer Aided Rescue Service. This prompted a massive revival in the organisation's fortunes. In five years, RAC membership doubled and profits trebled. These days RAC patrols reach over 80% of breakdowns in under an hour. The use of leading edge technology, including sophisticated diagnostic equipment and a complete library of technical data accessed within seconds via CD Rom, enables 1,350 expert RAC patrols to fix over 80% of breakdowns at the roadside and get members back on the move quickly and safely. RAC recently rolled out a new contact centre handling system – iCAD – which is focused on improving the speed and accuracy with which in-bound customer calls are handled and members are assisted. In addition, RAC is developing its approach to customer-centric management with the introduction of new software to better utilise customer information for those using multiple RAC motoring products and services.

RAC has developed a host of additional services, which are available both to breakdown members and non-members alike. The organisation offers a broad range of services completely dedicated to the needs of motorists – from roadside assistance, to car financing, insurance, legal services, driver training, travel services and glass repair and replacement.

History

Today's RAC has its roots in the Royal Automobile Club, the UK's oldest and most influential motoring organisation, established in 1897. In the early days, most motorists joined the RAC, which became the arbiter of matters relating to cars and driving. It promoted and enhanced the new 'motoring movement' by teaching driving, issuing road maps, approving garages and hotels, organising insurance and eventually establishing Road Patrols to help its members. These became the forerunners of the breakdown service for which RAC is best known today. The RAC carried great prestige and authority and became the governing body of motorsport; setting standards and advising governments. Its palatial Edwardian clubhouse in Pall Mall was the 'Vatican of motordom' and its word was treated as law on everything from automobile etiquette to engineering refinement.

However, complacency and lack of vigorous leadership saw RAC fortunes decline over time to crisis point in the 1970s, mirroring the woes of the domestic motor industry.

A renaissance in the 1980s and 1990s saw the RAC's motoring services revolutionised, setting new standards of service which its competitors struggled to match. And this attracted an enormous increase in membership. In 1998, the full members of the RAC voted to sell the motoring service division, and in June 1999 RAC Motoring Services was acquired by Lex Service plc, a motoring and vehicle services provider with businesses including the contract hire and fleet management of cars, vans and trucks. Over the next three years Lex structured its businesses to maximise the links with RAC and in September 2002 the company was renamed RAC plc. While still operating through the RAC, Lex and BSM brands, the corporate name change enables the company to leverage the value of the RAC brand for investors and potential employees. RAC plc is now established as an integrated company with a clear vision to be the first choice for motoring and vehicle solutions for consumers and businesses. The company is no longer related to the Royal Automobile Club.

Product

RAC's vision is to provide a full and comprehensive range of 'individual motoring solutions' for both the consumer and business marketplace – be it windscreen repair and replacement, driver training, vehicle inspections, legal and financial services or up to the minute traffic and travel information. Members enjoy discounts on a wide range of products and services, the scope of which has grown as a result of the integration of RAC plc.

Customers travelling at home and abroad have access to services including European breakdown assistance, travel insurance, travel accessories, route planning and hotel and holiday reservations.

Fully qualified engineers conduct vehicle examinations for individual motorists, manufacturers and garages, utilising online information sources to search a vehicle's background.

RAC's Financial Services team has been offering insurance for over 50 years and has a wide and growing range of motoring related products including: private motor, motorcycle and caravan insurance, personal accident insurance, classic car insurance, motor and all-purpose loans and personal leasing.

RAC Legal Services provides a wide range of legal products supported by an in-house team of qualified solicitors and barristers working in conjunction with a nationwide panel of solicitors. The Legal Services team helps RAC members pursue personal injury claims, recovering over £33 million on behalf of members in the last year alone. Legal Expenses Insurance is also available to members at a small premium. RAC Accident Solutions comes free with breakdown cover and can help by assessing the scene of an accident, providing vehicle replacement or pursuing compensation for personal injury.

RAC's driving school, BSM, is the world's largest driver training company and the only national driving school to have a high street presence with over 108 centres. BSM is at the forefront of training technology, having invested in driving simulators and computerised theory training. The latest of these is MAP – Mind Alertness Programme – a CD Rom based programme which tests drivers' cognitive skills.

RAC is also driving the development of in-car traffic and route-finding information using communications and satellite location technology. Through a joint venture with Trafficmaster, RAC has developed smart navigation services, such as SmartNav (the first any-car system to combine satellite navigation, live traffic information and operator support at the touch of a button) and RAC Live, the traffic and travel information service.

The award-winning RAC website provides online services, from live traffic news, route planners and hotel booking to vehicle examinations, car insurance and motoring advice.

Recent Developments

New product and service developments are constantly being explored at RAC. The brand identity has been thoroughly overhauled in recent years, bringing it up to date and shedding the last of the Royal Automobile Club associations. The most visible expression of this is the distinctive orange livery of RAC's fleet of breakdown vehicles, which is both eye-catching and safety-focused.

RAC continues to publish the authoritative annual Report on Motoring (previously produced by Lex), which has evolved into a suite of research reports on the key issues affecting motorists. Established in 1987, the report provides a consistent source of fact and reason amidst the heat of transport debates.

Despite the rapid expansion in the range of products and services it offers, RAC remains

focused on motoring and motorists. All new opportunities are focused in this area, with no expansion into non-motoring ventures. A good example of this is RAC's acquisition of Auto Windscreens, the glass repair and replacement company. RAC Auto Windscreens provides 24 hour a day replacement services for damaged glass, totalling more than 620,000 vehicles' windscreens and side and rear windows a year. Since becoming part of RAC, a rebranding process of its fleet of

800 vans, mobile units and 160 professional fitting centres has taken place, meaning that the distinctive orange RAC livery is even more visible up and down the country.

Promotion

RAC has a considerable history as a television advertiser. Campaigns have, for the most part, focused on roadside assistance, perhaps most memorably with the 'New Knights of the Road' campaign. The decision to adopt the positioning – 'Individual Motoring Solutions' – prompted a new advertising approach and the appointment of WCRS in March 2000. The new advertising campaign was developed to broaden the perceptions and understanding of RAC beyond its traditional role as a breakdown organisation. A selection of specific products and services were featured in the campaign, each highlighting a key benefit that RAC can offer to all motorists; not just its breakdown members. A new strap line: 'A to B – we RAC to it' was developed to communicate RAC's expanding vision and positioning. It is now used throughout all communications as an encapsulation of the company's proposition.

RAC's long-time association with motorsport was revived in 2002. As well as agreeing a sponsorship deal on behalf of RAC Financial Services with up and coming driver Edward Redfern in the Zip Formula, RAC has provided sponsorship support for Darren Manning in ASCAR and in Team St George at The Rockingham 500 on behalf of RAC Auto Windscreens. This activity has proved successful in building on RAC's heritage (harking back to RAC's role as the governing body of motorsports and sponsorships of the RAC Rally and British Grand Prix), and supporting a range of formulas well known to motorsports fans. RAC's sponsorship of Redfern and Manning has also proved useful for cross-marketing purposes, with the two drivers taking part in a number of events on the company's behalf including the Motor Show and the MPG Driving Challenge.

RAC also undertook to sponsor channel five's peak-time movies in 2002, which enabled the company to build awareness of over eighteen products and services via different idents shown at the end of multiple ad breaks.

Brand Values

RAC's brand positioning was reviewed in 2000, following an extensive programme of research. This resulted in the development of 'Individual Motoring Solutions' as a concept which describes the present and future role of RAC. This became the central brand positioning

statement to differentiate the organisation within the broader motoring market. RAC had a powerful set of imagery and values attached to it by consumers, but not all of these were relevant to the new positioning the brand sought to adopt. Too many were rooted in the past and the old, traditional RAC. Nevertheless, there were some inherent strengths in the way RAC was perceived, which provided a platform for the development of new attributes. The research project enabled RAC to clarify the differentiating attributes that together define its strong and distinctive personality. These have since been enhanced to encompass a set of attributes relevant to the whole of RAC plc. These attributes centre on providing a high quality, prompt service and showing commitment and integrity towards staff and customers.

RAC continues to invest in the development, positioning and communication of its brand. The future lies in respecting its traditions and heritage as a protector, partner, provider and champion of motorists, whilst developing the highest levels of service. The final cornerstone of this brand positioning is presented in RAC's vision to maintain the positive associations members have from belonging to RAC as a result of additional benefits, value offers and incentives.

www.rac.co.uk

Things you didn't know about
RAC

RAC devised the formula for measuring horsepower.

RAC has been conducting vehicle inspections for 100 years.

RAC's recovery services do not stop at just road vehicles. RAC has been called on to help recover a light aircraft that had crash-landed in a field and to jump-start the London to Edinburgh sleeper train whose diesel engine had failed.

RAC's flagship Supercentre at Bradley Stoke near Bristol has twin masts which tower 215 feet over the M4/M5 interchange.

Mrs G Stockport, an RAC telephonist, had a call from a member who wanted to know why, after joining RAC, he hadn't received his uniform.

ROYAL DOULTON
COMPANY

Market

Pottery and ceramics are a strong indicator of the art and lifestyle of a given age. Indeed archaeologists rely on shards of pottery fragments to establish the level of sophistication of past civilisations.

Today's consumers are more demanding and discerning than ever before.

The rise in home entertainment has been matched by the introduction of contemporary, functional tableware. At the other end of the spectrum however, the decrease in traditional family meals and rise in solo eating, TV dinners and convenience foods has seen the companies extend their casual tableware ranges.

Withstanding market fragmentation, ceramic giftware has enjoyed considerable growth – gift-giving, home decoration and investment being the main motivations. Despite the introduction of many alternative forms of gifts, the ceramic form is sought after as offering true qualities of heritage, traditional craftsmanship and real long lasting value for money.

The key markets worldwide for premium ceramic tableware and giftware are the UK and Continental Europe, North America, Asia Pacific and Australasia. In total the global market is estimated to be worth over £1.5 billion.

Achievements

The Royal Doulton Company is one of the world's largest manufacturers and distributors in the premium ceramic tableware and giftware market. Its illustrious brand names include Minton, Royal Albert and the core Royal Doulton brand.

With 200 years of heritage, The Royal Doulton Company is a thriving global organisation, with around £140 million annual turnover, employing around 3500 people across its UK production houses and numerous distribution operations worldwide. Approximately half of all sales are generated overseas.

The Royal Doulton Company is a market leader within the ceramics and chinaware markets, around 40% of all English bone china being produced by Royal Doulton as well as almost half of the UK's ceramic sculptures.

The company's Hotel and Airline division is also one of the world's largest suppliers of bone china to the international airlines industry. Indicative of its continuing favour, the division holds major contracts to supply chinaware to British Airways Club World and Club Europe.

In total, The Royal Doulton Company produces a range of 30,000 different items across a broad range of product groups. As well as the company having provided Royal Doulton devotees with their treasured collection pieces, its Royal Albert design 'Old Country Roses' has become the world's best selling bone china tableware pattern, with over 150 million pieces having been sold since its introduction in 1962.

History

The Royal Doulton Company has been producing ceramics and tableware for 200 years. As far back as 1815 the company founder, John Doulton, began producing practical and decorative stoneware from a small pottery in Lambeth, south London.

His son, Henry Doulton, built up the business, relocating it 60 years later to Stoke-on-Trent. By 1901 the quality of Doulton's tableware had caught the eye of King Edward VII, who permitted the company to prefix its name with 'Royal' and the company was awarded the Royal Warrant.

The Royal Doulton Company expanded its production facilities and by the 1930s was involved in the manufacture of figurines and giftware.

The company was awarded the Queen's Award for Technical Achievement in 1966, for its contribution to china manufacture – the first china manufacturer to be honoured with this award.

In 1972, Royal Doulton was bought by Pearson and merged with Allied English Potteries. The move introduced a number of key brands, including Royal Crown Derby, founded in 1748, and also Lawley's retail chain of china and glass giftware.

In 1993, The Royal Doulton Company was demerged from Pearson and became a publicly quoted company that was listed on the London Stock Exchange.

Product

Each of company's principal brands – Royal Doulton, Minton and Royal Albert – enjoys a long association of royal patronage, and holds at least one Royal warrant. They are also trademark registered.

When drawing up new product design, the designers study the market, analyse consumer research and often refer to their own museum and archives for inspiration.

The Royal Doulton Archives, located at the Sir Henry Doulton Gallery, a museum of Royal Doulton in Burslem, Stoke-on-Trent, house a variety of material dating from 1815 to the present day. Contents include Royal Doulton Pattern Books containing over 10,000 hand-painted water-colours illustrating the talent of artists employed over the years by the Burslem Art Studio.

Apart from providing an invaluable historical record of decorative ceramic styles – from the exquisitely gilded and delicately hand-painted cabinet and tableware of the Victorian and Edwardian era to the bright and bold angular design of the 1930s Art Deco – this collection is an inspirational source for Royal Doulton's current Design Studio.

Today, Royal Doulton provides a wide range

of domestic tableware manufactured in bone china and fine china the brand is also featured in an extensive range of crystal stemware and giftware.

Royal Doulton lists amongst its products an extensive giftware range, character jugs, china flowers and an array of collectable figurines often known as the Royal Doulton 'pretty ladies'. Some of the figurines are inspired by history and literature, for example the figure of Heathcliffe and Cathy from 'Wuthering Heights'.

For the junior members of the household, Royal Doulton also produces nurseryware, and many of these ranges are of interest to adult collectors. Its most popular collection is 'Bunnykins', while 'Brambly Hedge' giftware, the Disney collections, such as 'Winnie the Pooh', have also excited and sustained much interest.

Royal Albert, which traces its origins back to 1896, has become an internationally recognised brand, offering domestic tableware and gift items. Equally famous, with an illustrious heritage, dating back to its inception in 1793, is the Minton range, best known for its most popular pattern Haddon Hall, which is particularly favoured by the Japanese market. Minton is also renowned for its intricate gold patterns, where one plate can cost £5,000. These, however, are unique works of art, many of which are purchased as heirlooms. The artists in the Minton Studio also undertake special commissions.

The Royal Doulton Company has a manufacturing capacity of around 500,000 pieces per week. Its tableware production factories are considered amongst the most advanced in the world. In addition, the company runs around 3000 tests per week to ensure that the highest possible quality of manufacture is maintained. The Royal Doulton Company is noted for its high standard of working practices and technology which is heralded as being amongst the most advanced and professional in the entire international china industry.

As the corporate ambition is to generate 50% of its sales overseas, an extensive distribution chain is required to oversee global sales and marketing. The company currently operates in over 80 different markets and has distribution companies in the US, Canada, Australia and Japan.

Recent Developments

The Royal Doulton Company is undergoing an important period of change in its long history as it implements a three brand master strategy as a

first step in developing the company's brands. New global merchandising systems, in-store environments product packaging, point of sale and have all been identified as key to the branded development.

The Royal Doulton Company has continued to do what it does best – produce top quality chinaware collections. The new ranges of casual dining-ware are stylish, functional and user friendly, suited to all modern appliances including dishwashers, microwaves, ovens and freezers.

The Licensing Division, created in the mid 1990s to propel the three brands into new product sectors, has achieved considerable success, not least the launch of Royal Bathrooms created by Twyford. Other categories inspired by the company's rich heritage and design include an extensive collection of fine art prints and furniture sold in the US market as well as teas, textiles, jewellery and ties in Japan.

In the UK licensed products include, kitchen textiles, Flemish tapestries and throws, stationery, children/baby gifts and accessories.

Promotion

Central to The Royal Doulton Company promotional and marketing activities have been the development and rationalisation of the brand and their communication. The introduction of everything from new logos to in-store promotional material and branded fixtures have demanded that the focus of activity be centred on the communication and effective introduction of the recent significant changes.

The Royal Companies immediate goal is to become more global, offering greater consumer relevance through a diversity of products and an extension of its offering through contemporary creations.

At grass roots level, The Royal Doulton Company continues to employ a variety of traditional promotional techniques ranging from in-store promotions, seasonal magazine and selected press advertising including supplements in bridal and lifestyle magazines.

There is also a strong and effective public relations campaign in place, which is reviewed annually.

Added to this, the visitor centre which was opened at The Royal Doulton factory, Nile Street, Burslem in 1996, is very popular. Open seven days a week, it features the world's largest public display of Royal Doulton figures, numbering over

1500. Visitors are also able to tour the factory and see product being made during the week.

As an acknowledged leader in china tableware, The Royal Doulton Company is working to maintain its position at the cutting edge of product development. Through building on its investments in areas such as a company owned factory in Indonesia, The Royal Doulton Company can maintain close control of its production and marketing throughout the world, making the most of its high brand awareness recognition.

Brand Values

Around the globe, The Royal Doulton Company is valued for its sense of heritage and Englishness. As one of the oldest and best-recognised chinaware brands in the world, The Royal Doulton Company has earned itself a reputation for excellence, quality and distinctiveness of design – values which it intends to build on in order to take the brand forward in the millennium.

Prized by collectors the world over, The Royal Doulton Company has an international reach extending way beyond its English roots and product. To sustain its position, The Royal Doulton Company emphasis for future brand growth centres on its ability to focus on people, to understand its consumer base fully and then to produce products which suit individual tastes and needs.

The Royal Doulton Company identifies its core brand values as integrity, innovation, creativity, craftsmanship and decorative skills.

www.royal-doulton.co.uk

The Real Network™

Market

Royal Mail has a massive and diverse customer base – every single person in the UK who sends or receives something in the post is a customer of Royal Mail.

The brand operates in the market for distribution of physical text and packages for non-guaranteed and express delivery. Both markets are growing with volumes rising 1-4% each year, dependent on sector. Around 90% of mail originates from businesses and the majority is sent to consumers. Of the various applications for which mail is used, financial transactions are the biggest in terms of volume, followed by retail, government and health. Goods distribution continues to grow steadily and this trend is expected to continue. But the fastest growth area for mail is in advertising, promotion and customer relations management (CRM).

The market is currently undergoing massive change. Alternative media, such as fax, email and mobile phones, have created significant competition in the letter and packet delivery sector. Developments in e-commerce in recent years have also changed the distribution market.

External factors such as globalisation, the advent of the regulator and European cross-border mail liberalisation are shaping the marketplace and demanding that Royal Mail adapts to meet the changing needs of current and future customers. Most of the UK market will be opened up by 2004, several years ahead of the rest of Europe. The regulator has announced plans to abolish all restrictions on market entry by April 2007.

As well as Royal Mail's core market in the UK, it also has an international customer base. As one of the world's largest carriers of international mail, Royal Mail despatches mail on 1400 scheduled flights every week to over 280 postal gateways worldwide.

Achievements

Royal Mail's greatest achievement is the way in which it collects, sorts and delivers the nation's mail in a 24-hour process which continues all year round. Royal Mail consistently delivers nine out of ten First Class letters on time, the day after posting.

Less well known is Royal Mail's capability in warehousing and customer return logistics where its services are state of the art. Up to 35,000 bar-coded items can be picked, packed and dispatched daily enabling business customers to realise the cash tied up in the customer returns channel.

The opening of the world's most technically advanced international mail centre in early 2003 puts Royal Mail in a strong position. The new centre is situated five minutes from Heathrow airport. At an investment of £150 million, the 'art mail centre' is a 24-hour, 365-day operation and can process ten million letters and packets a day.

In 2001, Royal Mail launched its successful £1 million First Class stamp promotion at Christmas which won a coveted award from the Institute of Sales Promotion and achieved awareness levels which put it in the top three most familiar Christmas promotions (Source: NFO BJM January 2002).

Keen to maintain mail's position as the third largest advertising media, Royal Mail has set up the Mail Media Centre, a one-stop shop for advertisers, offering specialist information, help and advice on the development and use of mail media. Royal Mail is a partner in the Postal Preference Service which helps improve the targeting of mail. Response uplifts of between 20-400% have been achieved using this data compared with traditional lifestyle data files.

In response to customers' preferences, self-adhesive stamps have now been rolled out in First and Second class stamp books across the UK, combining stamp manufacturing technology with the distinctive values of the traditional postage stamp.

History

Royal Mail is one of the most trusted brands in the UK. It is a valuable asset which has evolved and grown since 1635 when the service of accepting and handling mail by the Royal Posts was opened to the public by Charles I. This royal proclamation and the establishment of the General Post Office in 1660 began the crucial social change which put the postal service at the centre of the community and heralded a communications revolution. Letters were originally collected from households and handed to the local postmaster. Occasionally he would arrange onward delivery, but this was not granted to all until Queen Victoria's Jubilee Declaration in 1897. This face-to-face contact began the relationship for which Royal Mail is well known today.

The awareness of Royal Mail grew considerably once the Mail Coach service was introduced in 1784, launching the national postal network. New postal routes were opened and mail volumes increased dramatically with the introduction of the uniform postage rate in 1840. The first road-side post boxes were introduced in 1852. The 150th anniversary of post boxes was commemorated in 2002 with a set of special stamps featuring post boxes from the 1930s and 1960s.

Around the middle of the nineteenth century, mail carriages began to use the words 'Royal Mail' for the first time alongside the Royal cypher. The term 'Royal Mail' is steeped in history and has been in use since the seventeenth century, but Royal Mail has only been established as a business since 1986 with its own identity following three years later. The Cruciform logo now used includes the royal crowns – St Edward's for England and Wales and St James's for Scotland. Stamps, postmen and postwomen, vans and postboxes continue to symbolise the Royal Mail brand. Its heritage provides a solid foundation for what is now the most far-reaching communications network in the UK.

Product

Royal Mail's core offering centres around a range of physical distribution products for both consumers and businesses, as well as an increasing portfolio of electronic and internet solutions.

Mail is increasingly used as part of the business communications mix to attract customers and nurture business relationships as well as strengthening brands. A range of services is available to business customers, including Mailsort, Presstream, Packetpost and Special Delivery and significant savings can be made on standard postal rates depending on how the customer pre-sorts mailings.

Royal Mail is investing a great deal in its flagship Special Delivery product which guarantees delivery the day after posting for about a fifth of the cost of most courier services. A collection on demand service has recently been introduced for all UK businesses. A number of new variations on this service are in the pipeline for the future.

Despite the advent of fax, telephone and internet, direct mail volumes continue to grow strongly and now represent 14% of all advertising revenues.

Royal Mail has launched a new business product, known as mailmedia, which aims to transform the way businesses advertise using the mail by making it easier for them to price, plan and control their mailings. There is also a range of tools available online at www.royalmail.com to help smaller businesses with their mailing campaigns.

Royal Mail has continued to develop special edition stamps which are renowned for their fascinating range of designs and technical excellence. The 2002 stamp programme commemorated events as diverse as the Centenary of Kipling's 'Just So' stories and the Manchester Commonwealth Games. Stamp collecting remains a popular pastime and a way of collecting a little bit of history.

One of the most popular new ranges of Special Stamps is known as 'Smilers' which can be personalised with a photograph printed alongside the stamp to celebrate a variety of occasions.

Recent Developments

In common with all industries, the distribution market has been significantly affected by the opportunities represented by e-commerce. Royal Mail has seized these opportunities and developed a presence in this marketplace. In a nation with a relatively high internet penetration, Royal Mail has maintained an extremely high level of growth through its activities.

Royal Mail is working closely with a number of online businesses, most notably Amazon.co.uk, for whom it is the contracted delivery arm. Online retailers face the challenge of creating a real brand in an e-world and this is where Royal Mail can add value to the experience of many brands by becoming the trusted carrier for online customer orders.

The revolutionary software application Decide & Deliver was launched to make home shopping easier. The service acts as a 'web-based electronic postman'. It saves consumers time when shopping online and provides them with a range of extra delivery options. In addition, the Local Collect

Promotion

Much of the continued growth in mail volumes is attributed to a carefully planned and well executed marketing communications strategy. Even though the Royal Mail brand is one of the most well known in the UK, it does not rely on this alone to ensure continued growth. Good marketing communications help strengthen the brand and enable reinforcement of the core brand essence of 'reach'. Promotional activity spans both businesses and consumers and actively seeks to guide customers through the many mailing options available.

For consumers, promotions focus on useful information such as how to find the correct postcode and the latest recommended posting dates for Christmas. Sales promotions encourage active participation using innovative techniques which engage the nation.

For example, Royal Mail's biggest ever Christmas promotion, launched for the first time in 2001, was based on a £1 million prize campaign which gave a boost to Christmas First Class stamp volumes. The successful campaign grew the volume of First Class Christmas cards by nearly 12%.

For Christmas 2002, the First Class promotion was based on a partnership with the feature film 'The Lord of the Rings: The Two Towers'. This high profile partnership saw Royal Mail venture into the world of movies for the first time. The promotion offered customers buying books of First Class Christmas stamps the opportunity to 'Find the One Ring and Win £1 million'.

Special Delivery, Royal Mail's hero product, has its own dedicated TV campaign. Special effects

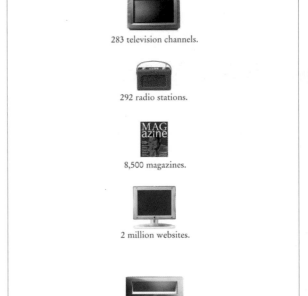

283 television channels.

292 radio stations.

8,500 magazines.

2 million websites.

Only one letterbox.

If your business advertises, always use direct mail as part of your media schedule to make sure the message gets picked up. It's the only medium that isn't fragmented and so goes directly to your target audience. For more information call 0000 000 000.

The Real Network

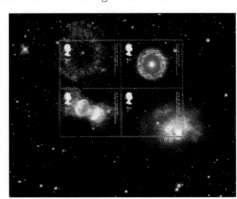

they have posted using Special Delivery.

Christmas 2002 saw the launch of a new online greeting card service which enables businesses and consumers to send real cards in the post anywhere in the world.

Brand Values

The Royal Mail brand is the biggest communications and distribution network in the UK. The core proposition for the brand is based on its unrivalled capability and the powerful fact that Royal Mail can reach virtually 100% of the UK population every day.

The network is powered by 160,000 postmen and women working in mail centres and out on delivery who daily interact with customers. 'The Real Network' strapline differentiates Royal Mail from other less tangible networks and plays to the inherent strengths of the brand as an enabler of UK business.

While the Royal Mail brand is well known for motivating consumers to send social mail, it is now positioned as a vital communications network at the heart of business life underpinned by the core brand values of speed, reliability and responsiveness.

www.royalmail.com

service allows consumers to choose delivery to a Post Office branch when ordering from participating retailers.

In the biggest shake-up of delivery services for many years, Royal Mail plans the national roll-out of a single delivery every day across the UK which will mean one million more First Class letters should hit their delivery target every week. This change to the pattern of national daily deliveries will also provide a five day week for the UK's delivery postmen and women, although deliveries will continue to be made six days a week. Business customers will be able to have their mail delivered from 6am with the Timed Delivery Service. Royal Mail is also planning to trial other variations to its standard delivery service including the choice of re-delivery in the evening or an option to collect mail from delivery offices.

are used to communicate the product's key features, boosting associations with both Speed and Reach by 8% in market research (Source: TNS, September 2002).

The focus of Royal Mail's latest television advertising is on highlighting the scale of the brand's capability and demonstrating its unrivalled reach throughout the UK.

Recognising the importance of new media, Royal Mail continues to develop its online presence in line with customer needs. The site has consistently achieved industry recognition as a well designed and customer focused site. It provides online information about products and services, as well as interactive services. 'Postcode Finder' allows customers to type in an address which then displays the relevant postcode. 'Track and Trace' enables customers to follow the delivery trail of items

Market

The UK adult soft drinks sector within the UK rose by 113% during 1999-2001 to achieve an annual consumption of 936 million litres at a total value of £639 million (Source: Mintel).

Schweppes, the original soft drinks brand, undoubtedly leads its category rivals in terms of the sheer durability of its brand heritage. The company that first set up shop in London's Drury Lane over three centuries ago, can rightfully claim to have pioneered the global carbonated soft drinks industry.

The total UK carbonates sector was valued at £8.4 billion during 2001, and is predicted to grow at a slightly faster rate than the overall soft drinks sector through until 2005 (Source: The Grocer 2001).

Competitive pricing and innovative new product development reflecting trends towards healthier life-style attributes is largely driving the sector's expanding consumer repertoire. The continuing challenge to brands will be to build upon established loyalty within the category via a greater understanding of changing preferences expressed through the customer base.

The Schweppes brand is owned within the UK by Coca-Cola Great Britain.

Achievements

Schweppes carbonated soft drinks, mineral waters and still drinks are available in over 200 different countries worldwide.

During its long history, Schweppes has picked up numerous awards for excellence, and has maintained an unbroken run of royal patronage since receiving its initial warrant in 1833.

History

Schweppes and, indeed, the global soft drinks industry, traces its origins to a German born Swiss jeweller enthused by the pioneering experiments with 'fixed air' carried out by Joseph Priestley in the mid eighteenth century.

Jacob Schweppe developed an amateur interest in physics and chemistry whilst training as a jeweller, which led to greater things. He may not have been the first to discover carbonation, but in 1783 he successfully applied the theory to inventing the first apparatus capable of producing artificial mineral waters. By 1792, Schweppe's early success in Geneva had prompted him to extend his developing business abroad. Encouraged by the positive interest of the British medical profession he began production of soda water from a factory in Drury Lane, London.

The business became a public limited company in 1887, by which time its manufacturing reach had extended as far a field as the US and Australia.

The company received a Royal Warrant which was renewed on the accession of Queen Victoria to the throne fourteen years earlier. Schweppes was subsequently invited to be sole supplier of soft drinks at the Great Exhibition of 1851. It was to be the single most influential event in establishing the company's worldwide reputation.

By the time the exhibition had closed, Schweppes had sold in excess of one million bottles. An eye-catching fountain flowing with the newly introduced Malvern soda water was placed centre-stage within the exhibition hall. This not only imprinted the brand's name in the minds of the six million visitors, but established a flair for promotion that has remained a continuing characteristic of the Schweppes brand profile.

Schweppes Indian Tonic Water is arguably the one product that is most readily identifiable with Schweppes worldwide. The strength of the branding is such that tonic water only achieved success within the US as an accompaniment for gin, once Schweppes commenced bottling operations there in the 1950s.

The pre World War II period was also marked by the formation of Schweppes (Colonial and Foreign) Limited in 1923, establishing the basis upon which a global network of local manufacture and franchised bottling operations soon replaced the hitherto traditional reliance upon exports.

The re-emergence of 'Schweppes' as an identifiable brand in the aftermath of World War II presaged a golden period of innovative advertising, incorporating a succession of creative campaigns presenting the name Schweppes in a witty and often irreverent tongue-in-cheek context; a tradition that continues to the present day.

'Schweppervescence' was quickly followed by the 'Schweppigram', 'Schweppshire',

and innumerable variations on a similar theme. Best loved of these was the 'Sch....you know who?' campaign, which dominated television and press advertising during the 1960s and 1970s.

In a less obtrusive, but equally impactful way, distinctive packaging has also played a major role in building consumer awareness to the brand; from the distinctive specially-designed 'egg-soda bottles' of the nineteenth century, through to the introduction of light-weight 'PET' bottles in 1994.

Product

Schweppes has extended way beyond its original carbonated water base, and now encompasses a wide selection of products. Schweppes provides an original range of intriguing blends and combinations. The fine blends of ingredients deliver crisp, clean tastes.

Schweppes product flavours are lifted by thousands of tiny bubbles and it is those bubbles, of which Schweppes has more per bottle than any other brand, that make Schweppes an ideal mixer and gives the brand its distinctive soundbite – 'Schhhhhh…'.

Schweppes Indian tonic combines a burnt citrus flavour and quinine and Schweppes Bitter Lemon combines the distinctive taste of quinine with real fruit juice and zest from whole fresh lemons.

Recent Developments

At the end of 2001, after twenty years in the same livery, Schweppes graphics were redesigned, keeping cues of authenticity such as the fountain device (originally introduced to mark the brand's involvement in the Great Exhibition) and introducing silver to reinforce the quality of the brand. New 180ml mini cans were brought in to further strengthen the offering of a perfect individual serving of a premium quality mixer.

Promotion

At the height of the original 'Sch…you know who?' campaign in the 1970s, the company's sophisticated, confident and witty interaction

been hugely successful and continues to drive media interest and anticipation whenever a new image is unveiled.

The 'Sch…You Know Who?' campaign and the subsequent debate around the theme of the 'real and unreal' has led to Schweppes further supporting photography as a medium which challenges viewers' perceptions and recent links have been made with exhibitions of a number of high profile photographers from the classic – Eve Arnold – to the contemporary – David LaChapelle. A specially commissioned 'Sch…you know who?' bar featuring hidden CCTV cameras that capture drinkers in 'off guard moments' has also become a regular fixture at photographic events at art galleries across the country. From this travelling bar, leading bartenders demonstrate the Schweppes perfect serve, creating Schweppes classic drinks for the event attendees.

Pursuing the theme of the perfect Schweppes serve, a large scale, modular travelling Schweppes bar was commissioned for summer 2002, inspired by London's Met Bar, to attend major outdoor events such as the Golf Open Championships, and Cowes Week to serve classic Schweppes mixed drinks in a stylish and contemporary surrounding.

with its market was so in tune with the times that research indicated that over 90% of the public were able to identify Schweppes as the product being advertised; despite the brand name never actually being mentioned. The campaign made a national star out of television actor William Franklyn, who returned the favour by making a television personality out of Schweppes.

In 2001 the brand returned to the 'Sch…you know who?' theme; the wit as ever in keeping with popular idiom and dependent upon capturing lookalikes of well known popular figures, ranging from the Prime Minister, 'Tony Blair' to the manager of the England football team, 'Sven Goran Ericsson' in off-guard moments. The award-winning campaign was created by Mother and shot by artist Alison Jackson in a distinctive black and white, grainy style. The photographs deliberately challenge perceptions of what is genuine and what is fake, by capturing moments that the viewer may have imagined, but never thought they would actually see. The campaign, targeted at an 'in the know' audience, has

Brand Values

Schweppes is 'the original soft drink brand' – a contemporary classic combining sociability with authentic heritage, quality, wit as well as confidence. Intriguing, effervescent and captivating, it has consistently kept itelf relevant, remaining prominent across three successive centuries.

Things you didn't know about
Schweppes

Schweppes Tonic Water has its origins in the days of the British Raj in India, where quinine (a bitter tasting drug made from cinchona bark) was the accepted antidote to numerous fevers. It was the custom to add citrus to lessen the otherwise bitter taste.

Schweppes pioneered the changeover to non-returnable bottles in 1966, effectively paving the way towards a major new sales market in supermarkets, off-licences and home consumption.

Market

Over the past 50 years, the adhesive tape market has expanded beyond its traditional home and office heartland to encompass applications especially developed for the DIY market. Demand for natural adhesives – including tape – has been fuelled by manufacturers' growing environmental consciousness and their concern to conserve resources and to use renewable raw materials where economically viable.

The total European clear sticky tape market is worth over £223 million per annum, while the UK adhesives tape market is valued at around £37 million. Office users account for 34% of the market, the DIY sector 30%, retail 28%, schools 2% and government 1%.

The market leader, Sellotape, enjoys the highest brand recognition in all sectors, and if Sellotape is available 71% of consumers have indicated that they would choose it over the competition (Source: Taylor Nelson Sofres). Sellotape holds 52% of the retail market, 45% of the office market and 11% of the DIY market. Sellotape sell more than 85 million rolls per year.

Achievements

Since it was launched into the stationery trade in 1938 Sellotape has become synonymous with clear adhesive tape and the word 'Sellotape' even has its own entry in the Oxford English Dictionary as a brand name.

Not surprisingly, given that Sellotape is to be found in most households, brand awareness is very high. Around 98% of UK consumers recognise the Sellotape brand name (Source: The Stationery Market in the UK Volume III 1993-1998 MPA International) and in unprompted research, it came out as one of the top ten best-known brands.

What is less well known is that Sellotape Original tape is made from completely biodegradable film in the UK tape market. All Sellotape products are manufactured under controlled quality management systems ISO 9001. The company has received environmental awards every year since 1996 from British Office Systems and Stationery Federation (BOSSF) and has applied for the highest British environmental standard ISO 14001.

Sellotape is the principal office tape in the UK.

History

Sellotape dates back to 1937 when Colin Kininmonth and George Gray coated cellophane film with a natural rubber resin to create a 'sticky tape' product that was based on a French patent. They registered their product under the name 'Sellotape' and began manufacturing in Acton, west London.

When World War II broke out, the company was put on war work and made cellulose tape for sealing ration and first aid packs and a cloth tape for sealing ammunition boxes. They also made a product in sheet form to cover windows to protect people from breaking glass.

In the mid 1960s Sellotape became part of the British packaging and paper conglomerate Dickinson Robinson Group (DRG). But in the late 1980s DRG was broken up and in 1991 Sellotape was given a new lease of life when it was restructured and endowed with new plant and systems. The brand flourished, adding new products for both the consumer and business sectors, and in 1995 it was relaunched as The Sellotape Company in order to take advantage of new market opportunities and exploit its innovation and new product development capability. Over the past few years, the company has extended its product portfolio into new market sectors, launching, for example, the Sellotape Office sub-brand.

Today, Sellotape products are as popular in the Retail market as they are in the commercial stationery market and they occupy as much space on the shelves of the DIY multiples as they do in stationers, high street shops and supermarkets.

Sellotape is a market leader abroad as well as at home. The brand is a registered trademark in 119 countries and has manufacturing sites in Dunstable in the UK and Auckland in New Zealand. The same rigorous manufacturing standards apply at each production location and the sharing of best practice ensures continuous improvement in customer service. All products are manufactured under controlled quality and environmental management systems.

In 2002 The Sellotape Company was taken over by Henkel UK Consumer Adhesives, part of the largest adhesive company in the world. Henkel Consumer Adhesives produces over 3000 specialised adhesives at 80 sites round the globe and sells them in 82 different countries.

Product

Sellotape Original is Europe's biggest selling clear cellulose pressure sensitive tape. A pressure sensitive tape is an adhesive tape that sticks to a wide

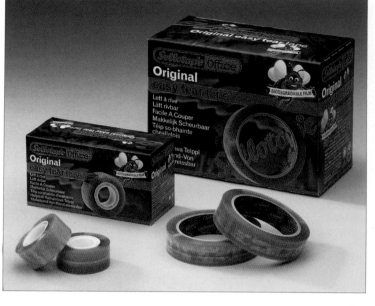

variety of clean dry surfaces with only the minimum of pressure applied. It is ready-to-use and does not need to be activated by water, solvent or heat. This kind of tape consists of a relatively thin, flexible backing or carrier, coated with an adhesive, which is permanently sticky at room temperature. The tapes can be manufactured with the adhesive coating on one side (single-sided) or both sides (double-sided) of the carrier.

Sellotape Original Tape is also made from the only completely biodegradable film in the European market. Whereas most other tapes are oil based, Sellotape is manufactured from cellulose, a natural wood pulp product. Its natural origins provide a number of intrinsic benefits over rival products: for example, it is naturally static-free which means it doesn't tangle while being handled, and it is easy to tear by hand without the need for scissors or teeth.

The way Sellotape is made is also environmentally friendly: the trees that produce the natural wood pulp are farmed on sustainable plantations, and it is produced in the UK so there are no long distribution chains.

Constant innovation has resulted in extensive development of both the consumer and office product ranges over the years. As well as the clear sticky tape that most people associate with Sellotape, products such as Original, Invisible, Double Sided and Sticky Hook & Loop have maintained the Sellotape brands standing within the market. Further developments have included Sellotape Diamond an 'ultra clear' strong tape, which is also waterproof and Sellotape Gift Tapes, a range of silver and gold holographic tapes which are designed to add a distinctive finishing touch to gifts. Pre cut sticky tape strips are the latest product to add convenience to the market. Sellotape also has products for other uses in the home such as Sellotape Pipe and Hose Repair, Sellotape Masking Tape, Sellotape Carpet to Floor and Sellotape Roof and Gutter Repair.

The company has used its brand heritage in recent years as a foundation to diversify into other business areas and Sellotape fast became as significant for the business user as it is for the householder. Furthermore, its chrome tape

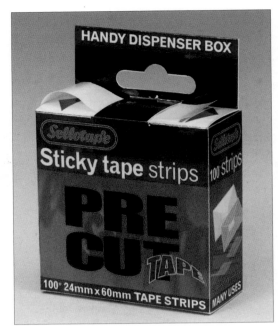

'Buzzy Bee' mascot. A free 'Buzzy Bee' soft toy was offered from January 2003 with every pack of twelve rolls of Sellotape Original. The relaunch was supported with consumer press advertising and a major initiative with schools to support the teaching of environmental awareness.

Sellotape has also launched an Environmental Themed learning pack for schools. Aimed at Key Stage 2 pupils, the pack contains teaching support material covering The Environment, Science, History and Geography and features the 'Buzzy Bee' character. The main topic of concern is to make children more aware of issues surrounding the 'health of the earth'.

dispenser is designed to expand tape usage, as well as being a stylish desk accessory. The New Wave™ dispenser allows the user to dispense and cut the tape in one.

Sellotape has used customer feedback and consumer research to design a complete range of over 70 products to suit every 'sticky' need around the home, office, garage and garden. Applications vary from binding books to repairing a broken hose – demonstrating the versatility of the Sellotape brand.

Recent Developments

Despite wide awareness of the Sellotape brand, the company isn't complacent and has kept abreast of the latest trends and technological developments in both the consumer and business sectors. Its most recent innovation is sticky tape strips – easy to use pre-cut tape strips in a convenient box which offers a good solution to present wrapping. They were launched in response to growing demand for convenient products.

For busy offices and post rooms the latest new development is Sellotape Printed Text Tape, a cost-effective, faster and more convenient alternative to sticky labels for marking up parcels and letters. Available in four messages: 'Urgent', 'Private and Confidential', 'Addressee Only' and 'Fragile', each roll of 'ultra clear' Sellotape is printed clearly in blue, giving a clean and professional look to post leaving the office. Each roll is supplied with its own dispenser, making it fast to use when post collection is looming, and at 33 metres long, the tape works out far more economical than labels.

The brand has also started to trumpet its green credentials with a major new rebranding of its core product Sellotape Original Tape. New packaging features bright blister cards with Sellotape's new

Promotion

Innovative promotional concepts now play a major role in Sellotape's marketing strategy, adding value to the Sellotape brand and generating customer demand.

For example, when teachers registered for a free environmental learning pack, they were entered into a prize draw to win a trip to the Eden project for two.

In the commercial stationery market, the company runs promotional campaigns to support its trade customers, encouraging office staff to specify Sellotape as their preferred office tape.

Promotional activity for the first three months of 2003 focused on relaunching Sellotape for the office market. New packaging featuring the 'Busy Bee' appeared in the new catalogue as the visible sign of the environmental benefits of cellulose, and Sellotape buyers were rewarded with a soft toy – a proven sales mechanism in the office market.

In the summer of 2002, Sellotape Office ran a major promotion with Coca-Cola™ to reward tape buyers with two free cans of the new Diet Coke with Lemon with every twelve roll promotional pack of Sellotape Original. The promotional packs had the coke cans shrink-wrapped

to the outside. It was the first time Coca-Cola™ had joined forces with a stationery brand for a major product launch.

This kind of support activity enables the Sellotape brand to sell at premium prices and generate strong sales. Indeed, EPOS data shows that Sellotape branded promotional packs achieve the highest stock turns of any stationery products in the supermarket and are among the highest of any non-food product.

Sellotape also has a website – www.sellotape.com – which give details of both consumer and dealer orientated promotions. The sites also include details of the Sellotape product range and the history of sticky tape.

Brand Values

Sellotape attests to the fact that a distinct and honest proposition can enjoy long-term popularity with the consumer and build itself a prestigious, highly valued brand name that produces high customer loyalty.

What's more, Sellotape's customer service is of a high standard. Delivery performance is measured both weekly and monthly in three operating countries. The company's emphasis on performance measurement has earned it prestigious supplier accolades from ASDA Wal-Mart and Homebase and 'Supplier of the Year' from Kingfield Heath.

Sellotape's wider impact on the environment and biodegradable properties has been recognised by The Sellotape Company receiving environmental awards every year since 1996 from the British Office Systems and Stationery Federation (BOSSF).

www.sellotape.com

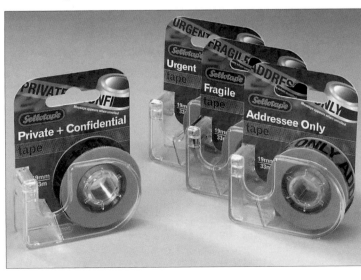

Sharwood's

Market

Over recent years, British tastes have changed enormously. With more and more of us cooking and eating food inspired by India, China and Thailand, stir-fries and curries are now part of our everyday lives. In 2001, the former foreign secretary, Robin Cook, highlighted this by declaring that Tikka Masala was the nation's favourite dish.

The market for home-cooked Asian food has grown by 74% since 1995. More than eighteen million UK households bought some form of it during the last year and the market is now worth £254 million. This growth has been fuelled by the rise of long-distance travel and the popularity of TV cookery programmes. Both have increased peoples' desire to experiment with and enjoy more exotic food in their own homes.

Sharwood's has been at the forefront of developing the popularity of Indian and Oriental cuisine. Having come into being in the 1880s, the brand now comprises an extensive range of products covering Indian, Chinese and Thai. The range includes cooking sauces and pastes, ingredients sauces, dipping sauces, curry powders, noodles, naans, puppodums, prawn crackers and, of course, its famous 'Green Label' mango chutney.

Today, Sharwood's 33% share makes it the biggest brand in the Asian sauces and accompaniments market by far. With its broad portfolio of products, the brand is able to cater for people with a range of tastes as well as for people with a variety of different cooking skills.

Achievements

Sharwood's track record has been a history of firsts. It was the first brand to introduce Tikka Masala to Britain in the early 1980s and since then the market for cooking curries at home has exploded. In the last twelve months, the UK population has consumed over ten million jars of Sharwood's sauces.

Sharwood's was also first on the market with cook-to-eat puppodums. In its quest to bring the best food from Asia to Britain, Sharwood's travelled to Chennai (formerly Madras) in India in the late 1980s to track down the perfect ingredients. Bought as small, uncooked discs, the puppodums are fried at home and expand to the size and freshness of those in Indian restaurants. The success of these cook-to-eat products led to Sharwood's subsequent launch of a selection of ready-to-eat puppodums in 1985. Eaten straight from the pack or warmed gently first, these convenient light and crispy accompaniments come in plain, spiced and garlic & coriander flavours. Over 1,000 ready-to-eat puppodums are eaten every hour in the UK alongside a curry or simply as a delicious and tasty snack and Sharwood's now owns over 80% of the ready-to-eat puppodums sector.

Over ten years ago Sharwood's was also the first to develop naan breads for the UK market. A traditional accompaniment for an Indian meal, naans are soft and lightly baked breads made from wheat flour blended with natural yoghurt. Alongside puppodums, naans can complete a Sharwood's curry, especially when eaten with a healthy dollop of mango chutney.

More recently, Sharwood's has successfully innovated within Indian and Oriental sauces.

In autumn 2000, Sharwood's launched a new range of Indian sauces that was inspired by peoples' favourite dishes from Indian restaurants. Based on high quality ingredients, this range of sauces allowed consumers to easily recreate the taste of their favourite restaurant meals in their own homes. Catering for a wide variety of different tastes, Sharwood's provides the familiar Korma, Balti and Madras sauces through to the more experimental Dopiaza, Bhuna and Dhansak dishes. This range also did something very different with its packaging. Made famous by Sharwood's 100-year-old 'Green Label' mango chutney, Sharwood's used its iconic square jar for the new sauces. In combination with striking pack designs that capture the vibrancy, colour and fun of Indian cooking, Sharwood's new range of Indian sauces stand out boldly on the supermarket shelves.

Sharwood's has been equally successful at pioneering Chinese and Thai food. As with curries, the brand's introduction of a range of Oriental stir-fry sauces during the 1980s heralded the rise of home stir-frying. The first Sharwood's products were based around the classic flavours typically associated with Oriental cooking. This range provided people with an inspiring range of convenient bases for making their own authentic stir-fry dishes and is still selling strongly today. Sharwood's has continued to innovate with its Oriental sauces by introducing consumers to new and exotic taste combinations from around the globe. Relying once again on the best ingredients, it has created a range of authentic sauces with a twist – Sharwood's does more than just offer people a straightforward sweet and sour and instead, its variant is combined with mango. The same is true of Hoi Sin & Plum, Sweet Chilli & Red Pepper and Black Bean & Green Pepper.

Not content with providing sauces, pastes, ingredients and accompaniments to create Indian, Chinese and Thai meals, Sharwood's also provide help and inspiration in the kitchen. The website (www.sharwoods.com) contains recipe ideas and suggestions and offers a 'recipe selector' service. Having understood the main ingredients that you want to use and the length of time that you have available to prepare the dish, it suggests a variety of recipes for you to choose from. The Sharwood's recipe selector was the first of its kind in the Asian food category and was found to be so useful and inspiring for people that it won the 'New Media' category at the Food and Beverage Creative Excellence Awards in 2000.

History

The origins of Sharwood's lie in the 1800s. In 1864, James Allen Sharwood, a city broker turned speciality food purveyor, travelled to India and the Orient in search of new spices to bring back to the West. In 1889, he founded J A Sharwood & Co as 'Importers & Exporters of Foreign Produce' in London. He was an avid traveller and was fluent in French, German, Spanish and Italian. Above all he was a gourmet who turned good food and travel into a business. The early price lists covered an extensive range of 'specialities, sweetmeats and delicacies' that James had discovered on his travels – even today his stock would put the most exotic food halls to shame. Indian foods like curry powders, pickles and chutneys from Bombay and Madras were first introduced to the UK under Mr Sharwood's expert guidance. By 1927, James had hung up his exploring gear, but his reputation for introducing Britain to some of the finest food from around the world lives on today in the brand that bears his name.

Since then, Sharwood's has twice been awarded the Royal Warrant. In 1947, the brand won the privilege as 'Manufacturers of Chutney & Purveyors of Indian Curry Powder' and in 1994, as 'Manufacturers of Oriental Sauces'.

In 1963, RHM acquired Sharwood's. Since then, it has further developed the popularity of Indian and Oriental cuisine and built up Sharwood's in the UK and in a few countries overseas. It has helped to transform the original

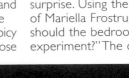

pioneering import and export business into one of the country's biggest brand names.

Product

Lying at the heart of Sharwood's success is a multicultural team of people who are experts in Indian, Thai, Chinese and British cuisines. All are dedicated to turning inspiration from delicious, authentic dishes into food that can be prepared and enjoyed by British consumers. This team ensures that Sharwood's is continually pioneering the introduction of new Asian flavours to the UK.

Whatever your cooking ability and whatever the occasion, be it a quick meal or one with all the trimmings to bring the full restaurant experience into your home, the Sharwood's range provides everything you need. In addition to offering quality Indian and Oriental cooking sauces, the brand has a wide range of accompaniments, from chutneys to naan breads and puppodums in Indian and noodles, prawn crackers and dipping sauces in Oriental. For those seeking a convenient but tasty meal, Sharwood's cooking sauces offers a good solution. For those with a little more time, Sharwood's also offers a variety of Indian and Oriental ingredients — curry pastes and curry powders, stir-fry bases and oriental essentials.

As an extension of this expertise, Sharwood's also offers a 'Kitchen Direct' service. This phone line allows people to get advice from a team of trained chefs in the Sharwood's kitchen on how to create their meal. The service can answer a very wide range of customer queries, from what to do with a curry that is too hot to suggestions for meals to prepare for vegetarians.

Recent Developments

With people increasingly experimental in the kitchen, Sharwood's has recently added some new flavours to each of its three sauce ranges. Bhuna is a well-known Indian restaurant dish, which uses a traditional cooking style to enrich a savoury onion sauce with warm aromatic spices, peppers and tomatoes. Makhani is the second new Indian sauce and has been predicted as the next big dish in the UK, being to India what Tikka Masala is to Britain. Its name means 'made with butter' and this sauce is enhanced further with cardomon and fennel. In the Oriental range, Cantonese Chop Suey and Spicy Sweet and Sour are the

newest products. When served with noodles and chicken, the first of these can be used to make Chow Mein and the second is a fruity medium spicy sauce that combines chilli with pineapple. For those

who prefer to make their stir-fries more from scratch, Sharwood's has added Lemon & Sesame and Teriyaki with Cracked Black Pepper to their stir-fry bases offering. With Lemon & Sesame, Sharwood's has once again taken a restaurant classic and given it an inventive new twist. In Teriyaki with Black Pepper, the brand has created a savoury and spicy sauce that blends the rich tastes of soy, garlic and black pepper.

Sharwood's accompaniments range has also seen an innovative new addition — the Feast Naan. Launched in May 2002 and true to the communal style of Indian dining, each Feast Naan is big enough to share, being twice the size of standard naans. Combining the best of new and old, the Feast Naan is produced using traditional Tandoor ovens alongside the latest baking technology. Each naan is individually finished by hand and then clay baked to create some of the most authentic restaurant quality naan on the market.

Promotion

In 2001, Sharwood's launched a new TV advertising campaign. Building on the colour and

vibrancy of its previous adverts, the new work is all about fun, experimentation and creativity. Based on the belief that cooking and eating Indian and Oriental food is both indulgent and rewarding, the ads use a playful tone to portray the kitchen as a place for inspiration and surprise. Using the recognisably seductive voice of Mariella Frostrup, the viewer is asked, "Why should the bedroom be the only place you experiment?" The campaign has adopted a new endline — 'Stirring Stuff'.

In addition to advertising, Sharwood's has pioneered a lot of activity with supermarkets to encourage everyday cooks to experiment with Oriental and Indian Food. 2002 was the sixth year in which Sharwood's led the celebration of Chinese New Year in several major stores. As a result, more than one million people tried stir-frying for the first time with Sharwood's jarred sauces and noodles (Source: ACNielsen). During the autumn, Sharwood's also works with retailers to bring the Indian 'Diwali' 'Festival of Light' to life for shoppers.

Brand Values

Sharwood's has always prided itself on its passion for and expertise in Indian and Oriental food. The brand's strengths lie in the breadth of its range and in the accessibility of the products that it creates for British consumers — all inspired by authentic dishes from Asia. The combination of the above means that people trust the brand and feel safe enough to have the confidence to be more experimental in their cooking.

www.sharwoods.com

Market

When thinking about Shell, many consumers might only connect it to the fuel they put in their car, or the service stations they see by the roadside. But, in reality, Shell is a brand which touches our lives in many more ways. Whether it is fuel for aviation, asphalt surfacing for roads, heating oil for homes, schools and hospitals, or the lubricants which keep the cogs of industry turning, oil and petrochemical products are all around us.

But Shell is not only an oil company. Like many of its competitors, it is in the energy business, exploring for, producing and marketing natural gas. This clean-burning, environmentally friendly fuel has become a major energy source in homes and businesses throughout the world and demand is already growing rapidly, up 75% in the last decade.

Being a provider of natural energy resources, Shell has a huge responsibility, not only to sustainable development, but also to its customers, who will punish those companies whose values and actions they don't respect. As such, when competing in the energy business, corporate responsibility and attention to environmental and business ethics is extremely valuable.

Furthermore, to be a competitive player in this huge industry, one needs to operate on a global scale. This, combined with reduced revenues from fuel has prompted the oil companies to consolidate over recent years. Total took over Belgian Petrofina, BP and Amoco merged, Exxon got together with Mobil, and most recently, Shell bought Texaco's US petrol retail business in a giant £2.6 billion deal.

Achievements

Over its long history, and thanks to continued marketing investment, Shell has one of the most instantly recognisable and valuable brands in the world. According to the marketing consultancy, Interbrand, Shell's brand, represented by the instantly recognisable Pecten logo, is worth nearly £2 billion. In addition, Interbrand's annual survey rates Shell among the globe's 100 most valuable brands. Another survey, by the Financial Times, said Shell's is the sixth most influential logo of the last century.

Shell's achievements in the energy business are countless. It has been a leader in North Sea oil and gas since production began in the 1960s, investing over £50 billion in the area and bringing a quarter of total North Sea oil production to the surface. Shell's development of the Brent oil field, the biggest discovery in the UK sector of the North Sea, is recognised to be one of the greatest technical feats of British enterprise.

On a corporate level, Shell has performed shrewdly. In 2001, it became the biggest petrol retailer in the US after signing the £2.6 billion deal to buy out Texaco's minority interests in two joint venture oil-refining and marketing operations.

The deal increases Shell's share of the US petrol market to about 15%, overtaking Exxon-

Mobil and BP, which each control about 12%. Once the rebranding programme is complete, Shell will have 55,000 retail sites around the world, making it the largest branded network in the fuel industry.

Shell's environmental and ethical record has also attracted plaudits. In 1998, the company initiated a top to bottom re-engineering of the business, making it more accountable and introducing a system of measuring its performance against a 'triple bottom line' of financial, environmental and social criteria.

In 2000, it began publishing the annual 'Shell Report', in which it reviews the group's progress in embodying sustainable development and details how it is meeting the environmental and social expectations of its stakeholders. The reports have become widely acknowledged as best practice in the field of corporate reporting. They invite stakeholder feedback through the 'Tell Shell' campaign, much of which, both positive and negative, is published.

Sustainable development is also a part of

another Shell success story – its partnership with Ferrari. By developing high performance racing fuels which take Ferrari to ever greater heights on the track, Shell is constantly improving the fuel and lubricants bought by the motorist. By working closely with Ferrari, Shell has been able to lead the fuel industry in producing fuels which burn more efficiently and are more environmentally friendly. Shell estimates its fuels sold worldwide reduce emissions to the same extent as creating a rainforest 100 times the size of Manhattan every year.

An example of how the consumer benefits from the Ferrari partnership is Shell Optimax and Shell V-Power, Shell's innovative unleaded high-octane fuels, which were developed as a direct result of developing fuel for the Ferrari Formula One team. As well as enhancing performance, the fuel also protects the environment by making the engine run more efficiently.

History

Shell's origins can be traced back to 1833, when Marcus Samuel opened a small shop in London's East End dealing in antiques, curios and oriental sea shells. His trade in shells – a fashionable item in Victorian households – became so profitable that he set up regular shipments from the Far East. Before long this had turned into a general import-export business.

The connection with oil was not established until early 1890, when Marcus Samuel Junior visited the Black Sea coast, where Russian oil was exported into Asia. Samuel started exporting Kerosene to the Far East, sending the world's first oil tanker through the Suez Canal. Samuel remembered his father's original business when he branded the kerosene 'Shell'.

In 1897, Samuel elevated the status of the shell name, calling his enterprise the Shell Transport and Trading Company. A Pecten Seashell emblem was chosen to give the name visual emphasis.

In 1907, Shell merged with a Dutch rival which was also active in the Far East, Royal Dutch Petroleum. Rapid growth followed, leading to the development of an international network of oil exploration and production facilities. As with many other petroleum companies, the new motorcar age literally fuelled their growth for decades to come.

By the late 1950s, oil had become the world's major energy resource. Supply and demand both boomed, and during this period, Shell supplied almost one seventh of the of the world's oil products. During the 1960s, there was a similar boom in the market for natural gas, leading to the exploration for and production of natural gas in the North Sea. Shell was a dominant player in these early years of North Sea operations, even more so when major oil fields were also discovered there in the early 1970s. The years ahead saw North Sea production and exploration become a major focus for Shell.

At this time, Shell also started diversifying into a new growth area – producing chemicals from petroleum products. Over the next twenty years,

its chemical product range grew enormously, manufactured in 30 locations around the world.

Nowadays, Shell focuses its exploration efforts on the Gulf of Mexico, where it discovered oil reserves at record depths of 3,000 feet in 1991.

Product

Shell's business is divided into four core areas: Exploration and Production; Oil Products; Chemicals, Gas and Power; and Renewables.

In the UK, Shell Expro is a leading operator in the UK sector of the North Sea, producing around 19% of the UK's crude oil and 23% of its gas. That's enough gas to supply over a third of the UK's domestic gas customers. The infrastructure needed to run this business is immense, with fourteen offshore production platforms, 57 oil fields and 23 gas fields.

The Oil Products business manufactures and distributes fuels, lubricants and other vital oil products, such as liquefied petroleum gas, bitumen and fuel oil.

Shell's range of fuels and lubricants, which are tested and developed through its relationship with Ferrari, are sold through its global network of 55,000 petrol stations. One of the most significant of these products is Shell Optimax, which was launched by Shell UK Oil in August 2001. Developed by the Shell scientists who fuel Ferrari's Formula One cars, Optimax's combination of optimum performance and maximum protection has been an outstanding

success, resulting in it winning 'New Brand of the Year' at the prestigious 2002 Marketing Society Awards.

Other brands in Shell's consumer product portfolio include the Helix lubricant range, which has also been developed in conjunction with Ferrari Formula One, and the ultra low sulphur Shell Pura Diesel. Shell has also developed Autogas liquefied petroleum gas for a new generation of LPG-powered road vehicles.

A network of more than 7,500 retail forecourt stores in 47 countries forms an important part of Shell's offer. The outlets are often open 24/7, offering a variety of food, drinks and other convenience items.

Recent Developments

Shell recently made motorsport history by becoming the first fuel and lubricant supplier to record 100 wins with one team. Michael Schumacher's win at Spa-Francorchamps in September 2002 completed the unprecedented run of victories for Ferrari and Shell, which began with Jose Froilan Gonzalez at Silverstone in 1951.

The success of the technical partnership was endorsed by Jean Todt, Ferrari's team principle, who described Shell as "the best development team in the pit lane". Shell continues to work with Ferrari on the optimum fuel and lubricants for the future.

As well as the successful launch of Shell Optimax, which was rolled out across the UK at the end of 2002, Shell also recently introduced Autogas LPG onto over 1,000 UK forecourts. At half the price of normal unleaded petrol, Autogas can cut over 30% off annual motor fuel bills.

Promotion

The fact that the Shell brand is so famous is, in part, down to the company's long-standing investment in marketing. Some of its campaigns still stick in the memory, such as the 'You can be sure of Shell' slogan, which dates back to 1932.

Nowadays, Shell's promotion takes place on many fronts. Strategic support for new products is an important area of activity, such as the £5 million UK launch programme for Shell Optimax in 2002. Charged with emotionally engaging consumers who often see fuel as a commodity product, Optimax is targeted at 'real' drivers who are willing to pay a premium for a fuel offering extra performance and engine protection. In an ultra-competitive, price-sensitive fuel market, this is an extremely valuable

positioning. Optimax has helped Shell win new customers, upgrade existing customers and improve margins.

Another major aspect of Shell's marketing activity is its corporate identity work, which has played a crucial part in communicating the company's environmentally and socially accountable stance. The first major marketing programme to communicate this new face of Shell broke in 1999, with the global 'Profits and Principles' programme, spanning TV, print, new media and public relations. A series of ads highlighted Shell's activities in key areas, such as reducing greenhouse gases, protecting endangered species and supporting renewable energy.

Another manifestation of this ongoing campaign is 'Experts', which highlights some of the individuals whose opinion Shell seeks when making its decisions, such as local fishermen in England, or botanists in the Philippines.

The Shell/Economist Writing Prize is another important promotional initiative in which people are invited to submit essays on key themes, such as globalisation, technological change and visions for the future. The 2002 competition asks for essays on the topic: 'How much freedom should we trade for our security'?

Brand Values

Shell is committed to carrying out its business operations efficiently, responsibly and profitably. In order to achieve this Shell will search for innovative energy solutions with the intent of improving the well-being of the planet and its people. Shell companies, therefore, are committed to making contributions towards sustainable development.

All communications from Shell are influenced by a company that cares about its customers and the world in which we live and hope to demonstrate how Shell innovates to help build a better future. A 'Waves of Change' theme is used to convey these values in all consumer communications, linking Shell with the sea. As the company's origins are linked to the sea, this provides a useful metaphor for communicating the values of the Shell brand, using a wide range of emotions and visual ideas.

www.shell.com

Market

Two thirds of the adult population wear glasses or contact lenses – a percentage that has been gradually rising with increased life expectancy.

The optical market is therefore driven by an ageing population, in particular the over 45s, as the older we get, the more likely we are to need glasses. By the time we are in our 60s, nearly 90% of us will require corrective vision.

Contact lens wearers, which account for only 6% of the population, tend to be in the younger age range, the under 35s.

The current market for eyecare products and services is estimated at more than £2 billion with just under half still being provided by small independent opticians.

For many years now Specsavers Opticians has been recognised as the market leaders in optics – today, one in four people who wear glasses buy them from Specsavers (Source: GfK Marketing Services).

The brand's market share is twice that of its nearest high street competitors. New brands in the market include Optical Express and supermarket suppliers ASDA Wal-Mart and Tesco.

With approaching 500 stores in the UK, Ireland and the Netherlands, Specsavers is one of the most successful brands in retail optics and is the fifth largest opticians in the world.

Achievements

With projected sales in 2002 of £500 million, Specsavers main achievement has been one of almost entirely organic continuous and sustained growth, despite a slowing down of the retail economy.

Specsavers' advertising campaigns, which are produced by an in-house creative team, regularly appear in Marketing Magazine's Adwatch, and the brand's TV commercials, in particular those featuring physicist Stephen Hawking, have been highly acclaimed.

Specsavers' customer magazine View, which is also produced in-house, has won several awards, including the British Association of Communicators in Business Award of Excellence. Its annual Drive Safe campaign has, over the past two years, been hugely successful in highlighting the need for drivers to have regular sight tests. So much so, that more than 5,000 people have signed a petition lobbying the Government to introduce a series of measures aimed at making UK roads safer.

Specsavers' Look of 2003 modelling competition, which aims to find the sexiest glasses wearer, is in its eighth year and attracts thousands of entrants, emphasising the fact that glasses are a fashion accessory as well as an optical necessity.

Above all, since its first store opened in 1984, Specsavers greatest achievement has been that it has revolutionised the optical market through its joint venture philosophy and transparent approach to pricing.

The abiding tenet of the Group is that professional and retail optics should be led by the opticians themselves, who own and run their own stores and are responsible for the day-to-day running of their business.

A full range of support services, expertise, experience and information is provided to stores by Specsavers Optical Group (SOG), based in Guernsey, ensuring partners receive help in all aspects of their business, tailored to their specific requirements.

Because the opticians own their own stores and keep all the profits, paying a management fee to SOG for their support services and marketing activity, they have a vested interest in serving the community and making their business a success.

Since its inception, Specsavers has been a consumer champion, demystifying eyecare products and services and offering the public real value for money and choice.

Specsavers was the first to advertise its products and services on television and still spends more on TV than any other opticians. Furthermore, it was the first to introduce Complete Price, whereby the cost of glasses includes single vision lenses. It was also the first to promote Two For One offers and free eyecare for children.

Specsavers was also the first to offer a full range

of contact lenses that could be paid for by monthly direct debit, making what was once seen as an expensive product, more widely available.

At a time when many British companies are pulling out of Europe due to poor sales and rapidly rising costs, Specsavers is forging ahead with its European expansion programme.

Specsavers Opticiens is already the third largest optical group in Holland, having grown from just three stores in 2000 to more than 40 stores today.

Such is its success that, somewhere in the UK or Europe, a new Specsavers' store opens every week.

History

The brand was founded in 1984 by Doug and Mary Perkins, who started the business in their spare bedroom on a table tennis table.

The Perkins had moved to Guernsey after selling a small chain of opticians in the West Country, but in the early 1980s they saw a gap in the optical market when the UK Government deregulated professionals, including opticians, freeing them to advertise their products and services for the first time.

Seizing this opportunity, Doug and Mary opened their first Specsavers value for money, quality eyecare opticians in Guernsey and Bristol, followed shortly by stores in Plymouth, Swansea and Bath.

From the outset, the Perkins wanted to offer a wide range of stylish, fashionable glasses at affordable prices.

Specsavers' first logo reflected its value for money approach with two pound signs replacing the lenses in a pair of glasses.

The strapline that went with this – Local Eyecare Nationwide – also demonstrated Specsavers' desire to be seen as trustworthy an optician as a local independent but with the huge buying power of a national company that meant savings could be passed on to the customer.

Having quickly established the brand in the marketplace as a provider of affordable eyecare, Specsavers changed its logo in 1996 to further reflect the quality of its products and services.

The new logo – two green overlapping ellipses – was coupled with a new strapline, Now You Can Believe Your Eyes, reflecting the customer's expectations that at last they could buy top quality glasses and contact lenses at a price they could afford.

With the onset of an ageing population, Specsavers commissioned research which revealed that people over the age of 40 were least attracted to Specsavers for their eyecare needs and would typically go to an independent, who they perceived as offering a more professional service.

To enhance the credibility of the brand among older people, a new campaign, and a new strapline, was introduced – Your Eyesight Matters.

Sophisticated TV commercials featuring artist David Shepherd and wheelchair-bound physicist Stephen Hawking, who depend a great deal on their eyesight, successfully illustrated that Specsavers is not just about special offers and promotions, but also about professionalism. The commercials demonstrate that Specsavers takes eyecare seriously.

The public's perception of the brand has changed significantly over recent years and in 2002 it was voted Britain's most trusted brand

of opticians by Reader's Digest, which surveyed nearly 40,000 consumers in eighteen countries.

The brand's current straplines – Number One Choice For Eye Tests and Number One Choice For Contact Lenses – reflect its position as market leader.

Product

Specsavers has always been known for its wide choice of glasses and now offers more than 2,000 styles and colours made from the latest high tech materials, including titanium and stainless steel.

Its glasses are sourced from all over the world and many are made by the same manufacturers that are responsible for some of the top name designer brands.

Specsavers is also market leader in contact lenses with its own brand of EasyVision monthly and daily disposable lenses. It has also pioneered the use of continuous wear lenses that can be worn for up to 24 hours a day for 30 days, and has estimated to have at least 40% of the UK market.

Furthermore, Specsavers is the largest provider of home delivery contact lenses in Europe through its Lensmail service, whereby customers can order their lenses by phone, post or online, as well as more conventionally in store.

Recent Developments

To satisfy younger customers Specsavers recently added glasses by Storm and FCUK to complement its own designer ranges Osiris and Ultralight. New styles are introduced continually to keep apace with changes in fashion and technology.

Its own lens manufacturing laboratories – two of the largest in Europe – mean that it can supply the latest high-tech lenses at high volume and low cost.

Specsavers' contact lens department is always on the look out for new lenses, such as varifocal contact lenses for older customers or lenses that help correct colour blindness.

Specsavers website, www.specsavers.com, has been developed and refined so that customers

can now view the latest frames, order contact lenses online and review the current offers and promotions available at their local store.

Ask The Optician provides the answers to many professional queries, while the press office features current news items and information.

As well as rapid expansion in Europe, Specsavers is now branching out into the hearing aid industry with the recent acquisition of the HearCare franchise. The deal, which will create 400 new jobs over the next four years, will see the roll out of 100 new private hearing aid centres retaining the HearCare brand and mirroring Specsavers hugely successful joint venture business model.

Promotion

Although most people should have a thorough eye examination at least once every two years, many choose to leave it much longer and are either oblivious of their declining vision or mistakenly think that an eye test is only about a prescription. The reality is that the eyes can also be an indication of poor health.

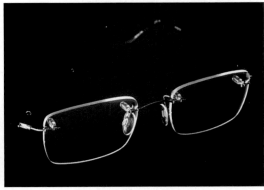

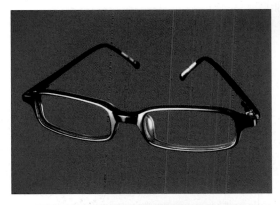

As well as highlighting visual problems, an eye examination can also help detect diabetes, glaucoma, high blood pressure, even the presence of a brain tumour. Through the eye test, opticians at Specsavers have saved lives.

Convincing people that they must have their eyes tested for the sake of their health as well as their sight is therefore of primary importance to Specsavers.

There is no fixed period for selling glasses or contact lenses – it is not a seasonal product – which is why the brand advertises year-round offers and promotions.

Specsavers therefore aims to reach as many people as possible throughout the year via carefully targeted promotions aimed at young people, contact lens wearers, fashion-conscious customers and older people who may need different types of lenses, such as varifocals and bifocals.

Specsavers in-house marketing and media buying departments make full use of the media mix, including television, radio, press and public relations, nationally and on a regional and local level to emphasise that Specsavers is fundamentally a professional opticians serving the local community and providing them with quality products.

It also has a duty of care to inform people when their next eye examination is due, which is done through direct mail. Specsavers sends out more than 220,000 letters a week reminding people that they are due a sight test, or that their

contact lenses are ready for collection or delivery, and of current and forthcoming offers.

Its in-store magazine View, which is published twice a year, is available free of charge in all stores and is mailed out to 600,000 customers.

Specsavers' website www.specsavers.com is another vital tool of which full use is made to convey key messages.

Specsavers also attends various trade fairs, such as the annual Optrafair, and exhibitions such as Clothes Show Live and the International Motor Show, and its Drive Safe trailer visits various towns across the UK to offer free vision screening to drivers, emphasising the need for regular sight checks.

Brand Values

Specsavers' brand values have remained consistent throughout its 19-year history – it aims to be the best value opticians, satisfying personal eyecare needs at affordable prices in a simple and clear manner that everyone can understand.

The brand is now the most well known of all the opticians – of those surveyed, 95% recognise the Specsavers logo (Source: NFO Worldgroup) – something of which the brand is immensely proud considering the age of some of the brands with which it competes.

www.specsavers.com

SPEEDO ®

Market

Demand for sports goods is growing faster than total retail sales in the UK, Germany, France, Italy and Spain, with the total market in the EU worth an estimated £23 billion. Ever since the 1980s, sportswear has crossed the line to become an integral part of general leisurewear, as the soaring demand for football replica kits, trainers and fleece clothing testifies. Like many other sports brands, Speedo has grown from a performance brand targeting athletes to compete in the wider fashion arena.

Speedo is best known as the world's leading swimwear brand – swimming is already a hugely popular sport and pastime – being among the top five sports participated in – and this is especially true in the UK. Since 1997, the proportion of the population who swim in their leisure time has risen from 20% to 24%.

to push the boundaries of technology and, in this regard, Speedo has excelled. An example of its achievements in innovation is Fastskin, which revolutionised the swimming world when it was first unveiled by Speedo in March 2000.

The company's objective was to develop the world's leading competition swimsuit through the use of the most scientific and technical expertise. Success would be gauged through its acceptance by the world's best swimmers.

The results exceeded all expectations, with swimmers from over 130 counties using the suit at the Sydney Olympics. As a result, thirteen of the fifteen world records set there were achieved by swimmers wearing a Fastskin and many more world records have been broken in Fastskin since.

It is not surprising that Fastskin scooped the coveted 'Best Designed Sport Kit' award at the inaugural Sport Industry Awards at the Park Lane

swimwear when the Swedish swimmer Arne Borg wore a Racerback to set a new world record. At the 1956 Melbourne Olympics, Speedo supplied the Australian team with their swimsuits and, within a week, they swept the board with eight gold medals, turning Speedo into a world famous name in the process.

Speedo began manufacturing in the UK in the 1970s and was the first company to produce nylon/lycra swimwear, which remains the most popular fabric today. The company also began producing beach and leisurewear, extending the Speedo name to encompass more than competition swimsuits.

In 1991, Speedo was acquired by the London-based brand management company, Pentland Group and continued to dominate the swimming world with the launch of the world's first 'fast swimwear' fabric, the S2000, at the Barcelona Games in 1992,

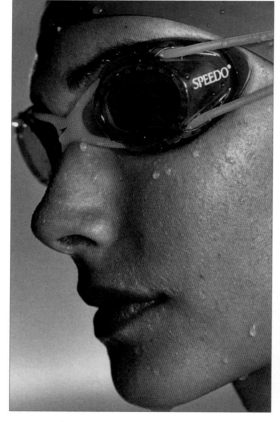

Swimwear and beachwear sales are also strongly linked to fitness, weather and holidays – all of which point to strengthening demand. Fitness club and gym membership is rising, and, with the British summer continuing to disappoint, more and more people are taking sun-seeking foreign holidays.

Achievements

In its 75-year history, Speedo has become an illustrious name in world sport. When it comes to swimwear, Speedo has been dominating the scene for years. Consistently meeting the demands of top athletes, Speedo equipped 27 of the 29 swimming gold medallists at the 1968 Mexico Olympics and, in 2002, 87% of all swimming medals at the Commonwealth Games in Manchester were won wearing Speedo.

Maintaining this level of credibility amongst the most demanding of users means continuing

Hilton in London, in April 2002. Speedo was also highly commended in the Sport Brand of the Year category at the Sports Industry Awards, 2002.

History

Speedo was founded by Alexander MacRae, who emigrated to Australia from Scotland in 1910. MacRae set up a hosiery manufacturing business, which expanded into swimwear in 1914. But it wasn't until 1928 that the Speedo name was born. This coincided with more liberal attitudes towards bathing and the growth of swimming as a sport. MacRae met this trend with a new 'Racerback' costume and a staff competition was held to find a new company name. A Captain Parsonson coined the slogan 'Speed on in your Speedos' – and the Speedo name was born.

The brand was an immediate success and quickly established itself as a leader in performance

where over half of the medals were won by swimmers wearing Speedo.

This culture of innovation also spawned the revolutionary Fastskin, unveiled in 2000. World class athletes who wear Speedo today include the legendary Australian swimmer Grant Hackett (1500m freestyle world record holder) and Mark Foster of the UK (world record holder in 50m freestyle short course).

2003 sees Speedo celebrate its 75th anniversary. The brand continues to make its mark in the pool and on the beach with an extensive and stylish range of beach and leisure wear for men, women and children.

Product

Speedo International is the world's leading brand of competition and training swimwear for men, women and juniors. Using feedback from top athletes, Speedo is constantly refining its designs and innovating to offer the ultimate in performance swimwear. It also incorporates the latest fashion trends to ensure that performance is not achieved at the expense of style.

The company also uses its expertise to produce an extensive range of swim accessories, including goggles, caps, footwear and learn-to-swim equipment. As always, the accessories incorporate the latest technology and the latest styles for the pool and beach.

Speedo is also active in beach leisure wear for men, women and juniors. This is an ever expanding range of products, incorporating not only swimsuits, but also beach shorts, tops, sarongs, and other contemporary clothing featuring a wide variety of prints, colours, styles and cultural influences.

Recent Developments

In all of these areas, Speedo is introducing new products for 2003. The Competition collection is being augmented with further development of the Fastskin suit to improve flexibility and performance. A new Drag Suit for female swimmers is another new addition, specially designed to help increase endurance in training.

The new Speedo Female Beach Leisure collection for Spring/Summer 2003 combines comfort, fit and style with cutting edge design and functionality. A key style in the new range is inspired by the kimono styling of the East.

The 2003 Men's Leisure Collection also features an Eastern theme with Japanese ethnic inspired prints and minimalist styling. Key to this season's collection is the introduction of 'Jetstream', a desirable new range offering a contemporary, style-leading look. New branding, with a slashed boom logo, differentiates Jetstream from the core Speedo range. Water shorts, jackets, hooded tops and trousers all feature in the Jetstream range.

Promotion

Speedo invests in a full range of communication channels to support its growing product range. With a rich heritage in advertising, Speedo has always been a strong believer in brand communications and hopes to continue developing in this area with the use of more effective use of marketing than ever. Its biggest challenge is to shift consumer perception that Speedo is a pool-only brand and make its presence felt in the growing and fashion-led beachwear market. Speedo aims to reposition itself as a desirable and fashionable brand, with a consistent and appealing image.

Speedo's connection with world-class competitive swimming is a strong marketing opportunity. Sponsorship of athletes, clubs, leagues, national teams and key sporting events gives Speedo an ideal opportunity to showcase its products at the highest level and leverage associated marketing opportunities. For instance, Speedo saw a surge in demand for its products following its high-profile marketing activity around the Sydney 2000 Olympics. The message that was conveyed was that 'winners' wear Speedo and that consumers aspire to the same values.

Advertising is important to Speedo in underpinning its sporting strength (such as taking out large press ads to celebrate the success of its sponsored teams), but it also plays an important role in building emotional attachment to the brand, which will be increasingly important in growing its share of the beach leisure wear market. Exploiting its 75th anniversary in 2003, Speedo introduced a stylish retro-looking logo to accompany much of its advertising and point of sale material. The anniversary also provides an excellent hook for PR activity, competitions and other marketing.

Brand Values

Speedo has a rich heritage and expertise in swimwear, apparel and equipment based in or near the water. The credibility of the brand is underpinned by technology, design and innovation and continues to be worn by the world's top athletes demanding the ultimate in technical equipment.

Communications combine technology, design and contemporary style that lies at the root of the Speedo brand.

www.speedo.com

Market

Tea may be historically regarded as our national drink, but, since the mid 1990s, 'coffee culture' has become firmly established in the UK. The biggest and most obvious expression of this trend has been the rise of branded coffee chains on the high street, starting in London and now spreading to towns and cities across the nation.

Viewed as a fashionable and comfortable alternative to the pub, the coffeehouse has become an immensely popular social venue. There are now over 7500 coffee shops in the UK, a growing proportion of which are branded chains like Starbucks, Costa Coffee, Coffee Republic and Caffe Nero. There are now over 1500 of these branded outlets in the UK but, according to Allegra Strategies, this number will grow to 2500 by 2003, accounting for 30% of the total UK market.

Starbucks is currently the market leader in the UK coffee shop business with over 330 stores. This fast-growth business, driven by lifestyle changes with more people eating and drinking on the move, has seen sales increase by 110% since 1999. Britons now spend nearly £544 million a year in coffee outlets, drinking around six million cups of espresso-based coffee every week.

Far from reaching saturation point, the UK coffee shop market is set to continue its rapid growth, particularly outside London. Regional expansion is expected to account for the lion's share of the market's growth over the next three years, with analysts expecting 38% growth, compared to 18% within the M25.

Achievements

If there's one company which has fuelled the global coffee shop revolution and, in the process, made

latte and cappuccino part of the vernacular, it is Starbucks. The company's founder, Howard Schultz, introduced coffee house culture to Seattle and then exported the concept around the globe. Many others have followed, but it all began with Starbucks – a journey that has taken the company from a single store to today's empire of over 4700 coffeehouses in 25 countries.

The Starbucks brand has become one of the best known in the world. According to the branding consultancy Interbrand, Starbucks is one of the 75 greatest global brands of the twenty first century. Furthermore in a recent brand tracking study Starbucks achieved twice the awareness and preference of any other brand in the branded coffee shop category as well as leading its competitors with regards to penetration and loyalty.

The company's growth has been truly dramatic. In 1997, it had an income of US$975 million but, in 2001, it reported incomes of US$2.65 billion. In becoming such a large and successful company, Starbucks has not lost sight of its responsibilities. It has worked hard to improve social and economic conditions for coffee farmers as well as contributing to the communities in which it does business and provides the best possible working environment for its employees.

An example of its achievements in this area is The Starbucks Foundation, which it launched in 1997 to benefit literacy programmes in communities where the company has coffeehouses. In addition, Starbucks works with The National Literary Trust (NLT) making regular donations to the charity as well as sponsoring 'fun days' at local libraries where books are distributed to children for free. It also backs this up with in-store promotional activities highlighting issues surrounding the NLT.

Starbucks is also very conscious of giving the farmers who grow the coffee used in its coffee shops a fair deal. They are paid approximately

three times above the recognised market price. Furthermore, the coffee sold in Starbucks sells Fair Trade certified coffee as 'coffee of the day' and within its whole bean packaged coffee range.

The principles on which Starbucks' conducts its business have been recognised in the many awards the company has won. For instance, in 2000 and 2001 it was named one of '100 Best Corporate Citizens', by Business Ethics magazine, and 'One of the 100 Best Companies to Work for' by Fortune Magazine in 1998, 1999, 2000 and 2002.

In 2002, Starbucks committed to publicising its progress in meeting targets for business ethics and corporate responsibility by publishing its first Corporate Social Responsibility Annual Report.

History

Starbucks opened its first location in Seattle's Pike Place Market in 1971. For the next ten years, Starbucks remained a quality coffee stall in the bustling city market, and only began expanding its horizons when the current chairman, Howard Schultz, joined the company in 1982. He spotted an opportunity to provide coffee to fine restaurants and espresso bars. The coffee bar concept was still undeveloped in Seattle and, following a trip to Italy where Schultz was impressed with the popularity of espresso bars in Milan, he decided to test the concept in his home town.

In 1984, the first Starbucks coffeehouse opened its doors in downtown Seattle, serving the first caffe latte. Following the success of this experiment, Schultz led a team to officially found Starbucks as a company in 1985.

By 1987, it became clear that coffeehouse culture had the potential to spread further afield, leading to Starbucks outlets opening in Vancouver and Chicago. By the end of the decade, Starbucks was growing fast, with 84 locations. It opened a new roasting plant in Seattle to cater for the volume.

Product

Starbucks sells more than 30 blends of coffee, espresso, blended drinks, teas and the Frappuccino range. It also sells home espresso machines, coffee brewers and grinders, freshly baked pastries, a line of premium ice cream, chocolate and sandwiches. And, as the Starbucks brand is now so well known, it also sees great demand for its branded merchandise, such as coffee mugs, and coffee accessories. In some of its 5000 global stores it sells CDs, books and gifts in addition to the regular merchandise.

Recent Developments

A major new product launch for Starbucks came during summer 2002, when it introduced the UK to Starbucks Frappuccino. Available in fruit tea, cream or coffee variants, the ice-blended Frappuccino is a revitalising and refreshing drink, ideal for a hot summer's day.

biosphere reserve in Chiapas, Mexico, that serves as a habitat for plants and animals. The partnership provides economic incentives to farmers who use environmentally sound agricultural methods to preserve tropical biodiversity.

On a more hi-tech level, Starbucks launched a new initiative to introduce high-speed wireless internet access to its stories, via a pilot programme with Hewlett Packard and T-Mobile. This is part of a global roll out of high-speed wireless internet access in Starbucks coffeehouses, providing customers with simple, fast and convenient connections for their wireless-enabled laptops or personal digital assistants.

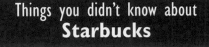

Promotion

Summer 2002 saw a major publicity drive behind the launch of Starbucks Frappuccino. A print and poster advertising campaign, which showed British people transported into a summery frame of mind as soon as they tasted an ice-cold Frappuccino spearheaded the launch. With executions including a man sitting on a rainy pavement bathing his feet in a puddle, a women lying in a child's sandpit as if on a beach, and an office worker reclining on his desk 'sunbathing' under an angle poise lamp, the poster campaign used the line 'Instant Summer – Free with every Frappuccino'. The campaign was commended in the respected Campaign Poster Awards 2002.

Brand Values

Starbucks is the world's leading retailer, roaster and brand of speciality coffee. It is a coffee company driven by its values and is inspired by a passion and dedication to quality. Furthermore, it is guided by strong principles to care for the environment, the community, and improve social and economic conditions for coffee farmers.

www.starbucks.com

But it was also beginning to combine size with social responsibility. In 1991, it established a relationship with CARE, the international relief and development organisation and also becoming the first privately owned US company to offer stock options to part-time employees.

The following year, it completed an initial public offering, making its debut on the Nasdaq exchange under the trading symbol 'SBUX'.

Having raised funds through additional stock offerings in the early 1990s, Starbucks began expanding abroad, opening its first coffeehouses in Tokyo in 1995 and Singapore in 1996.

In 1998, Starbucks acquired the Seattle Coffee Company in the UK, giving it 60 retail sites and giving it a springboard to help satisfy the new found British love affair with the coffeehouse.

Today, the company has over 5000 outlets, in 22 countries. Howard Shultz stepped down as CEO in 2000, but remains the company's chairman and chief global strategist.

Another important development in 2002 was the alliance between Starbucks Coffee Company and the Fairtrade Foundation to sell Fairtrade Certified coffee in Starbucks stores in the UK. The agreement means that Starbucks customers will be able to buy Fairtrade Certified coffee in all Starbucks stores, available as a 'Coffee of the Day,' for drinking in store, take-away, or as a whole bean product for customers to brew at home.

Another environmentally and socially responsible initiative was the recent introduction of Starbucks Organic Shade Grown Mexico™ coffee in Starbucks stores in the UK. Starbucks Organic Shade Grown Mexico coffee is a result of a partnership begun in 1998

between Starbucks and Conservation International. The shade coffee farms are located adjacent to a biosphere reserve in Chiapas, Mexico, that serves as a habitat for plants and animals. The partnership provides economic incentives to farmers who use environmentally sound agricultural methods to preserve tropical biodiversity.

Certified as organic by the Soil Association, Starbucks Organic Shade Grown Mexico coffee is a result of a partnership begun in 1998 between Starbucks and Conservation International (CI). The shade coffee farms are located adjacent to a

TESCO
Every little helps

Market

The UK grocery retail market is among the most competitive in the world. It is dominated by a core of four brands, Tesco, Sainsbury's, ASDA and Safeway, which battle fiercely for market share and customer loyalty. Tesco is the UK's leading retailer with a 16.6% share of the market (Source: IGD June 2001).

International mergers, including the arrival of Wal-Mart, through its acquisition of ASDA in 1999 and the growth of the internet have shaped the UK retail market in recent years. Tesco actively leads the way, not only by continuing to widen the gap between itself and its competitors' share of the market, but also by being the world's largest online grocer. The brand is also well positioned to be a leading retailer in Central Europe and South East Asia, with much expansion currently underway in these territories.

Achievements

Tesco has come a long way since its 'pile it high, sell it cheap' image of the 1970s. It pioneered the development of superstores and in the 1980s began investing heavily in the format. By 1986, its turnover was £3.5 billion and operating profit was £145 million.

These developments led to Tesco becoming the market leader in 1995 (Source: Audits Great Britain – AGB). In 2002, Tesco's customer loyalty stood at 36.7% (Source: Taylor Nelson Sofres). Furthermore, in 2002 Tesco's turnover reached £25.7 billion, with an operating profit of over £1.2 billion and an average spend in stores per trip of £24.42 (Source: Taylor Nelson Sofres).

In 1997, the company was voted the UK's 'Most Parent-Friendly Supermarket' by Great Ormond Street Hospital's 'Tommy's Campaign' award scheme. Tesco is also well respected in the business community, winning the Grand Prix in IPA Effectiveness Award 2000 and the Gold in Marketing Society Effectiveness Award in the same year. In 2001, Tesco's contribution to British society was recognised with the RBS/Sunday Times Business Enterprise Award.

The highly successful Tesco Computers for Schools scheme reached its eleventh year in 2002. Since 1992, the scheme has helped to equip 22,000 schools with over £77 million worth of computing

equipment. Tesco sponsored Race for Life for the first time in 2002. Over 250 thousand women participated by running, jogging or walking a five kilometre course at 100s of venues. Tesco smashed its target of raising £12 million and to date have raised £15.6 million for the charity Cancer Research UK.

History

Tesco was founded by Jack Cohen in 1919. After serving in the Royal Flying Corps during World War I, 21 year old Cohen invested his serviceman's gratuity of £30 in NAAFI surplus groceries to sell from a stall in the East End of London.

Cohen went on to trade successfully in a number of London markets and also started selling wholesale goods to market traders. By the late 1920s he switched his attention from market stalls to open fronted shops on the high street and in 1929 the name Tesco first appeared above a lock up shop in Edgware, North London. Cohen began to expand his business empire and by 1939 there were 100 branches of Tesco. After the war, the company floated on the Stock Exchange with a share price of fifteen shillings and Cohen began to acquire a string of other companies.

In 1960, Tesco began selling clothing and household goods and by 1968 it opened the UK's first superstore in Crawley, Sussex selling both food and non-food products. Throughout the decade it also introduced 'Green Shield Stamps' which consumers could collect and redeem against a range of household goods. These were replaced in 1977 by a price cutting campaign called 'Checkout at Tesco'.

In 1982, Tesco celebrated its fiftieth anniversary as a private limited company and raised £500,000 for charity. In the same year it introduced the first computerised checkouts. A year later Tesco changed its name to Tesco Plc and in 1985 a rights issue was launched to raise £145 million for a superstore development programme. This was followed by a £500 million investment program to build 29 new stores which provided 10,000 new jobs.

Over the years Tesco has been quick to adapt to meet evolving customer needs in order to improve the total Tesco offering and strengthen customer loyalty. A range of marketing and service initiatives have been employed, including long running and popular advertising campaigns, new store formats and continual development of the width and depth of the product range.

Product

Tesco maintains a strong core UK business and now has over 759 stores throughout the UK. It is also the biggest private sector employer with 195,000 staff. The brand continues its overseas expansion with stores 264 stores across Ireland, Hungary, Poland, Thailand, Czech Republic, South Korea, Slovakia, Taiwan and Malaysia. In total, Tesco has 65,000 staff overseas and is the market leader in six markets.

Tesco Metro stores were launched in 1992 to bring convenient shopping to the high street. Tesco Express stores were launched two years later and took supermarketing into a new era by focusing on convenience and fresh food. In addition to Tesco supermarket size stores (intended for use as a one stop weekly shop), Tesco Extra opened in 1997. It had a hypermarket feel, carrying a wider range of products including non-food items such as electricals, sportswear, designer clothing, computers and luggage.

In order to cater for a wide variety of tastes and budgets Tesco's aim is to offer a diverse range of premium, exotic and luxury foods as well as its more traditional and value for money items. Tesco launched the first economy own label range within the sector; the ' Value' range. This was followed by other ranges such as 'Finest*' to cater for the higher quality food market and is now worth £400 million and is sold internationally. Furthermore, the 'Organic' range now has in excess of 1,000 lines, making Tesco the biggest organic food retailer in the UK. Tesco has reduced the price of 50 top selling organic lines, making the range more accessible.

In addition to these very focused ranges, the brand is continually expanding its total range with 20,000 lines currently on offer. Tesco has expanded its fresh food counters and an increasing number of stores offer fish, hot chicken, take-aways, salad, and a new concept 'Grab and go' ready cut cheese at the delicatessen counters.

The non-food product range has expanded to include home entertainment items, sports equipment and home furnishings. Indeed, Tesco now accounts for almost 4% of the non-food retail market.

Improvements were also made in customer service including its 'One in Front' queue policy, no quibble guarantees, baby changing facilities, in-store opticians, photo processing and Pharmacy. Furthermore, 365 UK stores are open 24-hours a day, recognising the diversity lifestyles that exist in the UK.

Tesco Clubcard was launched in 1995 and was the first national loyalty card in the grocery sector. There are currently over ten million active Clubcard members and every quarter, millions of tailored mailshots are sent with a range of product and money off coupons, depending on the customer and the products they buy.

The Clubcard has been developed to enable customers to redeem their points for airfares, theatre tickets and other entertainment. In total, over £1 billion worth of reward vouchers have been issued to customers.

Tesco Personal Finance was launched in 1997 in a joint venture with The Royal Bank of Scotland and now has 2.5 million customer accounts. It offers fifteen products and services from credit cards to pet insurance.

Tesco initially offered home delivery in 1993 with the launch of its Wine Mail Order service. This has expanded over the years and Tesco is now the largest grocery e-tailer in the world with an average of 85,000 customers using the service each week. It has over 2.5 million products on offer including grocery items, flowers, books, CDs, DVDs and videos.

Recent Developments

Tesco's new 'Free From' range is intended for those with special dietary needs and is supported by a new healthy living club and website www.tesco.com/healthyliving.

Tesco's value line is also being strengthened with a move into non-food items and at the other end of the scale, the 'Finest*' range is being expanded with a further 300 items now in place in both foods and non foods.

Tesco Kids Club was launched in July 2001, following on from the baby and toddler clubs. A pack, sent directly to children, includes a range of activities which is backed up by a website, www.tesco.com/kids. Tesco has also launched a new Kids Range of healthy, great tasting foods for its youngest customers. The range includes ready meals, cereals, drinks and 'mini' fruit.

Instant Travel Insurance was rolled out in 2002 to 450 stores as a new and convenient way to buy travel insurance with no form filling required. Shoppers pick up a pack in store and pay at the checkout.

Developments in operational issues have included the introduction of a Continuous Replenishment system, where products are ordered automatically based on continuous information flows from checkouts. It is now operating on nearly all food and drink lines, improving availability and increasing efficiency. Using the world's first store-specific merchandising system, Tesco can now tailor each store range to specifically meet the needs of its customers. Linked to the Continuous Replenishment system, product space is allocated to demand.

Tesco is also very active in it charitable donations. ATM charity payout was a UK first, with Tesco donating 1p to charity for every withdrawal from its cash point machines; £265,000 was raised for The Alzheimer's Society.

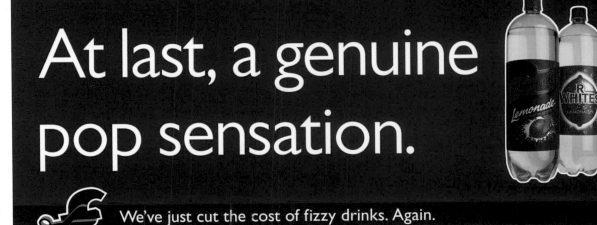

At last, a genuine pop sensation.

We've just cut the cost of fizzy drinks. Again.

Always committed to cutting prices.

Subject to availability in selected stores whilst stocks last, excluding Express & selected Metro stores, R.O.I., N.I. and I.O.M.

TESCO
Every little helps.

Promotion

Communication by Tesco is inevitably multifaceted through a combination of television, press, in-store and direct marketing. Advertising has made a significant contribution to changing perceptions of the brand by highlighting Tesco's improvements and innovations.

Tesco's 'Quest for Quality' advertising campaign ran from 1990-1992. It starred Dudley Moore as the Tesco buyer who scoured the world in pursuit of an elusive flock of French free-range chickens; en-route discovering other surprisingly high quality products to add to the Tesco range. The campaign

adopted a deliberately (and, at the time, highly unusual) light-hearted approach in order to present the changes at Tesco in a way that would build a more positive brand identity. The campaign was very impactful, peaking at 89% awareness (Source: BJM Tracking).

In 1992, a strategy review suggested a new direction focusing on a new shopping deal: 'quality + price AND service = value'. Tesco needed to adapt to new market realities shaped by the recession, the success of discounters and the improvement of its rivals' advertising campaigns. Tesco understood that shopping is so much more than the products you buy and realised that none of its competitors were making serious attempts to improve the whole shopping experience. Tesco capitalised on this by launching 114 new initiatives and ran an advertising campaign under the umbrella positioning of 'Every Little Helps' to demonstrate that whilst not everything in life goes perfectly, Tesco was doing its best to make at least one aspect – doing the shopping – a little easier. Between 1993-1995, Tesco ran twenty executions, each one focusing on a different initiative including Mother and Baby changing facilities, Tesco Clubcard and the removal of sweets from the checkouts. Awareness peaked at 64% and attracted new shoppers, helping to secure market leadership.

By 1995, the advertising needed a change. Britain had come out of the recession and Tesco could afford to mirror the public's increased confidence. Instead of focusing on Tesco's attitude to its customers, the tables turned and consumers' attitudes to Tesco were concentrated on.

The new campaign centred on the 'mother of all shoppers', Dotty Turnbull, played by Prunella Scales and her long-suffering daughter, Kate, played by Jane Horrocks. Dotty regards each of Tesco's initiatives as an opportunity to put the store to the test and in doing so allows the staff to shine. Even though the campaign is in its seventh year, and after 52 commercials, the humour and simple messages still strike a chord with the public. Despite Tesco's relatively low media spend versus its competitors, it has regular prompted recall scores of 90%, its highest awareness levels ever, thereby making the brand one of the most efficient advertisers in its category.

Tesco successfully communicated its commitment to offering low prices without damaging its service and quality image, by remaining true to its 'Every Little Helps' philosophy. Econometric modelling has shown that for every £1 invested in Dotty, Tesco has gained £38 in incremental turnover and £2.25 in incremental operating profit (Source: IPA Effectiveness Award 2000).

Brand Values

Tesco grew from a 'pile it high sell it cheap' approach and has maintained a reputation for value for money. The brand is however now highly regarded for its customer service, quality and its ever increasing range of products. The 'Every Little Helps' philosophy underpins the brand from how staff and customers are treated to how the brand acts within the community.

www.tesco.com

Tesco.com You shop, we drop.

Market

As a nation of tea-drinkers, the British population has a particularly strong bond with Tetley. An astonishing 1011 cups of tea are consumed per person per year in the UK, creating a retail tea market worth £540 million. Tea is by far the most popular hot drink, with only 507 cups of coffee consumed per person per year.

However, leading brands like Tetley are competing in a market where overall tea consumption is slowly falling. The old image of the traditional British 'cuppa' is giving way to a more modern environment of 'repertoire drinking' with consumers drinking more coffee and soft drinks. The popularity of coffee bars and a 'cappuccino culture' have been putting tea under particular pressure in recent years.

However, the sectors leading brands are continuously innovating to bring new products to market, keeping the thirst for tea alive.

We are also drinking different types of tea, such as fruit and herbal infusions. So, despite coffee's advance, we are still one of the biggest tea drinking nations – 100,000 tonnes per year. Over 26% of this volume is Tetley branded tea bags (Source: ACNielsen 2002), making it a brand that has become synonymous with our national drink. Tetley is a giant amongst consumer brands, being one of the biggest food and drink brands in the UK.

Achievements

Tetley is the second biggest tea bag brand worldwide, with sales in a number of key markets across the globe. It is one of the leading brands in both the UK and Canada and is a well established major brand within both the US and Australian tea markets. It also has a developing presence in France, Poland and Russia.

Despite its traditional image, innovation is particularly important in the tea industry and Tetley has established a reputation for being at the very forefront of new developments in the sector. For example, in 1953, it was the first to introduce teabags into the UK market and in 1989, it introduced the round bag. This was the result of extensive research and development and it helped Tetley to grow volume sales by approximately 30%, achieving market leadership.

This reputation for innovation continues, with the launch of drawstring tea bags in 1997, the UK's only mainstream organic tea in 2001 and in 2002, Tetley Tea:therapy: a range of three teas that created a new tea sector.

The Tetley Group employs over 1,000 staff worldwide in various offices and manufacturing sites, including those employed by its joint venture partner Tata Tea Ltd, in India.

History

Tea was first publicly sold in Britain by Thomas Garway in the middle of the seventeenth century. 150 years later, Joseph and Edward Tetley started to sell it in the Yorkshire Moors, peddling it from the back of the pack horse along with other provisions like salt. Soon, they were doing well enough to set themselves up as tea merchants, establishing Tetley Brothers in Huddersfield.

In 1856, the brothers moved the business to London, setting up in Callum Street, which was very close to Mincing Lane – the centre of the world tea trade in those days. However, soon the brothers parted company and Joseph was left to run the business alone, changing the name to 'Joseph Tetley and Company, Wholesale Tea Dealers'.

Tea with no loose leaves to empty away!

New, quick, easy way to make delicious tea for ½d. a cup

Just put a Tetley Tea Bag in the pot, add boiling water and infuse in the usual way. When finished simply remove the small, square Tea Bag—and rinse out the pot.

No more time-wasting bother of a heap of messy leaves to empty away! And each Tea Bag contains enough fine quality, full-flavoured tea to give you two good cups!

NO leaves to empty away
NO wasteful measuring
NO strainer
NO leaves in cup
NO slop basin

TETLEY *tea bags*
FULL-FLAVOURED, FINE QUALITY TEA...
1/5 for a box of 16

The brand's earliest success was in the US, distributing packet tea through an agreement with an American agent, Wright & Graham. This partnership established Tetley as a major trade name in the US (more effectively than had been so far achieved in Britain) and also led to the partnership becoming a world force in packet tea distribution. In 1913, Wright & Graham became Tetley Tea Incorporated.

Having introduced the tea bag to the US 33 years earlier, it wasn't until 1953 that Tetley brought it to the UK. In 1954, the Stock Exchange Gazette reported: "Joseph Tetley is particularly well-known for the introduction of tea in small bags for immediate use in the pot."

The company stayed loyal to its invention during a period of tumultuous market change, as the retail market began to be dominated by large multiples and strong, national brands began to take centre stage. With the tea bag giving it a clear point of differentiation, Tetley was in a good position to ride the storm.

Tetley has continued with its innovative approach ever since, launching round tea bags in 1989, drawstring bags in 1997, organic tea in 2001 and Tea:therapy in 2002.

Product

Tetley tea bags are blended and packed at the company's factory in Eaglescliffe, Teeside, one of the world's largest tea-packing facilities. It produces approximately 280 million Tetley tea bags every week, blending tea from over 30 different estates around the world.

As well as the core Tetley tea brand, the company also makes Tetley Decaf, which is the brand leader of the growing decaffeinated market in the UK, with a value brand share of 30.7%, up 34% year on year (Source: ACNielsen 2002).

Recent Developments

Tetley's reputation for innovation has remained strong with the launch in March 2001 of Tetley Organic, the only mainstream organic tea and the fastest growing. The brand also launched Tetley Tea:therapy in May 2002, a range of three teas designed to have all the taste of a normal cup of tea, but with added herbs. This product has created a new sector in the tea market.

In February 2002, the Tetley brand was successfully relaunched with a new consumer proposition supported by fresh TV advertising, poster and press support and advertised in gyms and leisure centres for the first time to emphasise health benefits. Indeed, these facets of tea are becoming more prevalent, with Tetley taking a leading role in communicating this news to consumers. Tea contains no calories worth counting; it is 100% natural, comes from a renewable source, has no additives and, what's more, can count towards your daily fluid intake (the recommended daily intake is usually measured as eight glasses of water).

In addition, all tea contains high levels of antioxidants, compounds also found in fruit and vegetables. Antioxidants form an important part of a healthy diet, so Tetley has been featuring this in almost all its communications.

In the first six months after its relaunch, Tetley's sales increased by 10% (Source: ACNielsen March 2001-August 2001 versus March 2002-August 2002).

For the foodservice sector however, the last eighteen months have been a difficult period. Whilst the tea market as a whole remains stable, Tetley's out of home market share grew by a third over this period – stopping the tea sector from showing dramatic decline. Tetley has managed to sustain considerable growth over this period, by working closely with both end users and distributors and introducing innovative promotions and high impact point of sale. Concentrating sales and marketing efforts on sectors that were not unduly affected by the tourism down turn (workplace and health), has also paid dividends with Tetley the leading brand in those markets.

Promotion

In February 2002, Tetley ran its first advertising campaign for 28 years that did not feature the Tetley Tea Folk – the brown-capped, white-coated band of characters led by Gaffer. The Tea Folk, the face of the brand from 1973 (one of the longest running TV campaigns ever), starred in over 55 commercials, using end lines such as 'Only Tetley will do',

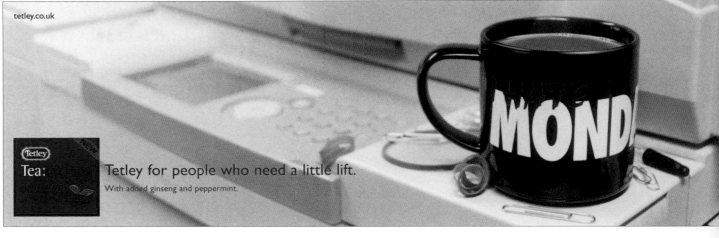

Tetley for people who need a little lift.
With added ginseng and peppermint.

'That's better, that's Tetley' and 'Tetley make tea bags make tea' and remain some of Britain's favourite TV ads.

The new communications focus is on 'living life to the full'. Poster advertising used lines such as 'Cup, up and away' and 'Go on, live a lot', with 30 'specials' sites around the UK which feature large flashing hearts.

The pack design was also revamped as part of the relaunch. A clean, bold design was chosen, to maximise its visibility on shelves. The design was implemented across all main variants and sub-brands.

Historically, Tetley sales promotion has focused on added value promotions. The brand has given away football characters, Tea Folk items, Disney merchandise and Roald Dahl children's books. As the highly competitive tea market has moved away from this, Tetley has focused more on multi-buys, extra product free, price promotions and cause related marketing.

As sponsors of Team GB at the Sydney 2000 Olympics, Tetley ran an on-pack promotion called 'Free Sports Stuff for Schools', giving consumers the chance to collect tokens that local schools could use to buy new sports kit. The scheme signed up over 80% of British schools and redeemed over fifteen million tokens.

Tetley has sponsored the British Heart Foundation since 2001. Aimed at communicating the benefits of a healthy lifestyle and raising large sums for the charity, it has been very successful – donating well over £400,000 in the first two years. On-pack communication, web activities and PR based in the British Heart Foundation's 440 charity shops have been the main threads of the activity to date.

Tetley has also begun utilising the power of the internet, with a brand new site, www.tetley.co.uk. In 2002 it scored in the top ten for FMCG site visits and ran highly successful online sampling campaigns. Consumers can also

purchase Tetley over the internet, which has proved very popular with ex-pats and tea fans the world over. A trade focused site, teaexperts.co.uk was launched in August 2001, allowing Tetley to offer an objective view of the tea market to everyone selling tea; from the main multiples buyers to small independent retailers and caterers. The information and advice contained in the website helps those businesses grow their total tea sales.

As part of its investment in one to one relationships with its consumers, Tetley runs a direct marketing campaign, talking regularly to hundreds of thousands of consumers about tea.

Brand Values

Generosity, commitment, devotion, enthusiasm and optimism are descriptives that form the cornerstones of how the Tetley brand aims to be viewed. Corporately, Tetley and its parent company Tata Tea have always been passionate about tea and are together involved at every stage of the tea process, from bush to cup.

Tetley are founder members of the Tea Sourcing Partnership, an organisation that represents the majority of the UK's tea companies. The Partnership believes in a shared responsibility for the ethical sourcing of tea, and it aims to monitor standards on 1,200 estates in seven countries. Independent social auditors visit the estates to check that the terms and conditions of employment, health and safety, maternity rights, education and housing, fully comply with local laws and union agreements.

www.tetley.co.uk

Tetley for people who need a little calm.
With added camomile, lemon balm and honey.

Market

The National Lottery was launched in November 1994. The lottery was positioned as a 'harmless flutter', which could be enjoyed by all adults in the UK. The Henley Centre concluded, after just fourteen weeks, that The National Lottery was "the most dramatic product launch in British history." Though the National Lottery is part of the UK gaming market its main competition does not come from this sector, instead it finds itself competing with other products available in newsagents which can be consumed for a pound or two.

The UK gaming market is worth £26 billion of which the National Lottery accounts for around 20%.

Achievements

The National Lottery created a powerful structure for raising money for good causes around the country. Indeed, over £12 billion (equivalent to over £24 million a week and over £2,300 a minute) has been donated to date.

The Lottery quickly became popular with the British public, with around 60% of the country playing regularly. It is estimated that more than 94% of the UK adult population have played at least once. By the end of its first week The National Lottery had raised £12 million. Parliament chose to divide the money amongst worthy causes in the areas of sport, the arts, heritage and charities as well as for the Millennium celebrations.

Nine years on, 72% of adults play Saturday Lotto, 43% play Wednesday Lotto and the total average spend per player per week is £3.86. Over £18.8 billion has been given away as prize money since The National Lottery was launched and over 1,400 millionaires have been created. On average, about 3.5 million people win an amount with the lottery every week and between them take home around £40 million in prize money. In the process, the UK has benefited significantly, with vast projects such as the Tate Modern, the Eden Project and the Millennium Stadium winning lottery funds as well as much smaller projects in every part of the country.

In terms of sales during the year to April 2002, Lotto and Instants led major brands by a significant margin. Sales of Lotto were £3,849.8 million and Instants £578.5 million, compared with Coca-Cola's £520 million, Walkers' £440 million, Müller's £335 million and Nescafé's £285 million. (Source: Annual Biggest Brands survey ACNielsen, compiled for Marketing August 2002).

History

In March 1992 the Government proposed the creation of a UK National Lottery with the aim of injecting massive funds into designated 'Good Causes' in the UK. Eight organisations tendered and Camelot was chosen to run The National Lottery in May 1994 for an initial period of seven years. Camelot had committed to raise £9 billion for Good Causes, a target it achieved in October 2000. This amont has subsequently increased to £12 billion.

Camelot Group plc was a consortium set up by five separate companies – Cadbury-Schweppes, De La Rue, GTECH, Racal Electronics and ICL.

Winning the licence was the first step on a long road. The newly formed company had just 24 weeks to set up the lottery from scratch and faced being fined £1 million a day for any delay. In that time it had to meet highly demanding technical requirements, establish a retailer network and a communications strategy. It created the largest

communications network in the UK – equivalent to the four biggest high street banks combined – capable of processing up to 400,000 transactions per minute. It installed terminals in over 10,000 retail outlets, including multiple and independent retailers, forecourt operators, off-licences and Post Offices and trained 80,000 individuals to operate them.

By launch, at least 93% of the UK adult population lived or worked within two miles of a lottery outlet. Getting the communications and education right at launch was essential: the public had to understand and believe in the brand and be inspired to purchase National Lottery tickets. The National Lottery was launched with the now famous advertising campaign featuring the slogan 'It Could Be You' with the 'Hand of Good Fortune' acting as the random hand of luck.

A total of 22 million viewers watched the first National Lottery draw which was broadcast live on BBC One. Four months later in March 1995 National Lottery Instants was launched, immediately becoming the UK's largest impulse brand. By September that year £1 billion had been raised for Good Causes. In March 1996, Lucky Dip was launched, a randomly generated selection of numbers for the draw based game, and February 1997 saw the first mid-week draw.

In June 1997 Camelot launched The National Lottery Thunderball game, followed in November 2000 by Lottery Extra. In December 2000 The National Lottery Commission awarded Camelot the licence to run the lottery for another seven years, starting in January 2002. In April of that year Camelot announced plans to relaunch the lottery, enabling The National Lottery to become the umbrella brand for all games, whilst the Saturday and Wednesday draws were renamed Lotto and Lotto Extra. In July 2002 Camelot launched a new way to play on the main Lotto game with the introduction of Lotto HotPicks.

Product

The National Lottery provides a wide range of games for its customers. There are two distinct types of game offerings. The first are the draw-based games – Lotto, Lotto HotPicks, Lotto Extra and Thunderball – which take place twice a week and are shown live on the BBC on Wednesday and Saturday nights. The second are Instants – a selection of Scratchcard games, which offer consumers, the chance of an instant win.

Lotto is the biggest game in the portfolio, representing 75% of turnover and offering a potential jackpot on Saturdays of around £6 million. In common with similar games around the world it is a long odds big jackpot game with a one in 52 chance of winning a prize and a one in fourteen million chance of winning the jackpot. A third of winners play in syndicates, and around 1.3 million people a week win something.

Thunderball offers a fixed jackpot of £250,000 and more lower-tier prizes give players a one in nineteen chance of winning. In 2002 Thunderball was

repositioned as the game you win on more often and a mid week draw was also introduced. Unusually for a 'powerball' game (common in most global lotteries) players don't have to match the Thunderball to win a prize.

HotPicks, the major launch of 2002 and a significant contributor to revenue, offers players the chance to win big prizes for picking and matching fewer numbers. Players pick two, three or four numbers and if they come up on the main Lotto draw they win £40, £450 or £7,000.

Extra is an escalating jackpot-only game with no lower prize tiers. The jackpot tends to roll which raises excitement levels. It has reached a high of £14 million and regularly offers a substantial prize to play for.

Christmas Millionaire Maker is a seasonal game which is held on Christmas Eve. The £5 tickets allow The National Lottery to create a millionaire for every million tickets sold.

The National Lottery distributes a new Scratchcard game every two weeks and the cards have the widest distribution of any of the lottery products, featuring prominently in 36,000 outlets. New play formats, greater promotion, better merchandising and the broader use of £2 price points boosted sales in 2002.

Recent Developments

In 2002 The National Lottery began to relaunch its offering, including changing the names of the Saturday and Wednesday games to Lotto and Lotto Extra. In July 2002 HotPicks was launched and rapidly became very popular with younger players and with more occasional customers.

Also in 2002 Thunderball became available on Wednesdays as well

as Saturdays, with the aim of generating increased interest and sales.

In the pipeline are instant win games on The National Lottery website, a daily game and a European game. The brand also has plans to make the current portfolio of games available to play online.

Also in 2002 The National Lottery promoted its Subscription service whereby consumers can purchase their tickets on an annual basis and not have to worry about checking their numbers as all winners are notified of any fortuitous results.

Promotion

Camelot spent £39 million on television, radio, press, poster, point-of-sale and direct mail for the launch of The National Lottery. Resulting in approximately 40 million adults seeing the TV commercial at least thirteen times. Furthermore, the direct mail push was the largest recorded and was sent to 21.8 million homes.

Four years after launch, as the number of people who believed 'it could be them' fell, so the campaign was updated to rekindle enthusiasm and excitement in the lottery. The new executions emphasised the 'possibility' rather than the 'probability' of winning, encapsulated in the slogan 'Maybe, just Maybe.' Also, for the first time, television advertising featured

some of the beneficiaries of the Good Cause funds, in an attempt to challenge the widespread misconceptions about how lottery money was spent and to encourage the general public to reassess its value to the nation.

National Lottery advertising has also supported new product development, including the launch of Thunderball in 1999, and Instants, where a TV vox pop campaign featured National Lottery retailers recounting stories of customer wins, accompanied by the message 'Anyone can win in an Instant.'

Camelot relaunched the Lottery in 2002, with marketing activity taking place during May, June and July. Billy Connolly featured in a series of commercials promoting the name change and two special draws in May and another to celebrate the Queen's Golden Jubilee in June. Posters were also used extensively and for the first time Lotto was promoted in a nationwide doordrop, containing a 'playslip', to eighteen million homes. Retail outlets enjoyed a facelift, as did the BBC draw show. In July the HotPicks game was successfully launched.

The Good Causes are what gives The National Lottery its competitive edge and are a significant driver of participation. Drawing on this, a new campaign rolled out in 2003 across all media, heavily featuring the beneficiaries of the Good Causes. The Good Causes became a platform through which the National Lottery was able to both communicate facts about the games and also to demonstrate how people all over Britain have directly benefited from the money raised through people playing the games from the National Lottery. Thereby showing that every time somebody plays the Lottery somebody in Britain is winning.

Brand Values

Keen to promote a consistent communications message after its relaunch, Camelot hopes The National Lottery will come to stand for great games and Good Causes. Values include 'dreams' (irrepressible, upbeat, resilient, optimistic, full of ideas), 'inclusiveness' (human, real, honest and engaging), 'Britishness' (populist, deep understanding of what the British like and are like) and 'betterment' (principled, behaves with integrity and conviction).

www.national-lottery.co.uk

THE Sun

Market

Every day over 24 million Britons reach for a daily paper, which provides everything from news and opinion to sport, celebrity gossip and business. According to research conducted by the Henley Centre, for an average person, newspapers are second only to their husband or wife as an influence on their thoughts and actions. Newspapers bring us up to date not only with what's happening at the end of our street but across the globe.

On any given morning, The Sun can make its readers feel informed, inspired, entertained or angered and maybe even experience all four emotions at once.

In today's technology-driven and media literate society, where consumers' potential points of contact with news are ever expanding, 'content' is still key and newspapers provide great breadth and depth of coverage and comment.

In addition to reporting the news, newspapers, not least The Sun, have a long history of setting political and social agendas. For example, The Sun's advice to its readers in the run up to the 1997 general election, advising them to vote for the Labour Party, caused as much international news comment as anything reported in the media that day.

In the UK, the newspaper market can be broken into three categories; the 'populars', the 'mid-markets' and the 'broadsheets'. Populars account for over 50% of the daily sales volume, with The Sun the undisputed leader in this category, outselling its nearest rival by 1.5 million copies every day.

Achievements

The Sun is the biggest English language daily paper in the world. Few brands have consistently led and shaped their market for as long and as successfully as The Sun. Every day almost ten million people across the UK purchase The Sun for their daily read; more than the other populars combined. It is renowned for its ability to capture the mood of the nation and communicate it in an individual way. Its straightforward, entertaining and easy to understand style of reporting has remained consistent for over 30 years and has won it legions of loyal readers. Over 80% of its average daily readership read at least three copies out of every four, making them the most loyal readers in the market.

History

The Sun as we know it today began life in 1969 when a failing title owned by the International Publishing Corporation (IPC) was rescued by Rupert Murdoch's News Corporation.

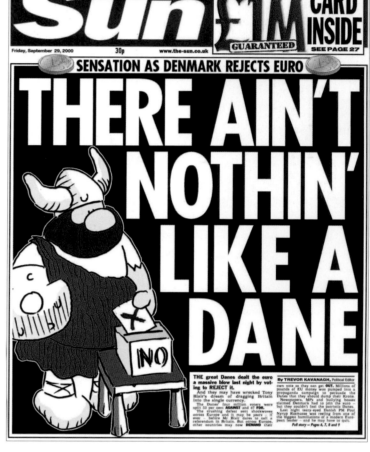

Its purchase, for £600,000, marked the beginning of its transformation into one of the most successful newspapers in the world.

However, its history dates back to 1911 with the launch of the trade union backed Daily Herald. By 1933 The Herald had become the world's biggest selling newspaper with a circulation of over two million copies per day. However, in the decades that followed, sales gradually fell to the point where, in 1964, IPC decided to replace the Herald with a new, more modern paper and so The Sun was born. This new paper was aimed at the newly affluent young, as well as graduates emerging from the recently established redbrick universities and technology colleges. Unfortunately it never achieved its target circulation of two million copies per day and within five years, sales had slumped to eight hundred thousand, with financial losses growing rapidly.

In stepped News Corporation, which recognised The Sun's huge potential and the opportunities for a paper that spoke out for and entertained the ordinary man and woman in the street. The relaunched paper with its fresh mix of news, opinion and fun was a success. The very first issue sold over a million copies. Within a year sales had doubled and after four years the circulation had grown to an impressive four million.

In 1970 another British institution, The Page Three Girl, was born. The most popular girls featured in the photographs quickly became famous in their own right and women such as Samantha Fox and Melinda Messenger became household names.

In 1986 The Sun was making the news itself, featuring prominently on all its rivals' front pages when production was moved to its present site in Wapping, East London. The trade unions' restrictive hold over the newspaper industry was broken and other papers quickly followed suit to reorganise and relocate their operations.

In 1990 News International again led the way in newspaper production, when a massive investment in new technology gave The Sun higher quality printing, with full colour reproduction, as well as extra supplements and pull-outs for its readers. Key innovations included the launch in 1996 of the first free TV listings magazine as part of the Saturday package, which reshaped not only the tabloid market but also the paid-for TV listings business. Another first, which built on The Sun's sports coverage, was the introduction in 1998 of 'Supergoals', the first football-dedicated pullout in the tabloid market.

Continuous investment, passion for what it does and commitment to being the best, helps ensure that The Sun is well placed to best meet its readers changing lives, their values and needs from a newspaper.

Product

The lifespan of an edition of a newspaper is very short as its content changes every day. What never changes though is what the product stands for and believes in; simply put, The Sun is passionate about life in Britain. It has led, questioned, challenged and provoked reactions for over 30 years. It has established itself as a leader and barometer of the mood and opinions of the great British public and is an essential part of their daily lives. In a world increasingly dominated by 'spin' and media hype, The Sun can always be relied on to give an opinion and tell the truth as it sees it. As a result, its readers will have different opinions and reactions to The Sun on different days.

The Sun aims to speak out for the ordinary man and woman in the street. It does so in a straightforward uncomplicated manner.

The reporting in The Sun aims to present news stories and celebrity gossip in a manner that reflects the concerns, humour, generosity and irreverence of the British people. It covers everything from who has been elected to parliament, to those who has been elected to be in the Big Brother house.

As a barometer of public opinion, its views are noted by a diversity of the population from Prime Ministers to pensioners, captains of industry to local volunteer groups and sports stars to ordinary sports fans.

Recent Developments

The Sun website www.thesun.co.uk has trebled in size since 2001 and the brand is now fully integrated into the new media landscape. It not only brings readers all the news and information available in that day's paper but also allows them to interact with the paper in a way never before possible. As well as reading up to the minute breaking news, readers can check how their 'Dream Team' fantasy football league team is doing. Indeed, Dream Team is the biggest game of its kind in the country. Visitors can also 'chat' to other Sun 'surfers' or visit the online shop where The Sun offers a range of top branded goods at discounts negotiated on behalf of its readers.

Promotion

As the leader in its market, The Sun brand enjoys incredibly high recognition levels, with over 99% of newspaper readers claiming to have heard of it. It is a brand that is both trusted and 'loved' by its readers, while its campaigning stance is equally respected and feared by anyone in a position of power looking to put one over on the British public.

Within the market, The Sun has always led the way for sales promotions and reader offers, the mainstays of newspaper promotion. Its first Bingo game in March 1988 entered the Guinness book of Records for the largest number of entrants in a newspaper competition — over 4.3 million. In return for collecting tokens, readers were offered £9.50 holidays, for a short break in holiday parks all over Britain. As a result, The Sun became the UK's largest travel agent for holidays taken in this country. Books for Schools, run in conjunction with Walkers Crisps, is about to enter its fifth year. This hugely successful campaign, which allows schools to swap tokens collected from The Sun, News of the World and special packs of Walkers crisps for free books, gave away over six million books worth £32.5 million in its first three years alone. Over 97% of schools in the UK have participated in this scheme since 1999 and it is supported

by extensive marketing activity by The Sun.

In recent years marketing for The Sun has become more sophisticated, with an increasing amount of consistency running through all of its communications. The Sun's advertising tag line 'We Love It', captures the passionate and inclusive nature of the product and can now be seen on all advertising from billboards to the regular TV campaigns as well as becoming an integral part of the editorial layout. In addition, The Sun is now in a position to tailor all of its offers to groups of readers and as their lifestyles have changed, so have the methods of communicating with them. This consistency of communication is continued through two million SMS messages, nearly one million emails and six million pieces of direct mail per year.

The Sun consistently brings its readers breaking news in its own individual style and recently readers have been able to access this online.

Brand Values

Long-term The Sun readers know that their paper of choice continually evolves and develops to reflect their changing lives, concerns, interests, values and beliefs.

Furthermore, The Sun aims to maintain a passion for reporting the news and a willingness to speak

out on their reader's behalf with a passion for life in the UK. The paper aims to bring people together, through shared emotions and reactions. It is this which has made the brand an icon of contemporary British culture.

www.thesun.co.uk

FREE BOOKS FOR SCHOOLS

EQUIPPING CHILDREN FOR THE FUTURE

The Brand Council

THE ✦ TIMES

Market

Newspapers still remain the one medium that can truly be taken anywhere, at anytime, whilst still providing the breadth and depth of coverage that today's media consumers demand. In Britain, the role of the newspaper is ingrained in the lifestyle of many people, with approximately half of the adult population reading a national newspaper daily. This alone shows the continuing strength of the newspaper sector, particularly in light of ever-increasing media fragmentation and the advance of the internet. Furthermore, newspapers still provide a unique role, one that has changed immensely over the decades. Once, a broadsheet newspaper's role was seen primarily as a serious informer, commentator, advertiser and campaigner. However, consumer demand has meant they must now also entertain, while providing conversation, lifestyle opinions and knowledge for personal welfare. Above all, a broadsheet newspaper now has to provide guidance, and impart clarity through the clutter of today's information overload. In today's hectic world, many find time for reading a newspaper as a reason to escape and relax from the hubbub surrounding them.

In the UK, the highly competitive national newspaper market sells approximately thirteen million daily copies and fourteen million Sunday copies. National newspapers are grouped into three sectors – broadsheets, mid-market and tabloids. The Broadsheet sector comprises of five daily and five Sunday titles, with the top three newspaper groups, News International, the Telegraph Group and the Scott Trust (Guardian and Observer), fiercely competing for market share of circulation and readership alike. Moreover, increasing competition of the two Mail titles from the mid-market has developed due to the change of social make-up in Britain over recent years.

Within the daily broadsheet sector, The Times (founded 1785) and the Daily Telegraph (founded 1855) are the two largest newspaper sellers and the greatest of rivals, but differ in their appeal. The recent trends in broadsheet national newspapers have been to appeal to many different types of consumer. However, due to the personal attachments and perceptions, many based on political leanings, that people have of newspapers it can be hard to shake the old images. For example, The Times has finally shaken off its 'bowler hat' image through aggressive marketing and modernising product changes.

THE ✦ TIMES
When war came to America

Times reporter James Bone was looking up at the World Trade Centre minutes before the twin towers fell from the sky

was modernised in many ways. By the beginning of 1999, the end result was a national newspaper that was clearly ahead of the rest of the market except the Daily Telegraph. Nevertheless, at an average of over 700,000 daily sales, The Times could also genuinely claim to be a serious competitive threat to the Daily Telegraph.

The Times has also won numerous awards over the years at the British Press awards and the What the Papers Say awards. Most recently, it won Newspaper of the Year Awards for 2000 and 2002, with the then Editor, Peter Stothard, winning the Editor of the Year award as well as several other writers who won awards. The Times' sports journalists received four out of the five major sports awards in 2001.

The Times can also be credited with launching the first major promotion of all broadsheet newspapers with the Eurostar offer in 1996. It was an unprecedented success driving massive trial of the product, and as a result, the broadsheet market now offers many strong promotions.

History

The Times has been at the forefront of British journalism since it was founded as The Daily Universal Register in 1785, and shortly afterwards changed its name to The Times. More than two hundred years later, it has adapted to the changing interests and lifestyles of its readers, leading to recent successes. One of the world's oldest surviving daily newspapers, it was first published by John Walter who wrote in his first issue, "A news-paper ought to be the register of the times and faithful recorder of every species of intelligence…The Register, in its politics, will be of no party". All subsequent editors have reaffirmed this position, and kept consistency in the brand.

The Times quickly gained the reputation as a hard-hitting newspaper and after an article in 1830, acquired the nickname 'The Thunderer', by which it is still known today. However, between 1908 and 1926 its position was under threat due to spiralling costs and strike action during the General Strike. Lord Thomson first brought the two different titles, The Times and Sunday Times, together in 1966. In November 1978, The Times was forced to close for almost a year due to union problems. By 1981, both The Times and Sunday Times were sold to News International. It was in 1986, with a new state-of-the-art printing works built in Wapping, that News International took the drastic steps that would change the newspaper industry immensely. Other newspaper companies soon followed News International by moving out of Fleet Street. The quality of newspapers in terms of print, colour, and variety would not have otherwise been as advanced as it is today.

The Times' stature in the market and the newspaper itself was transformed during the 1990s. 1991 saw the Saturday Times blossom into six sections and a new typeface, Times Millennium, was introduced. The newspaper's layout was re-designed, with much more emphasis on colour news pictures and informative graphics. In 1993 the newspaper embarked on the ambitious goal of breaking the stagnation in the market by using a series of price cuts. The Times also began printing in continental Europe, and in 1996 the first internet edition appeared. By 1998, The Times had the most foreign correspondents ever in its history, helping to secure its reputation for international news. Many further product changes ensued, including The Times' first true tabloid section called Times 2, which has given The Times the window of opportunity to introduce further tabloid sections to meet consumer demands.

Product

The Times newspaper has always been regarded as the definitive broadsheet. It is one of the most recognisable, trusted and respected newspapers in the world. With a continuous quest for objectivity, the product strives to give readers the most balanced arguments on matters of importance, so that they

Achievements

One of the most remarkable successes of The Times has been its 90% rise in sales over the past ten years. The Times used to sell an average of 390,000 copies a day, very similar to The Guardian and The Independent at the time. To break the stagnation of the market and improve its own position, The Times embarked on a five-year pricing strategy that saw the cover price of The Times fall as low as 10p on Mondays. At the same time, the product

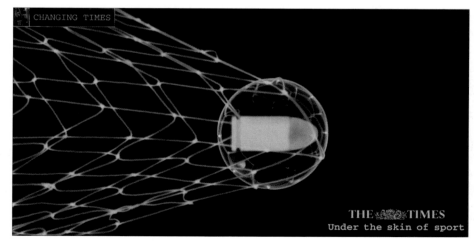

CHANGING TIMES

THE ✦ TIMES
Under the skin of sport

can make their own judgements; The Times offers its own opinions, it does not impose them. The Times is renowned for the breadth and depth of its coverage, and its image is one of being informative, responsible, assertive, British, and not sensationalist or trivial.

The core topics of The Times remain news, business and sports, yet its diversity has grown over the past decade. The product now offers much more feature-led topics and articles with the introduction of the new Times 2 tabloid section. Furthermore, recent re-vamps of the Business section have proved to be very successful and well regarded amongst The Times' business readers. The Times' Sport section is also vital to the title's continued success, and the section's reputation is strong. Sport supplements help strengthen The Times' reputation even further, especially with regards to football, such as the Football Handbook and The Game. Within the Saturday package, The Times' excellence in lifestyle features is borne through its magazine and travel section. All of these changes have had to be backed up by editorial investment and marketing above the line.

Extra supplements are a regular feature of The Times. This has a double benefit: it helps draw in trial readership and purchase, whilst at the same time strengthening the loyalty of its existing readers. The Times also takes pride in some of its more niche sections: The Times Appointments is seen

as one of the most prestigious advertisers of top jobs, whilst the Law section is highly considered by the legal profession. In fact, The Times Law reports are written by barristers and, carrying legal status, can be quoted in court.

Of course, there are also the items in The Times that to many people make the title what it is and are considered part of the fabric of the

product. The Times is famous for The Obituaries, Courts and Social, Birthdays and Anniversaries, the now new interactive Debate section – all of which are under the title of The Register section. Furthermore, The Times would not be The Times without its challenging crossword, the Letters to the Editor and the Comment section.

Recent Developments

The changes to The Times are continuous and evolutionary. Robert Thomson, an Australian, was recently appointed the new Editor, the first non-British editor of The Times. A change of Editor brings new developments to the newspaper. This has already been seen in very recent product changes; The Game, a new 24-page tabloid football supplement was launched on Mondays, further

enhancing The Times' image as best for football amongst many consumers. Another introduction has been Bricks and Mortar, a weekly supplement on Fridays that provides an irresistible mix of facts, figures and fantasies from the world of property.

To develop The Times' core strength on sport, sponsorship deals have been struck with both the ECB for cricket, which is also shown on Channel 4, and the PGA for golf. This means that, with The Game supplement, The Times is promoting itself in three major areas of its sports readers interests.

Promotion

The Times uses most elements of the marketing mix to promote the product and the brand. Like most newspapers, The Times uses TV and radio specifically to support promotions such as two for one flight offers or additional supplements, such as Premiership Handbook. To sharpen targeting, The Times also uses email to communicate with specific customers.

The brand's strategy is to continually contemporise itself, whilst giving it enduring relevance and accessibility. To do so, The Times uses more classic brand advertising to present its brand benefits. This is spearheaded by TV brand campaigns such as 'Feed Your Mind' and the recent campaign 'What's Important: The Times'. These communications aim to remind people that The Times is a modern, important newspaper that delivers the vital news and knowledge for its consumers needs.

The latest advertising campaign for the newspaper is designed to reinforce the theme of importance by showing that even the most innoccuous, everyday objects often have hidden or symbolic aspects of real importance to them. This idea is a metaphor for how The Times encourages its readers not to take events at face value, and how its coverage strives to look beneath the surface of those events for their true significance.

The Times marketing goes into overdrive when promoting new product developments. Campaigns use a variety of integrated marketing, including TV, radio, outdoor, online, direct mail, and email (CRM), to drive awareness and trial. The Times believes that whilst aggressive promotion is vital, real success lies in the presentation of superior products through advertising, and increased desirability of the brand itself.

Brand Values

The reputation of The (London) Times is global and based on the trust of the paper's readers. It aims to consistently represent a fair and honest view that reflects the concerns of both the British public and the international community. Those readers value its wisdom and objective scrutiny. Those strengths allow the paper to illuminate both sides of an argument, whilst remaining an authority on many topics.

The confidence of The Times in its own ability and reputation means that the brand remains relevant and influential. The power of knowledge is vital and The Times uses this to set agendas, form opinions and most importantly to guide its readers through the many complicated events that go on every day across the world.

www.timesonline.co.uk

Market

Tea is Britain's favourite cuppa and teabags are our preferred way of consuming the beverage. According to a recent survey by BMRB, tea is available in the majority of UK households with 94% of housewives claiming to use teabags. The overall market is worth £546 million, of which teabags take a 93% share of total sales (Source: ACNielsen).

However, the classic brew faces challenges. The success of teabags has meant that sales of instant and packet teas have suffered, and the overall tea market is facing a further threat from the youth sector which is favouring soft drinks and mineral water.

Fruit and herbal teas are showing growth, but they currently account for less than 5% of the market in value terms and just over 1% of total consumption (Source: ACNielsen). The picture is similar for green, organic and 'fair trade' teas.

Consumers are however being lured back to tea by packaging and design innovations – such as round or pyramid-shaped teabags. Furthermore, the therapeutic effect of tea may help to attract the younger end of the market. Research from The Tea Council suggests, "social, health and environmental benefits give tea opportunities to capitalise on its gradually changing image with the youth market to become a real lifestyle choice".

This rediscovery may coincide with a rise in tea drinking outside the home. Tea bars are already springing up in the US, having started in health-conscious California, and the trend is likely to gain ground in Europe. In the UK, coffee bars have proved popular, but tea bars are still few and far between.

Another plus point is that, unlike other products, tea brands are successfully defending themselves against supermarket own labels. In the last two years own label's share of the market declined by 3.7% (Source: ACNielsen).

Changes in the demographic state of the nation may also prove beneficial to tea. The beverage is traditionally consumed by older drinkers, and the 45-64 year old age group is, according to the 2001 census, expected to swell by nearly three quarters of a million by the middle of the decade.

This is likely to be beneficial to tea consumption, although manufacturers will need to work hard to stimulate demand.

Achievements

Since its launch at the beginning of the twentieth century, Ty.phoo has grown into a classic British brand. It has a 8.3% value share of the UK tea market (Source: ACNielsen) putting it in the top three with PG Tips and Tetley.

History

Tea is nearly 5,000 years old and was discovered, as legend has it, in 2737 BC by a Chinese emperor when some tea leaves accidentally blew into a pot of boiling water. The first European to personally encounter tea and write about it was the Portuguese Jesuit Father Jasper de Cruz in 1560 as Portugal was the first to gain the right of trade with China.

The first samples of tea reached England between 1652 and 1654 and quickly proved popular enough to replace ale as the national drink of England. The first record of adding milk to tea was recorded in 1680.

The popularity of the beverage continued to rise and importation rose from 40,000 pounds in 1699 to an annual average of 240,000 pounds by 1708. By the late 1880s top hotels in England began to offer tea service in tea rooms and tea courts. Served in the late afternoon, Victorian ladies would meet for tea and conversation. At the beginning of the 1900s, hotels began to host afternoon tea dances as dance crazes began to sweep the UK.

Ty.phoo was launched in 1903 by Birmingham grocer John Sumner, after his sister Mary had highly regarded tea as a cure for indigestion. Her enthusiasm for the product encouraged John to sell it in his shop. Sumner set himself three criteria when choosing a name for his tea. Firstly, the name had to be distinctive and unlike others. In addition, it had to be a name which would trip off the tongue as well as being one which could be protected by registration. After a few sleepless nights trying to think of a name, he finally came up with Ty.phoo Tipps – 'ty.phoo' being the Chinese word for 'doctor'. Sumners stuck with the name as he felt that it sounded attractively exotic and was alliterative with tea. The word 'Tipps', however, could not be registered even though it appeared on packets for years and was copied by many imitators – right down to the misspelling of the word 'tips' refering to the tea leaves. The double 'p' was originally a printing error. In 2003, Ty.phoo celebrates its centenary.

Ty.phoo grew in strength over the years and in 1968 merged with Schweppes. A year later, Cadbury's also joined the conglomeration, creating Cadbury Schweppes Ty.phoo. In 1986, however, Ty.phoo was sold to a company called Premier Brands, which since its recent takeover by the

American venture capitalists Hicks Muse Tate and Furst has been known as Premier Foods. As well as Ty.phoo, Premier Foods owns the Ridgways Organic brand, and London Fruit & Herb.

There have been many product developments over the years to cater for consumer's changing needs, not only in packaging innovations, but in the way in which tea is presented with loose, bagged and instant variants now included in the Ty.phoo range.

Product

All tea comes from the same tree Camellia Sinensis, which originates from China. Three basic types are produced, namely: black, green and oolong. In Britain the most popular products are made from black tea, however green tea blends are growing in popularity albeit from a low base. Ty.phoo were the first to introduce a green tea blend into the market in 1999.

Tea for the Ty.phoo blend is sourced from many different high quality tea producing countries. The backbone of the blend is vacuum packed Assam tea, the main tea growing area in the North Eastern part of Assam. The vacuum packed Assam tea has a malty, smooth character. The blend includes further high grown teas from the quality tea growing areas in Eastern Africa and Southern India. The combination of all these teas ensures that Ty.phoo consistently delivers a smooth, refreshing, 'golden' cup of tea, which caters specifically for the demands of the UK consumers. Ty.phoo is ideally suited to be drunk with milk and with sugar if so desired.

As well as teabags, Ty.phoo produces the brand leader in the instant white tea market with Ty.phoo QT. It is also brand leader with Decaffeinated tea, and Ty.phoo One Cup.

Recent Developments

The Ty.phoo brand was relaunched in April 2002, as the result of a £5 million overhaul of the brand. The aim was to position the brand as a contemporary, refreshing drink that would appeal to 25-40 year olds – exactly the market segment that had been lured away by soft drinks. Ty.phoo introduced fresh new packaging that crossed the entire range, with a striking red livery and a modernised logo, as well as a 'cut-out' effect which enables the purchaser to see the foil packaging inside the box. The revised look stood out on shelves and successfully drove sales.

Promotion

To maximise exposure for the brand's relaunch, Ty.phoo embarked upon an extensive advertising drive. The campaign consisted of TV, press, radio and posters. It revisited the concept of using the 'OO' in the brand's name to humorous effect, recalling previously successful campaigns with the slogans 'You only get an OO with Ty.phoo' and 'Only an OO will do'. This time, the ads featured deflated people who had, as the campaign put it, lost their 'OO' and needed revitalisation.

In one execution, an office worker begins to physically deflate during a meeting – until he flies around the room like a balloon, knocking over cups and saucers until he comes to rest on the boardroom table. Only when he takes a sip of Ty.phoo does he begin to re-inflate. In another execution, a decorator painting a trendy flat also takes flight, bouncing off furniture and spraying paint everywhere until he finally gets his hands on a cup of Ty.phoo. The press and poster executions reflected the same idea – all with the slogan 'Get back your OO with Ty.phoo'.

This campaign was supported by a competition in the women's press and regional publications, encouraging readers to nominate somebody who gives them back their 'OO'.

The overall strategy reinforced the 'refreshment' aspect of Ty.phoo, while concentrating on individual users – reflecting changes in lifestyle and

consumption habits. The element of humour also underscored a modern approach, differentiating Ty.phoo from the competition. The end result was an increase in market share to 8.3% (Source: ACNielsen) with significant new recruits to the brand from the youth segment.

Brand Values

The key qualities of Ty.phoo are freshness and premium quality, but it also has less obvious brand values that distinguish it from its rivals. From the beginning, Ty.phoo has been associated

Lost your 'OO'?

Get back your 'OO' with Ty.phoo

with renewing energy, revitalising its drinkers and providing tea with plenty of 'oomph'. This idea has featured in one form or another in all its marketing, and continues right up to the present day.

www.typhoo.co.uk

Market

The areas in which the Virgin brand operates are diverse and far-reaching, covering a spectrum of industries from insurance and music to soft drinks and travel. Virgin positions itself as a consumer champion, taking on big established players in every sector it operates in by seeking to offer customers better value and service – and fun – than the competition. Because of its diverse interests, Virgin has no single major rival. Virgin's activities span transport and travel, telecommunications, entertainment, retail and leisure and financial services. The group is best described as a cross between a branded venture capital organisation and a Japanese-style 'keiretsu' or family of businesses.

Achievements

Virgin is one of the UK's largest groups and has achieved its growth, mainly through organic development. Indeed, there are currently over 200 Virgin-branded companies trading round the world employing around 30,000 people.

Virgin applies its brand values of quality, value for money and innovation to every new market it penetrates. So it's not surprising that the brand has strong resonance and appeal to consumers: a recent survey showed that 71% of the public feel emotionally close to Virgin.

History

Richard Branson's career began at the age of seventeen with the launch of 'Student' magazine in 1968. Two years later he set up the first Virgin business – a small mail order record retailer that undercut the big stores' prices. In 1971 Branson and his cousin, Simon Draper, neither of whom then knew much about music, established Virgin Records. In 1972 at least one store opened every month and by the end of the year there were fourteen outlets throughout the UK. Virgin Records rapidly became the largest independent record company in the country, and the sixth largest in the world, signing acts such as Mike Oldfield, Culture Club and the Sex Pistols along the way.

Branson sold the company to Thorn EMI in 1992 to free funds for investment in other markets. As Virgin Music became increasingly successful, it

started to diversify. In 1983, it began to distribute films and videos through Virgin Vision – and so began Virgin Games, a computer games software publisher. The group's combined pre-tax profit climbed to £2 million on a turnover of just under £50 million. In 1984 it took perhaps its biggest gamble when it launched Virgin Atlantic Airways in direct competition with British Airways. Within five years the airline was making pre-tax profits of £10 million and has continued to expand and add further routes ever since.

Virgin Holidays was launched shortly after Virgin Atlantic. Two years later Virgin Retail Group and WH Smith announced a joint venture to develop the Virgin Megastore business in the UK and opened stores in Spain, the Netherlands, Australia and the US. By 1994, Virgin Retail had acquired the Our Price chain in the UK and Ireland and Virgin Retail became the UK's largest music retailer.

Branson then decided to take on the financial services sector and provide consumers with no-nonsense financial packages, cutting out sales people and their commission – and so Virgin Direct was born.

In 1996 Virgin acquired Euro Belgian Airlines, renamed it Virgin Express and began to operate a low cost, no frills service to a number of European cities. Furthermore, the V2 music label and music publishing company was launched as well as Virgin Net, to enable users to get the most out of the internet.

Also in 1996 Virgin Bride opened its doors for business and the Virgin Group was awarded the Cross Country Trains passenger rail franchise. A year later Virgin Vie, a cosmetics and beauty care company, opened its first four stores.

In September 1999 Virgin entered the Health Club market with the launch of Virgin Active. There are currently thirteen Virgin Active clubs in the UK, with the west London club becoming Europe's biggest 'life-centre'. The price of membership (approximately £45 a month) undercuts many competitors. On average, Virgin Active centres have 6,000 members each – more than any UK competitor. Virgin Active continues to expand globally; the first step in this was the purchase, completed in March 2001, of the Health & Racquets Clubs chain from Leisure Net in South Africa. The purchase of these 80 centres (approximately 300,000 members)

has resulted in Virgin Active becoming the world's fifth largest health club operator.

In November 1999 Virgin Mobile was launched as a 50:50 joint venture with One 2 One. It offered customers a simple, single tariff, with no line rental, monthly charges or hidden catches – with customers only paying for the calls they made. Virgin Mobile also offered customers an ever-expanding range of Virgin Xtras, services which gave discounts on shopping, a range of special offers, and a world of information and advice. It is also expanding its product range and was the UK's first operator to offer an integrated MP3 player. Virgin Mobile continues to expand globally with the launch of Virgin Mobile,

Australia and perhaps Virgin's most ambitious launch in the last decade the launch of Virgin Mobile, USA in July 2002.

In September 2000, V.Shops was launched as the first ever internet to high street retail offer in the UK to combine old economy retailing with new. A total of 100 stores were opened in the last quarter of 2000 utilising the ready-made network of premises, which formally housed the Our Price shops. The stores offer one-stop shops for entertainment, offering the latest in

music, Virgin Mobile phones, visual media and everything else to do with the virtual world. Purchases can be both traditional 'select a product and buy' or virtual – surfing a huge catalogue at in-store terminals for later home delivery.

Product

Virgin's Transport and Travel Group encompasses Virgin Atlantic, Virgin Aviation Services, The Airline Group, Virgin Express (Europe) & Virgin Blue (Australia), Virgin Travelstore, Virgin Holidays, Virgin Hotels, Virgin Rail Group, thetrainline.com and Virgin Cars, which are all major businesses in their own right.

Virgin Atlantic has grown from one plane and one route eighteen years ago to become Britain's second largest long haul carrier. It was the first airline to introduce a complimentary limousine service for Upper Class passengers and remains the only airline to offer a personal seatback TV for every traveller in every class. It recently ordered the Airbus A380 'superjumbo', dubbed 'the future of air travel'.

Virgin is also applying the Virgin brand values to rail travel. It is in the process of introducing 97 revolutionary tilting trains that are designed to reduce journey times by up to a quarter.

Launched in early 2000 Virgin Cars was one of the first car-buying sites on the internet and now plans to build a multi-franchise car business, focused on the 'clicks and mortar' retailing model. It has already expanded into direct motorcycle sales.

The Entertainment, Retail and Leisure business comprises Virgin Megastores, V.Shop, Radio Free Virgin, Virgin Cinemas Japan, Victory Corporation, Virgin Active, V2 Records, virginstudent.com, virgin.net, Virgin Energy and Virgin Wines.

The first Megastore, selling a range of home entertainment software, as well as music, opened in 1978 and there are now 93 throughout the UK. By 2004 there will be an estimated 192 around the world. Virgin links its Megastores with virgin.com as part of a 'clicks and mortar' strategy uniting e-commerce and mobile activities with retail.

Virgin prides itself on making a customer's

visit to its stores an 'experience', whether using interactive listening stations, playing the latest Dreamcast or Playstation game, enjoying a cup of coffee in one of the cafés, e-mailing a friend from the in-store internet terminals or even seeing a band play live in-store. In the US, Virgin Retail operates one of the most successful e-tailer sites with Virgin Megastore online at www.virginmega.com. Building on this success, Virgin rolled out the first genuine global offering on the internet with the launch of sites in the UK, Europe and Japan in 2000. Virgin Retail has also launched the Virgin JamCast service, www.virginjamcast.com, a web service that broadcasts digital music files directly to the consumer's computer.

Launched in 1991, Virgin Publishing has grown to become one of the major forces in British publishing, producing about two hundred new books each year and with an active backlist of around 500 titles. Virgin Publishing has built its reputation as a niche publisher of books on popular culture, particularly music, film, television and sport and also as an opportunist publisher in strong genres such as true crime and erotica.

Virgin has not completely severed ties with its musical origins, and still owns V2 records, whose signings include artists such as The Stereophonics, Moby, Liberty X and Tom Jones.

The Victory Corporation encompasses primarily cosmetics (Virgin Cosmetics) sold through established high street retailers, Virgin Active gyms and Direct Party Sales. There are thirteen Virgin Active clubs in the UK, with fees of around £45 a month. Virginstudent.com is a simple-to-use portal where students can access a collection of free tools and resources, while virgin.net, a content-rich entertainment and travel website as well as an ISP, helps the typical Virgin customer get the most out of their free time.

Virgin Energy promises to help customers save money on their gas and electricity

bills wherever possible and provides 24-hour service. While another off shoot, Virgin Wines offers online wine buying with a good level of choice and advice as well as attractive prices.

In the financial sector, Virgin Direct offers customers investment and insurance products free of the complexity, jargon and cost traditionally associated with middlemen. The Virgin One account, launched in 1998 offers a whole new way of banking, combining your mortgage with your current account.

Recent Developments

Virgin credit card was launched in 2002 as an extension of Virgin's financial services offering. Applications can be made online, with the customer given choices in terms of which combination of services to include on the card such as the interest rates for new purchases as well as balance transfers, the option of reward points, design on the front of the card (from a choice of five designs). Customers are also given exclusive access to the Virgin Card Members Shop, with deals from a vast array of products and services in the Virgin family.

Promotion

Owing to Richard Branson's high profile – whether on his round-the-world balloon trips or dressing up as a bride to launch Virgin Bride – and to the innovative, often audacious, nature of the products and services themselves, Virgin has always had high levels of recognition of the brand. Indeed, Branson's

activities have made such impact on public awareness of the brand that they resonate across the whole group and every sub-brand benefits. His autobiography, Losing My Virginity, published by Virgin Books, has been one of the best-selling business books in the world ever.

In recent years, Virgin has employed traditional forms of communication to launch new products and services. However, Virgin's sense of humour is always reflected in its communications. For example, with the launch of Virgin Mobile in November 2000 users were encouraged by television ads to 'get divorced' from their old networks and switch to Virgin Mobile. This was followed in 2002 with the 'Be careful what you sign' campaign, which featured Wyclef Jean signing his life away to an obsessive fan.

Brand Values

The Virgin brand is famous the world over for being prepared to take on established businesses – and win. The signature logo tells customers that something is a Virgin business, with all the associations and aspirations that it conveys. In a sense the Virgin logo is seen as Richard Branson's personal signature. The brand's personality embodies value for money, quality, service, fun and innovation. Each new Virgin product comes with a promise that it is delivered with the common thread of Virgin's distinctive DNA.

www.virgin.co.uk

virgin atlantic

Market

The airline industry was affected more than most by the tragic events of September 11th 2001. There was an immediate and significant reduction in passenger demand, particularly across the North Atlantic, and a number of airlines became bankrupt. The industry is slowly rebuilding passenger confidence but it will be some time before the long-term consequences are fully apparent. It is clear that in order to survive and compete in this challenging environment it is vital for airline companies to adapt and evolve, focusing on capturing the market with an ever-improving range of services. Airlines with strong brand leadership, like Virgin Atlantic, should be most likely to emerge from the challenge strengthened.

Achievements

The brand's achievements have been recognised by a number of prestigious award schemes. In 2001 Virgin Atlantic won OAG Airline of the Year and in 2002 won an array of awards including Best Business airline at Conde Nast Traveller Awards and The Guardian and Observer Awards and Best Transatlantic Airline at the Travel Weekly Awards. In addition, the brand was consistently voted as a Superbrand and in 2001 was given Cool BrandLeader status by the Superbrands organisation.

Despite tough trading conditions in 2001, Virgin Atlantic achieved a turnover of £1.3 billion and carried over 4.1 million passengers.

History

In the early 1980s, transportation – rather than customer care – appeared to be the top priority of the airline industry. Then Virgin Atlantic burst on to the scene offering not only better service and lower costs for passengers but a commitment to put the customer first – the effects were radical.

The company was set up in 1984 when an Anglo-US lawyer called Randolph Fields approached Richard Branson – the young and unorthodox chairman of the Virgin Group – with an idea for a new airline that would fly between the UK and the US. Better known at the time as the leading light in the world of pop and rock music, Branson was enthusiastic about the opportunity to diversify. His characteristic energy and enthusiasm meant

that within three months the airline began to lease its planes and June 22nd 1984 marked Virgin's inaugural flight from London to Newark.

From those early days the airline has gone from strength to strength. Now based at both London's Gatwick and Heathrow airports, it operates long haul services from Heathrow to New York (Newark and JFK), Los Angeles, Boston, San Francisco, Washington, Tokyo, Hong Kong, Johannesburg, Cape Town, Shanghai, Lagos and Delhi. Virgin also operates services from Gatwick to Miami, Orlando, Barbados, St Lucia, Antigua and Las Vegas. Virgin Atlantic has also introduced a service from Manchester airport to Orlando. In January 2003 the airline began twice-weekly services to Port Harcourt in Nigeria and in May 2003 the airline is due to commence services between Gatwick and Tobago and Grenada, bringing its total number of destinations to 22.

On December 20th 1999 Richard Branson signed an agreement to sell a 49% stake of Virgin Atlantic to Singapore Airlines to form a global

partnership. The cost of the transaction to Singapore Airlines was £600.25 million, which included a capital injection of £49 million and values Virgin Atlantic at a minimum of £1.225 billion. The deal was finalised in early 2000.

Virgin Atlantic has pioneered a range of innovations setting new standards of service, which its competitors have subsequently sought to follow. Virgin Atlantic has introduced a string of firsts including individual seat-back televisions for all economy passengers and the introduction of automatic defibrillators. Despite Virgin Atlantic's growth, the service still remains customer driven with an emphasis on value for money, quality, fun and innovation.

Product

Virgin Atlantic's Upper Class has changed the face of business travel by offering limousine pick-up and Drive-Thru check-in. Virgin Atlantic also has Clubhouses and Virgin lounges for Upper Class passengers at many of its destinations. The Virgin Clubhouses are deliberately designed to challenge the conventions of the airline industry and to create a different travelling environment.

In 1999 Virgin Atlantic transformed its Upper Class products and services in a £37 million relaunch. The cabin makeover, themed around 'The Modern Romance of Flight', has given the airline a striking look. The on-board bar can now seat up to seven people. The 'Freedom' meal service was also introduced which means passengers can eat 'what they want, when they want'. Virgin Atlantic's in-flight beauty therapy service, which celebrated its tenth anniversary in 2002, also introduced five new treatments and now has a dedicated area on-board the plane. The centrepiece of the new Upper Class experience is Virgin's new seat. The revolutionary new seat design, which uses the latest technology, transforms into a full length bed offering 6ft 8'' of sleeping space.

Virgin Atlantic also opened its first arrivals lounge called Revivals at Heathrow airport. Revivals is designed to provide everything a passenger could need to awaken, revitalise and prepare for their day ahead after a long haul flight.

Virgin Atlantic also operates 'flyingclub', one of the most generous frequent flyer programmes available. flyingclub was relaunched at the end of 1999. As well as restructured membership levels, flyingclub has even more partners with the introduction of more airlines and hotels than ever before.

Premium Economy was first introduced in 1992. It is a service aimed at the cost conscious business traveller who for budgetary reasons, travels economy but still requires extra space in which to work or relax. Premium Economy features 38'' seat pitch, complimentary champagne at take-off and a fully flexible ticket.

Virgin Atlantic's Economy class was the first to provide every passenger with a seat-back TV screen providing a selection of up to 21 video and audio channels and Nintendo and classic PC games. Virgin Atlantic also gives out K-ids Packs to children on-board and amenity kits containing useful items like socks and toothbrushes as well as more unusual items such as eye gel and lip cream.

Recent Developments

Virgin Atlantic continues to launch several new routes. In June 2000 Virgin launched the first ever scheduled services between London and Las Vegas – its 10th US destination and on July 5th 2000 direct services were launched between London and Delhi.

In summer 2002 the airline took its newest delivery becoming the launch customer for the A340-600 – the longest plane in the world. In total ten aircraft will be delivered by 2006 in a deal worth US$1.9 billion. The aircraft was named 'Claudia Nine' by supermodel Claudia Schiffer in front of an audience of media and VIPs. The new aircraft offers passengers many new on-board features including a redesigned on-board bar and in-flight beauty therapy area in Upper Class and new seats for both Premium Economy and Economy passengers. The aircraft has the most advanced in-flight entertainment system in the world which provides passengers with up to 300 hours of video on demand, fourteen audio on demand channels, fifteen computer games including multi-player games, on-board SMS text messaging service and a quick find search facility.

In Autumn 2002 the airline announced new services to Port Harcourt, Nigeria and Grenada and Tobago – all due to start in 2003.

Promotion

The greatest and most well known advertisement for Virgin is Richard Branson himself. Branson is often perceived as the consumer's hero, an entrepreneur operating in a style all of his own, and Virgin's brand values emanate from his personality. At the same time as being one of Britain's most admired businessmen,

Richard Branson's daredevil antics, such as ballooning across the Atlantic, have given the Virgin brand additional publicity. Branson also keeps a shrewd eye on promotional opportunities:

when he heard of British Airways' decision to remove the Union Jack from their plane exteriors, for example, he capitalised on the change by introducing the Union Jack onto Virgin planes.

Virgin Atlantic has proved an astute advertiser over the years. Its logo is highlighted on all its goods and services and is a highly protected property. Virgin Atlantic has implemented an integrated media strategy to promote its brands, including television, newspapers, posters, promotions, direct mail and the internet, often to wide acclaim. The 'Grim Reaper' ad, for example, won numerous marketing awards and creative accolades including a Golden Lion in the Travel Transport and Tourism category at the Cannes International Advertising Festival; a Silver in the British TV Advertising Awards, a Solis award for Travel & Air Transport TV at the International Tourism & Leisure Festival as well as winning the Travel category in the London International Advertising Awards. In 1999 it won The Guardian Newspaper Recruitment award for Best Commercial Advert and Best Written Advert.

Recent television advertisements have featured celebrities including Miss Piggy and Stephen Fry in a campaign for the Upper Class service. In addition, a selection of strip advertisements, emphasising Virgin Atlantic's services and fares have featured in the UK press and won several marketing awards.

Brand Values

Virgin Atlantic strives to provide the best possible service at the best possible value. It is a distinctive, fun-loving and innovative brand which is admired for its intelligence and integrity. Judging from the results of a poll conducted by research agency NOP the public also associates it with friendliness and high quality. Virgin Atlantic also recently won an NOP World Business Superbrands Award for the 'brand most perceived to keep its promises'.

www.virgin.com/atlantic

Market

Sausages are a well-loved staple of the British diet – we eat 226 million lbs of them each year (Source: ACNielsen September 2002). Furthermore, half of British households serve sausages for at least one meal every week. The total fresh sausage market is worth £305 million and is showing 8% growth year on year (Source: ACNielsen September 2002). Sausages are popular throughout the year – from sausage sandwiches, hearty sausage casseroles in winter, through to being a strong favourite for the BBQ in the summer months. There are over 50 million BBQs held per year and 300,000 tonnes of sausages cooked in this way (Source: National BBQ Week).

In recent years, sausages have been given a more modern image, having been embraced by the modern British cooking style. They are now popular in the increasing number of pubs serving up-to-date, satisfying English food, and sausages are enjoying a resurgence on restaurant menus.

Achievements

The Wall's brand has a total sausage (fresh & frozen) value share of 10% and is worth over £36 million (Source: ACNielsen September 2002). Thanks to a £4 million campaign involving billboard posters, press, radio and sampling in 2002, Wall's brand awareness has risen by fifteen percentage points (January - September 2002) and more consumers now associate Wall's with the 'tastiest sausages' and 'using the best ingredients' than ever before (Source: Millward Brown Brand Tracker 2002).

Since the repositioning and relaunch of Wall's Instants as Wall's Micro-Sausages in April 2002, value sales of the product have quadrupled over twelve months (Source: ACNielsen Scantrack May 2001-2002). The brand is currently worth £1.2 million at retail selling price (RSP), and has capitalised on the growing trend for consumers to snack at home, particularly on foods stored in the fridge. Wall's Micro-Sausages mean that consumers can now cook sausages in under 60 seconds.

Wall's has also seen significant growth within the bacon category at 98.2% year on year and now commands a 5% share of this market and is worth over £26 million at RSP (Source: ACNielsen October 2002).

History

The word sausage is derived from the Latin word 'salsicius', meaning 'salted', and was a general description for preserved meats. The original 'salsicius' was probably a dried sausage that would keep fresh in the hot Italian climate. Over the centuries literally thousands of sausage varieties have been created by butchers and chefs the world over. As far back as 9BC the Greeks had already established sausages as a standard food item.

Sausages were first introduced to Britain by the Romans and developed over the centuries with each county in the UK creating its own particular way of flavouring the local sausage.

Sausages also found their way into Royal households through the generations. Richard II loved sausages and Queen Victoria laid down a set of instructions concerning the making of sausages in the royal household. Recently, Prince William has declared his fondness for sausages and chips and participants in Channel 4's 'Big Brother' were heard to declare their affection for a plate of bangers and mash.

Wall's sausages first came about when Thomas Wall's father, Richard, opened his sausage and pie business in St James' Market, London, in 1786. He quickly earned a reputation as a pork butcher and word of his superb quality cuts of meat and delicious pork sausages soon reached the royal household of the time.

Wall's has had royal warrants since 1812, when Richard Wall received his first royal appointment as 'Pork Butcher to the Prince of Wales'.

The business then moved to larger premises at 113 Jermyn Street and the company continued to flourish under Thomas and his sons, gaining a series of further royal appointments.

Wall's continued to thrive up to and during World War II, when sausages were one of the few foods never to be rationed. However, it was at this point that sausages first earned the affectionate name 'bangers'. Due to the large water content of sausages during this period, they would spit then explode, when the water mixed with hot fat during frying.

In the 1950s Wall's were quick to spot the potential of television advertising and used the medium in its early years, continuing to have a strong presence ever since.

Throughout the 1980s and 1990s, Wall's grew its market share through TV advertising featuring Charlie and Sniff the dog. Kerry Foods purchased the Wall's brand in 1994 and continued with the same theme for several more years, until 2000 when the campaign changed to 'When your mind turns to bacon/sausages think Wall's'. The advertisements comprised of amusing scenarios involving prisoners, builders and even Humpty Dumpty. In 2002 Wall's launched its 'We Want Wall's' advertising campaign which was also supported by developments to the Wall's range in terms of both product and packaging.

Product

The Wall's portfolio stretches across both fresh and frozen sausages, including Wall's Lean Recipe Sausages, which contain less than 5% fat (one sixth of the fat of traditional sausages) but with all the taste, Wall's Micro-Sausages (ready in 60 seconds in the microwave) and Chef's Selection – the ultimate, premium family sausages – as well as the popular Wall's Pork Thick sausages. The Chef's Selection range comprises Pork, Lincolnshire and Cumberland which have 74% meat content, and come in the distinctive parchment 454g packs of eight.

Despite the proliferation of flavours launched into the sausage market, pork sausages are still Wall's most popular variant.

Wall's has also now significantly increased distribution in the bacon market with its range including three varieties: smoked, unsmoked and streaky.

Recent Developments

Wall's Instants were relaunched in 2002 as Wall's Micro-Sausages. Since the start of the campaign, awareness and trial of the product has significantly increased.

Easy to open, and packed in twos for extra freshness, the product aimed to reach a new audience of 20-35 year-old men. For many in this bracket, convenience in food preparation is of key importance. Furthermore, over 80% of the UK population own microwaves and cooking using this method is still on the increase (Source: Family Food Panel 2002).

The relaunch was supported by a £0.5 million national press and radio advertising campaign and sampling on railway station forecourts, at music festivals and in stores. An on-pack promotion during the World Cup 2002 offered consumers the chance to win the 'ultimate' Sony home entertainment package.

The other major launch was the introduction in October 2002 of a new flavour to the Lean Recipe sub-brand – namely Pork & Apple.

With the continued trend in healthy eating, Wall's Lean Recipe commands a 23.3% share of a £18.4 million market (Source: ACNielsen Scantrack September 2002). Pork & Apple came out top in a research study commissioned in 2002. Its appeal lies essentially in offering something different from the traditional flavours such as Lincolnshire and Cumberland within the low fat sausage market, but also an added ingredient that itself is seen as healthy, tasty and complements pork sausages. This launch was supported by an advertising campaign in the women's press with the theme of 'Golden Delicious'.

New Wall's Balls, launched in January 2003, are an innovation in the £926 million frozen kids tea market (Source: ACNielsen Scantrack September 2002). Wall's Balls are golden, crispy, crumb-coated Wall's sausagemeat balls that can be cooked in the oven straight from the freezer in fifteen minutes. The product, which is aimed at children aged between 7-11, has been created to give mums variety of choice at kids' teatime, which has, to date, been dominated by frozen chicken and fish-based products.

The launch support includes a national £2.2 million marketing campaign dominated by national TV advertising throughout 2003. The campaign also features cinema advertising during family movies, on-pack incentives to drive product trial, online activity, sampling, fixture point of sale, plus PR activity.

Promotion

A £4 million marketing spend was put behind Wall's in 2002 with an advertising campaign, extensive PR and promotional activity such as eye-catching fun billboard poster ads, radio commercials and press advertising, in-store sampling and the Wall's road show, with product sampling that took place at various locations including County Shows, BBC Good Food Show, V2002 and Reading music festivals. Product sampling also took place in-store and in store car parks with media relations and promotional PR work supporting this activity.

The campaign was deliberately tongue-in-cheek and humorous to give the brand a down-to-earth personality and a new positioning. It also helped to reinforce the Wall's positioning as 'the tastiest pork sausage on the market'.

Packaging was also redesigned across all Wall's products, adding to its contemporary appeal. Furthermore, the Wall's website – www.wewantwalls.co.uk – was updated to reflect the ongoing activity off line throughout the year.

With the aim of making Wall's the number one branded sausage during the BBQ season, Wall's was the official sausage sponsor of National BBQ Week – other sponsors included Fosters, Sainsbury's and Garnet Point. Wall's spent a total of £0.5 million on sponsorship, press and radio advertising, plus PR activity.

In terms of sampling results, over three quarters of a million people tasted Wall's sausage and bacon at over 30 events during the 49 national road show sampling days. In-store sampling had a total of 150,000 people sampling product over 503 sampling days and the nineteen National BBQ week events resulted in over 120,000 people trying Wall's sausages.

Brand Values

Wall's has been trusted to provide quality and taste for over 200 years, offering consumers a wide range of products and great choice – the Wall's expertise. The brand has a warm, fun personality and is seen as unpretentious and approachable, whilst still maintaining a contemporary appeal. Wall's stands for the satisfaction of good, honest grub, providing great sausages and bacon for everyone.

www.wewantwalls.co.uk

Nothing beats a Wall's banger off the barbie, just be prepared for the queue.

The best, best hangover cure.

WE WANT

Things you didn't know about Wall's

Wall's sausage meat was originally ground by a donkey working a treadmill in the cellar of Thomas Wall's prestigious butcher's shop at 113 Jermyn Street in 1834.

Wall's sausages are in the top five list of food products that Britons pack when going on holiday abroad (Source: Iceland survey).

Wall's Lean pork sausages each have 3g of fat – equivalent to half that of a chocolate cookie.

Wall's Pork Thick sausages contain 35% less calories than a bar of milk chocolate.

After carrying out a survey of the UK's sausage-eating habits, the results of which were released in January 2002, Wall's discovered that most men would like to share a sausage with Kelly Brook and most women would choose Jamie Oliver of the celebrities offered.

WATERFORD
CRYSTAL

Market

Between 1995 and 2000, the value of the glassware market was estimated to have risen by 17%, to reach £290 million – an increase of 11% (Source: Mintel 2001).

In recent years wine drinking has increased to a point where it has become an everyday occurrence in UK households. This has fuelled demand for stemware as increased usage naturally leads to an increased risk of damage from breakages, abrasion or dulling of glass from repeated immersion in an over-hot dishwasher. In addition, there is now a greater incentive to buy a wider repertoire of glasses to suit different types of wine, as well as other drinks, and to introduce a different look to the table according to the occasion.

Additionally, the use of vases has increased as flowers have become a more regular purchase for UK consumers both for themselves and as gifts. Not only are they more readily available via supermarkets and home-delivery services, but they are more frequently featured in magazines and weekend supplements. Individuals such as Paula Pryke and Jane Packer have completely changed the way flower arranging is perceived, especially among younger people.

The onset of the new millennium also played its part in promoting sales – very much a one-off factor. Sales of champagne flutes were particularly healthy during this time.

Waterford Crystal is the brand leader in the premium world crystal market. The Waterford brand's pre-eminence in the luxury tabletop market is unrivalled.

The Waterford brand is marketed around the world with dedicated distribution companies from North America, to Japan, Hong Kong and Singapore and the UK to Australia. One of the key factors in its success in recent years has been the continuous introduction of innovative, market-led, new products which have attracted new consumers to the brands while, at the same time, keeping existing consumers loyal.

Waterford's sales growth rate has been so dramatic year after year since the early 1990s that the business has almost doubled in size since 1991.

Achievements

Waterford's reputation for quality, excellence and attractive design has meant that Waterford Crystal's consumers regard the brand as simply the best crystal brand in the world for self and gift purchase.

Recent research has confirmed the standing of Waterford Crystal in both the US and the UK. Waterford is now the market leader in the US crystal market with a consolidated market share of more than 60% for its Waterford Crystal brand and its marquis sub-brand.

Furthermore, in the US, under the heading of esteem, Waterford emerged as the number two brand amongst luxury consumer products; that puts Waterford ahead of Rolex, Ralph Lauren and Gucci to name but a few. In Britain, amongst high income males, the Waterford brand was most highly regarded – rated above the likes of Rolls Royce and Burberry.

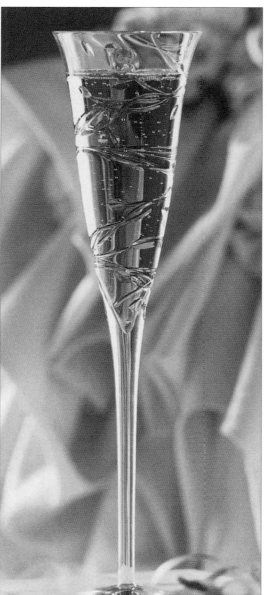

More recently, a survey of 600 major brands was conducted among 6,000 consumers in the US. Waterford scored eighth in that survey for perceived quality – ahead of such luminous brands as Ford, Hoover and Pepsi.

Furthermore, the great department stores of the world such as New York's Bloomingdales and London's Harrods value Waterford among the prestige goods they offer to customers.

Today, Waterford Crystal chandeliers hang in Westminster Abbey in London, the State Apartments at Dublin Castle as well as Dublin's National Concert Hall, the John F Kennedy Center for the Performing Arts in Washington DC, the Governor's Mansion in Maryland in the US and the Houses of Parliament, Melbourne, Australia.

History

The modern Waterford Crystal company was re-established in 1947 but it traces its roots back through the centuries. The beginnings of glass making in Ireland are lost in the mists of time but there is sufficient archaeological evidence to show that, from the early Iron Age, glass was regarded with respect. Indeed, medieval documents can prove glass making existed in Ireland back in the middle thirteenth century.

However, the Waterford Crystal story started to blossom in 1783 when two brothers, George and William Penrose, founded the Waterford crystal manufacturing business in the busy port of Waterford in Ireland. They were important developers and the city's principal exporters and told the Irish Parliament that the development cost £10,000 – obviously a great deal of money at that time.

The brothers employed 50-70 people, led by John Hill, who, like the brothers was a Quaker. Hill succeeded in producing crystal with a purity of colour unmatched in Ireland or England. Merchant ships sailed regularly from the port of Waterford with cargoes of crystal bound for Spain, the West Indies, New York, New England and Newfoundland.

In what seems a remarkably short time, Waterford Crystal acquired an unequalled reputation that has transcended the intervening centuries. But less than 100 years later the initial company failed due to lack of capital and excessive taxation.

Another century passed before the enterprise was fully revived. In 1947, while Europe was still in ruins after World War II, a small glass factory was set up in Waterford just one and a half miles from the site of the original glass factory.

Waterford Crystal today has very strong links with its illustrious predecessor. There is the same dedication to the purity of colour, to the same design inspiration and to the same pursuit of highest quality levels possible. The traditional cutting patterns made famous by the artisans of Waterford became the design basis for the growing product range of the new company.

The sparkle of today's Waterford Crystal is emphasised by these designs and further enhanced by the light refracting properties made possible by the distinctive formula used in blending Waterford's raw materials.

Product

At Waterford, the production process, in some respects, is little changed from medieval times. Base elements – silica sand, litharge and potash which, together with other trace elements, are mixed into a 'batch' – are brought to a temperature of 1400°C for 36 hours to produce the molten lead ready for blowing. Today, technology enables a computer-controlled batch to produce a purity of mix unequalled by Waterford's predecessors and modern furnaces provide the opportunity to ensure that the required temperature is sustained under ideal conditions. Waterford's most skilled artisans undertake ten years of training to attain master status in sculpting and engraving – longer than it takes to become a qualified physician.

Waterford Crystal, today, is the leading brand of premium crystal. Its products such as handcrafted crystal stemware, giftware and lightingware are designed and manufactured to the highest standards.

A new product development programme has led Waterford's master craftsmen and designers to produce ever more innovative and collectible gifts resulting in a vast range of animals, bowls and vases. A recent introduction is a range of crystal replica buildings based on the church, houses and shops in the heritage village of Lismore, which is the Irish seat of the Duke of Devonshire.

Waterford Crystal has become synonymous with finest quality crystal sought after by collectors and connoisseurs around the world. Each piece of Waterford can be recognised by the signature on the base with the word 'Waterford'.

Recent Developments

In 1991, the first new brand in the company's history, Marquis by Waterford Crystal, was introduced and has since been very successful.

In 1997, Waterford Crystal invited internationally acclaimed fashion designer John Rocha to design a contemporary collection of crystal. In collaboration with John Rocha, the craftsmen of Waterford Crystal created a collection of stemware and giftware that combines contemporary design and centuries of skill.

The collection, which was launched in Ireland in 1997 and rolled out to the UK, Canada, Australia and the US in 1998, was an immediate success.

Other products which extend the power of the Waterford brand beyond its core crystal products include Waterford China, Waterford Linens, Waterford Writing Instruments, Waterford Holiday Heirlooms and Waterford Crystal Jewels.

In 1995, Waterford acquired Stuart Crystal in the UK and, in 1998, the parent company Waterford Wedgwood completed the purchase

john rocha

WATERFORD
CRYSTAL

of more than 85% of the issued shares of Rosenthal in Germany.

Promotion

Waterford has extended the brand carefully, protectively and intelligently. It has invested in effective advertising and public relations. Furthermore, Waterford invests considerably

in marketing resources to ensure that the brand receives the necessary support to maintain its position as a leader in the cut crystal market.

The brand has also maintained the highest

standards of craftsmanship which, allied to the most suitable technology available, assures the beauty and quality of the products is maintained. Waterford has transformed a brand that was once heavily identified with stemware into a multi-faced brand that today and provides consumers all over the world with solutions to a wide range of gift-giving challenges.

Brand Values

In the past decade, Waterford has nurtured and promoted the brand with the utmost care. The company has made it more accessible to many more consumers. Waterford continues to refuse to sell seconds and discourages discounting, while insisting that the products are distributed only in the finest stores. Waterford has extended the brand carefully and protectively. It has invested in effective advertising and public relations to ensure that the brand receives the necessary support to maintain its position as the first name in crystal for consumers.

The company has maintained the highest standards of craftsmanship which, allied to the most suitable technology available, assures the beauty and quality of the products is up to standard.

www.waterford.com

YELLOW PAGES™

Market

Yellow Pages competes in the classified advertising market with other producers of classified and local advertising, as well as local, regional and national newspapers and classified advertising magazines.

Yellow Pages is part of Yell, an international directories business, which is the biggest player in the £4 billion UK classified advertising market (Source: The Advertising Association 2001). Almost 28 million directory copies were distributed in 2002 and there were an average of around 103 million directory uses each month. In 2002, Yellow Pages published 83 regional editions containing about 875,000 advertisements.

Yell, the publisher of Yellow Pages, operates in the market through printed, phone and internet-based media. Its business proposition is putting buyers in touch with sellers through a range of simple-to-use, cost-effective advertising solutions.

Achievements

Yellow Pages' achievements are evident in the brand's ubiquity, with 98% of adults having a copy of the Yellow Pages at home (Source: Saville Rossiter-Base 2002). Through close communication with advertisers and their audiences, Yellow Pages maintains a reputation for comprehensiveness and reliability.

Yellow Pages has achieved Superbrand status through its longevity as a household name. For more than 35 years, consumer awareness of the directory has been consistently high. Both consumers and advertisers trust Yellow Pages to deliver the results they require year after year. Consequently, Yellow Pages was used an estimated 1.2 billion times in 2002.

Yellow Pages and its parent Yell are very aware of environmental and social issues and their impact on the wider community. To reduce the impact of the printing of

directories on the environment, for instance, Yellow Pages works with local councils to encourage the recycling of old directories. By August 2002, 79.8% of UK councils had the facilities to recycle Yellow Pages directories. In 2002, 41% of people said that they recycled their directories.

In April 2002, Yell won a prestigious Queen's Award for Enterprise for its integrated approach to sustainable development. It demonstrated

LONDON CENTRAL 02/03

HISTORIC BUILDINGS AND STATELY HOMES

YELLOW PAGES

YELL.COM.

outstanding commercial success whilst at the same time ensuring work practices which benefit society, the environment and the economy.

Yellow Pages is also a supporter of Marie Curie Cancer Care and in 2002 was one of four finalists for the Corporate Community Involvement Award at the UK Charity Awards for its work with the charity in Northern Ireland.

History

The first directories were actually produced well before Alexander Graham Bell invented the telephone. In Elizabethan times, street directories were published detailing the names and addresses of local residences and businesses. By the 1840s, Kelly's London Post Office directories had begun to emerge.

The growth of the telecommunications industry offered further potential to publishers of directories. Yell's Yellow Pages first appeared in 1966, when it was bound into the standard Brighton telephone directory. By 1973, Yellow Pages had been rolled out across the UK and existed as a product in its own right. In 1979 it became a registered trademark.

Over the years Yellow Pages has continued to improve and enhance its product, as well as extending into new areas to keep up with the developing directories industry. Aside from Yellow Pages, Yell's products in the UK also include Business Pages, introduced in 1985, which is a specialist directory covering business to business suppliers. In 1994, the Talking Pages service was introduced enabling customers to find out details of businesses, shops and services throughout the UK by calling a 24-hour freephone number. Following deregulation of 192 directory enquiries in 2002, the service has now been enhanced with a directory enquiry offering and the overall package,

www.yell.com Think YELLOW PAGES

THINK YELLOW PAGES www.yell.com

operating on a new number, is now known as 118 247 from Yellow Pages. Yell.com, a leading online directory service enabling people to search for businesses and services on the internet, was launched in 1996.

In August 1999, Yell expanded into the US with the £430 million purchase of Yellow Book USA, the largest independent publisher in the US. In June 2001, a further milestone in Yell's development was heralded with the £2.1 billion sale of the company by BT to a private equity consortium made up of investment funds advised by Apax Partners and Hicks, Muse, Tate & Furst.

Since then there has been further expansion in the US, the most significant development being the £417 million purchase of McLeodUSA Media Group Inc in April last year. This consolidated Yell's position as the largest independent publisher of Yellow Pages directories in the US, doubling its geographical footprint to about 520 markets in 38 states and Washington DC.

Product

In 1999 the Yellow Pages was redesigned and launched with a vibrant sunflower front cover. Subsequently, every year has seen a new front cover design, including fish in 2000, and the 2001 chick cover which was promoted by pop trio Atomic Kitten.

The 2002 edition, whose twelve-month roll-out started in July 2002, features sandcastles on the front cover, to represent the classification 'Historic Buildings and Stately Homes'. The new edition was launched alongside a national Yellow Pages survey to find the 'Seven Wonders of Britain', which named Stonehenge, Hadrian's Wall, the London Eye and the Eden Project as amongst Britain's top man-made attractions. This campaign positioned Yellow Pages as a supporter of British tourism and aimed to encourage people to discover the 'wonders' in their own home region.

Recent Developments

Yellow Pages is constantly looking at new and innovative ways of attracting new advertisers and retaining existing ones, as well as ensuring the directory is easy to use and relevant to local needs.

In October 2001 full-colour advertisements were published in the Yellow Pages for the first time. This significant development came after successful trials lasting over eighteen months, and research

amongst advertisers who felt that colour advertising offered flexibility of style and enhanced the impact of their advertising (Source: Critical Research Agency). It is an initiative which has proved to be popular with advertisers.

In July 2002, a new bound-in section – the Internet Guide – was introduced into the Yellow Pages. The Internet Guide offers advice to new and inexperienced web users and covers issues such as shopping online and safe surfing. The guide is split into two sections to allow easy reference for users. The first section features practical help on topics from how to get online to successful internet searching tips. The second part comprises various advertising sections, enabling advertisers to reach internet users.

As a general policy, Yellow Pages also regularly reviews the traditional geographical boundaries of its directories to ensure that users can find the information that is most relevant to them. Where necessary, and only if there is overwhelming local support, boundaries will be redrawn to split an area into separate, new directories.

Promotion

Yellow Pages has consistently used strong advertising campaigns to build and reinforce awareness of the brand. The famous JR Hartley TV advertising, where an elderly man used Yellow Pages to search for a book that he had written years before, aimed to remind consumers that Yellow Pages is 'Not just for the nasty things in life'. The advert won a British Television Silver Award in 1983, and in 2000 'Fly-Fishing' came 13th in a Channel 4 poll of the '100 Greatest TV Ads of all Time'. Award-winning and memorable advertising campaigns have kept Yellow Pages at the forefront of consumers' minds for many years since. For instance, the memorable 'Cleaners' advert was awarded a British Television Gold Award in 1998.

In 2002 a new wave of television advertising was launched, comprising several short, humorous executions. These featured the use of Yell classifications as thought bubbles to remind the consumer to turn to Yellow Pages on a wide range of occasions. The new executions were punchy with a modern feel, giving consumers frequent reminders of the advertising and the variety of uses of Yellow Pages. The strapline 'Think Yellow Pages' aimed to keep the directory at the forefront of consumers' minds when requiring a service.

The 'Think Yellow Pages' message has also been applied to an outdoor campaign, with adverts appearing on posters and bus-sides. Awareness of Yellow Pages is consistently strengthened in the capital with branded taxis, tube maps and pocket tube maps.

Brand Values

Even in today's competitive environment, Yellow Pages plays a crucial role in people's everyday lives, both at home and in the workplace. More than 35 years' experience has enabled Yellow Pages to offer an unparalleled service to suppliers and buyers, and it has become a trusted and familiar source of information. In keeping with the brand's friendly and helpful personality, Yellow Pages' involvement with charity and environmental projects reflect its concern with issues that affect individuals and communities throughout the UK.

Yellow Pages has worked with Marie Curie Cancer Care since 1999, supporting the annual 'Daffodil Campaign', which has raised more than £6 million for the charity. Yellow Pages also sponsored the Marie Curie 'Garden of Discovery' at the Chelsea Flower Show in May 2002, celebrating the centenary of Marie Curie's discovery of radium and helping to promote the charity's work.

Yellow Pages' support of The Directory Recycling Scheme (DRS) forms part of the company's ongoing commitment to the environment. A major schools recycling initiative – The Yellow Woods Challenge – was launched in October 2002, with Kirk, a woodland creature, as its mascot. The aim is to educate children about recycling, conservation and to encourage them to recycle old Yellow Pages directories. Up to 1000 schools across the UK are competing for national and local cash prizes in the scheme organised by Yellow Pages, The DRS and the Woodland Trust in partnership with local authorities.

The Challenge also aims to put something back into the environment through links with the Woodland Trust. For every pound awarded to schools by Yellow Pages in prize money, a pound will be donated to the Woodland Trust to help keep native woodland alive.

www.yell.com

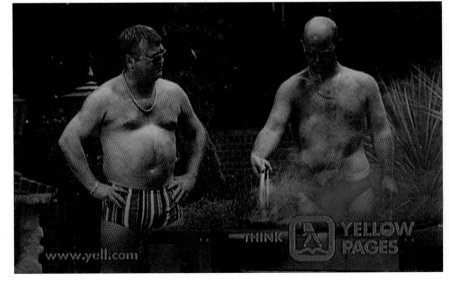

TIM BROADBENT
Executive Planning Director
Bates UK

About Bates UK

Bates claims to be the best as well as the largest truly integrated communications group in the UK. Its power is derived from being able to draw on the knowledge and expertise from all communications disciplines across all different market sectors. The work that Bates produces motivates and inspires, it builds and develops brands and most importantly, it drives sales.

Bates was established in 1905 under the name of Dorland Advertising. It is one of the oldest agencies in Britain and has been a thought leader and key influence within the communications sector for almost 100 years.
www.batesuk.com

The irresistible rise of branding

Ten years ago brands were said to be on the way out. On 'Marlboro Friday', April 2nd 1993, Philip Morris cut the price of its best-selling brand by 20% in response to competition from cheap cigarettes. Its shares collapsed, followed by many other consumer goods companies, because this was taken, according to the Wall Street Journal, as "the most dramatic evidence yet of a fundamental shift in consumer buying habits... More and more, shoppers are bypassing household names for cheaper, no-name products. Even the biggest and strongest brands in the world are vulnerable."

With hindsight, Marlboro Friday looks like a mere hiccup in the irresistible rise of branding. Branding has been called "probably the most powerful idea in the commercial world".

Nowadays it seems everything can be branded, from political parties to football clubs. Recently we spent an afternoon with the Duchy of Cornwall's archivist, to see if any of the Prince's ancient heraldic devices or titles might serve as the basis of a new brand. The latest idea from America is to brand yourself – Personal Branding magazine excitedly urges readers to "develop your own Personal Brand, so others don't decide how you are perceived!"

Well, if brands are not on the way out after all, and if everything can be branded, including you, what makes the brands in this book super? There are perhaps two main schools of thought about what lies behind exceptionally strong brands.

What makes brands super?

One school might be called Phenomenalists, after the philosophical theory of George Berkeley. It holds that ultimately brands are collections of perceptions in consumers' minds. Their esse (essence) is percipi (how they are perceived).

Phenomenalists cite the remarkable fact that consumer preferences in blind tests are often reversed when the brands are revealed.

A chairman of Quaker famously endorsed the primacy of perception over reality: "If this business were to be split up, I would be glad to take the brands, trademarks, and goodwill, and you could have the bricks and mortar – and I would fare better than you."

The other school of thought might be called Empiricists, after the philosophical theory of John Locke. Empiricists hold that, on the contrary, what matters is how brands choose to behave in the real world. For instance, if McDonald's had sold franchises to anybody, had allowed them to decorate the restaurants in any way they saw fit, and to serve any food they cared to cook, McDonald's would not be the global icon brand it is today. Virgin and Nike are also examples of brands that have been built by consistently sticking to self-selected rules.

Phenomenalists and Empiricists offer powerful perspectives on the nature of brand strength and how ordinary brands can become Superbrands. But a simpler, even more fundamental insight underlies both schools.

Choice depends on differences

The most salient marketing feature of our age is the unprecedented level of competition.

A category starts as a single entity and then, like an amoeba in a petri dish, divides again and again. The process is unstoppable. To take a single example, the launch of Clover in 1983 created the dairy spreads category. Today there are 24 dairy spread brands on supermarket shelves (as well as all the butter and margarine brands alongside them).

Killer competition is driven by consumer affluence. Britain officially entered the Leisure Age in 1999. This was the first year since records began that household spending on leisure overtook spending on food and drink to become the largest element of the average household's budget. It marked a profound change in consumer priorities.

Our main problem is no longer, 'Which one can I afford to buy?' Our main problem now is, 'Which one shall I choose from the hundreds of brands staring back at me from retailers' shelves?' Choosing between multiple options is always based on perceived differences. Differences are the raw material of selection.

Reinventing the USP

The simple yet profound insight into the importance of "differences" led Jack Trout and Steve Rivkin to dedicate their new book, Differentiate or Die, "To Rosser Reeves, the man who made the "Unique Selling Proposition" famous. He was truly a man ahead of his time. Little did any of us realise just how competitive the world would become."

The Unique Selling Proposition (USP) stems from the will to differentiate. Reeves, a former creative director and chairman of Bates, thought of the USP as a precise term so he gave it a three-part definition in his book, Reality in Advertising:

1 Each advertisement must make a proposition to the consumer.

2 The proposition must be one that the competition cannot or does not offer. It must be unique – either from a uniqueness of the brand, or a claim not otherwise made in that particular field of advertising.

3 The proposition must be so strong that it can move the millions, i.e. pull over new customers to your product.

The USP may come from the Empiricist model of exercising behavioural control over every aspect of the brand experience. Or it may come from the Phenomenalist approach of re-engineering consumer perceptions of the brand's imagery. But either way, it must come. Otherwise the brand will decline under wave after wave of competitors.

Some advertising experts who ought to know better say there isn't enough "difference" in the product or brand to talk about. What they ignore is the fact that faced with almost excessive choice (24 dairy spreads!), a prospect still has the problem of deciding what to buy or not to buy. Decisions have to be made. That is why Theodore Levitt, one of the fathers of marketing, wrote: "Differentiation is one of the most important strategic and tactical activities in which companies must constantly engage. It is not discretionary." In fact you can differentiate anything if the will exists.

The four sources of differentiation

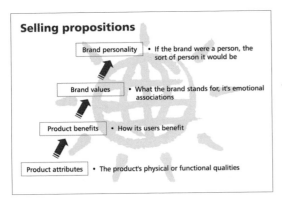

Selling propositions

- Brand personality — • If the brand were a person, the sort of person it would be
- Brand values — • What the brand stands for, it's emotional associations
- Product benefits — • How its users benefit
- Product attributes — • The product's physical or functional qualities

At Bates, we use a simple four-step model to help identify what kind of differentiation to talk about (we think simple is good when it comes to communications).

To bring this schematic to life, there follow some real life examples, and to illustrate the effectiveness of differentiation we have included the payback results that each campaign delivered. The sales results are taken from 2002 IPA Effectiveness Awards papers.

Watch an evening's TV, and you will see the largest number of advertisements fit into the category at the bottom of the ladder: news about the product. Retailers talk about this week's special offer, media brands talk about this week's content or promotion, shampoos talk about their new formulations, car manufacturers launch new models.

When Bates UK launched Benadryl Plus for Pfizer, the differentiating proposition was based on the new product attribute that it cures hayfever fast. Each £1 spent on advertising generated £4.30 in incremental sales.

When there is no differentiating news about the product, the task for advertising moves to the next step up the ladder, namely to redefine how its users benefit.

The Real Network™

When Bates UK "relaunched" the Royal Mail as a business rather than a consumer service, with no change to the product, the differentiating benefit was that the Royal Mail is the only communications network that reaches EVERY customer. Each £1 spent on advertising generated £9.33 in incremental revenue.

Ocean Spray's problem was typical of many packaged grocery brands. The product (100% cranberry juice) and its benefit (health) are much the same as own-label competition. Differentiation came from the next step up the ladder, brand values.

When Bates UK advertised the brand as a modern-day elixir, each £1 spent on advertising generated £2.81 in incremental sales, compared to £1.90 for each £1 spent on promotions.

B&Q has achieved a dominant share of the DIY market, offering the product attribute of widest range at lowest prices. However, in order to increase spend per

customer, it needs to compete for higher-value purchases beyond just nails and timber, important though those are. The source of differentiation also included the top of the ladder, the brand personality.

Advertising through Bates UK differentiated B&Q from other DIY chains as the approachable expert. Each £1 spent on advertising generated £12.90 in incremental sales.

Importantly, B&Q advertising also talks about the differentiating product attribute too — a crucial element in its success.

Keeping the brand in the market

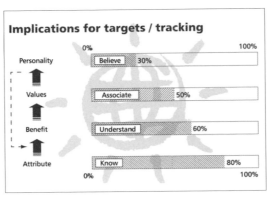

Implications for targets / tracking

- Personality — Believe 30%
- Values — Associate 50%
- Benefit — Understand 60%
- Attribute — Know 80%

Clients and agencies can get bored with effective selling propositions long before consumers stop responding. We continually need to remind ourselves what keeps the brand in the market in the first place. One of the mistakes made by "new economy" marketeers was to ignore the basic product benefit and leap straight away into brand values or personality advertising.

The advertising may have been "cool" but it did not sell. In fact the linear progression we have just described is an over-simplification. There is a continuous feedback loop from the top of the ladder to the bottom, as shown above:

Suppose we set a target for awareness of a certain product attribute at 80%. That means we want 80% of the target market to be aware that, for instance, B&Q offers the widest range of DIY products at the lowest prices. (All the numbers cited here are solely for illustrative purposes and do not reflect actual B&Q targets.)

We might also want 60% to understand the benefit of that attribute. In this case, for instance, that DIYers can tackle any job. And we might want 50% to associate certain brand values with B&Q. For instance, that B&Q is a helpful, friendly brand full of DIY ideas. And so on up to a brand personality target of 30% believing in B&Q as an approachable expert.

This framework gives a research template for evaluating how successful the advertising has been at differentiating the brand. A brand might carry out two or three waves of consumer research a year to find out whether the targets are being met. Usually we find that awareness of the core product attributes and benefits continuously declines under competitive pressures — you don't mow the lawn just once!

Then it is necessary to re-direct the advertising budget back to the bottom of the ladder again, until awareness of what makes the product different is once again at the target level.

Introduction

Successful brands are hard to identify, because there are many measures of success – market share, market growth, margin and so on. However these may be transitory, and we believe that a more enduring and consistent measure of brand success is the equity a brand has with the consumers in that category. Fortunately, at JWT we have access to what is probably the world's biggest database of consumer brand equity – the WPP BrandZ™ study.

BrandZ™ is a very big study. Based on the methodology that Millward Brown developed for their Brand Dynamics* studies, the BrandZ™ study now has some impressive statistics behind it. We have interviewed over 500,000 consumers, across 30 countries. Those consumers have allowed us a much better understanding of over 15,000 brands in 150+ categories.

The UK brand elite

What makes a brand an Elite brand, we shall explore later – but to begin with, lets have a look at what brands have 'made it' in the UK.

The Top ten brands across the 80 categories we have looked at in the UK since 1998 are given below

BRANDZ ™ - UK Top Ten

1	**Gillette**	6	**NESCAFÉ**
2	MARKS & SPENCER	7	**Heinz**
3	BBC	8	**Kellogg's**
4	McDonald's	9	**whiskas**
5	Nike	10	**Colgate**

Source : WPP BrandZ study, JWT Special Analysis

Other brands that have made it are: BT, British Airways, Pedigree Chum, Dairylea, Tesco, Coca-Cola, Cadbury's Dairy Milk, British Gas, Persil, Walls Ice Cream – and Barbie.

We can identify the Elite brands – which is a start – but more importantly, we can establish some of the causes of their success and the consequences thereof. Importantly, the learning is not UK specific. As the BrandZ study has covered so many countries, so many categories and so many consumers, we are able to establish the general 'rules' which govern success.

Defining elite brands

Brands, like people, go through lifestages. They are born, mature, and unfortunately, die. One of the key outputs of the BrandZ™ study is the ability to identify where a brand is in its lifecycle – is it still a developing brand, or is it in its prime, or like some, has it passed it's 'best by' date?

We can see this natural lifecycle for brands in figure 1 (BrandZ™ Map – The Lifecycle of Brands). The typology a brand is assigned is dependent on a number of factors, but these can most

simply be defined as 'Presence' (or fame), and 'Voltage' (or dynamism). Brands start off as Clean Slates where nobody knows much about them, pass through Little Tigers where they begin to develop a small but loyal fan base, achieve greatness as a Classic or Olympic brand, then die away slowly, like a Fading Star. We can plot brands on the BrandZ™ Map (see figure 1), and identify the most successful brands. The place most brands would like to be is in the top right hand corner; a famous and vital brand among the brands we call the BrandZ™ Elite. (Note that this is not to say that brands cannot be profitable elsewhere – e.g. Specialist brands with a small, but loyal and profitable user base – but the top brands, or the BrandZ™ Elite have both scale and profitability).

And only 1 in 16 brands are achieving this level of success.

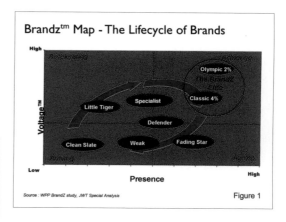

Brandz™ Map - The Lifecycle of Brands

Source : WPP BrandZ study, JWT Special Analysis

Figure 1

These Olympic and Classic brands that make up the Elite are generally very successful, and by comparing the nature of the consumer's relationship with those brands versus other brands, we have been able to identify the signifiers of success.

What elite brands have in common

At the heart of Elite brands' success is the concept of domination. These brands become virtually synonymous with the category, they have huge market shares, and they relegate most other brands in the category to second best status. But to achieve this requires considerable effort.

More, More Bonded Customers: As you might expect, successful brands have a lot of customers – but more than that, they have established a deeper relationship with them. The consequence is that they have a great many more consumers who feel close to, or are 'Bonded' with the brand. Now most consumers bond with only one brand in a category, and the average bonding level for an individual brand is around 5%. For brands in the BrandZ™ Elite, the number is nearly five times that, at 24%. i.e. 1 in 4 category users express a strong level of commitment to that brand.

This 'bonding' with the brand is important financially, because customers who bond with a brand generally give a much higher share of wallet to that brand. The share of wallet varies by category, but in the case of McDonald's, 45% of revenues come from bonded customers, while for Nescafé 51% of revenues come from these bonded customers.

DAVE COCKBURN
Director of Branding Intelligence
JWT London

J Walter Thompson

About J Walter Thompson

J Walter Thompson's own Business Superbrand status comes from its ability to create, build and sustain tough, enduring brands. It does this by creating powerful branding ideas that connect with consumers and work across all communication channels. Shell, Boots, Unilever, Kraft, Nestlé, Diageo, Vodafone, Kimberley-Clark and Kellogg's are among its notable clients.
www.jwt.co.uk

Achieving this level of bonding is a function of the quality and quantity of effort that is put into supporting the brand.

Emotional Advantage: Consumers rate the BrandZ™ Elite as being rationally advantaged in comparison with other brands. In fact they rate them 30% better on brand attribute statements. So to win, you do need a product or service that performs well, and is differentiated. However, good products are not enough. The best brands may outscore their competition on rational measures, but it is in emotional connection that they really score well. The elite (Olympic) of the Elite brands, like McDonald's and Nike, may have substantial rational advantages versus all other fast food outlets, or sports clothing, but often, these

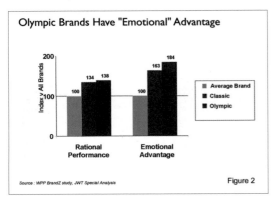

Olympic Brands Have "Emotional" Advantage

Source : WPP BrandZ study, JWT Special Analysis

Figure 2

advantages are minor when the comparison is made with their closest competitors (like Burger King and adidas). Then, the real difference is to be found in the emotional connection the brands make with category users, and here, they are way ahead. The Olympic top one third of the BrandZ™ Elite dominate their categories, and reap the rewards on measures such as perceived popularity, momentum (setting trends) and overall attractiveness (See figure 2).

Functional benefits give the brand permission to develop deeper relationships – but it is the brands emotional connection that really drives success

The secrets of success

The BrandZ™ study does not directly tell us why some brands are successful, and others are not. But by comparing winning brands against the rest, we are able to isolate the most common contributors to success.

As we have already mentioned, a good product is the launching pad, and along with strong emotional appeal, this will lead to a high proportion of bonded users. However, we have also identified some patterns in the identity of members of the BrandZ™ Elite. Individually, few of them have the power to give Elite brand status, but collectively, they seem to be overpowering to the consumer.

Provenance: The best brands come from somewhere. At a literal level, this can be something as simple as the country of origin. The national telecom companies, the airlines, and national energy suppliers are all examples of categories where a mixture of national pride, previous monopoly position, and sheer size seem to conspire together in a positive way. The only exception to this pattern is in America, where national public services are virtually non-existent

– but even here AT&T makes it into the BrandZ™ Elite.

Then there are a few companies/brands which are national institutions – despite not having the country name in the title. Samsung in Korea is one such company, as is Tuborg in Denmark, and M&S here in the UK. These are local heroes which have the potential to travel – but do not always succeed.

Another way of looking at provenance is to think of the lifestyle, values or history of the source of provenance. These are local hero brands that have taken their core associations, and found them desirable elsewhere. For example, Levi's has historically been successful in the UK in part by building on their Americana feel. Mercedes-Benz leverages the perceived expertise of German engineering, and Fosters and Castelmaine XXXX tapped into beliefs about Australian beer drinkers. What is generally the case, however, is that brands that tap into these beliefs have been successful at home first, before they succeed abroad.

Category Definition: The most successful brands come almost to define the category. They often do this by creating the category in the first place, by transforming it, or by bringing something new to the market which consumers want, but are presently not being offered. What Hoover once did for vacuum cleaners, McDonald's now does for fast food, with its mixture of cleanliness, service, and value.

Innovation: Closely linked to the above, is the area of innovation, and many Elite brands have successful track records in innovation. We have already seen that some brands define or redefine the category (with the PlayStation being a good example), but even in categories which are less dramatically innovative, brands can successfully inspire consumers with R&D initiatives (such as Dairylea in processed cheese, or Colgate in toothpaste).

Of course for established brands, cannibalisation is always a concern when launching newer more innovative products. However, what we see is that to remain successful, such brands must innovate if they are not to end up among the 'Fading Stars'. That is one of the major reasons why Persil, Pantene and Smirnoff are in the BrandZ Elite, but Daz, Vosene and Martini (all once great brands) are not.

The role for innovation for a brand is crucial to the brand's development, and ultimate persona. For brands like Sony, innovation almost appears to be the brand's raison d'être. But some brands innovate within their category, and do so regularly and powerfully – here we are talking about brands such as Gillette, Pampers and Nokia. Finally, there are brands which stretch, like Nike and Virgin. These brands leverage their distinctive personalities, and apply them to new markets where they can come in as innovators.

Values: Another potential component of success we have identified, is the use of 'values' to differentiate the brand. Pre-eminent in this area is Coca-Cola, and the power of this approach can be seen in that Coca-Cola is a member of the BrandZ™ Elite in all 26 of the 29 countries where we have looked at Soft Drinks – and furthermore is Olympic in 25 of them! Coca-Cola is not alone in spending its brand investment on things other than product communication – but it is probably

the best at reaching customers through sponsorship, charities and 'corporate brand ' communications.

Investment & Consistency in Communications: Finally, and importantly, they are consistent communicators – they invest for year after year at high levels to retain their dominant presence, and ensure that their consumers always know what the brand is up to. Of course campaigns and media mixes may change, and brands move with the times, but what is generally the case is that the most Elite brands have done three things consistently.

• They usually dominate communications in their category. Not only do they tend to have the highest measured advertising spends in their category, they are usually present in lots of other communication channels. They have consistently invested in marketing support over a number of years. For example, Gillette, was the number one spender in the category between 1999 and 2001 had a 62% share of voice in 2001.

• They have consistently portrayed the brand's identity (differentiators, personality and values). One thing that Nike has done particularly well has been to maintain its fundamental focus on the attitude of the sportsperson's mindset.

• And they have had management who has kept to that vision – difficult, when the search for short-term share gain (and share price support) is a constant threat to building an enduring brand.

In conclusion

It is not easy becoming a member of the BrandZ™ Elite. A great product is a great start – but that is all. Building longer term value (and short term sales) requires the development of closer bonds with a large proportion of category users – and it is here that emotional connection is most important.

The brand's persona, history and provenance can all be leveraged – especially if global expansion is the aim, but long term management commitment to, and financial investment in, the brand are crucial.

Finally, Elite brands can never rest on their laurels. They need to constantly innovate if they are to keep their prestigious position.

References:
JWT: http://www.jwt.co.uk
WPP: http://www.wpp.com
Brand Dynamics:
http://www.millwardbrown.com/html/solutions/branddyn.html

Introduction

What do brands do for us and what do we get from developing a great brand? In economic terms, the answer is simple. Brands favourably affect both the demand and supply curves.

On the demand side, brands enable a product to achieve a higher price at a given sales volume. Strong brands can also increase sales volumes and reduce churn rates. Price and volume impacts are in some instances achieved at the same time.

Brands also establish more stable demand, through their relationship with consumers. They establish barriers to entry. The relationship with consumers is due to both functional and emotional attributes. On the functional side, brands ensure recognition and further aid the purchase decision through a guarantee of quality. From an emotional perspective, they satisfy aspirational and self-expression requirements. This is most evident in luxury and fashion sectors.

A further benefit of branding, which has increased in importance in recent years, is the ability to transfer the equity or values associated with a brand into new product categories. In order for brand stretching to be effective, it is necessary that the core values of the brand are image, rather than product, based.

Whilst there are numerous examples of successful brands that have achieved significant price premiums or higher volumes, the impact of branding on the supply curve is often ignored. Brands tend to shift the supply curve downwards due to the following reasons:

• Greater trade and consumer recognition and loyalty. This results in lower sales conversion costs and more favourable supplier terms.

• Lower staff acquisition and retention costs.

• Lower cost of capital.

• Economies of scale achieved through higher volumes.

Defining 'brand equity'

'Equity' is a financial term that has been adopted by marketing people to reflect the fact that the brands they manage are assets, which create significant shareholder value.

It reflects a growing recognition that responsibility for brands must be shared between the finance and marketing functions. The marketing department will always have responsibility for the creative aspects of brand building, maintenance and support. But as brands grow in importance, ensuring that return on brand (as an asset) is measured, monitored and maximized is the responsibility of both marketers and financiers.

However, while 'brand equity' is often talked about it is seldom clearly defined. How it works is not clearly understood. Tim Ambler, of the London Business School, defines 'brand equity' as a marketing asset 'between the ears' of consumers, trade customers, staff and other stakeholders, which stimulates long term demand, cash flow and value.

He uses the analogy of a reservoir that needs to be topped up if the out flow of water is to be maintained at a constant or increasing rate.

If the 'brand equity' reservoir is depleted revenues and cash flows may remain strong for a period, but eventually the reservoir empties and cash flows dry up. A great visual analogy, but we need to really understand the flow process.

Paul Feldwick, planning Director of BMP, points out that the term 'brand equity' is often used indiscriminately to describe different points along the stream:

Consumer images, associations and beliefs. These are high up the flow towards the source. A brand may be described as 'young', 'green' or 'exciting'. It is possible to measure and report how such brand images, associations and beliefs vary from consumer group to consumer group, how they change from time to time and how they affect purchase decisions. This provides great diagnostic insight into the consumer segments around which a financial brand valuation is structured.

Consumer brand strength or loyalty. These intermediate outputs may be measured in terms of attitudes or awareness, price elasticity, demand volume, purchase frequency. There are many different ways of tracking 'brand strength'. Econometric modeling of empirical data, experimental trade-off analysis and 'share of category requirements' analysis are just a few of the techniques available. Such measures help forecast future cash flows used in a financial brand valuation.

Financial brand value. Brand valuations are a snapshot of future brand earnings taken at a point in time. They reflect the sustainable out flow and put a firm financial value on it. They depend on an accurate prediction of future brand health because they are based on forecast cash flows generated by the brand. They rely on an accurate estimate of the future flow, which the reservoir has yet to produce. The flow rate may be falling or rising depending on the amount of 'brand equity' left in the reservoir.

Brand Finance definition of 'brand equity'

'Brand equity' measures 'the propensity of specific audiences to express preferences which are financially favourable to the brand'. Brand equity measurement systems isolate and analyse the attributes that explain changes in this propensity and predict future financial behaviour.

Figure I illustrates how the flow referred to by Tim Ambler works in practice and how the measures referred to by Feldwick fit together in determining the rate of that flow.

In determining the brand's value at a point in time we consider the current and future financial performance, the expected flow rate from the reservoir. The output measure that allows us to value the brand is ultimately the volume and value of sales generated by the brand.

Volumes and values can be explained and predicted by consumer behavioural measures such as trial and repeat purchase rates, or willingness to pay a price premium. These are determined by brand preference.

Moving back up the flow, we see that brand

DAVID HAIGH
Chief Executive
Brand Finance

About Brand Finance

Brand Finance is the world's leading independent brand valuation consultancy. It specialises in brand valuation, evaluation, tracking, measuring, economics, strategy and communications.

Brand Finance's comprehensive research methods, enables the company to advise strongly branded organisations, both large and small, on how to maximise shareholder value through effective brand management.
www.brandfinance.com

preference is driven by a mixture of functional attributes (such as perceived product quality, value for money or convenience of distribution) and by image attributes (such as status, ethics or association with the brand).

Brand preference is affected to different degrees by different attributes. We typically use conjoint or trade off analysis to understand the weight of these attributes on preference and brand choice. These intermediate measures are really the predictive heart of a 'brand equity' measurement framework. These intermediate measures allow us to measure and understand how the flow rate will change in the future.

At the source are the inputs or direct actions which can be taken by brand owners to affect the perceptions and preferences further downstream.

By understanding which perceptual attributes affect brand preference most, and by understanding which actions have the greatest impact on the perceptual attributes, the brand owner is able to decide where to allocate resources to maximize value.

Should resources may be applied to functional changes, like service or product improvement? Or to marketing communications, shifting image attributes?

Brand Valuation allows the brand management team to take the brand equity process and give a financial value to the flows coming from it. By creating a segmented brand valuation model it is then possible to understand where the greatest value is being created and help make those decisions at the source of the flow as to where resources will be best deployed.

Figure 2 illustrates the framework of a typical brand valuation. We first conduct a market review to understand all the trends driving the size, growth and profitability of the market within which the brand operates. We review the competitors and conduct brand strength assessments. We review the internal landscape, reviewing current and forecast cost structures. Critically the valuation is segmented into discrete pieces to allow an understanding of the brand contribution by segment.

So a brand valuation provides a framework for valuing the brand into segments (by geography, product, channel or consumer demographic) which matches with the analysis of brand equity. By understanding brand equity in aggregate and for the individual segment we are able to better diagnose how and where future value can be maximized.

Figure 3 illustrates how the flows described can be turned into a Brand Scorecard. The purpose of a Brand Scorecard is to record the input, the intermediate and the output measures along the flow. They allow managers to measure and report actions taken, perceptual attribute changes, developments on awareness and preference, behavioural measures, their impact on volumes and values and finally the financial value that all this implies. If this is reported regularly to the management and the Board it provides a framework for decision making and corrective action.

Figure 4 provides an example of a typical scorecard picking out some key measures for management reporting. Such a scorecard is provided for each key brand and segment or market in

which the key brands operate. It is a summary and behind the headlines there is usually a wealth of data kept in a relational database for enquiry once a problem or opportunity has been spotted.

Conclusion

There is no simple measure of 'brand equity'. There are several measures which, taken together, inform management decision-making. What major companies are beginning to realise is that all of the measures available need to be gathered, reviewed and prioritised in a structured brand audit and considered as a whole in the brand evaluation process. Ideally data should be statistically analysed to find persuasive if not definitive relationships which can be tested empirically.

To this end more and more companies are building brand monitoring and forecasting systems with large volumes of detailed research and financial data incorporating brand equity and brand value measures.

Applications of 'brand equity' tracking:

Brands will be major drivers of corporate value in the twenty first century. Investors and business leaders have recognised this. Financial managers and planners are increasingly using brand equity tracking models to facilitate business planning. They should go one step further. Investors need and want greater disclosure of brand values and marketing performance. Financial managers should play a lead role in ensuring that such information is adequately communicated to investors, rather than waiting for statutory disclosure requirements to catch up with reality.

Having detailed information on the brand, not just a brand value in financial terms, including information on perceptual, performance and customer measures can aid the investor relations function. By utilising detailed brand equity trackers it is possible to show the investment community the contribution of the brand as well as its actual value.

Other key areas in which a greater understanding of brand equity aids company performance includes the setting of marketing budgets, resource allocation, internal communication and brand performance tracking.

Many organisations suffer from a surplus rather than a lack of market and consumer information. Unfortunately, much of this is gathered and stored in isolation. The old functional boundaries of a bygone era still prevent the effective flow and integration of information. Even if brand tracking data makes it onto the intranet or a shared directory, it tends to remain in 'research speak' and tends not to be used by financial and strategic planners.

What marketers, and brand owners need to ensure is that adequate data is collected centrally and regularly, that relationships between the data variables are understood, that the financial value of the brand is understood and that it is monitored. It is now best practice to have a brand equity and value system of this kind and will be further driven by the financial community.

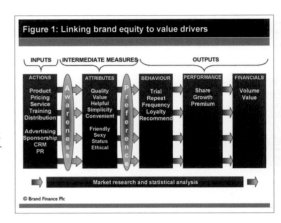

Figure 1: Linking brand equity to value drivers

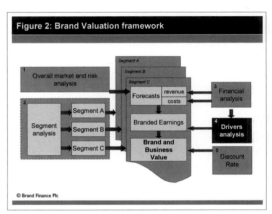

Figure 2: Brand Valuation framework

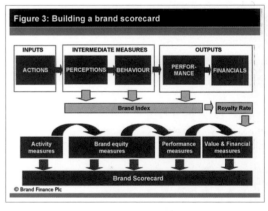

Figure 3: Building a brand scorecard

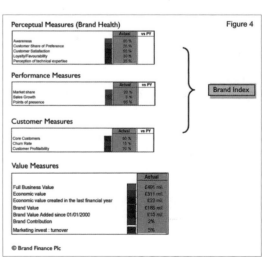

Figure 4

SARA MURRAY
Founder, Ninah Consulting

NINAH
Optimising Marketing Investment

About Ninah

Ninah was launched in 1995, with the specific aim of increasing strategic profit growth for major investors in the sales and marketing mix. Ninah has developed a UNIQUE business tool, which builds a bespoke profit simulation of a business and analyses the profit impact of infinite marketing investment scenarios. The Ninah process is deemed to be unique in its ability to compare the returns from investment in advertising, consumer promotions and trade promotion, creating a common currency across these variables. Ninah works with brand leaders in many categories to maximise their return on sales and marketing investment.

In early 2003, Ninah became a member of the Publicis Groupe of companies, through its acquisition by ZenithOptimedia. Since then, Ninah has strengthened its global presence and is the established leader in marketing investment optimisation.
www.ninah.com

Integrated communications planning

is a current 'hot topic' in marketing. Brand owners are always seeking 'something different'. The question is – does that 'something' lie in the planning, or somewhere else?

The normal reason for a marketing campaign by a brand owner is indisputably to move the target customer (here meaning purchaser and/or consumer) along the purchase cycle.

What then is an 'integrated' communications plan?

This has been described as the 'fairy dust' of a marketing campaign. So, let's examine from where this fairy dust may be sprinkled.

When looking at what integration might mean in communications planning, and, therefore, who should be responsible for it, there are three obvious areas to investigate. The first is the creative. Is it that every message that I take in, as an average customer, shuffles me a little further along the path of the purchase cycle? Hence, each message is carefully tailored to move me one step further than the last, increasing my knowledge of the brand through an understanding of the proposition, and an increased preference, to a prompt action. The integration of the key messages follows the dictionary definition – 'Unification into a whole, e.g. of diverse elements in a community; the state of being integrated' – only if the key messages really are 'diverse elements'.

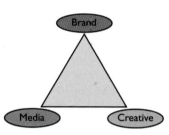

The second area to investigate is the media planning. (Media buying here is assumed to include only execution of the media plan at the best price, and is, therefore, excluded from analysis. The media buyer should never have to sacrifice the quality of the plan due to cost.) Is it that every communication that I observe, whatever message it contains, during the week of my average media diary, is delivered in the right way, at the right time, to move me along the purchase cycle? Hence, the brand is with me throughout my decision process and, with timely reminders, encourages me to action. If each communications vehicle were a diverse element, then the total impact of all these elements coming together to build my propensity to act could be considered to suit the definition of integration. However, isn't my action the result of my growing propensity, which was caused by the communications, rather than being the unification of them?

So, we reach the third area of responsibility in communications planning – the client. The client is the brand owner and represents the brand. Most major brands are ubiquitous. In my daily life, everywhere I go, I am within ten miles of a McDonald's, driving my Lexus or Land Rover, insured by the AA, carrying my Nokia mobile, which pronounces the receipt of Vodafone or Orange, smoking Marlboro, drinking Coca-Cola or Kenco, and glancing at my Rolex as I look forward to a Smirnoff Ice. Brands that become Superbrands never let me down in this daily life. The quality of the products, and the service

surrounding them, are consistent across the brand. Is it, then, that every experience I have of the brand unifies my belief in its quality and relevance?

It seems clear that in each of these three areas, one must answer affirmatively. Every additional message that I take in, which is delivered at the right time, and assuming that I have no negative brand experiences, increases my propensity to action. Revisiting the definition of integration is helpful, as the unification of 'diverse elements'. The diverse elements, which exist in a brand marketing campaign, are not the diverse messages, nor are they the diverse media or the different products. In fact, the diverse elements are the messages, the media and promotions, and the products.

Integration in communications planning, therefore, cannot be provided by the creative or media agencies, or the client alone. An integrated communications planning process must be a process, which brings together all these diverse elements of the brand marketing campaign – a process, which brings together the creative agencies, the media and promotions agencies and the client.

NINAH Consulting has such a process. The Ninah process brings together all the key elements of the communications plan to objectively forecast the impact of every possible option for brand investment.

Increasing numbers of Superbrands use this process to establish the impact of their brand investments in terms of additional brand value, short and long term sales and profit and changing customer attitudes.

The need for an integrated planning process is widely accepted for the following reasons:

- There is increasing demand for ACCOUNTABILITY in advertising, with companies seeking to quantify the returns they are getting from brand investment. Integrated planning delivers highly efficient consumer communications, reaching consumers cost-effectively and persuasively at all stages of the purchase cycle, from communicating emotional brand attributes (personality) to point of purchase.

- Media audiences are becoming more FRAGMENTED, increasing the cost of effective reach. Many brand owners are shifting marketing spend from traditional media advertising, particularly TV, into direct media, where the sales effect is more easily quantifiable.

- Current marketing industry jargon focuses on MEDIA-NEUTRALITY, which requires an objective choice from all communications vehicles, based on their ability to deliver against key criteria, rather than their creative interest, or habitual inclusion in a media plan. Given the tools and research currencies available before Ninah, delivering media neutrality was more fantasy than reality.

- Integrated communications often requires planning across ORGANISATIONAL BOUNDARIES, where an objective process can bring together business silos, and media and promotional activity.

- Diminishing budgets require more sophisticated PORTFOLIO MANAGEMENT. Reallocating budget between brands in a portfolio, or variants in a brand, has shown increases in profit in excess of 10%.

The Ninah process was developed to overcome some of the limitations of previous approaches to integrated communications planning.

Some brand activity is more easily measurable:

- Brands using direct and interactive media can tie media spend to response and sales.

- Consumer promotions can be directly correlated with clear short-term sales impacts.

Where good data is available, econometrics is helpful in understanding what has worked in the past and it attempts to evaluate all communications vehicles in a single model. However, it has well-documented draw-backs:

- Whilst advertising expenditure generally requires an extended payback period to show a positive return on investment, it is much easier to show short-term sales effects in econometric models, compared to effects that are spread out over time.

- Models require individual media to have been used consistently in several periods, but at variable levels of weight. Often, few media have these characteristics.

- 'Driving looking in the rear view mirror'. Econometrics can tell us how brands responded to different communication vehicles historically. This does not provide a dynamic model of the future, allowing us to predict the effects of using different media, or in a different way.

- 'Black box approach'. Econometrics is a complex and specialist science. Models are difficult to communicate to the marketing team, and do not create the buy-in, which is needed for the results to be implemented.

The Ninah solution is an integrated financial model, which evaluates all communications vehicles within a single model, including those never used before. It evaluates all communications vehicles in a common currency, including advertising, consumer promotions and trade spend, allowing the user to understand the returns in terms of brand value, sales and profit, or changing consumer behaviour. It takes account of both the short and the long-term effects of investment.

The Ninah model is a pragmatic synthesis of both quantitative and qualitative approaches. It leverages sources, such as econometrics, promotion evaluation, tracking studies and panel data to provide valuable quantitative inputs. It uses a unique and clear team process to quantify judgemental inputs from brand and media experts, engendering buy-in from a cross-functional team. The resulting model learns from the past, but is focussed on a changing future. Results are actionable.

Case study: Vodka

In this case, the brand was in a highly competitive market with complex distribution channels. The client was interested in determining the most cost-effective media and promotional mix to maximise long term profit, while achieving the following year's sales target. The communications mix included TV, cinema, radio, magazines, internet, in-venue posters, party kits, in-store displays, price discounts and beer mats.

The approach taken combined an analysis of historical data with facilitated management judgement about how the brand would be different in the future. The experience of a cross-functional management team was included – marketing, on-trade and off-trade sales, research, finance and agencies, which built a common understanding of, and commitment to, the project. Inputs were sense-checked against the Ninah database of consumer goods benchmarks.

At the first stage of the six step process, the communications mix was revised and it was agreed that the model would be built initially at the level of four segments.

The historical data was then collected and analysed to produce objective forecasts and learnings.

For example: An analysis of the different competitors in the market showed that beer is the biggest competitor of vodka.

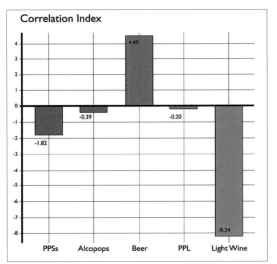

The historical analysis was used to produce a robust current plan, built up from the four key segments – a plan of the next three years investment, with expected returns.

Ninah then used a variant of the Delphi technique to facilitate judgement around key variables, to build a dynamic model of the future for the brand. This involved bringing together

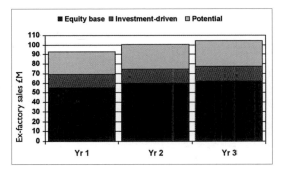

all experts in the brand and its marketing, to investigate 'what if' options for the future of the brand at extremes of investment.

This resulted in an understanding of the level of sales, which were driven by momentum in the brand, and the potential upside in brand sales, which was achievable through marketing. This facilitated an analysis of the impact of changing investment levels.

The analysis showed that an increase in overall budget of £7 million would deliver an incremental profit of more than £25 million, whilst still delivering an ROI the following year in excess of £1,000 per 1000.

However, the improvements in profitability from an optimisation of the marketing mix were even more exciting. The analysis confirmed that the brand had fallen prey to discounting and that this was taking its toll, quantifying the long-term impact on profitability. Consumers were considering the brand as increasingly equal to own-label. Although the price discounts were delivering short-term sales, they were diminishing long-term profit, and the long-term value, of the brand. Reallocating the current budget size within the marketing mix showed an increase in profit in excess of £40 million.

This client implemented their findings from the Ninah model, and delivered an increase in marketing contribution of 24.8% above the original plan.

The fairy dust?

So, given that there now exists an integrated process for planning marketing investment in an objective way, which translates all media and promotions, in a common currency, to their impact on the P&L or the consumer, where is the fairy dust?

The fairy dust lies firmly in the hands of all the parties to the campaign plan. The real magic is in that exceptional idea that we all seek – in creativity. If the process is there to deliver the number crunching and the hard 'behind the scenes' work, that leaves more time for talent, for imagination and for creative flair. Using Ninah gives more opportunity for the agencies and the client to take that little extra time to come up with something cleverer than the competition; a better use of media, a more compelling promotion, a stronger message, a new product idea.

1 What is a consumer powerbrand?

2 Why is it desirable and who is in search of it?

3 What are the 'golden rules' to create one?

4 How do you know you've arrived and what can you do to maintain your status?

Like the comic superheroes of our collective imagination – what business or organisation doesn't want to possess the extra-ordinary powers of strength, success and popularity that a Powerbrand commands? In today's challenging and fickle consumer marketplace – global marketing and management leaders are concentrating their focus, energy and investments to create consumer Superbrands/Powerbrands. These are brands that can survive the vicissitudes of economic growth and stagnation; can attract investment capital, confidence and clout on global exchanges whilst delivering shareholder returns and value. At the same time these brands create mesmerising consumer bonds to their products and services that defy the laws of customer loyalty and lifetime value.

So, who are the global consumer Powerbrands and how do they attain this status? What are the critical factors for success and maintenance? And – what does the future hold for them as determined by consumer preferences, knowledge and power? Firstly, Powerbrands share a few common traits and qualities.

1 They are leaders and innovators in their respective category or sector of consumer goods. Evidenced by either marketshare (#1, 2 or 3); Awareness and recognition (spontaneous and unprompted); or share price value and return on investment. These Powerbrands dominate consumer consciousness and the media landscape.

2 They excel across at least three continents. To truly be 'super' a brand must appeal to globally diverse consumer cultures and geographies. They understand the strengths and challenges of global vs. local, continually experimenting, sharing, learning and rolling out new product developments and innovations to catch 'trendwaves' and re-define tastes and preferences. International brand owners such as Unilever, Nestlé, Danone, L'Oreal and Procter & Gamble leverage their global capabilities with local knowledge and experience to adapt and modify brands. They realise the importance of cultural tastes, rituals and preference in branding.

3 Consumer Powerbrands also span product or service sectors often redefining their category and consumer expectation, constantly refreshing the experience of consuming their brand. Defying the laws of description – these consumer Powerbrands resist being pigeon-holed or positioned based on a single product feature or sector description. More often than not, these Powerbrands re-define models, categories and terms that their consumers intuitively understand and believe in. For example, Starbucks redefined themselves from coffee wholesalers to retail experiences that provided consumers with a 'third space' to enjoy their time and a venti latte!

4 Powerbrands are dynamic. They never stand still and are continually experimenting and challenging the norm to offer consumers a 'better' or more memorable choice. They value and encourage consumer opinions so that they can listen and adapt. With one eye on their competitors and one eye on the future – consumer Powerbrands get product and pricing right. They carefully balance and manage their resources and capital to deliver strong margins. Perhaps most importantly they understand that image and marketing are a brand's oxygen, however they never confuse marketing hype with product quality.

Ultimately, a consumer Powerbrand is loved. It is an object of desire that can both whet the appetite with anticipation while also assuring that the product or service 'experience' will not fail to disappoint. These Powerbrands connect on an emotional level with human need states and desires to offer more than just a flight (British Airways), a photograph (Kodak), a fizzy drink (Coca-Cola) or a cup of coffee (Starbucks). They connect by fulfilling a role in their consumers' lives, which gets them invited into an intimate and personal world. Just like in human relationships, consumers come to them with above average expectations. A failed promise or tarnished ethic can break the faith and trust in even the most powerful brands. The ubiquity of these brands means that if they do slip up, they have nowhere to hide. Powerbrands must present themselves as truthful and honest, without appearing cynical.

The fact of the matter is that many try, but few succeed. The current race is on for the large twentieth century manufacturers to become Powerbranded. The likes of Unilever, Nestlé and Danone are harnessing talent and investment funds to focus their portfolios, generate returns and get a foot in the consumers' household door before the power of the internet and retailers make them obsolete or subservient. Of course, the key learning for these marketing and manufacturing behaviours is that 'brand emotion' cannot roll off of a conveyor belt like a packaged good. A 'brand experience' is not a 'flagship' store that has 'profile' but makes no money. A true Powerbrand is more than a world wallpapered with logos, slogans, product placement and advertising ubiquity.

A true Powerbrand dares to lead not follow; takes risks not research; stays close to consumers by understanding where, how, why and when they live their lives. The start point is never what role does a washing powder brand play in my life – but rather, what is my life like – what are the influences, demands, and memories that create and destroy brand preferences? How does the future and my consumer perception of it affect my decision making and loyalties today? The challenge for Powerbrands is to focus their brand essence on a compelling truth that is relevant to consumers and true to the product or service reality. Next, Powerbrands must establish a 'territory' that they can own with consumers that has strong, meaningful and differentiated associations. This 'territory' will allow the marketing communications, sales activation and product R&D to develop a deeper and broader presence in consumers' lives and homes.

CHRISTOPHER NURKO
Joint Managing Director
FutureBrand UK

FutureBrand

About FutureBrand UK

FutureBrand's philosophy is to give its clients the knowledge and conviction to create and sustain fresh and innovative brands. Brands that are simple, rewarding and original. It achieves this by being future focused and having an intimate understanding of consumers, trends affecting brands, and creativity. Ideas for brands lie at its core. www.futurebrand.com

A Powerbrand manager or owner knows they have achieved Powerbrand status when the momentum of its success begins to challenge the business to maintain control with growth.

A few of the signs of success include:

• New partners or complementary brands seek association with the Powerbrand to reach new audiences, extend brand loyalty or derive enhanced value.

• Consumer awareness and increased preference create pressures and demands for the Brand driven from 'grassroots level' upwards. Increased profile and exposure begins to create demand for more information and transparency not only for the product or service – but, for the owner/manufacturer as well.

• Analysts and investors begin to not only take interest but also notice in the Powerbrand, the knock-on effect of share price sensitivity and performance means the Powerbrand and its management require greater levels of diligence to protect and manage all aspects of the brand whereas previously it was purely marketing or promotions oriented.

• Lastly, the best and brightest talent in all areas of business seek to work for or with the Powerbrand. Resumés and Curriculum Vitæ's of the highest calibre arrive on the desks of HR teams with a willingness to sacrifice status, pay or package benefits for the opportunity to have the Powerbrand added to their career history.

To maintain Powerbrand status a manager must be vigilant and professional. Once achieved, it is as easy to lose Powerbrand status as it was difficult to attain. By staying in touch with consumers, monitoring trends and competitive threats, keeping focused on the brand's essence and 'territory' whilst also continually renewing the brand experience a true Powerbrand can, and will, stand the test of time.

JULIAN SAUNDERS
Executive Planning Director
McCann-Erickson

About McCann-Erickson

McCann-Erickson WorldGroup is comprised of best-in-class specialist global marketing communications companies. Launched in late 1997, the WorldGroup has expanded rapidly to become the world's leading networked marketing communications group, now working with more than 25 key worldwide clients in three or more disciplines.

The WorldGroup now includes McCann-Erickson Advertising, MRM Partners – relationship marketing, Momentum – experiential marketing and sales promotion, FutureBrand – brand development and design, Zentrophy Partners – digital marketing, Torre Lazur Healthcare, Universal McCann – media planning and buying, and Weber Shandwick – public relations.
www.mccann.com

Experienced marketeers are familiar

with the deathly phrases in the research debrief. "Your brand has drifted to the back of the store cupboard", "You are seen as a bit tired and dusty", "The brand is out of touch" "The typical user is seen as a middle aged man in a suit standing in a pub cradling a pint of bitter". In short, your brand is no longer contemporary.

What sort of brands are we talking about? Not 'cool brands'. They are cool because they are 'discovered'. Not 'challenger' brands – life is more straightforward for them; they have a simple mission and a focus. My theme is big established brands with multiple audiences and that have challengers snapping at their heals. How should these brands think and behave to stay contemporary?

The media dynamic affects values and imagery

Try this simple exercise, put together a reel of ads from ten years ago for (say) household brands and compare them with today. In the scheme of history ten years is a very short time, but when it comes to décor, hairstyles, clothes, dialogue, it seems like a life time ago. The media seeks out the fresh, the new, the exciting, the significant and exposes it to our gaze, then overexposes it and continues seeking out the fresh, the new, the exciting and the significant. Brands exist in this world and have to constantly evolve to stay fresh. We study what we call media ethnography every week as part of our Pulse programme. (1)

We're looking for what is becoming truly popular and can become the currency of communication for big brands (which need to be inclusive). In Pulse we talk to both style leaders and customers so we can also track how trends that start with élites and at the margins move into the mainstream. This is important for big brands like Coca-Cola which need to 'lead', but do not necessarily wish to be 'leading edge'.

Demographic change, social change and shifting values

Nothing transforms the culture of society so dramatically as demographic and social change. Contemporary family life is the product of profound shifts in society. Contrast the 'mum centered' world of the Oxo family of a decade ago with the todays 'democratic family' with its complex sets of negotiations between mum and kids, mum and dad, mum alone with the kids. The underlying causes of 'the democratic family' are well known – more women working, more divorce, children fending for themselves, time shortage, and stress – and its consequences for the family are profound.

For brands, it's an opportunity to be seen to understand, to be contemporary. The pressure cooker lives of many women create reactions – for freedom, for escape, for relaxation, for getting back to your true self, for indulgence, for the authentic, for maternal love and much more.

Think of how the category of adult ice cream has grown by accessing these values shifts: ten years ago Walls ice cream was mainly for kids, now we have Carte D'Or, Ben and Jerry's, Häagen-Dazs and each of these brands connects with a different psychological need.

Children are getting older younger. It is the result (amongst other things) of the pervasiveness of the media and children also having to fend for themselves more. For many food brands it means that they sit at the epicentre of complex negotiations between mums and kids. If your brand can communicate vividly with both and make it into the lunchbox then you can be truly contemporary. Walkers crisps are there, Golden Wonder are not.

Understanding the dynamics of the food negotiation also sparks innovation; Dairylea was a mum brand, Dairylea Lunchables are in the lunch box. It creates harmony in the negotiations between mum and kids; for mums it's good food, for kids it's fun and she knows that they'll eat it. This is a complex and exciting area and so we have established a specialist unit – McCann Junior – to advise on innovation and communication for family and kids brands.

Innovation and reframing the brand

Innovation is, as ever, an important behaviour for contemporising brands. Its absence can lead to a brand seeming tired in contrast to the greater sense of energy and purpose of more innovative competitors. Nurofen's record of innovation has helped it to achieve a premium position in pain relief leaving brands like Dispirin in its wake. In the mid 1990s Levi's went off the boil by believing that Jeans would never go out of style; so it targeted new products (Trusted, Vintage) at more leading edge consumers, which have subsequently moved more mainstream.

Bacardi was a brand that was losing its role; other than Bacardi and Coke, people didn't know how to drink it. The launch of Breezer provided the platform to reframe the brand. It targeted younger drinkers. It projected a new world for Breezer to live in – intense, memorable evenings out. And a new role for the brand – the way to release the Latin Spirit in all of us.

Innovation galvanises a company because it provides a focus for reappraisal – as it did in the Levi's and Bacardi cases. The combination of innovation, finding new audiences, using different media and fresh communication is how tired brands can get themselves right back into the mainstream of contemporary life.

Be contemporary and true to yourself

Change always carries risk. In the pursuit of new markets, brands can overstretch themselves and lose their essential identity. From our Pulse work, Virgin is emerging as a case in point. Once we knew where the brand stood; it had a point of view. It would champion fresh thinking where the consumer appeared not to be getting value. Now the brand appears to have lent itself to a miscellaneous set of ventures. A brand's customers understand this instinctively. It's as if a friend they have known for a long time starts to behave out of character. Once they understood his taste in clothes, where he would go, how he would behave and talk. Now the things that made him tick are Nuclear. So as a brand changes it needs to be constantly check that it is being true to itself. Unilever's recent brand cull – from 1600 down to 400 with 40 Global brands – is partly motivated by the ambition to build power brands that can be stretched across categories. Dove is an undoubted success; starting life as a cleansing bar with moisturising cream, it has developed stretchable values of 'care', 'softness' and 'gentleness' which have provided a platform for moving into skincare and haircare. By contrast Domestos's extension into all purpose cleaning has been more problematic. Domestos started life as a bleach (which is a poison) and has an advertising heritage in 'germ kill' ("kills all known germs, dead"). The brand values are rooted in 'abrasion' and 'power' which may be limiting when it comes to (for example) extension into surface cleaning wipes.

As a brand changes, stretches and innovates we have to keep asking the difficult questions – is it a meaningful evolution or a step too far? Customers today are acute in reading not just advertising but also brand strategy, and it can backfire. Nowhere is this truer than in the thoroughly contemporary issue of corporate social responsibility.

Social responsibility, business and brands

The role of business in society is a highly topical. Corporate social responsibility is one of the big contemporary themes. People are increasingly knowledgeable and interested in the companies that own brands (and their behaviour). And, as trust in institutions and government have declined, the spotlight has fallen on business (and therefore brands). CSR will be no passing fad. Having a CSR strategy will increasingly become a test for how in touch with customers a brand is. Doing good can be highly motivating for staff and keeps a brand contemporary by demonstrating an understanding of the broader lives and concerns of it's 'customers' rather than merely seeing 'consumers' and 'transactions'.

The Tesco's computers for schools programme is one of the most high profile examples of CSR in the UK. However, business today operates in an environment of intense public scrutiny. Vigilante consumers and pressure groups are ready to expose any lapses in probity. For example if you espouse sustainability – a highly contemporary issue on which McCann's WorldGroup (2) has conducted an in-depth study – it means you have to live up to the promise in other aspects of business practice. You also have to be consistent over time to avoid the suggestion that your true motivation was just a 'short-term reputation hit'. Any CSR programme will require vigour, transparency and consistency if it is not to backfire.

That said, for Dupont sustainability has transformed brand perception and, vitally, workforce motivation. The campaign 'To do list for the Planet' shows what Dupont is, what it has achieved and what it will do in the future. Dupont's is no longer perceived as an old-fashioned smokestack company but as a leading force in the dynamic world of life science.

Retailers – model contemporary brands?

Surveying all the above strategies prompts a question. Is there one type of brand that is most successful at remaining contemporary? My answer is supermarket brands.

They are less inhibited than other types of brands (except possibly media brands) when it comes to innovation. They can afford a few mistakes. It's less expensive for retailers to innovate – they own the channel to market, can launch within the parent brand rather than investing in the establishment of a new one. They are well placed to be 'magpies' of new ideas – say new pack forms – and rapidly apply them across markets. They benefit from a culture of constant evolution. Famously, Marks & Spencer launched vichyssoise, which failed. It was relaunched as leek and potato soup and succeeded. Ten years on and after many hours of cookery programmes and gastroerotica, we are now ready for vichyssoise.

Retailers are closer to customers. They are, literally, in the community. Through loyalty cards they have a holistic view of customers' purchasing and are best placed to spot innovation gaps. Customers spend hours of their time 'inside the brand' so supermarkets are able to prove themselves each week, resulting in growing familiarity and trust.

Trust, of course, will never go out of fashion. Declining trust in institutions (the monarchy, parliament) and brands (Equitable Life, Arthur Andersen, Enron) makes it perhaps, the most important of contemporary values for a brand and when it comes to brand stretching and entering new markets, it means supermarkets are well placed. Commoditised markets like petrol and insurance are particularly happy hunting grounds but that is the start; car retailing will be next and so on.

So perhaps there is therefore one lesson in the complex task of contemporising big brands:- If you're managing a big brand that is just that little bit off the pace, think and behave more like a Supermarket Brand.

Footnotes:
(1) Pulse
Pulse is a McCann-Erickson proprietary consumer insight programme. It is the largest programme of its kind in the world and operates in over 90 countries. It is designed to constantly monitor and anticipate changing consumer moods and attitudes on a local, regional and global basis.
(2) McCann-Erickson WorldGroup (see bottom left)

Andrex®

ALEX PICKERING
Brand Manager
Alex Pickering joined Boots as a marketing graduate trainee in 1998, having read French & Spanish at Durham University. Alex worked in the UK & Spain for Boots in brand management and later brand development, before joining Kimberly-Clark in 2002 to work on the Andrex® brand.

AILSA TILEY
Brand Manager
Ailsa Tiley joined Kimberly-Clark as a graduate trainee in 1997, having gained a degree in Management Studies & French at Nottingham University. After a two-year placement in France on Infant & Child Care, Ailsa worked on Huggies in the European Headquarters for three years, before transferring to Andrex® UK.

Ask Jeeves

AYLIN SAVKAN
Vice President, Marketing & Strategy

Aylin is responsible for developing and managing the marketing communications and brand strategy for the consumer web properties at Ask Jeeves. She comes to Ask Jeeves from Elida Faberge, part of Unilever plc where she was responsible for marketing and product development for various personal products such as Sure Deodorant, Organics Shampoo and Impulse Bodyspray.
Aylin is a graduate of Cambridge University where she studied English Language and Literature.

BBC

HELEN KELLIE
Head of Marketing Strategy & Planning, Marketing Communications

After graduating from Oxford, Helen began her career in consumer goods marketing at Reckitt and Colman. In the ten years Helen spent there, she was responsible for the marketing of a range of diverse products in the UK and around the globe such as Lemsip, Disprin, Lysol and Harpic. From 1994 to 1998 Helen was global Category Manager for the household cleaner business in New York. From August 1998, Helen was European Category Director for two household categories in Paris. Helen joined the BBC in January 2000 as Head of Brand Strategy and is currently Head of Marketing Strategy & Planning, for the BBC public service business.

Black & Decker

ANDRZEJ ALEKSANDER
UK Brand & Communications Manager
Andrzej graduated from Brunel University in 1998. He undertook various sales and marketing roles in the Black & Decker Consumer division before being appointed in September 2002 to his current role to implement the new branding statement 'Make it your own home™'.

ANDREW WESTCOTT-PITT
Head of UK Marketing
Andrew began his current role as head of Black & Decker UK Marketing in 2001. He oversees all aspects of Black & Decker product and brand offering, as well as developing commercial plans with the sales team to maximise Black & Decker's distribution and consumer opportunities.

British Airways

ROD EDDINGTON
Chief Executive
In January 1997 News Limited appointed Rod as Executive Chairman of Ansett Airlines in Melbourne. He held that post until April 2000 when News sold its 50% share in Ansett. He remains on the Boards of News Corp and John Swire & Sons Pty Ltd. Rod was appointed Chief Executive of British Airways on May 2nd 2000.

MARTIN GEORGE
Director of Marketing & Commercial Development
Martin joined British Airways in 1987 and following his role as Director of Marketing became Director of Marketing & Communication in October 2000 and then Director of Marketing & Commercial Development in March 2002. Martin's responsibilities include Worldwide Marketing, eBA, Network Planning, Revenue Management, Fleet Planning and Corporate Communications.

Classic FM

ROGER LEWIS
Managing Director & Programme Controller
Roger Lewis was appointed to his present position and as a Board Director of Classic FM's parent Company, GWR Group plc in 1998. Immediately prior to this he spent eight years in the record industry as a Managing Director at EMI Records and President of the Decca Record Company.

GILES PEARMAN
Brand Controller
Giles started his marketing career in 1989 at Birds Eye Wall's where he managed Unilever's impulse ice cream brands like Magnum, Cornetto and Solero. His interest in radio was nurtured during a two year sabbatical in the Philippines where he broadcast a show on a national commercial radio station before being appointed Classic FM Brand Controller in the Spring of 1999.

Direct Line

JIM WALLACE
Marketing Director

Jim Wallace joined the Direct Line Group in March 1999. Previously he was Sales and Marketing Director for Privilege insurance, the specialist insurer, now part of the Direct Line Group. Prior to this, Jim was Sales and Marketing Director for Car Care Plan, Europe's leading vehicle warranty company.

Duracell®

GEORGE ALLAN
Business Unit Director
George joined Duracell® in 1985 and has worked in various sales, marketing, and finance roles for Duracell® and Gillette. George moved to Holland in 2000 to look after Duracell® Benelux before returning to the UK to manage the Duracell® UK and Ireland business. As Duracell® Business Unit Director, George is responsible for Duracell® Major Cells and Specials.

SUREN RAYMOND
Senior Business Manager
Suren has been responsible for the Duracell® brand, at Gillette, since 2000. He has seen the successful launch of both the Duracell® Plus and Duracell® UltraM3 ranges in the UK and Ireland, with the Duracell® 'Battersea Power Station' launch campaign winning the prestigious 2001 Gold Lion award at the Cannes International Advertising Festival.

easyJet

DAVID MAGLIANO
Sales and Marketing Director
David joined easyJet in August 2002 following the acquisition of Go. David was a founder director of Go and responsible for creating the Go brand. He helped lead the company from start-up to management buy-out, and is now responsible for the sales and marketing of Europe's number one low cost airline.

TOBY NICOL
Head of Communications
Toby joined easyJet in 1999 from the agency world. He is responsible for running the easyJet communications department with a brief to maintain and build the easyJet brand across all markets, stakeholders etc. As head of communications for the airline, Toby is responsible for all aspects of media, corporate affairs, government relations and campaigning.

firstdirect

PETER SIMPSON
Commercial Director

Peter was one of the original team to set up and launch firstdirect back in 1989.

He began his career in Midland Bank in the 1970s in a number of roles before becoming Head of Marketing in the early 1980s. Peter joined "Project Raincloud" (the initial firstdirect project in 1988), before returning to run the Midland marketing function until 1991, when he joined firstdirect full time as Commercial Director.

Since then, he has been responsible for many developments at firstdirect including the launch of internet banking, SMS text messaging, and smartmortgage (fd's offset mortgage proposition). He is passionate about leading the firstdirect brand in terms of identity and personality.

FT

JOANNA MANNING-COOPER
Director of Communications

Joanna Manning-Cooper is Director of Communications. Her global remit covers corporate communications, media relations, brand PR and internal communications for the Financial Times Group, including the FT newspaper and FT.com.

GORDON WILLOUGHBY
Global Marketing and Content Sales Director

Gordon Willoughby is Global Marketing and Content Sales Director for the integrated Financial Times and FT.com operation. He sits on the FT Management Board and joined the FT as Circulation, Sales and Marketing Director in September 1998.

Häagen-Dazs

REEMAH SAKAAN
Marketing Manager

Reemah graduated from Bath university with a Business degree in 1997. After a graduate training programme with Reckitt Benckiser where she worked on household products such as Finish and Vanish she joined General Mills in 1999. In her marketing roles at General Mills she has worked across a range of their well known food brands. Now heading up the Häagen-Dazs marketing team, she is responsible for the brands significant ad spend and advertising legacy, their new product strategy, as well as communication through the brands network of 70 cafes.

Heinz

MICHAEL MULLEN
General Manager, Corporate Affairs Heinz Europe

Michael Mullen has worked for Heinz for the last four years in both the US and UK. Recently Michael has moved to the UK and is the General Manager of Corporate Affairs, responsible for the development, implementation and management of all internal and external communications across Europe.

A native of Ireland, Michael earned his bachelor's degree from the University of Wisconsin and his master's degree in public and international affairs from the University of Pittsburgh.

Huggies

BETH BENNETT
UK Brand Manager

Beth joined Kimberly-Clark in 1999 after graduating from Edinburgh University with Bsc Hons in Developmental Biology. Since joining she has progressed through the graduate training scheme, gaining experience in category management and Regional & European marketing. Having worked on Huggies and KLEENEX®, Beth is now responsible for the day to day running of the Huggies brand.

Intel

DAVID MITCHELL
Head of Brand Marketing

David Mitchell is Head of Brand Marketing for Intel in the UK. He is responsible for all Intel's brand activities in the UK, including advertising and marketing activities in the consumer and retail markets.

Since joining Intel in 1996, David has worked in a variety of marketing roles addressing both the retail channel and PC Manufacturers.

Prior to Intel, he worked as a sales manager at Compaq and Dell in the UK, after starting his career with a number of years as an account director in retail marketing agencies.

Jack Daniel's

DENISE DEWAR
Marketing Manager

Denise joined Brown-Forman in November of 2000 from Glenmorangie plc where she worked in an International role, responsible for Glenmorangie and Ardbeg, along with own label brands in five of their top International Markets.

She has been responsible for the Marketing of Jack Daniel's in the UK since September 2001.

ANDREW WILBY
Managing Director

Andrew joined Brown-Forman as Vice President UK and Ireland in January 2000. His association with Jack Daniel's and other Brown-Forman brands spreads over fifteen years as he was previously employed by their then UK distributor, Diageo; where he worked as Finance Director and Sales Director for IDV UK and latterly as Managing Director for their Morgan Furze sales area.

Jaguar Cars

IAN CALLUM
Design Director

As a child, Ian sent his vision of Jaguar styling to the company and was encouraged to continue. Now his team is designing the cars of the future.

For Ian, Jaguar styling is about elegant, flowing lines ... and what is left out is as important as what is put in.

IAN MAJOR
Marketing Director, UK

Ian was Director of Operations for the Middle and Far East, Japan, Australia and South America before becoming Sales Director for Southern Europe.

As a brand, Jaguar inspires passion and Ian is proud to be part its renaissance. He sees his role as an opportunity to build on this in the UK.

Johnnie Walker

JIM BEVERIDGE
Technical Manager, Liquid Science & Technology

Jim joined the company in 1979, working as an analytical chemist, investigating the origins of malt and grain spirit character. He has worked extensively with project teams involved particularly with distillation and maturation. Over time he gained the insights necessary to lead the Johnnie Walker team of Master Blenders. He is now one of the most respected blenders of whisky in the world.

STEPHEN MORLEY
Global Brand Director

Stephen joined the company in 1982 as a salesman. Since then, he has worked in a variety of Senior Sales and Marketing roles, which led him to General Management positions throughout Latin America, Europe and Asia. This gave him the skills and experience necessary to head up the Johnnie Walker business as Global Brand Director – a position he has held for the last three years.

KLEENEX®

LOUISE CURRAN
Associate Brand Manager

Louise joined Kimberly-Clark in 2000 as a graduate trainee. She spent her first twelve months as a marketing assistant working on the KLEENEX® brand, then spent ten months as a national accounts manager working mainly on Huggies products. Louise is now associate brand manager on KLEENEX® responsible for the day to day running of the brand.

JOHN WATERS
Marketing Manager

John joined Kimberly-Clark in 1977 after graduating from Nottingham University. He has held various roles including thirteen years in Sales and National Accounts. For most of the last ten years he has worked in marketing, responsible for the KLEENEX® brand in the UK and Eire.

Kodak

DAVID ALGAR
Director and General Manager
Consumer Imaging, UK & Ireland
David has previously worked for
Danone, Kraft and ICI in a number
of different roles including marketing,
factory management, sales management, international
development as well as general management. He
joined Kodak in October 2000 as Director and
General Manager of Consumer Imaging, UK & Ireland.

PETER BLACKWELL
Chairman & Managing Director
Kodak Ltd, and Director and
Manager Human Resources
Peter began his career with Kodak
in 1970 in Sales and Marketing.
In 2000 Peter was appointed as Manager
Warehousing Western Europe, European African
and Middle Eastern Region.
In May 2001 Peter became Director and Manager,
Employee Relations and then in July 2001 was appointed
Chairman and Managing Director, in addition to his
responsibilities for Human Resources.

Land Rover

JOHN EDWARDS
Director, Global Marketing
John, was appointed as Director
of Global Marketing on the day Ford
Motor Company formally acquired
Land Rover from the BMW Group.
Previously, John was Managing Director of Mini/MG
UK, a new division with the BMW Group established
to manage sales, marketing and distribution of Mini
and MG vehicles in the UK.

COLIN GREEN
Marketing Director,
Land Rover UK
Colin has spent over 23 years with
Land Rover. He has been in his current
role since June 1st 1999 and prior to
that had two years as a Regional Business Manager.
From 1994-1997 he was Land Rover's first Brand
Director and other previous roles include Brand
and Product Marketing and Product Planning on
the original Discovery project.

Marks & Spencer

ROGER HOLMES
Chief Executive

Roger was appointed Chief Executive in September
2002, after joining Marks & Spencer as Managing
Director, UK Retail, in January 2001.
He joined the company from Kingfisher where he was
Chief Executive of the Electrical Sector and a main
Board Director. Previously, he was Finance Director
with B&Q and Managing Director of Woolworths.

MARS bar

SOPHIA NADUR
UK Marketing Manager

Sophia Nadur joined Masterfoods in 2001. A Marketing
Professional with over ten years of international
experience with Coca-Cola Latin America, Unilever
and PricewaterhouseCoopers, Sophia has an MBA
from Warwick University and a BSc (McGill). Sophia is
also a member of the Chartered Institute of Marketing.

Mr Kipling

IAN AYLING
Marketing Director

Ian is Marketing Director at Manor Bakeries, the
company behind Mr Kipling.
He is working with teams across the business to
make sure Mr Kipling continues to provide all the
best bits of eating cake. Ian has previously worked
on other great British brands including Bisto, Paxo
& Pot Noodle.

NIVEA

NORBERT KRAPP
Corporate Vice President,
International Brand Management,
Skincare Beiersdorf AG, Hamburg

"To work for NIVEA is a challenging marketing
experience. In the last 30 years we have extended
the brand and at the same time we have kept the
core of the brand 'NIVEA Creme' young. Today
NIVEA is by far the largest skincare brand in
the world".

Oxfam

CAROLYN MEDD
Creative Services Manager
"My role is to develop Oxfam's
brand. The way we treat people
when they buy a second-hand jumper,
the way we work with partners overseas
and the way we address donors in a mailing, all
contribute to the way we're perceived – that's
our brand and we're all guardians of it."

JOHN WHITAKER
Director of Marketing
"Everyone knows the Oxfam brand.
We work with poor people and with
supporters to find new ways of ending
poverty. Our brand tells people that
we do this by being listened to as an authority, by
involving and empowering the people we work
with, and through ingenious use of money."

PG Tips

WILLIAM BROWN
Beverages Business Director
William Brown joined Unilever
in 1986 and has had a number
of key marketing roles within the
UK Business including Batchelors
soup, Red Mountain coffee and most notably
responsibility for the launch of Chicken Tonight,
Marketing Manager of Colmans at the time of
acquisition by parent Van den Bergh Foods. He
took up his role on Tea in 1997 and was appointed
to the Unilever BestFoods board in January 2000.

ANNEMIEKE TROMP
PG Tips and Scottish Blend
Marketing Manager
Annemieke joined Unilever in 1992
as a Marketing Trainee and after a
few years on culinary brands – Ragu
and Chicken Tonight, joined the Beverages Group.
She was responsible for the successful roll-out of the
PG Tips pyramid and her most recent success is the
successful replacement of the longest running
commercial TV ads – the PG Chimps with the
Aardman T-Birds.

RAC

FINDLAY CALDWELL
Managing Director
Findlay Caldwell has been with RAC
Motoring Services for four years. In his
current role, he heads up the consumer
side of RAC's business, which includes
breakdown assistance, financial and legal services,
glass replacement and driver training. He has overall
responsibility for the consumer face of RAC's brand
and is leading the development of RAC's offering
into a wide range of motoring related products
and services.

ANDY HARRISON
Chief Executive
Andy Harrison joined Lex Service
PLC as Chief Executive in 1996.
The business acquired RAC Motoring
Services in 1999 and changed its name
to RAC plc in September 2002 and now provides
motoring and vehicle solutions to consumers and
businesses through the RAC and Lex brands.

Royal Doulton

GARY MYLUM
Group Marketing Director
Key marketing champion, Gary Mylum
joined Royal Doulton in 2002
following a career in fashion. He has
been a key figure since his arrival,
helping to develop The Royal Doulton Company.
His main tasks in 2003 centres upon developing
the three main brands within the company, Royal
Doulton, Royal Albert and Minton.

WAYNE NUTBEEN
Chief Operating Officer
Chief Operating Officer since January
2000, Wayne Nutbeen joined Royal
Doulton in 1996 as Managing Director
of Royal Doulton Australia. In 1999,
he became president of Royal Doulton's North
American business, and shortly afterwards was
appointed to the Board as Director of Sales and
International Markets. In his earlier career, he worked
with leading brand names including Lladro, Lalique,
Baccarat and Waterford Wedgwood.

Royal Mail

TOM HINGS
Head of Brand & Advertising

Tom Hings began his career in advertising at Cogent Elliott and then at Lintas. In 1990 he joined Allied Breweries and relaunched Castlemaine XXXX. As Marketing Manager at Carlsberg-Tetley, Tom was responsible for Carlsberg's sponsorship and advertising programmes. As Marketing Controller for Lagers, he relaunched Carlsberg and Carlsberg Export. He joined Royal Mail in 2002.

PAUL TROY
Brand & Communications Director

Paul Troy is Brand & Communications Director for Royal Mail. Paul has held marketing management positions in Smithkline Beecham, Allied Domecq and Weetabix. More recently he has been a Brand Marketing Director with Cadbury Schweppes, and LloydsTSB.

Sharwood's

The responsibility of bringing delicious and exciting Asian food into the Kitchens of the British public is shared by all the staff at Sharwood's. From 'factory assistants' to specialist 'product designers' employees are all committed to promoting and bringing to life the passion of the Sharwood's brand.

Shell

VENETIA HOWES
Global Brands Strategy Manager

Venetia Howes has responsibility for the strategic development of the Shell brand. Her experience includes B2B marketing in chemicals, shipping and lubricants, and she was previously the Marketing Manager for Shell's global aviation business. She took the CIM post-graduate Diploma mid-career and is an active member of the Worshipful Company of Marketors, as well as being a school governor.

RAOUL PINNELL
VP, Global Brands & Communications

Raoul Pinnell developed an early interest in business whilst at school, Bradfield College, leaving to pursue Business Studies, subsequently followed by a post graduate Diploma in Marketing. Following seventeen years with Nestlé, five years at Prudential and three years at NatWest, Shell International appointed him to the post of VP, Global Brands & Communications in 1997.

Specsavers Opticians

ANDREW MOLLE
Marketing Director

Andrew has been instrumental in establishing the brand as a market leader and was responsible for changing and developing the logo so that it is now recognised by 95% of the population. He has also led the team that keeps the face of the brand fresh and up to date on the high street.

DOUG AND MARY PERKINS
Founders

Doug and Mary founded the Specsavers Optical Group in 1984. The couple, who met at Cardiff University where they were both studying ophthalmics, still have a pivotal role in the success of the company and take a hands-on approach to ensuring the long-term security of the joint venture partnership.

Tesco

Titles and positions held vary from Chief Executive to Customer Assistant, but the responsibility for understanding and promoting the Tesco brand is shared by all staff. 'We all believe that in order to win our customers' lifetime loyalty, we must try harder than any other and treat people how we like to be treated'.

Tetley

NICK KILBY
Marketing and Development Director

Nick joined Tetley in 1984 and has held a number of senior marketing positions within the company. After a period of time developing the Tetley brand in Canada, Nick became General Manager for its French business until July 2002 when he was appointed Marketing and Development Director with responsibility for the GB marketing as well as International NPD and brand co-ordination.

JOHN NICHOLAS
Commercial Director

John joined Tetley within Marketing in 1986 following marketing roles with Mars and RHM Foods. He became Marketing Director of the GB business in 1993 and joined the Tetley Group Board in 2000. He is now Managing Director – Developed Markets, responsible for a number of Tetley businesses around the world.

The National Lottery

PHIL SMITH
Commercial Director

Phil joined Camelot's Board in January 2002 with responsibility for overseeing everything to do with players and Camelot's 35,000 retailer estate. He was previously Deputy Managing Director of Improveline, an online home improvements business. From 1996 to 1999 Phil was on the board of Kwick Save plc, first as Group Marketing Director and then as Trading Director.

DIANNE THOMPSON
Chief Executive

Dianne joined Camelot in February 1997 as Commercial Operations Director, taking over as Chief Executive when the company was finally awarded the second license in December 2000. Dianne was named Veuve Clicquot Business Woman of the Year for 2000 and was voted 2001 Marketer of the Year by the Marketing Society. She is a member of the Advertising Standards Authority (ASA) and also currently President of the Chartered Institute of Marketing.

The Sun

ANDY AGAR
Marketing Director

Andy Agar joined News International in 1998. Andy has taken several roles within the company including Group Promotions Director with responsibility for both tabloid and broadsheet publications. He is currently responsible for overseeing the Marketing and Promotions strategy for News Group Newspapers.

SEAN MAHON
Marketing Manager

Sean Mahon has been responsible for the marketing output of The Sun since March 2002. He joined News International from The Telegraph Group in January 2000 as Direct Marketing Manager for News Group Newspapers and has worked as Marketing Manager for the News of the World before taking up his current position.

The Times

ANDREW MULLINS
Marketing Director

Andrew's marketing career began at Lever Brothers with his key role being Marketing Manager for the Fabric Detergents Portfolio – Persil, Radion and Surf. After nine years he moved to Diageo as Global Brand Director for the UDV Gin Portfolio – Gordon's, Tanqueray and Gilbey's. In June 2001, Andrew joined NI as Marketing Director for The Times and Sunday Times.

ROB PAINTER
Senior Brand Manager

Rob moved to News International in 1998. He spent four years in the NI Strategic Planning department working on the Times and Sunday Times brands where he was responsible for Consumer insight, Research and Brand Planning. Rob moved into Marketing in 2002 and is now charged with the management of The Times brand. Recent activity includes the launch of The Game and Bricks and Mortar.

Virgin Atlantic

ALISON COPUS
Marketing Director

Alison Copus has worked for Virgin Atlantic Airways for seven years and is now Marketing Director. She joined Virgin from American Express where she was Head of Advertising in the UK Market. She oversees the brand strategy including the development and implementation of the airline's corporate identity.

PAUL MOORE
Director of Corporate Affairs

In his current role Paul is responsible for all the airline's public relations activities worldwide from day to day operations to product, service and route launches, and including the occasional stunt. Virgin Atlantic's public relations is absolutely integral to defending and promoting the brand. Paul is also a PR Director for Virgin Management and The Airline Group.

DAVID CONNELLY
Senior Brand Manager

David is currently senior brand manager on the Wall's (sausage & bacon) brand. He has been with Kerry Foods for over five years during which he has also worked on the Mattessons brand. In 2002 David has overseen the £4 million 'We Want Wall's' campaign, and the brand is currently showing strong growth in both sausage and bacon categories.

TOBY LANGTON
Marketing Controller

Toby joined Kerry Foods in 1999 following his brand marketing roles at Anchor and Colgate-Palmolive. Toby is responsible for Wall's, Richmond, Porkinsons, Mattessons as well as Homepride Flour and the Green's brand.

He is currently heading up the marketing programme to drive ambitious growth in all of Kerry's brands through increased marketing investment and innovation.

JOHN FOLEY
Chief Executive Officer

John Foley has worked in Senior Marketing positions in Beecham, Johnson & Johnson, Chesebrough Ponds and Bord Na Mona.

In 1991, John joined Waterford Crystal as Marketing Manager and was appointed Director of Sales and Marketing in June 1995. In 1997 he was appointed to the Waterford Crystal Board and in September 1999 John was appointed Chief Executive Officer of Waterford Crystal.

BRIAN MCGEE
Director of Sales and Marketing

Brian worked in product design in Ireland, Paris and the US and then moved into product management with Dyson Kissner Moran and later with Newell Rubbermaid in Ohio, working on the Anchor Hocking Glassware Brands.

Brian has been with Waterford since 1999 in New Product Development and in Strategic Management.

PHILIPPA BUTTERS
Head of Design

Head of Design for Yellow Pages, Philippa Butters ensures they only work with agencies that deliver exciting and innovative design solutions for the product and its range of service brands. Philippa has received numerous awards including the Grand Prix Award at the 1999 Design Effectiveness Awards for her work on the Yellow Pages directory re-design project.

Abbey National
Abbey National plc
Abbey House
201 Grafton Gate East
Milton Keynes
MK9 1AN

adidas
adidas UK Ltd
PO Box 39
Pepper Road
Hazel Grove
Stockport
Cheshire
SK7 5SD

Anadin
Wyeth Consumer Healthcare
Huntercombe Lane South
Taplow
Berks
SL6 0PH

Andrex®
Kimberly-Clark Ltd
1 Tower View
Kings Hill
West Malling
Kent
ME19 4HA

ASDA
ASDA Stores Ltd
ASDA House
Great Wilson Street
Leeds
LS11 5AD

Ask Jeeves
Ask Jeeves UK Ltd
53 Parker Street
London
WC2B 5PT

Avis
Avis Rent a Car Ltd
Trident House
Station Road
Hayes
Middlesex
UB3 4DJ

BBC
BBC
Broadcasting House
Portland Place
London
W1A 1AA

Black & Decker
Black & Decker
210 Bath Road
Slough
Berkshire
SL1 3YD

British Airways
British Airways plc
Waterside
PO Box 365
Harmondsworth
UB7 0GB

BT
British Telecommunications plc
BT Centre
81 Newgate Street
London
EC1 7AJ

Classic FM
GWR Group plc
7 Swallow Place
Oxford Circus
London
W1B 2AG

Coca-Cola
Coca-Cola Great Britain & Ireland
1 Queen Caroline Street
Hammersmith
London
W6 9HQ

Comfort
Lever Fabergé
3 St James Road
Kingston-upon-Thames
Surrey
KT1 2BA

Direct Line
Direct Line Group Ltd
Direct Line House
3 Edridge Road
Croydon
Surrey
CR9 1AG

Duracell®
Gillette Group UK Ltd
Great West Road
Isleworth
Middlesex
TW7 5NP

easyJet
easyJet
easyLand
London Luton Airport
LU2 9LS

Eurostar
Eurostar Group Ltd
Eurostar House
Waterloo Station
London
SE1 8SE

Evian
Danone Water UK
2nd Floor International House
7 High Street
London
W5 5DW

firstdirect
firstdirect
40 Wakefield Road
Leeds
LS98 1FO

FT
Financial Times
Number One
Southwark Bridge
London
SE1 9HL

Gillette
Gillette Group UK Ltd
Great West Road
Isleworth
Middlesex
TW7 5NP

Häagen-Dazs
General Mills UK Ltd
Harman House
1 George Street
Uxbridge
Middlesex
UB8 1QQ

Heinz
H J Heinz Company Ltd
South Building
Hayes
UB4 8AL

Hertz
Hertz Rent a Car
Hertz House
700 Bath Road
Cranford
Middlesex
TW5 9SW

HMV
HMV UK Ltd
Film House
142 Wardour Street
London
W1F 8LN

Huggies
Kimberly-Clark Ltd
1 Tower View
Kings Hill
West Malling
Kent
ME19 4HA

Intel
Intel Corporation UK Ltd
Pipers Way
Swindon
Wiltshire
SN3 1RJ

Jack Daniel's
Bacardi Brown Forman
West Bay Road
Southampton
Hampshire
SO15 1DT

Jaguar Cars
Jaguar Cars Ltd
Browns Lane
Allesley
Coventry
CV5 9DR

Johnnie Walker
Diageo Amsterdam
Molenwerf 10-12
1014 BG Amsterdam
The Netherlands

Kellogg's Corn Flakes
Kellogg's Company (UK) Ltd
The Kellogg Building
Talbot Road
Manchester
M16 0PU

KLEENEX®
Kimberly-Clark Ltd
1 Tower View
Kings Hill
West Malling
Kent
ME19 4HA

Kodak
Kodak Ltd
Kodak House
Station Road
Hemel Hempstead
HP1 1JU

Land Rover
Land Rover UK
Banbury Road
Liththorne
Warwick
CVB5 ORG

lastminute.com
lastminute.com
4 Buckingham Gate
London
SW1E 6JP

Lemsip
Reckitt Benckiser Healthcare UK Ltd
Dansom Lane
Hull
HU8 7DS

MALTESERS®
Masterfoods
Dundee Road
Slough
Berkshire
SL1 4JX

Marks & Spencer
Marks and Spencer plc
Michael House
Baker Street
London
W1U 8EP

MARS bar
Mars Confectionery UK Ltd
Dundee Road
Slough
Berkshire
SL1 4JX

McDonald's
McDonald's Restaurants Ltd
11-59 High Road
East Finchley
London
N2 8AW

Michelin
Michelin Tyre plc
Campbell Road
Stoke-on-Trent
ST4 4EY

Mr Kipling
Manor Bakeries Ltd
3rd Floor
Minton Place
Victoria Street
Windsor
Berkshire
SL4 1EG

Müller
Müller Dairy (UK) Ltd
Shrewsbury Road
Market Drayton
Shropshire
TF9 3SQ

NIVEA
Beiersdorf UK Ltd
3500 Parkside
Birmingham Business Park
Birmingham
B37 7YS

Nurofen
Crookes Healthcare
D80 Building
Thane Road
Beeston
Nottingham
NG90 1LP

Oxfam
Oxfam
274 Banbury Road
Oxford
OX2 7DZ

Oxo
Campbell Grocery Products Ltd
Building 2020
Cambourne Business Park
Cambourne
CB3 6EZ

Persil
Lever Fabergé
3 St James Road
Kingston-upon-Thames
Surrey
KT1 2BA

PG Tips
Unilever BestFoods
Brooke House
Manor Royal
Crawley
West Sussex
RH10 9RQ

Philips
Philips DAP UK
The Philips Centre
420-430 London Road
Croydon
CR9 3QR